Critical Acclaim for
Blowback
by Christopher Simpson

"Startling, thoroughly documented. . . . Simpson concludes that the true scope of the association between United States intelligence agencies and Nazi criminals should be exposed. He has done just that in *Blowback.*"
—Herbert Mitgang, *The New York Times*

"Christopher Simpson is a wizard and an expert in the field. . . . Two cheers for the Freedom of Information Act, and three cheers for Mr. Simpson."
—Marcel Ophuls, Director of *The Sorrow and the Pity*

"A bloodhound of a book. . . . In establishing facts he does an impressive job—and it is not a pretty story (although certainly a fascinating one)."   *—Foreign Affairs*

"*Blowback* is a riveting story of considerable historical importance, well documented and well told."
—Richard J. Barnet, author of *The Alliance: America, Europe, Japan—Makers of the Post-War World*

"Path-breaking research. . . . Simpson succeeds in making this shocking story all too believable. . . . A policy that proved, as the saying goes, worse than a crime, a blunder."   —Merle Rubin, *The Christian Science Monitor*

BLOWBACK

America's Recruitment of Nazis
and Its Effects on the Cold War

Christopher Simpson

COLLIER BOOKS
Macmillan Publishing Company
New York

Collier Books
Macmillan Publishing Company
866 Third Avenue, New York, NY 10022
Collier Macmillan Canada, Inc.

Due to limitations of space, permissions and credits appear on page 381.

Library of Congress Cataloging-in-Publication Data

Simpson, Christopher
    Blowback: America's recruitment of nazis and its effects on the
Cold War/Christopher Simpson.—1st Collier Books ed.
        p. cm.
    Bibliography: p.
    Includes index.
    ISBN 0-02-044995-X
        1. War criminals—Germany—Recruiting—History—20th century.
    2. World War, 1939–1945—Collaborationists—Recruiting. 3. Secret
    service—United States—History—20th century. 4. Spies—Europe—
    Recruiting—History—20th century. 5. Brain drain—Germany—
    History—20th century. 6. United States—Emigration
    and immigration—History—20th century. 7. World politics—1945–
    8. National socialists. I. Title.
    D804.G4S54   1989   89-7331   CIP
    940.53'73—dc20

Macmillan books are available at special discounts for bulk purchases for
sales promotions, premiums, fund-raising, or educational use. For details,
contact:

Special Sales Director
Macmillan Publishing Company
866 Third Avenue
New York, NY 10022

First Collier Books Edition, 1989

10 9 8 7 6 5 4 3 2 1

Printed in the United States of America

For my mother and father

Acknowledgments

My special gratitude goes to the Freedom of Information Act officers, archivists, and librarians without whose generous professional assistance this project would not have been possible.

The following institutions and their staffs deserve special mention: National Archives and Records Service, Washington, D.C.; Berlin Document Center, Berlin, Germany; Staatsanwaltschaft bei dem Landgericht Wiesbaden, Federal Republic of Germany; National Archives and Records Service, Suitland, Maryland; New York Public Library; John F. Kennedy Library, Boston, Massachusetts; Harry S. Truman Library, Independence, Missouri; Center for Military History, Washington, D.C.; McKeldin Library, University of Maryland, College Park, Maryland; Butler Library, Columbia University, New York City; Hoover Institution, Stanford University, Stanford, California; Library of Congress, Washington, D.C.; Chicago Public Library; Special Forces Museum, Fort Bragg, North Carolina; Simon Wiesenthal Center, Los Angeles, California, and Vienna, Austria; RFE/RL Library, New York; *Washington Post;* Group Research Reports, Washington, D.C.; Association of Former Intelligence Officers, McLean, Virginia; and the U.S. Army Intelligence and Security Command, Fort Meade, Maryland.

My personal thanks to the following people, who helped out in one way or another when the chips were down: Richard Barnet, Peter Carey, William Corson, Konrad Ege, Benjamin Ferencz, John Friedman, Ron Goldfarb, John Herman, Elizabeth Holtzman, Lisa Klug, Jonathan Marshall, Marcel Ophuls, David Oshinsky, Constance Paige, John Prados, Fletcher Prouty, Marcus Raskin, Eli

Rosenbaum, Allan Ryan, Jr., Gail Ross, Thomas Simpson, Robert Stein, and several others who must remain nameless.

Thanks, most of all, to my wife, Susan, whose help was essential in the completion of this manuscript.

Christopher Simpson
Washington, D.C., 1988

Contents

Prologue

The press briefing room at the U.S. Department of Justice in Washington, D.C., is designed as a modern-day lions' den, with the department's spokesperson cast in the role of Daniel. The focus of the design is the lectern at the center of the room, which is filled with serpentine microphones and wires when a big story is about to be announced. The lions of the press are arranged along broad rising steps like the seats in an amphitheater.

On August 16, 1983, U.S. government Nazi hunter Allan Ryan strode into that briefing room to announce an unprecedented 600-page report on the activities of a certain Klaus Barbie (alias Klaus Altmann, alias Becker, alias Merten, etc.) and on that one man's relationship to the American intelligence agencies more than thirty years ago.

"I didn't really know how much of a bombshell this would be," Ryan recalled later. "I was so immersed in the details of the investigation that I wasn't quite sure what the reaction would be."[1] When he arrived, he found more than 100 reporters crammed into the briefing room, about two dozen cameras complete with newscasters representing every major television organization in the world, hangers-on of every description, and so many microphones clipped to the lectern that they had to be rearranged before he could find a place for his notes. It was, one press corps veteran commented, the biggest crowd to turn out for a news briefing since the stormy investigations of Watergate days.

The Justice Department had printed up the 200-page Barbie study, along with about 400 pages of documentary exhibits, and distributed it on schedule at the event. Ryan made a short presentation of the study's conclusions about fifteen minutes after the reporters had those books in their hands.

In a nutshell, the Justice Department's study acknowledged that a U.S. intelligence agency known as the Army Counterintelligence Corps (CIC) had recruited Schutzstaffel (SS) and Gestapo officer Klaus Barbie for espionage work in early 1947; that the CIC had hidden him from French war crimes investigators; and that it had then spirited him out of Europe through a clandestine "ratline"—escape route—run by a priest who was himself a fugitive from war crimes charges. That was point number one.

Point number two, on the other hand, was that the CIC agents who had recruited Barbie "had no reliable indication . . . that he was suspected of war crimes or crimes against humanity [until much later]," that Barbie was the *only* such war criminal that the United States had protected, and that he was the *only* such fugitive from justice that the United States had smuggled out of Europe. The Central Intelligence Agency (CIA), in particular, was given a clean bill of health in the Barbie case and, by implication, in other incidents in which the agency is alleged to have had traffic with fugitive war criminals.

Point number one was true enough. Point number two was, and is, false.

At the time of the news conference Ryan stated point number two with what appeared to be genuine conviction. His extensive investigation had convinced him that "no other case was found where a suspected Nazi war criminal was placed in the ratline, or where the ratline was used to evacuate a person wanted by either the United States government or any of its postwar allies," he said carefully, as the television cameras recorded his words.

He noted, it is true, that his investigation had been limited to the Barbie affair, so he could not be certain that some other case might not have escaped his scrutiny. His mild qualification on that point was almost entirely ignored, however, by both the press and Ryan himself in the weeks that followed.

United Press International, for example, headlined PROBER: BARBIE THE EXCEPTION, NOT RULE, and quoted Ryan as indicating that the Justice Department's search had "uncovered no evidence [that] there was any other former Nazi that the U.S. shielded from justice." ABC TV's *Nightline* program featured Ryan on its broadcast that evening. Ryan said that the United States had "innocently recruited Barbie, unaware of his role in France . . . [and that] the

Barbie case was not typical." Under Ted Koppel's questioning, Ryan expanded on the theme: It was "very likely there were no other Nazi officials who were relied upon as Klaus Barbie was . . . [and] this closes the record."[2]

Since the Barbie case broke open, however, there has been a chain of new discoveries of Nazis and SS men protected by and, in some cases, brought to the United States by U.S. intelligence agencies. One, for example, was SS officer Otto von Bolschwing, who once instigated a bloody pogrom in Bucharest and served as a senior aide to Adolf Eichmann. According to von Bolschwing's own statement in a secret interview with U.S. Air Force investigators, in 1945 he volunteered his services to the Army CIC, which used him for interrogation and recruitment of other former Nazi intelligence officers. Later he was transferred to the CIA, which employed him as a contract agent inside the Gehlen Organization, a group of German intelligence officers that was being financed by the agency for covert operations and intelligence gathering inside Soviet-held territory. The CIA brought the SS man to the United States in 1954.[3]

Following the revelation of the von Bolschwing affair, new evidence turned up concerning U.S. recruitment of still other former SS men, Nazis, and collaborators. According to army records obtained through the Freedom of Information Act (FOIA), SS Obersturmführer Robert Verbelen admitted that he had once been sentenced to death in absentia for war crimes, including the torture of two U.S. Air Force pilots. And, he said, he had long served in Vienna as a contract spy for the U.S. Army, which was aware of his background.

Other new information has been uncovered concerning Dr. Kurt Blome, who admitted in 1945 that he had been a leader of Nazi biological warfare research, a program known to have included experimentation on prisoners in concentration camps. Blome, however, was acquitted of crimes against humanity at a trial in 1947 and hired a few years later by the U.S. Army Chemical Corps to conduct a new round of biological weapons research. Then there is the business of Blome's colleague Dr. Arthur Rudolph, who was accused in sworn testimony at Nuremberg of committing atrocities at the Nazis' underground rocket works near Nordhausen but was later given U.S. citizenship and a major role in the U.S. missile program in spite of that record. Each of these instances[4]—and there were others as well—casts substantial doubt on the Justice Department's assertion that what happened to Barbie was an "exception."

And in the Barbie affair itself an independent review of the department's evidence raises considerable doubt whether one of its most important conclusions is justified—namely, that the American agents who recruited that particular Nazi had no reason to suspect that he had been responsible for crimes against humanity.

In fact, those agents did have evidence to indicate that Barbie had committed serious crimes against innocent people. The French government had submitted a statement to the United Nations War Crimes Commission as early as August 1944—almost three years before Barbie was recruited—charging him with "murder and massacres, systematic terrorism and execution of hostages." These accusations led to repeated notices concerning Barbie in U.S. arrest lists of fugitive war criminals, beginning in 1945 and continuing through the late 1940s. Confirmation that the CIC knew that Barbie had been Gestapo police chief in Lyons may be found scattered throughout his CIC dossier.

The question of what the CIC knew of Barbie's wartime career is of considerable significance, for upon it hangs an unspoken premise of the Justice Department report—that is, that American recruitment of former Nazis or Gestapo officers was justified by the pressing "national security" needs of the day, as long as the U.S. agent who recruited him did not know of *particular* atrocities committed by that *individual* Nazi. Barbie's recruiters, the government asserts, made a "defensible" decision, and those who reject it are arguing from a "visceral" revulsion against the Nazis' Holocaust, rather than from a "pragmatic" point of view that "looks to the future."[5]

The practical effect of the Justice Department's premise, if accepted, is to provide a ready-made excuse—namely, "We just didn't know"—for any U.S. official who chose to protect Nazi criminals for their supposed intelligence value.

The fact is, U.S. intelligence agencies did know—or had good reason to suspect—that many contract agents that they hired during the cold war had committed crimes against humanity on behalf of the Nazis. The CIA, the State Department, and U.S. Army intelligence each created special programs for the specific purpose of bringing selected former Nazis and collaborators to the United States. Other projects protected such people by placing them on U.S. payrolls overseas.

The government employed these men and women for their expertise in propaganda and psychological warfare, for work in American laboratories, and even as special guerrilla troops for deployment inside the USSR in the midst of a nuclear war. CIA recruiting in Europe in particular often focused on Russians, Ukrainians, Latvians, and other Eastern European nationalists who had collaborated with the Nazis during Germany's wartime occupation of their homelands. Hundreds, and perhaps thousands, of such recruits were SS veterans; some had been officers of the bloody Sicherheitsdienst (SD), the Nazi party's security service.

Most of the U.S. government has given every indication that it hopes that queries concerning U.S. intelligence agencies' use of these Nazis will fade away. But as each new bit of evidence accumulates, the questions about this practice become more insistent and more disturbing.

BLOW BACK

CHAPTER ONE

A Discreet Silence

The basic rationale U.S. policymakers used after 1945 to justify employment of former Nazis and collaborators was the possibility— no, the *imminence*—of the outbreak of a new war between the United States and the USSR.

The American anticipation of a cataclysm was reinforced by the East-West geopolitical confrontation in Europe and the Mideast in the first years after World War II; by the shortage of reliable information about actual conditions in the east; and not infrequently by religious doctrine that asserted that the Communists were Satan's army on earth.[1] Such perceptions varied from individual to individual, of course, but were by no means a fringe phenomenon.

The actual balance of forces in Europe during the decade following 1945, however, meant that neither the United States nor the USSR was capable of unilaterally imposing its will on the other through military force alone. The Soviets' advantage in troop strength and geographical position gave it powerful leverage in Eastern Europe, America's atomic bomb and economic wealth notwithstanding.

Given that situation, President Harry Truman ordered a program of psychological warfare, covert operations, and intelligence gathering aimed at the USSR and its satellites that began as early as 1945 and significantly accelerated in the years that followed. Recently declassified records make clear that by 1948 Truman had approved

3

a multimillion-dollar program initiated by his National Security Council (NSC) secretly to finance and arm "underground resistance movements, guerrillas and refugee liberations [sic] groups . . . against hostile foreign states," meaning the USSR and its Eastern European satellites.[2]

Many of these "refugee liberations groups" were, in fact, extreme right-wing exile organizations that had collaborated with the Nazis during the German occupation of their homelands. Some of their leaders were major war criminals who had directed massacres and deportations of Jews during the Holocaust. Despite this background, U.S. clandestine operations experts convinced the National Security Council and other senior policymakers that U.S. sponsorship of these organizations, and of their German agent handlers, would yield substantial benefits for the United States.

Exile organizations such as the Natsional'no-Trudovoi Soyuz (NTS, Russian Solidarists) and the various factions of the Ukrainska Povstancha Armia (UPA, or Ukrainian Insurgent Army) claimed to have large networks of sympathizers behind Soviet lines. German intelligence specialists like General Reinhard Gehlen, who had run these networks during the war, asserted that a modest infusion of American money and arms could produce secure organizations of espionage agents, saboteurs, and strong-arm specialists inside the East bloc countries and in the teeming refugee camps that then dotted western Germany. The idea, in a nutshell, was secretly to underwrite the work of these groups in much the same way that the Allies had backed resistance forces inside German-occupied territory during the war.

Contrary to the promises once made inside secret U.S. government councils that the use of such persons would be of practical benefit to this country, the truth is that these Nazi utilization programs have frequently been disasters, even when all ethical considerations are laid aside. Their behind-the-lines spy teams are now known to have been largely nonexistent, and those that did exist were laced with Soviet double agents. Instead of building a relatively airtight anti-Communist spy service, the same old boy circles used to recruit former Nazis ended up giving the USSR a relatively easy way to penetrate legitimate U.S. intelligence gathering on Soviet military capabilities and intentions. U.S.-sponsored secret warfare campaigns employing these recruits failed consistently, leading to the arrests, imprisonments, and sometimes executions of thousands of Eastern Europeans.

The government's use of Nazis and collaborators in intelligence programs has also left a mark on life in the United States itself. This impact is what is known in spy jargon as "blowback," meaning unexpected—and negative—effects at home that result from covert operations overseas.

Often blowback from CIA clandestine work abroad has been no more (and no less) alarming than, say, a fraudulent news report planted in a European magazine that later shows up in U.S. publications as fact. Sometimes, however, the problem has become far more serious. In a case revealed here for the first time, an organization of former SS and German military intelligence experts provided false information that nearly led to World War III. In another instance Senator Joseph McCarthy employed a secret U.S. espionage squad made up in part of Nazi collaborators to gather slanderous information used to smear political opponents.

Despite these negative consequences, the existence of U.S. operations employing ex-Nazis has remained a carefully kept secret in the West. There has been a certain convergence of powerful interests, rather than the great conspiracy that some critics have alleged, that has kept this story buried. The American government, for example, has not been inclined to publicize the men and women involved in sensitive "national security" missions. Many U.S. documents concerning these programs have been systematically purged from the files and destroyed, and the majority of the records that remain are still classified above "secret." Most of the men who put together the U.S. program—including the CIA's former chief of clandestine operations Frank Wisner and his boss, CIA Director Allen Dulles—are dead. Most of those who are still alive refuse to talk.

Until recently the U.S. media could usually be counted on to maintain a discreet silence about émigré leaders with Nazi backgrounds accused of working for the CIA. According to declassified records obtained through the Freedom of Information Act, several mass media organizations in this country—at times working in direct concert with the CIA—became instrumental in promoting cold war myths that transformed certain exiled Nazi collaborators of World War II into "freedom fighters" and heroes of the renewed struggle against communism.[3] The general public, for the most part, has had little reason to suspect that anything was amiss.

But the facts concerning government protection of selected former Nazis and collaborators cannot remain buried forever. Smuggling collaborators into the United States for clandestine work during the cold war was never as easy to keep hidden as it might seem. The entry of former senior Nazi Foreign Office official Gustav Hilger is a case in point. Senior U.S. State Department officials, including George F. Kennan, intervened personally on the German's behalf, leaving behind a trail of telegrams.[4] Then secret visas had to be arranged and the Immigration and Naturalization Service (INS) had to be quietly informed, producing still more records. Transport for Hilger aboard a U.S. military aircraft was necessary to get him out of Germany. Later new identification and a top secret security clearance had to be obtained for Hilger before he could begin regular work in Washington, D.C.

Despite the fragmented nature of the evidence left by these activities, it is now possible to reassemble much of the story of Hilger and other collaborators. The careers—and the explanations—of the specific American leaders who protected such men and put them to work can be brought to light. Equally important, it is now possible to begin to trace the otherwise invisible imprint that the government's secret sponsorship of former Nazis and collaborators has left on the United States.

America's own initial plan to enlist the brains of Nazi Germany concentrated on scientists, declassified U.S. Army records show. Some American intelligence officials were clearly aware from the very beginning that they were recruiting former Nazis, including SS officers and others alleged to have personally participated in executions of concentration camp inmates. Even so, top Pentagon officers believed that these Germans could be put to work in the then continuing war with Japan and the emerging conflict with the USSR. A highly secret U.S. military intelligence coordinating center advised the U.S. Army to alter its dossiers on those scientists so as to bring them into this country with supposedly clean wartime records. The United States soon stopped "beating a dead Nazi horse," as Bosquet Wev, executive officer of the Pentagon's intelligence coordinating office, put it, and began importing German chemical warfare experts, submarine specialists, and the scientists who had once built Germany's rockets using slave labor from Nazi concentration camps.[5]

At about the same time these experts were conscripted, the United States also began a small, extremely secret program to enlist German espionage and covert operations specialists at an American camp for high-ranking Axis POWs near Wiesbaden. There the chief of U.S. Army intelligence in Europe, General Edwin Sibert, gave the go-ahead to a gaunt former Wehrmacht (German army) general named Reinhard Gehlen to construct a new espionage organization made up of German experts on the USSR. Sibert, in what was at the time a clear violation of President Franklin D. Roosevelt's orders concerning denazification of Germany, assumed personal responsibility for the project. Before the 1940s were out, Sibert and Gehlen's small seed had grown into an organization upon which the Americans depended for much of what they knew about Eastern Europe and the Soviet Union.[6]

With Gehlen's group at its core, former Nazis and collaborators went on to play an important, though largely unnoticed, role in the interlocked evolutions of the cold war and of American intelligence capabilities. Gehlen provided U.S. Army intelligence and later the CIA with many of the dire reports that were used to justify increased U.S. military budgets and intensified U.S./USSR hostilities. He exaggerated the Soviet military threat in Europe, says the CIA's former chief analyst on Soviet military capabilities Victor Marchetti,[7] in order to ensure further protection and funding for his U.S.-financed operation. The German intelligence group, as it turns out, usually received at least part of any new budget appropriations that accompanied escalation of the conflict with the USSR.

At about the time the Gehlen organization was getting on its feet, the U.S. Army Counterintelligence Corps (CIC) gradually moved from investigating underground Nazis for war crimes prosecution to using some of these same Nazis and collaborators to track Communists. By 1948 the CIC found itself in a sub rosa bureaucratic battle with both the U.S. Air Force and the then newly founded CIA over funding in the spy war against the Russians. One of the most valuable prizes in this intra-American conflict was control of several thousand former Waffen SS soldiers and officers whom the army had hired and equipped for use in a guerrilla war against the USSR. The army ended up actually integrating these SS troops into U.S. nuclear strategy.*

---

*Since the end of the war a protracted debate has taken place in West Germany concerning the character of the Waffen SS or "Armed SS" and its relationship to the rest of Himmler's police apparatus. Former members of the Waffen SS sometimes glorify the role of the group as a select type of Marine Corps that was not, they contend, involved in war crimes or crimes against humanity.

The Waffen SS originated in 1940 as specially trained and indoctrinated German troops under SS leader Himmler's command who were assigned special tasks ranging from duty as

Policy concerning clandestine use of former Nazi collaborators during the early cold war years was shaped by a series of National Security Council directives and intelligence projects sponsored by the Policy Planning Staff of the State Department, then under the leadership of George F. Kennan, according to records discovered recently in U.S. State Department archives. Kennan was at the time assigned the task of internal policy oversight of all U.S. clandestine operations abroad. His initiatives—along with those of Allen Dulles, Frank Wisner, and a number of other latter-day CIA executives—helped convince Truman's NSC to approve a comprehensive program of covert operations that were explicitly modeled on the Vlasov Army, an anti-Communist émigré campaign created by the SS and the Nazi Foreign Office during World War II.[8] Scholars and propagandists who had once collaborated in formulating the Nazis' political warfare program were brought into the United States to provide brains for the new operation.

Wisner, the dynamic director of the CIA's clandestine operations directorate, gradually gathered many of the threads of earlier Nazi utilization efforts into agency hands. Wisner believed in the tremendous espionage potential of the Eastern European émigré organizations, their value as propagandists and agents of influence, and the unique advantages of using soldiers who had no provable ties to the U.S. government for certain particularly sensitive missions, including assassinations. More than that, Wisner was convinced that Communist rule would be soon overthrown in Eastern Europe and possibly in the USSR itself. America was already at war,

---

Hitler's personal bodyguards to serving as custodians and executioners at concentration camps. As the war proceeded, many were placed under the operational command of the Wehrmacht (the German army), and were often employed in brutal antipartisan strike force operations. By 1944 the increasingly desperate Nazis had begun conscripting men, including many foreign-born collaborators, into these previously all-volunteer divisions. These draftees have since argued, in some cases truthfully, that they did not participate in the mass murders for which the SS has become infamous. Therefore, they say, they should not bear the same burden of guilt as other members of that group.

The International Tribunal at Nuremberg concluded that the entire SS (including the Waffen SS) was a criminal organization. "[T]he shooting of unarmed prisoners of war was the general practice in some *Waffen SS* divisions," the Nuremberg judgment reads. "[They] were responsible for many massacres and atrocities in occupied territories, such as the massacres at Oradour and Lidice. . . . [They] supplied personnel for the *Einsatzgruppen* [murder commandos], had command over the concentration camp guards," and operated under the direct authority of SS headquarters in anti-Jewish operations. The tribunal made an explicit exception, however, for those individuals who "were drafted into [SS] membership . . . in such a way as to give them no choice in the matter, and who had committed no [war] crimes."

as he saw it, and there was no time to quibble over the pasts of its new foot soldiers.

Wisner's clandestine campaigns were originally aimed at the USSR and its satellites. Before the decade was out, however, the American people also became an important target for CIA propaganda programs. It is at that point, over the winter of 1951–1952, that the blowback from the CIA's overseas operations reached a new and more dangerous stage. According to National Security Council records, Wisner began large-scale programs designed to bring thousands of anti-Communist exiles to the United States as a means of rewarding them for secret operations overseas and to train others for guerrilla warfare against East bloc countries. The CIA secretly subsidized the work of right-wing refugee relief organizations aiding such immigrants, including some groups with clear ties to extreme nationalist and Fascist organizations in Europe.[9] The agency simultaneously funneled millions of dollars into advertising and staged media events inside the United States during the same period, with support for these overseas "refugee liberation" projects as a primary theme.

Tens of thousands of Eastern European refugees emigrated to the United States throughout the late 1940s and 1950s. Clearly the overwhelming majority of these new immigrants have proved themselves to be valuable citizens, who have made great contributions to science, culture, medicine, sports, and the American work force as well as to the defense of values like democracy and national pride. But just as any large group of humans contains some criminals, so, too, did this emigration. The difference this time was that of the criminals who did come, many were experienced right-wing political activists who were highly organized and blessed with the patronage of the CIA.

Shortly before the presidential election of 1952 the agency sharply expanded its media operations with a multimillion-dollar publicity campaign inside the United States designed to legitimize expanded U.S. cold war operations in Europe.[10] This program was guided by a theory known as "liberationism," and an important part of that strategy held that certain exiled Fascist leaders left over from World War II should be regarded as democratic "freedom fighters" against the USSR. The CIA's propaganda campaign inside the United States was clearly illegal; but the agency concealed its ties to the effort, and the enterprise prospered.

Right-wing émigré organizations, which had once been little

more than instruments of German (and later U.S.) espionage agencies, began to take on a distinct life and authority of their own during the cold war, particularly inside America's large Eastern European immigrant communities. Through organizations such as the CIA-funded Assembly of Captive European Nations (ACEN), certain Ukrainian fraternal groups, and the Latvian Daugavas Vanagi alliance (each of which included in positions of leadership persons whom U.S. investigators have alleged to be Axis war criminals[11]), these extreme-right-wing exiles gradually expanded their reach in American affairs.

Although never the mainstream voices for their particular nationality groups, these organizations and others like them succeeded in creating genuine power bases on the far right of the U.S. political spectrum. Before the decade of the 1950s was out, the activities of extremist European émigré organizations combined with indigenous American anticommunism to produce seriously negative effects on U.S. foreign policy and domestic affairs under both Republican and Democratic administrations. By 1959 these exile groups had articulate defenders inside the staff of the National Security Council and had won a measure of influence on Capitol Hill. Observing their impact on U.S. policy toward the USSR and Eastern Europe had become, as columnist Walter Lippmann wrote, "a morbid experience."[12]

In short, U.S. clandestine operations employing Nazis never did produce the results that were desired when they were initiated, but they did contribute to the influence of some of the most reactionary trends in American political life. This lesson has increased in significance over the years. More recent U.S. interventions abroad have facilitated the entry into America of extremist and even terrorist émigré organizations that have subsequently gained political footholds in ethnic communities in this country, often through the use of violence and intimidation. The influence of Bay of Pigs veterans in Cuban-American enclaves or of the former Saigon police among Southeast Asian refugees comes to mind in this regard. "Blowback" of this type has not been limited to cold war Nazi utilization operations; it is a much more widespread characteristic of the CIA's émigré operations than is generally recognized and one which deserves further study.

The pages that follow focus in detail on one example of blowback: the Nazi utilization operations during the cold war and their influence on America. Why did the U.S. government decide to employ war criminals? Why did it admit such persons to this country? To understand the answers, it is first of all necessary to look at what is meant by the term *war crimes* and to trace back to their roots the careers of some of the men and women who committed those iniquities.

CHAPTER TWO

Slaughter on the Eastern Front

"Crimes against humanity," states the Allied Control Council Law No. 10 of 1945, are "atrocities and offenses, including but not limited to murder, extermination, enslavement, deportation, imprisonment, torture, rape, or other inhuman acts committed against any civilian population, or persecutions on political, racial or religious grounds. . . ."

This statute, together with earlier joint declarations by Allied governments concerning war crimes, became the formal foundation upon which the Nazis and their collaborators were tried after World War II. The Control Council law as written is comprehensive. It also includes prohibition of *war crimes*—including murder or deportation of civilian populations by occupying armies, plunder, killing of POWs or hostages, wanton destruction of cities or towns, etc.—and *crimes against peace*, meaning the launching of an invasion or waging an aggressive war in violation of treaties. Punishment for those convicted under the law range from deprivation of civil rights to the death penalty, depending upon the circumstances of the crime.[1]

While this declaration prohibits specific acts by individuals, it also implicitly acknowledges that the genocide and slavery perpetrated by Nazi Germany required a high degree of coordination. Criminal culpability explicitly extends to the administrative apparatus of the SS, to the Nazi party, and to the chiefs of German industry that profited from concentration camp labor. It includes pro-Fascist newspaper publishers who promoted racial hatred in the pages of their publications and the senior officers of Axis ministries and local governments that carried through the day-to-day business of mass murder and persecution.

This text uses the term *war crimes* to refer to those activities banned by Allied Control Council Law No. 10, such as murder, torture, deportation, or persecution on the basis of race or religion. A "war criminal," logically, is one who has committed those crimes. But as is well known, many persons directly responsible for the Holocaust against the Jews, the mass murder by starvation of millions of Soviet prisoners of war, and other atrocities have escaped and never been tried for their deeds. Therefore, any serious discussion of who can properly be called a "war criminal" must of necessity consider all the historical evidence of what took place during the war and the Holocaust—not just the relatively small number of cases that were formally tried before the International Tribunal at Nuremberg or other courts. The term *war criminal,* as used here, is narrowly defined, but it goes beyond simply those persons who have been convicted in a court of law. It applies to the responsible officials of the political parties, police organizations, or wartime Axis governments whose records of terror, extermination, and anti-Semitism are beyond dispute; to the individuals who voluntarily participated in genocide or mass murders; and, in a small number of cases, to propagandists or publicists who actively promoted persecution on the basis of race or religion.

To understand how certain people in the pages that follow escaped punishment for their crimes, it is necessary to look briefly at one of the most prominent features of the Nazi political philosophy: extreme anticommunism and particularly fanatic hatred of the USSR.

The slaughter that followed the German attack on the Soviet Union in June 1941 is without equal in world history. Next to the Nazis' operation of the anti-Jewish extermination centers at Treblinka, Sobibor, Birkenau, and elsewhere, the most terrible crimes of the entire war took place in name of anticommunism in the German-occupied territories on the eastern front. Civilian casualties in these areas were so enormous, so continuous, and so extreme that even counting the dead has proved impossible. Scholars have attempted to deduce the numbers of fatalities from captured German records, reports of *Einsatzgruppen* (mobile execution squads), prisoner of war (POW) camp mortality reports, and Soviet census statistics. The evidence indicates that between 3 and 4 million captured Soviet soldiers were intentionally starved to death in German POW camps between 1941 and 1944. About 1.3 million Jews were exterminated inside Nazi-occupied Soviet territory, mainly through mass shootings but also through gassing, deportation to extermination camps, looting and destruction of villages, hangings, and torture. The generally accepted figure for all Soviet war dead is 20 million human beings—about 15 percent of the population of the country at the time—but the destruction was so vast that even this number can be only an educated guess.

The Nazis deliberately used famine as a political weapon in the East, and it soon became the largest single killer. As the German invasion of the USSR began, General (later Field Marshal) Erich von Manstein ordered that "the Jewish-Bolshevist system must be exterminated. . . . In hostile cities, a large part of the population will have to starve." Nothing, Manstein continued, "may, out of a sense of mistaken humaneness, be distributed to prisoners or to the population—unless they are in the service of the German Wehrmacht."*

This was a war not only of conquest but of extermination. Entire regions of the USSR were to be cleared of the existing Communist apparatus and of Slavic "subhumans" to make way for settlement by "Aryan pioneers." Above all, it was believed necessary to conduct an ideological war to wipe out the "Jewish-Bolshevist plague" and those who were its "carriers."

The Nazis' mass killings at Lidice, Czechoslovakia, and Oradour, France—where the Germans rounded up the town's population in retaliation for the assassination of a German official, murdered the captives, and shipped any survivors to concentration camps, then

*Other features of military regulations promulgated by Manstein on the eve of the war include orders for the immediate liquidation of all captured Soviet political officers or leaders, summary executions for civilians who "participate or want to participate" in resistance to German troops, and "collective measures of force"—which soon came to mean murder of entire populations of villages, including children—to punish hamlets in which "malicious attacks [against the Wehrmacht] of any kind whatsoever" had taken place. German soldiers who had committed what would otherwise be crimes under Germany's own military code were not to be prosecuted if their acts had taken place "out of bitterness against . . . carriers of the Jewish-Bolshevik [sic] system."

Manstein later claimed at his trial for war crimes that the starvation order had "escaped my memory entirely." He was convicted by a British tribunal and sentenced to eighteen years in prison, but he obtained release in 1952 after serving fewer than three years of his term. The former field marshal eventually became an adviser to the West German Defense Ministry.

burned the place to the ground—are well remembered in the West today.

But inside the Nazi-occupied USSR there were not just one or two Lidices. There were hundreds. Mass killings of the Lidice type took place at Rasseta (372 dead), Vesniny (about 200 dead, mainly women and children), and Dolina (469 dead, again mainly women and children), to name only three. In the Osveya district in northern Belorussia alone, in the single month of March 1943, the Nazis and collaborationist troops devastated some 158 villages, according to *Times* of London correspondent Alexander Werth. "All able bodied men [were] deported as slaves and all the women, children and old people murdered," Werth reports. This pattern of massacre and scorched earth warfare was repeated again and again throughout the war on the eastern front.

Nazi warfare against partisans was consistently brutal throughout Europe, and the Germans and their collaborators committed numerous violations of the "laws and customs of war," such as torture, mass killings of innocent persons in retaliation for guerrilla attacks, and murder of hostages across the Continent. It was in the East, however, that such killings reached a truly frenzied level. At Odessa, for example, the Nazis and their Romanian collaborators destroyed 19,000 Jews and other so-called subversive elements *in a single night* in retaliation for a partisan bombing that had killed about a dozen Romanian soldiers. Axis troops rounded up another 40,000 Jews and executed them during the following week. The SS used gas wagons disguised as Red Cross vans to kill about 7,000 women and children in the south, near Krasnodar. At least 33,000 Jews were slain in a single two-day massacre at Babi Yar, near Kiev, and so on, and on, and on.[2]

Hitler's high command carefully planned the extermination campaign on the eastern front, drawing up directives for mass killings and distributing them to Wehrmacht and SS commanders. They established special SS teams devoted exclusively to mass murder— the *Einsatzgruppen* and their subgroups, the *Sonderkommandos* and *Einsatzkommandos*—and set up liaison between the killing teams and the army commanders at the front to ensure that the killing teams received the necessary intelligence and logistical support. The SS carefully tabulated the results of the carnage as it took place, wrote it up, and sent word back to Berlin. Teams of inspectors and experts (among them men who were later employed as experts on Soviet affairs by U.S. intelligence agencies) traveled the eastern front throughout the war to make sure the exterminations or confiscations of food from occupied territories were going properly and were being carried out, as one *Einsatzgruppe* leader was to testify at Nuremberg, in a manner which was "humane under the circumstances."[3]

What has since come to be termed "political warfare"—that is, the use of propaganda, sabotage, and collaborators to undermine an enemy's will to fight—played an important role in German strategy from the beginning of the conflict. Specialized Nazi-trained propaganda and terror teams made up of native collaborators were among the first units that marched with the German armies across Europe.

The Nazis originally planned to conquer the USSR in a matter of months, and for a time it looked as though they might succeed. But the German offensive bogged down, their supply lines stretched longer and became more vulnerable, and the partisan movement in the German rear grew stronger. As the fall of 1941 turned to winter, army commanders on the eastern front began to place increasing stress on using native anti-Communist collaborators to administer regions under Nazi occupation and to supplement Germany's fighting troops, particularly in antipartisan warfare.

Germany's Soviet affairs specialists contended that a systematic program of employing collaborators and quislings, not unlike that which Germany had used in the occupied zones of Western and Central Europe, was a necessary tactic to achieve a military victory over the USSR. They argued that the invading Nazis should attempt to convince the Soviet people that the Germans would permit collaborators to enjoy a measure of wealth and power under Nazi sponsorship, that the occupied territories would be granted some sort of limited "national independence," that churches would be reopened, and that the collective farm system would be dissolved. The more extreme types of Nazi brutality should be temporarily restricted, they asserted, in order not to interfere with stabilizing Nazi power in the occupied areas. Anti-Communist émigré groups already on the Germans' payroll, such as the Natsional'no-Trudovoi Soyuz (NTS) and the Ukrainian nationalist movement, Organizatsiia Ukrainskikh Natsionalistov (OUN), were promoted as the Nazis' best instruments for applying this combined political/military strategy inside the occupied zone.[4]

Hitler, however, rejected such reasoning. His hatred of the Slavs in the East was both racial and political, and he had already laid plans to exterminate the majority of the Slavic people once he had finished with the Jews. He had little interest in setting up any sort of Slavic states in the East, not even those ruled by Nazi quislings.

But political warfare tactics continued to gain popularity among Wehrmacht and some SS officers who were alarmed by Germany's disastrous losses in the field. These men began to criticize some aspects of the German occupation of the USSR, a fact which has been repeatedly raised in their defense since the end of the war. Such "criticisms" of Hitler's strategy cannot be taken at face value, however. One leading advocate of political warfare, Karl-Georg Pfleiderer, for example, followed up a 1942 inspection tour of the Ukraine with a report that the famine created by the German army was a bad practice—but only because it would interfere with Nazi efforts to extort more food from the occupied areas the following year.

Even that sort of logic did not apply to the treatment of Jews. The political warfare faction of the German leadership "washed their hands of the Jews of Russia," notes Holocaust historian Gerald Reitlinger. Mercy for the Jews "had nothing to do with winning the war against Stalin" for the Germans, he writes; "it was not essential to the war effort." Indeed, according to Reitlinger, advocates of political warfare in the East often used aggressive anti-Semitism as a means of legitimizing their otherwise controversial program.[5]

As the military situation of the German troops worsened, German intelligence experts on the USSR found themselves in increasing demand. Several of these consultants had been born in czarist Russia, all spoke the language, and all of them had made careers out of their expertise in Soviet affairs. Some such authorities, like Franz Six and Emil Augsburg, were senior SS officers and true believers in the Nazi cause who had personally led mobile extermination squads in the East. Others, like Gustav Hilger in the Foreign Office and Ernst Köstring, Hans Heinrich Herwarth, Reinhard Gehlen, and Wilfried Strik-Strikfeldt of the Wehrmacht, appear to have been motivated primarily by a sense of duty and a nationalistic pride in what they perceived to be a historic mission to eradicate communism.[6]

Native collaborators and defectors became the key to the German political warfare group's plans. In the course of the war, the Nazis enlisted about a million such collaborators, including Ukrainians, Azerbaijanis, Cossacks, and, of course, large numbers of

Russians. The *Osttruppen* (eastern troops) program, commanded by Köstring and Herwarth, embraced all eastern collaborationist troops under German army administration, while the SS recruited its own defectors into units that eventually became part of the Waffen SS. A variety of auxiliary police, militia, and other antipartisan formations organized directly by the Nazis or by collaborationist local administrations under Nazi control filled out the picture.

The jobs assigned to these collaborators ranged from hauling ammunition for frontline troops to mass executions of Jews—the dirty work, in short, that the Nazis often did not want to do for themselves. For the Germans, these units became a living laboratory for the development of sophisticated propaganda, guerrilla warfare, and intelligence techniques for use against the Soviet government. After the war was over, as will be seen, they became the raw material from which the new U.S. political warfare capability was built.

The most important common cause among the German political warriors during (and after) the war became a "Russian Liberation Movement," which they financed and armed. Their aim was nothing less than uniting all the squabbling collaborationist groups throughout the Nazi-occupied USSR into a single anti-Stalin army. The plan never succeeded, in part because of obstruction from Hitler, who feared the prospect of any all-Russian army, even one commanded by Nazi officers.

Hitler was, however, willing to go along with the pretense of a supposedly independent "Russian Liberation Movement" as a propaganda ploy, so a psychological warfare operation built around those themes was undertaken by Gehlen and Strik-Strikfeldt as early as 1941 and continued throughout the war. In 1942 this effort became known as the Vlasov Army after Andrei Vlasov, a former general in the Red Army whom the Germans had chosen to be the crusade's leader. Vlasov, who had been personally honored by Stalin in 1941 for his courage in the defense of Moscow against German attack, had defected to the Nazis the next year following a humiliating defeat. A tragic figure of Dostoyevskyan proportions, Vlasov apparently sincerely believed that the Nazi government would back his effort to raise an anti-Communist army from among German-held POWs and refugees, then train and equip that army, all the while asking next to nothing in return. Such dreams, of course, were bound to lead to ruin. In the end Vlasov lost both his army and his life.*

In 1942, however, Vlasov was just the man that the political warfare faction was looking for, and the creation of an army of Soviet defectors under German control using him as a figurehead became its central preoccupation for the remainder of the war. "The Germans started a form of blackmail against the surviving Russian war prisoners," war correspondent Alexander Werth notes. "[E]ither go into the Vlasov Army or starve." The overwhelming majority of Soviet POWs refused the offer, and about 2 million POWs who were given the choice of collaboration or starvation between 1942 and 1945 chose death before they would aid the Nazis. But many thousands of Russians did join the invaders as porters, cooks, concentration camp guards, and informers, and later as fighting troops under German control.[7]

As will be seen, the Vlasov Army has frequently been portrayed in the West since the war as the most noble and idealistic of the Nazis' émigré legions. Vlasov was "convinced that it was possible to

---

*Vlasov was seriously ill with alcoholism throughout the war, and his condition worsened as defeat neared. Still, he clung to the conviction that his Nazi-sponsored army might somehow contribute to the overthrow of Stalin. Wilfried Strik-Strikfeldt, Vlasov's German liaison officer, remembered one of his last encounters with the general as follows: "That night when he had gone to bed I went up to his room. 'Forgive me, Wilfried Karlovich,' he said. 'Of late I have been drinking heavily. Of course I used to drink before, but it never got hold of me. Now I want to forget. Kroeger keeps filling up my glass and perhaps he thinks that is the way to manage me. He is wrong. . . . I miss nothing I just want to get away. . . . Wilfried Karlovich . . . [you must] tell the others that Vlasov and his friends loved their country and were not traitors. Promise me. . . .' " A broken man, Vlasov lapsed from these reflections into a fitful sleep.

In the very last days of the war Vlasov and his troops also betrayed the Germans and briefly assisted Czech partisans in Prague who were fighting the Wehrmacht. Following a short battle there, the general surrendered his men to the U.S. Third Army in early May 1945. The Americans, operating under wartime orders to cooperate with the Red Army in POW matters, turned Vlasov over to the Russians shortly after his capture.

There are several versions of how Vlasov passed from American into Soviet hands. The most colorful one is offered by Jürgen Thorwald, a German publicist who enjoyed close personal ties with a number of Vlasov's senior officers. Thorwald asserts that an unknown American officer lured Vlasov to a secret conference at a "mysterious locality" near where the Russian was being held under house arrest. "While the party was passing through a wooded lane . . . it was suddenly surrounded by Soviet troops. Vlasov and his staff were overpowered before they knew what was happening." Other versions claim the United States simply turned the general over to the Soviets during a routine POW transfer. Whatever the truth on that point is, it is clear that Vlasov and ten of his senior officers were tried for treason in Moscow during the summer of 1946. On August 12 the Soviet radio announced that "all of the accused admitted their guilt and were condemned to death. . . . The sentences have been carried out."

overthrow Stalin and establish another form of government in Russia," writes U.S. psychological warfare consultant Wallace Carroll in a widely circulated 1949 feature story promoting American recruitment of Vlasov's veterans. "What he wanted was a 'democratic' government, and by 'democratic' he meant . . . [a] republican and parliamentary system."[8]

In reality, Vlasov's organization consisted in large part of reassigned veterans from some of the most depraved SS and "security" units of the Nazis' entire killing machine, regardless of what Vlasov himself may have wanted. By 1945 about half of Vlasov's troops had been drawn from the SS Kommando Kaminsky, which had earlier been led by the Belorussian collaborator Bronislav Kaminsky. *

The Kaminsky militia's loyalty to the Nazis won it an official commission in the Waffen SS, quite an honor for Slavic "subhumans," coming from the Germans. They went on to spearhead the bloody suppression of the heroic 1944 Warsaw rebellion with such bestial violence that even German General Hans Guderian was appalled and called for their removal from the field. The Germans eventually caught Kaminsky pocketing loot that he was supposed to have turned over to the Reich. They executed him in the last days of the uprising.

With Kaminsky himself gone, the SS then folded together his remaining troops with other Russian turncoats from POW camps, plus a variety of other ethnic Russian and Ukrainian *Schumabataillone,* or security units.[9] Many of these new soldiers had histories similar in all important respects to those of the Kaminsky men. They are who made up the "idealistic" Vlasov Army.

The German political warriors were themselves split over the traditionally knotty question of the minority nationalities in the USSR. Advocates of political warfare tactics within the Nazi Foreign Office, the SS, and German military intelligence, for example, generally favored uniting all the defectors and collaborators from the USSR into the Vlasov Army. The figureheads of that force were generally of Russian ethnic background and sharply opposed to the

---

*These troops were among the actual triggermen of the Holocaust, and were particularly active in machine-gun slayings of civilians. Some of Kaminsky's men were also known to have titillated themselves by photographing naked Jewish women moments before murdering them. Some of the militiamen seem to have enjoyed "before and after" pictures, for a number of such prints were later discovered on the bodies of fallen Kaminsky soldiers. The Germans, however, fearing that premature publicity might wreck their "race and resettlement" schemes, soon put an end to Kaminsky's picture-taking sessions at the edge of the executioner's ditch.

nationalistic ambitions of the Ukrainians, Caucasians, and other minority groups within the USSR.

Alfred Rosenberg's nonmilitary (but thoroughly Nazi) ministry for the occupied eastern territories argued, on the other hand, that the Baltic, Ukrainian, and Islamic minority groups from the periphery of the USSR should be encouraged to create separate "national liberation armies" to free their homelands from both "Jewish-communism" and the imperialism of the Russians. Rosenberg's ministry created about a dozen "governments-in-exile" for Belorussians, the Crimean Tatars, Soviet Georgians, and other minority groups inside the USSR to carry out this program.

The old czarist Russia, it will be recalled, had been an expansionist empire for centuries and had gradually conquered much of Central Asia and the northern approaches to the Middle East. The subject peoples of those territories—the Uzbeks, Kazakhs, Kalmyks, and others—were primarily Muslim by religion and of Turkic or Mongolian ethnic background, with languages and cultures sharply different from those of the Orthodox Christian czars who attempted to rule them from Moscow.

Similarly, czarist Russia had also repeatedly attempted to assimilate the peoples along its European border to the west of Moscow. There Russians had historically clashed with the Lithuanians, Poles, and Romanians over a long strip of disputed territory stretching north to south from the Baltic to the Black Sea. Perhaps the most important prize in those early conflicts was the Ukraine, a rich, ethnically distinct area on the southeastern border of modern-day Poland.

The revolution of 1917 had added still another layer of complexity to the bitterness among these groups and had intensified the existing ethnic, class, and religious antagonisms. Many of the subject peoples—notably the Ukrainians, Armenians, and Georgians—attempted to set up new nation-states in their territories in the wake of the fall of the czar. All the major European powers, now including the predominantly Russian Bolsheviks, jockeyed for power in the contested regions, each of them backing a favored faction of the rebellious minority groups in a bid to expand its influence. By 1923 many of those struggles had been settled through force of arms in favor of the Soviets, particularly in the south and east of what was now the USSR. But the Baltic countries of Latvia, Lithuania, and Estonia in the north had managed to preserve a fragile national independence, and Poland had gained thousands of square miles of the Ukraine under the armistice that ended World War I.

These earlier upheavals had left a powerful legacy of ethnic and religious discontent inside the USSR and had led to the creation of large anti-Communist émigré communities in several major European capitals. The violence and bloodshed that accompanied Stalinist land reform and the suppression of religion during the 1930s ensured that many of those wounds remained open.

Alfred Rosenberg's vision was to make use of these conflicts as a means of advancing what he perceived to be Germany's racial and national mission in the East. The German intelligence services had also systematically recruited sympathizers among the various émigré groups and by the eve of World War II had trained and armed several large squadrons of Ukrainian nationalists for use in both the 1939 division of Poland and the later blitzkrieg attack on the USSR.

The relationship between these forces and their German sponsors was complex and shifted repeatedly in the course of the war. As some minority nationalist leaders saw it, it was *they* who were using the Germans, not the other way around, in order to pursue their own aspirations of power. The German response to such ambitions reflected all the classical dilemmas of an imperial power caught between its desire for absolute control and the practical necessity of relying on minor allies with dreams of their own to achieve that end. The various factions of the Nazi state fought bitterly among themselves over how to deal with their unruly pawns. The émigré nationalists and the Vlasov forces were alternately supported and temporarily suppressed, then supported again as Germany's military fortunes in the East changed.

There was one thing, it seems, on which all the German political warfare specialists could agree: Most of the blood to be spilled in the envisioned anti-Communist revolution would be that of Russians, Ukrainians, Cossacks, and other natives of the USSR, not that of Germans. "Every Russian who fights for us," the Nazi Foreign Office propaganda expert Anton Bossi-Fedrigotti argued, "saves German blood."[10]

The German generals who commanded the émigré anti-Communist legions had no illusions about the motivations of most of the defectors who agreed to work for the Nazis in the East. "The bulk of the volunteers . . . I am convinced, did not enlist to fight for the [anti-Bolshevik] cause," writes Lieutenant General Ralph von Hey-gendorff, a commander of the eastern legions (under Köstring's authority) from 1942 through 1944. Instead, the majority came "solely for the purpose of gaining personal advantages, immediately or within the near future. Many of these men attempted to demonstrate strongly an idealism which neither existed nor governed their actions." In reality, it was the "horrible conditions prevailing in most of the [POW] camps," according to Heygendorff, that led most of the collaborators to seize on cooperation with the Nazis as a "last hope."

The few "true idealists" among their ranks, the German general continues, "who combined a pronounced anti-Bolshevik attitude with a fanatical love for their own people" were among the most brutal and violent of all the Nazis' legions when it came to dealing with the civilian population in the German-occupied regions, precisely because they were generally regarded as traitors by their own people. "They were extremely harsh toward fellow countrymen who failed to share their ideals," Heygendorff writes. "In dealing with undependable individuals they were *so severe that we frequently had to intervene*" (emphasis added)—a German euphemism that indicates that the "idealists" were often responsible for mass murders of innocent civilians during the antipartisan campaigns.[11]

The Nazis selected the more promising and talented collaborators for intelligence missions behind Soviet lines, propaganda, sabotage, and—most commonly—the interrogation of the millions of Soviet POWs and civilians who had fallen into German hands during the opening months of the war. Multilingual defectors were often attached to the interrogation teams because of their language skills, knowledge of the local area, or, as noted above, enthusiasm for dealing with their compatriots "who did not share their ideals." The German army and the SS specifically authorized torture and frequently employed it as a means of extracting information. Inside the POW camps local collaborators specialized in *Durchkämmung,* the "combing out" of Jews, "commissars" (Communist party members), and other undesirables from among the captured soldiers. The SS turned the "combed" ones over to the mobile killing squads for execution.

The work of these interrogators and interpreters was essential to the broader Nazi effort to locate and exterminate the Jews and Communists who had fallen into their hands. After the war the

German political warfare experts rarely discussed their own roles or those of their defectors in these interrogations, despite their clear participation in them. This is perhaps because, as noted by the Nuremberg tribunal in its decision on SS man and political warfare specialist Waldemar von Radetzky, "by admitting the translation functions, [they] would be admitting that [they] knew of executions which followed certain investigations."[12] The political warfare experts were deeply involved in these interrogations throughout the war. Wilfried Strik-Strikfeldt, for example, who was later a central figure in CIA-financed émigré operations in Munich, spent much of the war as chief interrogator of the Russian intelligence directorate of the Abwehr (German military intelligence) on the eastern front.[13]

Otto Ohlendorf, the commander of Einsatzgruppe D mass execution squads in the Caucasus, offers a glimpse into a part of the careers of the leaders of the political warfare faction and their collaborationist troops that might otherwise be lost to history. According to Ohlendorf, the collaborator units formed one of the most important—and incriminating—links between the German military officer corps, on the one hand, and the SS's *Einsatzgruppen* extermination squads, on the other. "The Army units had to sort out political commissars and other undesirable elements themselves"— that is, through use of native quislings and collaborators—then "hand them over to the *Einsatzkommandos* to be killed," Ohlendorf testified. "[T]he activity of the *Einsatzgruppen* and their *Einsatzkommandos* was carried out entirely within the field of jurisdiction of the commanders in chief of the army groups or armies under their responsibility."[14]

Collaborators often played an important role in mass murders. The officers of these killing squads were, like Ohlendorf, primarily Germans attached to various police units under SS jurisdiction. But many of the troops in the killing squads, significantly, were not Germans. They were, according to Ohlendorf, collaborators on loan from the army known as *Notdienstverpflichtete* (emergency service draftees, later to be designated *Osttruppen,* or eastern troops), local militias or companies of defectors that were destined to be directly recruited into the Waffen SS.

"The importance of these auxiliaries should not be underestimated," notes internationally recognized Holocaust expert Raul Hilberg. "Roundups by local inhabitants who spoke the local language resulted in higher percentages of Jewish dead. This fact is clearly indicated by the statistics of the *Kommandos* which made use of local help." In Lithuania municipal killing squads employing Lithuanian Nazi collaborators eliminated 46,692 Jews in fewer than three months, according to their own reports, mainly by combining clocklike liquidation of 500 Jews per day in the capital city of Vilnius with mobile "cleanup" sweeps through the surrounding countryside.

Such squads were consistently used by the Nazis for the dirty work that even the SS believed to be "beneath the dignity" of the German soldier. In the Ukraine, for example, Einsatzkommando 4a went so far as to "confine itself to the shooting of adults while commanding its Ukrainian helpers to shoot [the] children," Hilberg reports. "We were actually frightened," remembered Ernst Biberstein, the chief of Einsatzkommando 6, "by the blood thirstiness of these people."[15]

The collaborationist troops of the eastern front were, in sum, an integral part of German strategy in the East and deeply involved in Nazi efforts to exterminate the Jews. The Western powers recognized this fact during the war. Collaborators captured by Western forces were treated as prisoners of war, and many were turned over to the USSR as traitors and suspected war criminals in the first months after Germany's surrender. The predominant opinion in the U.S. command at war's end was that it was now up to the USSR to decide what to do with the Nazis' eastern troops and other traitors, just as it was up to the Americans to decide what to do with Tokyo Rose and similar captured defectors from this country.

But a parallel development that would soon have a powerful impact on how Axis POWs were treated in the West was taking place. There was at the time in American hands another group of Axis prisoners, who, unlike the collaborators from the East, were regarded as quite valuable: scientists who had put their skills to work for the Nazi cause.

All the major powers considered German scientists part of the booty of war. The Americans, British, and Soviets each had established special teams that concentrated on the capture and preservation of German laboratories, industrial patents, and similar useful hardware of the modern age. Scientists were generally regarded as another technical asset to be appropriated.

The United States and Great Britain jointly created a Combined Intelligence Objectives Subcommittee (CIOS) to coordinate their efforts to seize particularly valuable targets. Actual raids were carried out by subordinate teams designated by a letter, like the "S Force" (also known as the "Sugar Force" in cable traffic) in Italy, the "T Force" in France, Holland, and Germany, and so on.[16] These units had only minimal armed strength, but they traveled complete with accomplished linguists, Western scientists, and police specialists who permitted them to identify rapidly and capture useful experts and materials.

The stakes in the search for the scientific expertise of Germany were high. The single most important American strike force, for example, was the Alsos raiding team, which targeted Axis atomic research, uranium stockpiles, and nuclear scientists, as well as Nazi chemical and biological warfare research. The commander of this assignment was U.S. Army Colonel Boris Pash, who had previously been security chief of the Manhattan Project—the United States' atomic bomb development program—and who later played an important role in highly secret U.S. covert action programs. Pash succeeded brilliantly in his mission, seizing top German scientists and more than 70,000 tons of Axis uranium ore and radium products. The uranium taken during these raids was eventually shipped to the United States and incorporated in U.S. atomic weapons.[17]

The U.S. government's utilitarian approach to dealing with German science and scientists, however, proved to be the point of the wedge that eventually helped split American resolve to deal harshly with Nazi criminals, including the captured collaborators who had served on the eastern front. It is clear in hindsight that the Americans in charge of exploiting German specialists captured through Alsos and similar programs became pioneers of the methods later used to bring other Nazis and collaborators into this country. Equally important, the philosophical concepts and psychological rationalizations expressed by U.S. officials in dealing with the German experts were gradually stretched to cover utilization of almost any anti-Communist, regardless of what he or she had done during the war.

CHAPTER THREE

"Chosen, Rare Minds"

German General Walter Dornberger is a case in point. Dornberger—a military, not an SS, officer—was never indicted or tried on any war crimes charge. Instead, he became a famous man in aerospace industry circles and remains much respected by U.S. corporate and military associations to this day. Dornberger is often cited as an example of the sort of German who was really innocent of Nazi crimes and who was appropriate for the United States to recruit once the war was over.

The U.S. Air Force, it is now known, secretly brought Dornberger to this country in 1947 and put him to work on a classified rocketry program at Wright Field (now Wright-Patterson Air Force Base) near Dayton, Ohio. By 1950 he had gone into private industry with Bell Aircraft, and he eventually rose to be a senior vice-president in the Bell Aerosystems Division of the massive multinational Textron Corporation. There he specialized in company liaison with U.S. military agencies. He enjoyed high U.S. security clearances and many public honors, including the American Rocket Society's Astronautics Award in 1959. He died peacefully in June 1980.[1]

Prior to his arrival in the United States Dornberger had been a career German artillery officer. He had recognized as early as the 1920s that the Versailles Treaty prohibited Germany from building more than a handful of cannons, bombers, naval guns, or similar conventional weaponry. Rockets, however, had been unknown as modern weapons at the time of Versailles and thus had not been banned by that agreement. Dornberger was one of the first who figured out that these scientists' toys could be put to use to propel high explosives. He labored hard from 1932 on to make missiles an integral part of the arsenal of the Third Reich.

It was not easy being a military rocket chief in Nazi Germany. The SS, in particular, tried to muscle in on Dornberger's work. Money, engineers, and slave laborers used in construction seemed always to be in short supply. And in March 1943 a terrible blow fell: Adolf Hitler had a dream in which Dornberger's pet project, the giant liquid-fueled V-2 rocket, failed to cross the English Channel. The Führer put great stock in these nightly visions, and soon the general's project had fallen to the bottom of a heap of high-priority "secret weapons" that were supposed to extricate Germany from the mess it had created.

But General Walter Dornberger was nothing if not determined. He requested and got a private audience with Hitler during July 1943. With films, little wooden rocket models, and other audio-visual aids, Dornberger personally convinced Hitler to authorize the creation of a gigantic underground factory near Nordhausen for mass production of his machines. This factory would also house one of the major crimes of the war.[2]

The Nazis used slave labor from the nearby Dora concentration camp to build the Nordhausen rocket works. In fewer than fifteen months of operation the SS drove Dora's inmates to hack a mile-long underground cavern out of an abandoned salt mine to house the facility. The starvation diet and heavy labor generally killed the toilers after a few months. The assembly line workers who actually built the missiles once the cave was finished were not much better off.

At least 20,000 prisoners—many of them talented engineers who had been singled out for missile production because of their education—were killed through starvation, disease, or execution at Dora and Nordhausen in the course of this project.[3]

The question of who bears responsibility for these deaths has been the subject of considerable controversy since the war. After 1945, of course, Dornberger and his subordinates denied that they had had anything to do with the Nordhausen production line. The SS, not they, they said, had controlled the labor force at the underground factory.

The SS surely deserves to bear part, perhaps even the largest part, of responsibility for the crimes at Nordhausen. But it is a mistake to think it acted alone. In truth, Dornberger and his aides fought a long bureaucratic battle with the SS over control of Germany's rocket program, and the degree of Dornberger's personal authority over what took place on the production line shifted with Hitler's moods. In late 1944 the general reached an agreement with Heinrich Himmler, head of the SS, under which the SS's representative, Hans Kammler, took over day-to-day management at Nordhausen on the condition that selected Dornberger subordinates (like latter-day U.S. rocket program administrator Arthur Rudolph) retained their positions of authority at the facility. Dornberger himself retained explicit jurisdiction over production schedules, including the number of missiles to be built and the mix of the various models.[4]

Dornberger, in short, did not directly control the slaves at Nordhausen. His production orders, however, set the schedule by which they were worked to death. And he was, it seems, an enthusiastic taskmaster. He demanded more and more rockets—more than there was even fuel to launch—until the very last moments of the war. Food for the slaves at Nordhausen—never much in the first place—ran out altogether sometime in February 1945. But Dornberger's orders for more missiles never stopped, and the labor battalions worked around the clock without nourishment. The SS simply crammed more prisoners into the Dora camp, used the strong ones for labor until they dropped, and let the weak ones die.

Thousands of inmates starved to death. Cholera raged through the camp, killing hundreds each day. At first the SS cremated the dead so as to keep down disease among the surviving slaves. As the end neared, however, the ovens couldn't keep up with the demand and the corpses were simply left to rot. Inmates piled the bodies up in corners, under stairways, anywhere that was a little out of the way. And the rocket work continued.

Dornberger visited the Nordhausen factory on many occasions. He knew—or should have known, for the atrocity was evident to any eye—that the prisoners who worked on his rockets were being systematically starved to death. And he knew, for he has said this much himself, that Germany's defeat was inevitable.[5] Dornberger could have shut down the assembly line on some technical pretext. He could have demanded adequate rations for the prisoners. He could have cut back his missile orders to the number that Germany was capable of launching. He chose instead to accelerate production.

The general's postwar autobiography, which was received with some critical acclaim in the West, is filled with anecdotes about his rocket tests, bureaucratic struggles, and technical achievements. His machines are described in endless detail with precise information on takeoff weight, fuel consumption, thrust, and other minutiae of physics. Yet there is not a phrase of acknowledgment for the prisoners who actually constructed these machines at the cost of their lives. He presents events in his book as though his missiles had simply leaped off their drawing boards and into the skies with no intermediate steps, as though rockets could somehow build themselves.

When many Americans think of the Holocaust—those, that is, who were not eyewitnesses—they often think of the images on a certain piece of grainy motion-picture film, on which cadaverous inmates resembling living skeletons are shown leaning out from filthy wooden bunks to weakly greet U.S. Army liberators. The movie then cuts to a scene in which hundreds of corpses are laid out in a row. They appear hardly human even in death. The legbones are etched clearly against the ground, but the limbs seem too big somehow, as though they don't fit with the bodies. This is because there is no flesh left on the remains, only skin; the Nazis and their rocket factory have made off with the rest. The film flickers as an American officer walks past the atrocity, his face a mask.

That documentary film was taken by the U.S. Army Signal Corps at Nordhausen in April 1945.[6] The Dora camp and its underground missile works were the first major slave labor facility liberated by American forces.

The U.S. liberation of the Nordhausen complex set off a scramble between U.S. and Soviet scientific raiding teams that proved to be one of the opening shots of the cold war. The Soviets attempted to claim the captured scientists and the buried technical booty at Nordhausen as their own, in part because they considered the camp inside their zone of military operations. The United States, however, ended up with the larger share of the scientific legacy of the Nordhausen complex. This included tons of partially assembled V-2 rockets, technical documentation, and about 1,200 captured German rocketry experts—Dornberger and Wernher von Braun among them. The value of the scientific documents alone has been conservatively estimated at $400 to $500 million.

And there was more, much more: scientific and technical booty from all over Germany. The U.S. share of these spoils included the engineers, technicians, and fifty ME-162 jet turbines—the most advanced in the world—from the Messerschmitt factory at Schönebeck; virtually the entire scientific staff from the Siemens and Zeiss companies; leading chemical and electrical engineers and their equipment from I. G. Farben and Telefunken; scientists, radium, and all traces of atomic research from the Physical and Technical Institute in Weida; and the technical staff and all designs for new motors from the underground BMW works at Unsenberg, to name only a few.[7]

The Soviets, for their part, regarded virtually all the wealth of Germany as potential compensation for the massive destruction that the Nazis had wreaked inside the USSR. Soviet troops seized almost any industrial or scientific equipment that could be located in the Russian occupation zone. Printing presses; chemistry labs; office furniture; dentistry tools; hospitals; steel mills; railroad track; machine tools—anything and everything of productive value that could be located were systematically dismantled, crated, and shipped east.

Before the summer of 1945 was out, the United States and the USSR were publicly accusing each other of looting German scientific and industrial wealth in violation of their wartime agreements. These East-West conflicts over seizures soon spilled over into the August 1945 Potsdam Conference, where contentious arguments over who had prior claim to Germany's scientists and technicians seriously soured the already tense negotiations. Each side at the conference appears to have regarded its rival's clandestine raiding operations as an acid test of its opponent's postwar intentions, regardless of what the diplomats may have said at the conference table.

American spokesmen, interestingly enough, replied to Soviet charges concerning captured German scientists with the assertion that all such experts then in U.S. hands were either suspected war criminals or former top executives of Germany's war machine. They were therefore appropriately subject to arrest, the United States said.[8] But despite these early public claims concerning the character of the captured German specialists, many of the same experts were soon considered too valuable to bring to trial. Instead, the United States began to integrate scores of top German scientists into American military research projects only weeks after Hitler's final collapse. Before two years were out, hundreds of German scientists, including some suspected of crimes against humanity, were on the American payroll.

Most of the German specialists who actively engaged in military research during the war were longtime Nazi party members. There are many complex reasons for this phenomenon. Some of them, of course, simply believed in the Nazi cause. U.S. Army investigators were informed shortly after the war that Dornberger's chief of staff, Dr. Herbert Axster, for example, beat and starved inmate workers on his two estates, while his wife had been a national spokeswoman noted for her pro-Nazi speeches on behalf of the NS Frauenschaft, a Nazi party women's auxiliary.[9] Many senior German academic figures promoted elaborate "scholarly" theories of Aryan genetic superiority, which had been popular in some intellectual circles for decades by the time the Nazis came to power, and the Axsters are said to have been among them.

Hitler's government had given party members and sympathizers among the intelligentsia control of most major centers of German scholarship well before the war, and they maintained an effective carrot-and-stick system to keep Germany's academic community in line. Research grants and professional advancement were open only to those experts who were willing to associate themselves publicly with the party or with a variety of Nazi-controlled professional associations and licensing bodies. Researchers engaged in rocketry, electronics, and other highly sensitive fields of interest to the military were carefully screened for reliability before they received security clearances. Leading technical thinkers were often given honorary party membership or SS ranks; Wernher von Braun, for example, had been an honorary SS officer for almost a decade by the end of the war. A brief review of the German scientific literature of the period makes it clear that many experts who were accorded such "honors" clearly felt it was prudent to display them and use them for professional advancement.

At the same time Jews and scientists thought to be hostile to Nazi precepts were systematically purged from academe, and not a few brilliant minds who refused to aid the Nazis died in concentration camps or as cannon fodder on the eastern front. Of those who continued work during the Nazi period, many have since said that they supported the Nazi state out of fear, German national pride, or the feeling that they could not abandon their country in wartime.

By the end of the war many U.S. military intelligence officials believed that a distinction should be made between scientists like von Braun who had joined the Nazi party and SS for what the Americans termed "opportunistic" reasons, on the one hand, and the various German experts who had supported Nazism for ideological reasons or who had directly participated in atrocities, on the other. The former were viewed as prized captives and given special dispensation from the general Allied policy on handling former Nazi officers and SS men.

The U.S. Army and Navy brought some German scientists to this country as early as the summer of 1945. On July 6 the Joint Chiefs of Staff (JCS) specifically authorized an effort to "exploit . . . chosen, rare minds whose continuing intellectual productivity we wish to use" under the top secret project code-named Overcast. The chiefs directed that up to 350 specialists, mainly from Germany and Austria, should be immediately brought to the United States.[10] These "rare minds" included, for example, specialists in submarine design, chemical warfare, and, of course, missile research.

Under Overcast, it soon became the custom for U.S. intelligence officers to ignore German scientists' past memberships in the Nazi party and the SS in order to recruit these presumably valuable experts. There were several reasons for this. For one thing, the first scientists were enlisted under a program that was clearly limited to "temporary military exploitation," as the JCS order put it, and thus was in effect an expanded type of interrogation of German POWs. All the Axis scientists (and their families, who were permitted to accompany them to the United States) were to remain under War Department control during their stay in this country, and all of them were supposed to be returned to Europe following completion of their particular research projects.

At first this was justified on the grounds that German scientists might be useful in the continuing war against Japan. But the Americans' own terror weapon, the atomic bomb, decided the Pacific conflict within a few months after the surrender of Hitler's Germany. The "Japanese threat" rationale evaporated.

Subsequent events have made clear that the emerging conflict with the USSR was often not far from policymakers' minds when Overcast was created. As early as June 1945 RCA chief David Sarnoff argues in a confidential letter to President Truman's chief science adviser that "the security for any nation henceforth depends . . . to a very large extent on its place in the scientific sun. That sun may shine brightly for those who know, and it may be a total blackout for those who don't." Sarnoff continues: "It is not only important that we get [Germany's] scientific information but that we lay hands on their scientists as well. If we do not find them and remove them to a place perhaps on this side of the water where they can continue their scientific experiments under our guidance and control, our Russian friends may do so first."[11]

At the same time the U.S.-USSR rivalry was heating up, the mystique of white coats and high technology was also at work, separating the captured specialists from responsibility for their wartime deeds in all but the most horrific cases. A special committee of the U.S. National Academy of Sciences, for example, put forward in 1945 the rather surprising theory that its brethren's wartime research for the Nazis had actually been a form of resistance against Hitler's regime. The majority of German scientists, the academy asserted, composed what was termed "an island of nonconformity in the Nazified body politic" which had withdrawn into "the traditional ivory tower [that] offered the only possibility of security" during the Nazi rule.[12]

By 1946 the Pentagon's Joint Intelligence Objectives Agency (JIOA) began pushing for a revised and bigger program of recruiting German scientists. (The JIOA, which was handling the Overcast program for the War Department, had superseded the earlier Combined Intelligence Objectives Subcommittee, the group that had organized the capture of many of the scientists in the first place.) The JIOA now wanted 1,000 former enemy specialists. More important, it wanted authority to grant them American citizenship as an inducement to participate in the program.

The Pentagon's agency generally refused to ship back the German experts who were already in the United States. These men and women were now viewed as too valuable to return to Europe, particularly because many of the Overcast scientists already knew almost as much about several of America's most secret military research programs as they did about Hitler's. Letting such specialists fall into Soviet hands back in Germany was seen as a serious security threat.

The JIOA needed President Truman's direct authorization precisely because so many of the German scientists and technicians had once been Nazi party members and SS officers. U.S. immigration laws at the time strictly prohibited entry into this country by any former Nazis. The fact that a person might have joined the Nazi party "involuntarily" or simply in order to advance his career could not be taken into account as the law then stood. What the JIOA and the War Department were asking for, in effect, was an exemption from this statute for up to 1,000 former enemy specialists.

President Truman accepted the idea of putting selected Germans back to work on America's behalf during the cold war, as long as the effort could remain secret from the public. American government attitudes toward Nazism in general were changing as early as the spring of 1946. "In the beginning everyone was a hard-liner," commented a former U.S. military government official engaged in Overcast who requested anonymity. "In the end, though, very few people were [hard-liners]." The recruitment of former Nazis through Overcast was not a dark conspiracy, he insisted, but rather what he termed "a natural process of learning what the role of the Nazi Party had been in Germany." Among his own conclusions, this retired official said, is that a useful distinction could be made between ordinary Nazis, on the one hand, and actual war criminals, on the other. Former Nazi party members could be put to profitable use by the United States, many of Truman's top advisers believed. War criminals, on the other hand, should be prosecuted.

Truman authorized the JIOA's plan in September 1946. He insisted that only "nominal" Nazis—that is, people who had joined the Nazi party out of what the Americans considered opportunistic motives—be permitted to participate in the program. Known or suspected war criminals were supposed to be strictly barred. The relevant presidential directive states in part: "No person found . . . to have been a member of the Nazi Party and more than a nominal participant in its activities, or an active supporter of Nazism or militarism shall be brought to the U.S. hereunder." Even so, "position [or] honors awarded a specialist under the Nazi Regime solely on account of his scientific or technical abilities" would not disqualify a potential candidate. This program took the code name Paperclip.[13]

Truman's authorization did not define exactly what an "active supporter" was. Instead, it left the sorting out of former Nazis up to a secret panel made up of experts from the departments of State and Justice, who were required to rule directly on each scientist the JIOA wanted to bring to this country. The question of who was—

and who was not—an "active supporter of Nazism or militarism" soon became a highly politicized issue within the American national security establishment. The decision often depended at least as much on the attitudes of the person who was judging as it did on the actual behavior of any given suspect.

JIOA Director Bosquet Wev presented the first group of scientists' dossiers to the U.S. departments of State and Justice for approval about six months after Truman's authorization of Paperclip. Wev's files did not contain raw investigative reports on the German specialists' activities, which might have permitted the outside agencies to decide for themselves about the characters of the recruits. Instead, the key document in each folder was a security report on each scientist filed by OMGUS (Office of Military Government—US), the U.S. occupation administration inside defeated Germany. The OMGUS report presented the gist of any earlier CIC investigations into the specialist's wartime activities. If OMGUS said the scientist had been an "ardent Nazi," there was little prospect that he would ever be permitted into the United States. If it didn't, he was probably home free.

Wev's job was to shepherd the experts' dossiers past the review board responsible for ruling on scientists nominated for the Paperclip program. Unfortunately for Wev, however, the State Department's representative on the committee was Samuel Klaus, a stickler for detail who made no secret of his belief that Nazis—"ex-" or otherwise—were a threat to the United States.

The OMGUS reports in Wev's first batch of folders had been prepared by OMGUS agents who served in Germany prior to the rapid revision of American intelligence attitudes toward former Nazis that was then under way. The reports bluntly pointed out that some of Wev's recruits, who had actually already entered the United States under Project Overcast, *had* been "ardent Nazis." The records on other specialists on the Paperclip recruiting list were not much better. Some of the experts were accused of participating in murderous medical experiments on human subjects at concentration camps, for example, and of brutalizing slave laborers. One was a fugitive from formal murder charges. Another was known to have established an institute for biological warfare experimentation on humans in Poland. At least half of Wev's recruits, and probably more, were Nazi party members or SS veterans.

Klaus refused to be a team player. He rejected Wev's first batch of applicants,[14] arguing that accepting them was against Truman's orders.

The JIOA chief was furious. In a scathing secret memo he warned that returning his scientists to Germany "presents a far greater security threat to this country than any former Nazi affiliations which they may have had, or even any Nazi sympathies that they may still have." Wev complained to Major General Stephen Chamberlin, then the director of intelligence for the War Department general staff, that Klaus and another State Department official, Herbert Cummings, were "sabotaging by delay" his efforts to import scientists. "The most positive and drastic action possible [must] be taken," Wev insisted, "in order to break the impasse which currently exists."[15]

The solution to Wev's problems proved to be surprisingly simple. If Klaus and Cummings would not accept the OMGUS dossiers as they were, then the files could be changed. In November of that year Wev's deputy returned seven OMGUS folders to General Chamberlin with a note explaining that the JIOA did not believe it "advisable" to submit the candidates to State and Justice "at the present time." Among the withheld records, it is worth noting, was Wernher von Braun's OMGUS report, which stated that the scientist was wanted for a denazification hearing because of his SS record, although he "was not a war criminal." JIOA also held back its file on Dornberger's wartime chief of staff, Dr. Herbert Axster.

Shortly thereafter JIOA Director Wev wired the director of intelligence at the U.S. European Command (EUCOM). His message was blunt: "[T]here is very little possibility that the State and Justice Departments will agree to immigrate any specialist who has been classified as an actual or potential security threat to the United States. This may result in the return [to] Germany of specialists whose skill and knowledge should be denied to other nations in the interest of national security." Therefore, Wev concluded, "it is requested . . . that *new security reports be submitted* [emphasis added] where such action is appropriate" so that von Braun and his associates might be permitted to stay in the United States.

OMGUS sent the new dossiers back from Germany a few weeks later. The offending language in each file had been changed. Von Braun and other leading specialists who had been initially held up because of their Nazi party and SS histories were now described as "not constitut[ing] a security threat to the U.S."[16] From that point on OMGUS investigators didn't send Washington any more reports that claimed its scientific recruits might be "security threats" because of their service in Hitler Germany. Klaus and Cummings soon left the screening board, and Paperclip recruitment of German scientists ran smoothly for almost a decade.

Von Braun insisted throughout this minor ordeal that his appointment as an SS *Sturmbannführer* in 1937 had been purely honorary and without political significance. Yet von Braun, like Dornberger, had every opportunity to know what was happening at Nordhausen. Still, he continued to work industriously on behalf of the Reich until its final collapse. He tinkered away on the missiles' design, adding special insulation to prevent the machines from blowing up in flight, then improving the guidance system so that a greater percentage of the V-2's high-explosive warheads succeeded in hitting London. Like Dornberger, von Braun pushed for increased production from the slaves at Nordhausen. After the war, of course, von Braun asserted that he had been opposed to the National Socialist ideology all along. His real reason for working in the Nazi missile program, he said, had been the potential usefulness of his machines in "space travel."

Dornberger himself did not experience the immigration difficulties that von Braun did. He was permitted to enter the United States without State Department opposition even at the height of the 1947 controversy, much to the dismay of the British, who had been, after all, the target of Dornberger's rockets. The British had held Dornberger as a POW for two years following the war, and they had made no secret of their desire to bring him to trial as a war criminal. Even the Americans had been leery of him at first but had gradually come around to believing him indispensable as the United States' own military rocket program gradually got off the ground. In the end Dornberger appears to have slipped through Klaus's and Cummings's security screen because he had never been a member of the Nazi party or the SS. No party or SS membership meant that OMGUS did not investigate him as a "security threat," and no negative report from OMGUS meant that he could enter the United States under Paperclip without opposition.

Between 1945 and 1955, 765 scientists, engineers, and technicians were brought to the United States under Overcast, Paperclip, and two other similar programs. At least half, and perhaps as many as 80 percent, of the imported specialists were former Nazi party members or SS men, according to Professor Clarence Lasby, who has authored a book-length study of Paperclip. Three of these experts, so far, have been forced out of the country. They are Georg Rickhey, a former official at the Nordhausen factory who arrived in 1946 but who left the country in 1947 when he was tried (and acquitted) for war crimes by a U.S. military tribunal; Major General Walter Schreiber, who had once been instrumental in medical experiments on concentration camp inmates by the Luftwaffe (German air force) and who fled the United States in 1952 following an exposé by columnist Drew Pearson; and Arthur Rudolph, another Nordhausen veteran who quietly moved to West Germany in 1984 following the U.S. Department of Justice's discovery of his role in the persecution of prisoners at the underground factory.[17] Rudolph is generally given credit for having been instrumental in organizing the construction of the powerful Saturn V rockets that launched America's astronauts to the moon.

Overcast and Paperclip were just the beginning. American intelligence agencies, which are, after all, research institutions of a sort, also wanted European specialists, just as the more conventional scientific laboratories did. The most fruitful potential source of new recruits for them was obviously the defeated intelligence agencies of Nazi Germany.

But unlike the scientists, many of whom could plausibly claim not to have been personally involved in war crimes, veterans of Hitler's clandestine services could hardly claim to have been ignorant of Nazi criminality. Hitler's spy agencies had been at the cutting edge of Nazi efforts to locate and exterminate Jews, Communists, and other enemies of the German state throughout the war.

CHAPTER FOUR

The Man at Box 1142

Reinhard Gehlen, Hitler's most senior military intelligence officer on the eastern front, had begun planning his surrender to the United States at least as early as the fall of 1944. Germany's inevitable defeat had become obvious by that time, and a number of senior Nazi security officers—including SS chief Heinrich Himmler and Himmler's adjutant, SS General Karl Wolff—had also undertaken secret surrender plans. The common features in their tactics were, first, the offer of something of value to the Western Allies, like espionage information or a quick (though not necessarily unconditional) surrender of German forces, and, second, an attempt to create an alibi that downplayed their participation in war crimes and genocide. The price tag for their cooperation with the West, they hoped, was insulation from prosecution. In the end Gehlen, Wolff, and several hundred other senior German officers succeeded in making deals with Britain or the United States, while a smaller number of top-ranking Nazis, apparently several score, made their peace with the USSR and its Eastern European satellites.

General Gehlen, however, proved to be the most important of them all. He was a scrawny man—at five feet eight and a half inches he weighed less than 130 pounds at the time of his surrender—with an arrogant demeanor and a violent temper that got worse as he grew older. But he also had extraordinary powers of concentration and a jeweler's attention to detail, both of which served him well in his remarkable thirty-seven-year career as a spy master.

In early March 1945 Gehlen and a small group of his most senior officers carefully microfilmed the vast holdings on the USSR in the Fremde Heere Ost (FHO), the military intelligence section of the German army's general staff. They packed the film in watertight steel drums and secretly buried it in remote mountain meadows scattered through the Austrian Alps. Then, on May 22, 1945, Gehlen and his top aides surrendered to an American Counterintelligence Corps team.

Luck was with them. Captain John Bokor was assigned as their interrogator at Camp King, near Oberursel, in the American occupation zone. Bokor had been interned by the Germans early in the war, had been treated well, and had later served as an interrogator of captured German officers at Fort Hunt near Washington, D.C. Though he was unquestionably anti-Nazi, Bokor's contact with the German officer corps had left him with a certain amount of respect for the enemy and a disdain for the narrow-minded anti-Germanism of many American officers of the time. He was, as Gehlen recalled later, "the first American officer I met with expert knowledge of Russia and with no illusions about the way political events were turning . . . we became close friends and have remained so."[1] During the weeks following Bokor's new assignment Gehlen gradually laid his cards on the table. Not only did the former Wehrmacht general know where the precious archives were buried, but he had also maintained the embryo of an underground espionage organization that could put the records to work against the USSR. Captain Bokor was interested.

There were serious obstacles to the plan. For one thing, the U.S. command mistrusted any type of deals offered by desperate Germans. For another, the Yalta agreements required the United States to turn over to the Russians captured Axis officers who had been involved in "eastern area activities" in exchange for Soviet help in returning the thousands of American POWs who had been picked up by the Red Army.

According to Gehlen's memoirs, Captain Bokor decided to proceed on his own, regardless of official policy. He kept the details of Gehlen's offer secret from the other Americans at the interrogation center and worked quietly to remove the names of Gehlen's senior command from the official lists of POWs in U.S. hands. Bokor and

Colonel William R. Philp (chief of the CIC's sprawling interrogation headquarters at Camp King) arranged for seven senior Gehlen officers to be transferred to the camp, where they were constituted as a "historical study group" supposedly working on a report on the German general staff. Gehlen's precious cache of records was located and shipped to the interrogation center under such secrecy that not even the CIC's chain of command was informed of what was being born at Dulag Luft, as the Germans called the garrison. "Bokor feared . . ." Gehlen related thirty years later, "that if he had reported our existence too early to [U.S. headquarters at] Frankfurt and the Pentagon, we might have become exposed to hostile forces [within the U.S. chain of command] and then we would have been beyond salvation. I now know . . . that Captain Bokor was acting on his own" during the earliest days.[2]

By the end of the summer, however, Bokor had won the support of Generals Edwin Sibert and Walter Bedell Smith, respectively the highest ranking U.S. Army intelligence officer in Europe and the chief of staff of the Supreme Allied Command. General William ("Wild Bill") Donovan and Allen Dulles of America's wartime clandestine operations agency, the Office of Strategic Services (OSS), were also tipped off about Gehlen's offer by a Dulles double agent inside the German Foreign Office. The OSS was soon jockeying with U.S. military intelligence for institutional authority over Gehlen's microfilmed records and, before long, over control of the German spy master himself.

Sibert shipped Gehlen and three of his assistants to Washington, D.C., for debriefing in August 1945. By December Sibert had won permission to proceed "under his own authority" with financing and exploitation of the German's espionage group. In the jargon of the spy trade, Sibert became a "cutout," in effect, for the policymakers in Washington—that is, Sibert could have his German operation, but if it went sour, he would be the one to take the blame. At the same time, however, Dulles's Secret Intelligence Branch (SIB) of the OSS enjoyed direct liaison with Gehlen. Frank Wisner, a dashing young Wall Street lawyer who had distinguished himself in underground OSS intrigues in Istanbul and Bucharest, headed the coordinating team.[3]*

---

*Frank Wisner's Special Intelligence Branch staff, which was engaged in work with Gehlen, had more than its share of brilliant operatives who were to leave their marks on the history of U.S. espionage. They included Richard Helms, for example, later to become CIA deputy director for clandestine operations and eventually agency director under Presidents

The documentation that might establish exactly how much President Truman knew about American recruitment of Gehlen and his organization remains classified. It is known, however, that the Soviets made vigorous protests against this secret agreement at least as early as the Potsdam Conference; thus it is unlikely that the matter escaped Truman's attention altogether. Considering the senior status of Donovan, Dulles, Sibert, and the other U.S. intelligence officers known to have been directly involved, and considering that two competing American intelligence bureaucracies were attempting to share Gehlen's archives, it is reasonable to suspect that the president had been well briefed about this operation. Further, the extreme political sensitivity inevitably involved in recruiting an enemy spy chief for missions against a country that was still officially an ally of the United States suggests that Truman's personal approval may well have been necessary before full-scale exploitation of the German general began. Either way, it is clear that before a year was out, the Americans had freed Gehlen and most of his high command, then installed them in a former Waffen SS training facility near Pullach, Germany, which has remained the group's headquarters to this day.

A sampling of Gehlen's earliest reports is illustrative of much of the German espionage chief's work during his first years of work for U.S. intelligence. According to a newly discovered secret summary of Gehlen's interrogation at "Box 1142"—the coded address for Fort Hunt, outside Washington, D.C.—Gehlen's first reports consisted of a detailed history of the German intelligence service on the eastern front, followed by a thirty-five-page summary on "Development of the Russian High Command and Its Conception of Strategy." By August 1945 new reports on Soviet land war tactics and the political commissar system within the Red Army had been completed.

Gehlen's case officer at 1142 waxed enthusiastic about the "potentialities [of] future reports" and offered a closely typed list of twenty-eight new intelligence studies based on Gehlen and his hoard of records that were to be available within a few weeks. Every one of them concerned the USSR. They included surveys of Russian tanks, manpower, war production, propaganda, the Soviet

---

Johnson and Nixon; William Casey, CIA director under President Reagan; Harry Rositzke, soon to become chief of CIA clandestine operations inside the USSR and later CIA chief of station in India; and, of course, Wisner himself, soon to be chief of all American clandestine warfare operations worldwide.

secret police (the NKVD), "employment of German methods . . . [for] evaluation of various new information received by the US," and "suggestions as to the employment of sources for gathering information in the Central European Sector."[4]

One would imagine that some U.S. intelligence officer must have asked Gehlen exactly how he had obtained his information, but the record of this inquiry, if it took place, has yet to appear. Instead, the source of Gehlen's data is simply referred to in the secret U.S. records that have surfaced as "Gehlen" himself or as "Gehlen's organization."

In reality, Gehlen derived much of his information from his role in one of the most terrible atrocities of the war: the torture, interrogation, and murder by starvation of some 4 million Soviet prisoners of war. Even Gehlen's defenders—and there are many of them, both in Germany and in the United States—acknowledge he was instrumental in organizing the interrogations of these POWs. The success of this interrogation program from the German military's point of view became, in fact, the cornerstone of Gehlen's career. It won him his reputation as an intelligence officer and his major general's rank.

But these same interrogations were actually a step in the liquidation of tens of thousands of POWs. Prisoners who refused to cooperate were often tortured or summarily shot. Many were executed even after they had given information, while others were simply left to starve to death. True, Gehlen's men did not personally administer the starvation camps, nor are they known to have served in the execution squads. Such tasks were left to the SS, whose efficiency in such matters is well known.

Instead, Gehlen's men were in a sense like scientists who skimmed off the information and documents that rose to the surface of these pestilent camps. Now and again they selected an interesting specimen: a captured Russian general ready to collaborate, perhaps, or a Ukrainian railroad expert who might supply the locations of vulnerable bridges when given some encouragement to talk. Gehlen's officers were scientists in somewhat the same way that concentration camp doctors were: Both groups extracted their data from the destruction of human beings.[5]

Gehlen officially promised the Americans after the war that he would refuse "on principle" to employ former SS, SD, and Gestapo men in his new intelligence operation. His reassurances are not surprising; those groups had been declared criminal organizations by the Supreme Allied Command in Europe during the war, and every former member was subject to immediate arrest. By 1946 these groups had been convicted as organizational perpetrators of war crimes and crimes against humanity by the Nuremberg tribunal, and the earlier assertion of criminality had taken on the force of international law.

But Gehlen's reassurances on the SS issue proved to be false. At least a half dozen—and probably more—of his first staff of fifty officers were former SS or SD men, including SS Obersturmführer Hans Sommer (who had set seven Paris synagogues to the torch in October 1941), SS Standartenführer Willi Krichbaum (senior Gestapo leader in southeastern Europe), and SS Sturmbannführer Fritz Schmidt (Gestapo chief in Kiel, Germany), each of whom was given responsible positions in the new Organisation Gehlen.[6] The earliest SS recruits were enlisted with phony papers and false names; Gehlen could, if necessary, deny that he had known that they had Nazi pasts.

It is reasonable to suspect that some Americans were aware of this ruse. It is, after all, the job of any professional intelligence officer to learn everything there is to know about the groups on his payroll and to collect information concerning his contract agents that might reveal their loyalty. General Sibert, who by then had become the leading American sponsor of the Gehlen Organization, had not gotten to be chief of U.S. Army intelligence in Germany by being naïve. It is hard to believe that Gehlen would have attempted to trick Sibert if the American had bluntly asked the German general if he was employing SS men; such deceit would have seriously undermined Gehlen's credibility had he been caught in the lie. The most likely scenario, according to intelligence veterans of the period, is one that repeated itself over and over again at virtually every level of contact between U.S. intelligence and former Nazis. Quite simply, Sibert knew what was going on—but didn't ask.

"Nobody had legalized, really, the functions of intelligence in those days," says Lieutenant Colonel John Bokor, the son of the man who first recruited Gehlen and a career intelligence officer in his own right. "Today maybe things have changed, but back then the intelligence agent was on his own. . . . There just wasn't any sheet music for us all to sing from in those days. That's how a lot of those guys [former Nazis] got hired."[7]

* * *

Nazis and collaborators became integral to the operation of Gehlen's postwar organization, and nowhere was this clearer than in control of émigré operations. As early as 1946 Gehlen had resumed limited funding of the Vlasov Army, the Ukrainian underground army OUN/UPA, and collaborationist leaders of other exile groups originally sponsored by Berlin. The cooperation of these groups was seen as crucial to successful interrogations of newly arrived refugees in the displaced persons (DP) camps. Although it is certainly true that the majority of the postwar refugees in Germany were not Nazi collaborators and had not committed war crimes, it is also true that the minority who had done such things were exactly the ones who were carefully sought out by the "Org," as Gehlen's group has since come to be known. "The main source of informers," noted a secret Gehlen study on recruitment of that time, "will . . . be the refugees from German minorities and ex-members of the Nazi organization."[8]

By the end of 1947 Gehlen had restored, for the most part, the lines of command that Berlin had once used to control its assets inside the collaborationist organizations during the war. Two SS veterans, Franz Six and Emil Augsburg, took charge of essential aspects of émigré work for Gehlen. The careers of these Gehlen men illustrate the depth of the Nazi influence both within the Org and in the émigré organizations it had penetrated.

Each of them was a veteran of Amt VI ("Department 6") of the SS RSHA, Nazi Germany's main security headquarters. This SS section had been a combined foreign intelligence, sabotage, and propaganda agency and was, in effect, the CIA of Nazi Germany. By war's end SS RSHA Amt VI had consolidated not only the foreign sections of the Nazis' police intelligence apparatus but military intelligence (Abwehr), Gehlen's own FHO, and much of the Nazi party's internal foreign espionage network as well. Amt VI was an extraordinarily rich collection of trained agents, intelligence files, saboteurs, and propagandists. Both Gehlen and the United States drew many of their most valuable recruits from this department after the war. Its hoard of files on the USSR and Eastern Europe, in particular, was without equal anywhere.

There was another side to the agency. Most of Amt VI's top officers had been instrumental in the mass extermination of Jews. Both Six and Augsburg had led mobile killing squads on the eastern front. Others had participated in the Holocaust as administrators, paper shufflers, and idea men.

Gehlen's man in émigré enterprises, SS Brigadeführer Franz Six, is a major war criminal and is still alive at last report. He was once described by Adolf Eichmann as a *Streber* (a "real eager beaver") on the so-called Jewish Question and as a favored protégé of SS chief Himmler's. Eichmann should have known: His own first efforts in the Holocaust were carried out under Six's personal command in the "Ideological Combat" section of the security service. In 1941 Six led the Vorkommando Moskau, an advance squad of the Nazi invasion, whose job it was to seize Communist party and NKVD archives in order to compile lists of hunted Soviet officials and to liquidate those who were caught. Six's *Vorkommando* never made it to Moscow, but his own reports indicate that his unit murdered approximately 200 people in cold blood in Smolensk, where they had stopped on the march to the Russian capital. The Smolensk victims, Six wrote headquarters, included "46 persons, among them 38 intellectual Jews who had tried to create unrest and discontent in the newly established Ghetto of Smolensk."

As late as 1944 Six spoke at a conference of "consultants" on the "Jewish Question" at Krummhübel. The stenographic notes of the meeting indicate that "Six spoke . . . about the political structure of world Jewry. *The physical elimination of Eastern Jewry would deprive Jewry of its biological reserves,*" he announced. *"The Jewish Question must be solved not only in Germany but also internationally"* (emphasis added).[9] Himmler was so pleased with Six's work that he lifted him out of projects in Amt VI and gave him a newly created department, Amt VII, of his own.

But Six was not simply a killer. He was a college professor with a doctorate in law and political science and a dean of the faculty of the University of Berlin and was regarded by some of his peers as one of the most distinguished professors of his generation. Six—Dr. Six, as he preferred—had joined the Nazi party in 1930, then the SS and SD a few years later. He was, along with Walter Schellenberg and Otto Ohlendorf, one of the nazified professors and lawyers who supplied a thin cover of intellectual respectability to the Hitler dictatorship. A number of such men enlisted in the security service and became the brains of the party, the intelligence specialists who presented dispassionate analyses to the Nazi high command concerning ideological warfare, racial questions in the East, and tactics for the Final Solution.

One of Six's most important projects in Amt VI was the Wannsee Institute, an SS think tank located near beautiful Lake Wannsee in the suburbs of Berlin. This was the SS's most sophisticated effort to gather strategic (i.e., long-term or long-range) intelligence on the USSR. It included collection and analysis of details on Soviet defense production capabilities, for example, activities at scientific research institutes, details of five-year plans, locations of oil and mineral deposits, identities of party officials, as well as the hoarding of Russian maps and technical books of every description.

Wannsee's work also involved, in characteristically Nazi fashion, studies of the location and size of the various ethnic groups in the USSR. Wannsee's highly secret reports were distributed to fewer than fifteen persons at the very top of the Nazi government, including General Gehlen (in his capacity as military intelligence chief on the eastern front), propaganda boss Paul Joseph Goebbels, and Hitler himself. The studies, which were among the most reliable information on the USSR produced by the Reich, were essential to the process of setting military strategy and selection of targets on the eastern front. The ethnic reports, which were the most accurate information available to the SS concerning locations of concentrations of Jewish population inside the USSR, provided a convenient road map for the senior SS leaders assigned the task of exterminating Jews.*

Most of the twenty-man staff at Wannsee were defectors from the USSR or scholars in Soviet studies from top German universities. It was this group that Gehlen sought out after the war to form the heart of his staff for émigré operations aimed at Eastern Europe and the Soviet Union. At least one Wannsee veteran, Nikolai N. Poppe, lives in the United States today.[10]

Dr. Six was sought for war crimes after the fall of Berlin. He went to work for Gehlen in 1946, however, and was given the task of combing the Stuttgart-Schorndorf area for unemployed German intelligence veterans who might be interested in new assignments.

*The Wannsee Institute also provided the setting for the January 1942 meeting in which SS leader Reinhard Heydrich announced the "Final Solution to the Jewish Question" to representatives of other branches of the German government. That gathering was the first time that Adolf Eichmann, then an enthusiastic young SS officer, had met quite so many "high personages," he was to remember. Eichmann's recollections of the Wannsee session—a crucial watershed in the development of the Holocaust—are almost rhapsodic: "[A]fter the conference, [then SS chief] Heydrich, [Gestapo leader] Mueller and your humble servant sat cozily around a fireplace," Eichmann noted later. "I noticed for the first time that Heydrich was smoking. Not only that, he had cognac. . . . We sat around peacefully after our Wannsee Conference, not just talking shop but giving ourselves a rest after so many taxing hours."

Unfortunately for Six, however, one of his subagents was a certain SS Hauptsturmführer Hirschfeld, who was also working for a joint U.S.-British operation tracing fugitive war criminals. Hirschfeld betrayed Six to the American CIC, which disregarded his protests and charged him with several war crimes, including murder. Once the capture of Six had been announced in the newspapers, there was little that Gehlen—or Gehlen's U.S. patron, General Sibert—could do for Six, at least not publicly. Six was tried before an American military tribunal in 1948, convicted of war crimes (including the murders in Smolensk), and sentenced to twenty years in prison.

The man who led the team of U.S. prosecutors at his trial, Benjamin Ferencz, remembers Six as a "clever man, one of the biggest swine in the whole [mobile killing squads] case. . . . Personally, I had more respect even for Ohlendorf, because he said, 'Yes, I did it [commit mass murder].' Six, on the other hand, would say, 'Who me? They were killing Jews? I had no idea!' "[11]

In the end, Six served about four years in prison before being given clemency by U.S. High Commissioner in Germany John McCloy. Even if the Americans had not known who Six was when he went to work for the Gehlen Organization in 1946, they could hardly plead ignorance after having convicted him in a U.S. military tribunal. Nevertheless, McCloy's clemency board specifically approved the former SS man for work in the Org, and Six was back at work in Gehlen's Pullach headquarters only weeks after his release from prison.*[12]

The second important member of Gehlen's eastern affairs staff was Dr. Emil Augsburg, a former SS *Standartenführer* from Himmler's staff in Poland. Augsburg, like Eichmann, had begun his career in Six's "Ideological Combat" section in the SD, where, according to an account found in SD records, he had become adept at using Jew baiting to smear political opponents within the SS by claiming they had Jewish ancestors.

During the war Augsburg led a murder squad in German-occupied Russia, according to his Nazi party membership records. He obtained "extraordinary results . . . in special tasks" during the invasion,[13] as a recommendation in his personnel dossier puts it. ("Special tasks," in SS parlance, is generally a euphemism for the

*In 1961 Six gave testimony as a defense witness during Adolf Eichmann's trial for crimes against humanity. Six had retired from the Gehlen Organization by that time and was employed as an agent for Porsche automobiles. Eichmann was a department head for Porsche's rival, Daimler-Benz.

mass murder of Jews.) The SS found him to be an "absolutely trust-worthy National Socialist" and appointed him a *Direktor* at Wann-see, overseeing the highly successful index of Soviet personalities used to target intelligence gathering and behind-the-lines assassina-tions—a job he later did for the Gehlen Organization as well. Augs-burg was no mere technician, however. Under Six's and Wannsee Direktor Mikhail Akhmeteli's* tutelage, he became recognized as one of the Nazi regime's most influential experts on Eastern Europe. Although never a public figure, Augsburg maintained this reputation among German foreign policy cognoscenti after the war as well.

The Gehlen Organization's ability subtly to manipulate other intelligence agencies is clearly illustrated by Augsburg's career in the first years after the war. In addition to his work for Gehlen, Augsburg was simultaneously employed by the U.S. Army Coun-terintelligence Corps; a U.S. military intelligence unit known as the Technical Intelligence Branch (TIB) that was supposedly interested only in German scientists but was actually also recruiting former German intelligence agents; a French intelligence agency; and a private network of ex-SS officers headed by former SS General

---

*Professor Mikhail Akhmeteli was a third noteworthy member of Gehlen's postwar émigré affairs apparatus that had been drawn from the staff of the SS's Wannsee Institute. During the war Akhmeteli led much of the work involved in compiling lists of Soviet officials slated for execution, related strategic counterintelligence operations, and development of Nazi racial theory as it applied to peoples of Eastern Europe. His personal contributions to the latter field included a theory (which Nazi ideologue Alfred Rosenberg eventually adopted) that the Georgians in the south of the USSR were "Russia's Germans" and as such were suitably "superior" SS recruits for use against Jews, Slavs, Gypsies, and other "racially in-ferior" peoples. It was on the basis of this work that Akhmeteli became one of the very few non-Aryans admitted to the Nazi party—quite an honor in Germany of that time. His party number was 5360858.

Akhmeteli was the son of an oil-rich Georgian family that had been dispossessed during the 1917 Russian Revolution. He helped finance the White Army's resistance to the Bol-sheviks for a time but was eventually forced to flee to Germany. There he established an anti-Communist center for Soviet studies at the University of Breslau that eventually emerged as the seat of the most comprehensive collection of materials on the USSR outside the Soviet Union. In time the Breslau collection became the heart of the SS archives on the USSR, complete with a card file index of notable Soviet personalities and an extensive collection of information on Soviet railroads, industry, communications, and other infrastruc-ture.

The Georgian became one of the primary liaisons between the SS team at Wannsee and Gehlen's military intelligence headquarters in the East. After the war Gehlen provided Akhmeteli with a chalet near Unterweilbach purchased with U.S. funds drawn from his discretionary account. Akhmeteli, a restless, stubby figure with deep-set eyes and a fleshy potato of a nose, was one of the very few men welcomed for visits in Gehlen's home.

Bernau,[14] all of whom appear to have been aware that Augsburg was a fugitive from war crimes charges.

Augsburg's specialty was the use of émigrés and defectors to collect information on the East. According to top secret U.S. CIC records, the Bernau SS network provided Augsburg with U.S. EEIs (essential elements of information) that served as a shopping list of information the Western Allies were most interested in buying. Augsburg then acted as gatekeeper for exchange of information among groups of informants working for each of his employers, a position that permitted him to promote selected information or to "confirm independently" a report that he himself had placed through another informant network. Theoretically Augsburg's primary loyalty could have been to any one of his employers, to the Soviets, or to anyone else. His subsequent lifelong devotion to the Org, however, makes it clear that he was first and foremost a Gehlen man.

Augsburg's postwar work for Gehlen's organization was an extension of what he had done for the SS at Wannsee: administration of the painstaking compilation of extraordinarily detailed records on the USSR. One specialty was preparation of remarkable cover stories for Gehlen agents scheduled to cross into the Soviet Union on both espionage and covert action missions. These "legends" included not only false documentation, such as travel passes and food ration books, but also carefully prepared stories of families, jobs, and events that appeared genuine but would be impossible for Soviet police officials to check. Details of geography, climate, local culture, even jokes were carefully collected and cataloged to provide realistic cover stories.[15] Augsburg and Six maintained close relations after the war with the émigré groups that had been supported by Berlin and assisted in the selection of agents that were used by the CIA in behind-the-lines operations in Eastern Europe.

CHAPTER FIVE

The Eyes and Ears

Of all the networks of former Nazis and collaborators employed by the United States after World War II, it is Gehlen's organization that has left the most substantial imprint on the United States. Gehlen's analysis of the forces that guide Soviet behavior, which were forged in part by his personal defeat at the hands of the Russians during World War II, became widely accepted in U.S. intelligence circles and remain so to this day.

Gehlen's singular error, says Arthur Macy Cox, a career Soviet affairs analyst who has served with both the CIA and the Department of State, is that he presented the *political* threat posed by the USSR as though it were an imminent *military* problem, thus "ingratiating himself," as Cox puts it, "with the unreconstructed cold warriors in the Pentagon and on Capitol Hill."[1] Gehlen's influential intelligence and analysis also strongly reinforced the "Communist conspiracy" model of foreign affairs, in which the hand of the Kremlin could be seen in almost every labor dispute and student strike on the Continent.

It is probably impossible to determine with certainty the extent to which Gehlen influenced American policymakers' decisions concerning European affairs during the cold war. The complex, dynamic relationship between information gathering, analysis, and policy-making is difficult to deduce under the best conditions. In Gehlen's case the problem is still more recondite as a result of the layers of secrecy that surround nearly every aspect of his long relationship with the Americans. Neither the West German nor the U.S. government is known to have released official documentation concerning Gehlen's work on behalf of U.S. agencies, although there have, of course, been leaks. Source material on the subject is often limited to the recollections and memoirs of persons who participated in these events, some of whom have requested anonymity in exchange for cooperation.

Gehlen's impact on the course of the cold war was subtle, but real. Self-avowed pragmatists in the U.S. intelligence services have consistently argued that the otherwise questionable employment of Gehlen and even of unrepentant Nazis through the Org was justified by their significant contributions to fighting a powerful and ruthless rival: the Soviet Union. "He's on our side," CIA Director Allen Dulles later said of Gehlen, "and that's all that matters."

During the first decade following the war the United States spent at least $200 million and employed about 4,000 people full-time to resurrect Gehlen's organization from the wreckage of the war, according to generally accepted estimates.[2] The Org became the most important eyes and ears for U.S. intelligence inside the closed societies of the Soviet bloc. "In 1946 [U.S.] intelligence files on the Soviet Union were virtually empty," says Harry Rositzke, the CIA's former chief of espionage inside the Soviet Union. "Even the most elementary facts were unavailable—on roads and bridges, on the location and production of factories, on city plans and airfields." Rositzke worked closely with Gehlen during the formative years of the CIA and credits Gehlen's organization with playing a "primary role" in filling the empty file folders during that period.[3]

Intelligence gathered by the Org was "essential to American interests," asserts W. Park Armstrong, the longtime head of the Office of Intelligence and Research at the Department of State. "Our German ally's contribution to knowledge of the Soviet military was at times a standard against which we measured our own efforts."

During the first years of the CIA under Rear Admiral Roscoe H. Hillenkoetter's administration, according to a retired executive of the CIA's Office of National Estimates, Gehlen's reports and analyses were sometimes simply retyped onto CIA stationery and presented to President Truman without further comment in the agency's morning intelligence summaries. Gehlen's organization "shaped what we knew about the Soviets in Eastern Europe and particularly about East Germany," he continued. Heinz Höhne, an internationally recognized historian and senior editor at *Der Spiegel* magazine, asserts that "seventy percent of all the U.S. government's information on Soviet forces and armaments came from the Gehlen organization" during the early cold war. While any such precise number is bound to be arbitrary, the thrust of Höhne's comment is certainly accurate.[4]

Contrary to the accepted wisdom, however, U.S. dependence on Gehlen's organization for intelligence on the Soviet military was quite likely a blunder from a strictly practical point of view. For one thing, enlisting Gehlen was in itself a substantial escalation of the cold war that undermined what little hope was possible for East-West cooperation during the pivotal years of 1945 to 1948. Once on board, Gehlen's Nazi-tainted operatives often gave the Soviets an easy target for denunciations of war criminals being sheltered by the West. This has since become a highly successful Soviet propaganda theme—in part because there is some truth to it—that is replayed regularly to this day as a means of undermining U.S. and West German relations with Eastern Europe. Financing Gehlen's organization also appears to have made infiltration of Western intelligence by Soviet spies easier, not more difficult, as will be seen. Most important, Gehlen's operatives and analysts strongly reinforced U.S. intelligence's existing predilection toward paranoia about communism and the USSR, contributing significantly to the creation of a body of widely believed misinformation about Soviet behavior.

"Gehlen had to make his money by creating a threat that we were afraid of," says Victor Marchetti, formerly the CIA's chief analyst of Soviet strategic war plans and capabilities, "so we would give him more money to tell us about it." He continues: "In my opinion, the Gehlen Organization provided nothing worthwhile for understanding or estimating Soviet military or political capabilities in Eastern Europe or anywhere else." Employing Gehlen was "a waste of time, money, and effort, except that maybe he had some CI [counterintelligence] value, because practically everybody in his organization was sucking off both tits."[5] In other words, Gehlen did not produce the reliable information for which he was employed, but careful monitoring of the Org might have produced some clues to Soviet espionage activity because the group had been deeply penetrated by double agents, thus giving the United States a vastly expensive and not very efficient means of keeping up with Soviet spies.

"The Gehlen Organization was the one group that did have networks inside Eastern Europe, and that is why we hired them," international affairs expert Arthur Macy Cox says. "[But] hiring Gehlen was the biggest mistake the U.S. ever made. Our allies said, 'You are putting Nazis at the senior levels of your intelligence,' and they were right. It discredited the United States." According to Cox, the Gehlen Organization was the primary source of intelligence that claimed that "the Soviets were about to attack [West] Germany. . . . [That was] the biggest bunch of baloney then, and it is still a bunch of baloney today."[6]

The crucial period of 1945 to 1948, when East-West relations moved from a wary peace to an intense political war, provides one case study of the damage that Gehlen's intelligence and analysis could produce. Among the most basic elements in the American interpretation of European events during the early cold war years was the evaluation of the Red Army. That subject, it will be recalled, was Gehlen's specialty.

In mid-1946 U.S. military intelligence correctly reported that the Red Army (then in control of most of Eastern Europe) was underequipped, overextended, and war-weary. Its estimate of the number of Soviet troops in Eastern and Central Europe was quite high—some 208 divisions—but the U.S. Army concluded that these forces were almost entirely tied down with administrative, police, and reconstruction tasks in the Russian-occupied zone. Soviet military aggression against Western Europe was highly unlikely for at least a decade, if only for logistical reasons, the army determined.

Particularly intriguing were 1946 U.S. Army reports concerning railroads in eastern Germany. The Red Army, it was well known, lacked the motorized strength of Western forces and relied heavily on the railroads to move troops to the front and for logistic support.* The U.S. Army intelligence reports drawn from military attachés inside the Soviet zone, from the U.S. strategic bombing survey research teams in Eastern Europe and from other on-the-spot reports prior to the Soviet decision to close its occupation zone to

---

*As late as 1950 fully half of the Soviets' transport for their standing army was horse-drawn. This actually had some advantages in the trackless frozen north, where Russian ponies were useful long after tanks and trucks had frozen up or bogged down in snowdrifts. Western Europe, however, was quite a different place.

the West made it clear that the Russians were *tearing up* much of the German railroad network and shipping it back to the USSR as war reparations. The Soviets uprooted about a third of the entire German railway system, including such strategic lines as Berlin–Leipzig and Berlin–Frankfurt, seizing train yards, switches, and thousands of miles of track.[7] Whatever else may be said of this form of Russian industrial development, it was clearly not the behavior of a military power contemplating a blitzkrieg attack.

Over the next two years, however, the U.S. appraisal of the capabilities and intentions of the Red Army fundamentally shifted, and this change was pushed along by misleading reports and mistaken warnings from the Gehlen Organization. By the time the reappraisal was over, it had become an article of faith in Washington, D.C., that the war-weary Soviet *occupation* forces were actually fresh *assault* troops poised for an attack on the West. The Americans' new estimate of the number of those troops, furthermore, was also greatly exaggerated because it did not take into account the large-scale demobilization of Soviet forces after 1945. As U.S. intelligence's primary source of information on the Soviet military during this pivotal period of the cold war, Gehlen's organization played an important role in the creation of the American evaluation—or rather misevaluation—of Soviet power in Europe that has not been adequately appreciated until recently.

Important changes took place within the U.S. intelligence community in the course of those years that reinforced the overall drift toward open hostilities with the USSR. Colonel John V. Grombach of the Pentagon's Military Intelligence Service (MIS), who appears later in these pages, played a significant role in one such change: the U.S. purge of the foreign intelligence analysis teams at the Pentagon and the Office of Strategic Services (OSS). This self-imposed purge, which appears to have been carried out primarily for political reasons, helped lay the foundation for Gehlen's growing influence within the U.S. intelligence community.

Grombach served during the war as chief of espionage for MIS, the War Department's in-house secret information gathering group. His department maintained an intense and sometimes vicious rivalry with America's more glamorous spy agency, the OSS. The competition revolved around funding, access to policymakers, manpower levels, control of agents, long-term strategy, and a myriad of other minor irritants. This contention grew so severe that each group accused the other—apparently with some justification—of actually revealing its contract agents to the enemy.[8] When World War II drew to a close, the tug-of-war between the two agencies escalated sharply. The fight against the common enemy that had united them in an uncomfortable alliance was over. Both organizations saw their budgets cut deeply. Both believed—accurately, it turned out—that they were fighting for their institutional lives.

Grombach was not one to ignore a challenge. A beefy, barrel-chested man, he had once been an Olympic heavyweight boxer and an award-winning decathlon athlete. Victories—in professional life as well as in sport—had come easily to him in his early years. As he matured, however, Frenchy Grombach, as he was known to his friends, became "an opportunist of the first order," according to his army intelligence file, "a man who lives on his contacts and one who would cut the throat of anyone standing in his way."[9]

One of Grombach's clearest targets in this bureaucratic firefight was the OSS's Research and Analysis (R&A) branch, which specialized in making overall sense of the thousands of fragmentary reports on foreign activities that flooded into Washington each day. OSS R&A was skeptical of reports that the USSR was massing troops for a military attack on the West and was not afraid to say so inside the secret councils of government. R&A singled out Grombach's espionage reports as unreliable and even as pro-Fascist. His reply to these accusations was a countercharge that the R&A branch had been infiltrated by Communists and that this accounted for both its low opinion of his efforts and its supposedly soft line on the USSR.

Grombach turned a squad of his men loose in captured German espionage files in 1945 to search for evidence proving that R&A's wartime reports were "soft on communism" as the result of penetration by Soviet agents. Not surprisingly, he found some evidence to support his suspicions. His investigation discovered that one mid-level R&A employee had probably joined the U.S. Communist party more than a decade previously and then had failed to admit it on his application for a government job. In a second case, he used uncorroborated reports from the state-controlled newspapers of Francisco Franco's Spain to "prove" that State Department official Gustavo Duran was not only a Communist but supposedly a Russian spy as well. A handful of university professors who had been recruited to R&A during the war had connections with a wide variety of liberal or left-wing organizations, though not with the Communist party itself. Finally, both Pentagon and OSS intelligence analyst *had* downplayed negative reports on the USSR during the war. The Germans' revelations of the Soviet NKVD's massacre of Polish officers in the Katyn Forest, for example, had been largely ignored in the interest of preserving Allied solidarity.

Grombach argued, according to army intelligence records obtained through the Freedom of Information Act, that the minimization of Soviet war crimes by U.S. analysts was not simply a political decision but rather part of a Communist plot. The analysis groups at both the OSS and the Pentagon "seemed to have 'liberal' tendencies," he asserted. They "consistently eliminated all anti-Communist information" that his unit had developed. "Pro-Communist or pro-Marxist personnel and actions" had been permitted to proliferate inside the U.S. intelligence analysis teams, he contended.*[10]

One Communist inside R&A was enough to prove his premise. Grombach leaked the results of this search—code-named Project 1641 inside the Pentagon—to Republican members of Congress and the press in the midst of a sensitive and difficult showdown over budget appropriations for American intelligence agencies. Rightwing senators on Capitol Hill, armed with Grombach's leaks, succeeded in breaking the R&A branch into some seventeen subcommittees, virtually ensuring the demise of the OSS's analytic group. The American capability to make sense of intelligence reports from Eastern Europe and the USSR, never strong in the first place, was deeply wounded. The R&A director, Colonel Alfred McCormack, who had also served with distinction during the war as director of U.S. military intelligence analysis in the War Department, soon resigned in disgust.[11]

As intelligence veteran and historian William Corson notes, both the acceptance of the theory of "ten-foot tall Russians" among U.S. intelligence specialists and the beginnings of what was later called McCarthyism may be dated from the destruction of McCormack's organization of skeptical experts on the USSR. The purge of the R&A branch served as clear warning to analysts all over the government that hard-line hostility toward the USSR was necessary for

---

*Some measure of Grombach's personal approach to the question of Soviet capabilities may be gleaned from his later published writings. In 1980 Grombach cited wartime Abwehr records as proof that "the Panama Canal giveaway . . . is the direct result of its definite selection by the USSR and Stalin as the first priority domino along with Cuba in the Communist play for world domination as far back as . . . 1942." Soviet efforts throughout the decades leading up to this supposed Russian victory were said to have been helped along by "criminal subversion [and] naive stupidity . . . in Washington," Grombach continued, including squads of Communist agents inside the State Department, CIA, and the Pentagon intelligence staffs.

professional survival during the Truman administration.¹² Colonel McCormack's downfall, moreover, became an opportunity for Reinhard Gehlen to expand his influence, which was more in tune with the precepts of U.S. intelligence agencies in the new administration.

The radical shift in U.S. and Soviet attitudes toward each other during this period was a product of a very complex, politicized process, of course, one that has been the subject of considerable debate ever since. To put it briefly, the U.S. government desired to stabilize events in Western Europe and expand American political and economic interests in Eastern Europe. This aim, however, ran headlong into Stalin's intention to draw new Soviet borders at the outer edges of the czars' old empire and to solidify the USSR's control over the same Eastern European countries that the United States viewed as allies and potential trading partners. This collision was aggravated by a multiplicity of ideological and cultural factors, not the least of which was the sometimes violent disputes between Communist party activists and Catholic church officials.

American officials made their own decisions concerning how to cope with the cold war, and it is evident that many factors in both domestic and international politics played a part in those decisions. Within that framework, however, it is enlightening to draw new attention to the influence of the covert operations and espionage agencies of both East and West, which played a powerful but largely overlooked role in the evolution of these tangled conflicts. Undercover organizations considered themselves the frontline armies of the cold war, and in several cases discussed in this book they appear to have been the proximate cause of dangerous incidents in East-West relations. The same clandestine agencies that had an evident interest in this clash were frequently the primary or even the sole source of information used by senior policymakers in evaluating the intentions of foreign governments. This privileged access of covert organizations to senior officials is, after all, the reason for having a *central* intelligence agency in the first place.

Gehlen's perspectives on the cold war are of interest because of his relatively influential role in defining U.S. policymakers' understanding of the capabilities and intentions of the Red Army. "Gehlen's approach, particularly during those [early cold war] years, took as its premise, first, that Moscow intended to control and/or disrupt all of Europe in the relatively near term, through military force if need be," says a retired Office of National Estimates

(ONE) staff member, "and, second, that every Communist in Europe was working in concert on that plan. He provided us with very detailed information along these lines for many years, and we made use of it in numerous ways. There is some truth to the theory. In the final analysis, however," he concludes, "he was mistaken."[13]

U.S. officials became convinced, writes Professor John Lukacs in *Foreign Affairs,* that "communism was a fanatical ideology and that, contrary to the wartime illusions about [Stalin's] nature, Stalin was wholly dedicated to it. But this seemingly logical, and seemingly belated, realization was not accurate. It concentrated on ideology, not geography. What mattered to Stalin was the latter, not the former. . . . There was no communist regime (with the minor and idiosyncratic exception of Albania) beyond the occupation sphere of the Soviet armies; and there would be none, either." However brutal Stalin may have been in the areas under his control, Lukacs concludes, he had no intention of invading Western Europe, and he even gave short shrift to the then powerful French and Italian Communist parties in the West.

By late 1947, however, Gehlen had become "an alarm signal" (as Höhne of *Der Spiegel* puts it) in a series of secret conferences with General Lucius Clay, then the U.S. commander in Germany. He reported to Clay that there were no fewer than 175 Red Army divisions in Eastern Europe, that most of them were combat-ready, and that quiet changes already under way in Soviet billeting and leave policies for these troops suggested a major mobilization could be in the wind. The Soviets' behavior should be interpreted as a prelude to military aggression, he argued.[14]

Then, in February 1948, two important events took place. The coalition government that had governed Czechoslovakia since the end of the war collapsed, in part because the United States declined fully to support Czech President Edvard Beneš (a Social Democrat) on the ground that he was insufficiently anti-Communist. The Czech Communist party took power with Red Army backing, thus strongly reinforcing Western apprehensions about the possibility of an eventual Soviet military attack on Western Europe. Within days of the Czech events, the U.S. Army general staff chief of intelligence, General Stephen J. Chamberlin (who had earlier been instrumental in the scientists' affair) met with General Clay in Germany. In these encounters Chamberlin stressed "the fact that major military appropriations bills were pending before congressional committees," as Jean Edward Smith, the editor of Clay's papers, has noted, "and the need to galvanize American public opinion to support increased defense expenditures." The public in the United States was unwilling to finance the military adequately, Chamberlin argued, unless it was thoroughly alarmed about an actual military attack from the USSR.[15]

Acting in response to Chamberlin's requests, Clay issued sharply worded telegrams that strongly implied a full-scale Soviet military offensive against Western Europe was brewing. "For many months, based on logical analysis, I have felt and held that war [with the Soviets] was unlikely for at least ten years," Clay cabled to Washington on March 5, 1948. "Within the last few weeks, [however,] I have felt a subtle change in the Soviet attitude . . . which now gives me a feeling that it may come with dramatic suddenness. . . ."[16]

Gehlen's studies of the Red Army provided the intelligence underpinning for Clay's comments, according to the Office of National Estimates (ONE) source; they were the "facts" that supported his argument. Clay's officially top secret telegram was quickly leaked to the U.S. press and was whipped up by the media into a full-blown war scare that is generally recognized today as one of the most important watersheds of the cold war. Policymakers in Washington accepted the contention that 175 fully armed Red Army divisions stood poised in the Soviet-occupied zone, waiting restlessly to attack. Gehlen's central contention that the USSR had not substantially demobilized its troops since the war, while the United States had, was accepted without question at the time and widely regarded as proof of an aggressive Soviet intent toward Western Europe.

Equally revealing, the same troops that the 1946 U.S. Army analysis had described as being tied down with "immediate occupation and security requirements" were now described in Gehlen's estimates (and later in the intelligence summaries of the Pentagon as well) as "a highly mobile and armored spearhead for an offensive in Western Europe," according to a crucial Joint Chiefs of Staff war plans summary. The U.S. Army's earlier acknowledgment of the transport and logistic problems faced by the Red Army disappeared from the top secret appraisals of Soviet capabilities. Instead, the Russians were said now to be able to launch large-scale offensives in Europe, the Middle East, and the Far East all at the same time.*[17]

*The U.S. war contingency plans of 1949 are a vivid illustration of the degree of self-deception that had taken hold among U.S. intelligence analysts at the time, in part as a result of the efforts of the Gehlen Organization. According to a top secret estimate declassified as

"Russia, at this stage, is the world's No. 1 military power," head-lined *U.S. News & World Report* in a feature story on the new crisis. "Russia's armies and air forces are in a position to pour across Europe and into Asia almost at will." The United States had fewer than a score of divisions to stand guard against this horde and seemed to be losing troops every day because of budget cutbacks and a widespread desire at home to return to normality. The Truman administration's response to this dilemma seemed obvious: Stop the cuts in the military budget, accelerate construction of the atomic weapons that appeared to offer more bang for the buck than conventional forces, and dump millions of dollars into a variety of covert operations and intelligence programs, including

a result of a Freedom of Information Act action by the author, U.S. military planning was based on the following "conclusions as to the strategic intentions of the Soviet Union in the event of war in 1949." It is worth noting that these same "conclusions" were also used to justify Defense Department budget requests. ·

The following would be undertaken [by the USSR] simultaneously, according to the intelligence estimate:

(1) A campaign against Western Europe (including Italy and Sicily, but not the Iberian Peninsula initially) to gain the Atlantic seaboard in the shortest possible time and to control the Central Mediterranean;

(2) An aerial bombardment against the British Isles;

(3) A campaign to seize control of the Middle East, including Greece and Turkey, and the Suez Canal area;

(4) A campaign against China, and South Korea, and air and sea operations against Japan and the United States bases in Alaska and the Pacific, insofar as the Soviet Union can support such operations without prejudice to those in other areas;

(5) Small scale one-way air attacks against the United States and Canada, and possibly small scale two-way air attacks against the Puget Sound area;

(6) A sea and air offensive against Anglo-American sea communications;

(7) Subversive activities and sabotage against Anglo-American interests in all parts of the world;

(8) A campaign against Scandinavia and air attacks on Pakistan may also be undertaken concurrently with the foregoing, or as necessary;

(9) On successful conclusion of the campaign in Western Europe (and possible Scandinavia) a full-scale air and sea offensive would be directed against the British Isles;

(10) The Soviet Union will have sufficient armed forces to undertake campaigns simultaneously in the theaters indicated and still have sufficient armed forces to form an adequate reserve.

The strategic estimate went on to report that the Soviet capabilities in 1956–57 were projected to be the same as those in 1949, with the exception that "South Korea and a large portion of China will have been absorbed into the Soviet orbit."

The British chiefs of staff also approved this estimate for their own military and intelligence planning, apparently at U.S. insistence. In an official communication with the U.S. Joint Chiefs of Staff, the British commented that the American estimate of Soviet capabilities "is probably an overestimate, [but] little purpose would be served in re-examining [it]."

the newly born CIA and its chief client, the Gehlen Organization.

It is clear in hindsight, however, that the estimates of Soviet military power that Gehlen provided to the Americans were simply wrong and grossly overstated both the Soviets' ability and their desire to fight. While it "is still commonly believed that the Soviet Union did not demobilize its ground forces at the end of World War II," writes Matthew Evangelista in the MIT journal *International Security,* "[t]his is not the case. . . . [The] overall manpower strength of the Soviet armed forces was considerably exaggerated in the West during the early postwar years."[18] Even Paul Nitze, whose hawkish credentials are well established, suggested recently that only about one-third of the Soviet divisions in Europe at the time were actually full strength. About one-third more were partial-strength forces, Nitze continued, and fully one-third were cadre—that is, paper—forces.[19]

Ironically, it is clear that the Soviets' own extreme secrecy played an important part in reinforcing Gehlen's status within America's growing national security complex. In the decade following the war many of the types of satellite surveillance photos and radio interception now used for keeping track of, say, Soviet bomber production or troop movements did not exist. Instead, the collection of that type of information was done in large part from the human sources in which Gehlen then specialized, like refugees, defectors, and spies.

Stalin's police agencies worked overtime to undermine every independent U.S. avenue to confirm (or disprove) the information that Gehlen's émigré agents were bringing in. While this was apparently viewed in the USSR as a wise security policy, its actual results were clearly negative from the point of view of long-term Soviet—or, for that matter, American—interests. Instead of slowing U.S. arms expansion, which is presumably a goal of Soviet security policy, it had exactly the opposite effect. Faced with the unknown, American military planners assumed the worst. The vacuum of information on Soviet military affairs that was ruthlessly enforced by the Kremlin ended up providing the environment in which America's own paranoia festered.

The dynamics of the process by which intelligence estimates are created also tended to lend credence to Gehlen's alarming assumptions about Soviet capabilities. "You'll never get court-martialed for saying [the Soviets] do have a new weapon and it turns out that they don't," Marchetti says. "But you'll lose your ass if you say that they don't have it and it turns out that they do."[20]

Gehlen's role in the 1948 crisis was one of the first—and still one of the most important—examples of blowback created by the Nazi utilization programs. His seemingly authoritative intelligence reports played a very real role in shaping U.S. perceptions of the USSR during this pivotal period. Furthermore, the reports became an important ingredient in the domestic American debate over military budgets and defense policy.

In those events, General Chamberlin of army intelligence solicited General Clay's telegram because he knew that once leaked, it would be a potent weapon in budget battles on Capitol Hill. The idea succeeded almost too well. The arrival of Clay's warning on the heels of the collapse of the government in Czechoslovakia and related crises came perilously close to triggering a war itself.

Had Gehlen's role been limited to the preparation of top secret studies for the use of America's own most expert intelligence analysts, it is unlikely that his project would have done much harm during the postwar period, and it might actually have done some good. But that is not how intelligence agencies actually work. In reality, contending factions in the government leak their versions

---

*Gehlen also played a role in the creation of the famous missile gap of the 1950s. "Gehlen provided us [the CIA] with specific reports on the Soviet ICBM program," Victor Marchetti says. "He said, 'We have two reliable reports confirming this,' and they [the Soviets] have just installed three missiles at that site,' et cetera, claiming that he had contacts among the German scientists captured by the Russians at the end of the war." The intelligence reports were transmitted to the Pentagon through interagency channels, and word about the alarming new development eventually leaked from there into the press.

Walter Dornberger added fuel to this fire in 1955 by publishing alarming speculations that the Soviets might attack from the sea, using shorter-range missiles deployed in floating canisters off the coast of the United States. He was deeply involved in the United States' own ICBM program at this point, and his opinions were given considerable weight in public discussions.

The CIA soon dispatched some of the first of the revolutionary new U-2 surveillance planes on secret missions inside Soviet airspace to gather more data. "We figured that if the Soviets had ICBMs before the U.S., that could be damn serious," Marchetti continues. "We also figured if they had them, they'd have to move them by railroad, particularly to Siberia, where they would be most useful against the United States. So we sent out Frank Powers and the U-2s and they plotted the whole [Soviet] rail network. U-2s scoured the Trans-Siberian Railroad, every railroad spur, and every missile R and D station. And nothing was found that remotely resembled the implementation of an ICBM [capability] at that time. . . . It was all bull."

By that time, however, the missile gap story had already taken on the status of a fact, one which appeared to be backed up by authoritative leaks from the Pentagon. The issue subsequently played a major role in debates over the defense budget and in several election campaigns.

of events to favored members of Congress or reporters and from them to the public at large. "Secret reports" revealed in this way—especially those that frighten or titillate us—take on a mystique of accuracy that is undeserved. These "secrets" become potent symbols that rally constituencies whose concern is not with the accuracy of a given bit of intelligence but rather with the use to which the leak can be put in the domestic political arena. As time goes on, a self-reinforcing process sets in, each new leak lending credibility to the next, which in turn "confirms" those stories that have already been revealed.

"The agency [CIA] loved Gehlen because he fed us what we wanted to hear," Marchetti concludes. "We used his stuff constantly, and we fed it to everybody else: the Pentagon; the White House; the newspapers. They loved it, too. But it was hyped up Russian boogeyman junk, and it did a lot of damage to this country."[21]

CHAPTER SIX

CROWCASS

Regardless of the high-level intrigues involving scientists and the Gehlen Organization, the United States Army was often an exemplary institution when it came to pursuit and prosecution of Nazi war criminals. Army investigators captured more suspects, conducted more interrogations, secured more evidence, and contributed to the prosecution of more war criminals than any other institution in the world, with the possible exception of the NKVD, the Soviet secret police. And unlike the NKVD, the U.S. Army made much of the war crimes data it had gathered available to the entire world. Repositories of evidence and investigative files originally created or financed in large part by the U.S. Army, such as the Berlin Document Center and the records of the international team of prosecutors at Nuremberg, have provided the foundation for thousands of war crimes prosecutions by more than a dozen countries.

It is ironic, then, that the same institution was knowingly responsible for the escape of a substantial number of Nazis, including Klaus Barbie, the "Butcher of Lyons," and, in fact, organized entire paramilitary brigades made up of Nazi collaborators. But the *pursuit* of fugitive Nazis and facilitating their *escape* were not really two separate phenomena. These two apparently opposite policies were actually connected and are found interlocked at the heart of many army intelligence operations in Europe following the war.

Army projects such as CROWCASS—the central registry for tracing war crimes suspects—and the big U.S. interrogation center at Camp King were officially used to hunt Nazi fugitives. At the same time, however, they were secretly employing and protecting some of the very men whose names were on their wanted lists.

During these first years after the war one of the most important interfaces between the army and fugitive Nazis—and a good example of how they gradually became connected—was the Central Registry of War Crimes and Security Suspects, known as CROWCASS. CROWCASS cross-referenced the names of fugitive war crimes suspects, on the one hand, with the rosters of the more than 8 million people being held in POW and DP camps at the war's end. Although it was in operation for only three years, the CROWCASS system proved to be a singularly effective tool for locating tens of thousands of suspects, several thousand of whom were eventually tried for war crimes by national authorities in Europe or at the tribunals at Nuremberg. It was the CROWCASS registry, for example, that helped locate men who had committed atrocities at Buchenwald, Mauthausen, and Dachau, a number of whom were subsequently found guilty and executed.

The CROWCASS operation began in May 1945, following a call by General Dwight Eisenhower, then supreme Allied commander in Europe, for international cooperation in hunting and prosecuting war criminals. By the time it suspended operations in 1948, CROWCASS had processed 85,000 wanted reports, transmitted 130,000 detention reports to investigative teams from a dozen countries, and published a total of 40 book-length registries of persons being sought for crimes against humanity—probably the most extensive data base on such suspects ever created.[1]

But the CROWCASS system, like many intelligence projects, had a dual personality. The same cross-checking capabilities that permitted the location of thousands of fugitive Nazis also created a pool from which the names of thousands of "suspects" who might be useful for police or intelligence work could be drawn. The operations chief of CROWCASS, Leon G. Turrou, coordinated that task.

Turrou had served in the czarist army during the First World War but had found his way to the United States and begun a modest living as a translator for the anti-Communist "White" Russian émigré newspaper *Slovo* after the Bolshevik Revolution. During the 1920s he joined the FBI, specializing in countersubversion investigations in New York City's large Eastern European immigrant community. By all accounts Turrou did well at his job, and by 1938 he had gained fame by breaking up a large spy ring run by undercover German Abwehr (military intelligence) agents based in New York.

Turrou joined the U.S. Army's Criminal Investigation Division (CID)—the investigative arm of the military police—in 1942. There he caught the eye of General Eisenhower's chief of staff, General Walter Bedell Smith, and was appointed chief investigator and assistant director of, first, the CID's North African division and, by 1945, of the CID's combined European and African theater operations. Smith personally selected Turrou to head operations for CROWCASS in early 1945.[2]

"Under Turrou, CROWCASS . . . operated on two distinct levels," writes intelligence veteran and historian William Corson: "[first], to catalog war crimes and the locations of war criminals; and [secondly] to recruit former Nazis to serve as U.S. intelligence agents and sources." Turrou became the contact man inside CROWCASS for American intelligence agencies that wished to frustrate unauthorized attempts to locate Nazis who had gone to work for the West. Concealment of a recruited agent was generally achieved by simple deletion of the suspect's name from the list of those in U.S. custody, thus ensuring that the new employee would be officially considered missing. Vienna OSS chief Charles Thayer acknowledges that he did just that for German political warfare expert Hans Heinrich Herwarth in 1945. And Reinhard Gehlen himself chuckled over the irony that he was still officially a "fugitive" as late as 1949 owing to the fact that notice of his surrender had been intentionally deleted from POW lists with Turrou's assistance. As will be seen, CROWCASS intelligence "assets"—meaning agents or sympathizers who could be tapped for clandestine missions—eventually became an important element in many U.S. intelligence operations in Europe during the late 1940s.[3]

In the first months after Germany's surrender the relationship between army counterintelligence agents in Europe and their targets had been clear enough. U.S. investigators hunted down fugitive Nazis in order to penetrate and destroy any underground Fascist movements that had survived the collapse of the Hitler government. The army took the threat of such movements quite seriously. Germany had, after all, risen from the ashes of World War

I and evaded the restrictions of the Versailles Treaty through use of a variety of underground organizations, and Hitler and his top lieutenants had repeatedly pledged that they would do it again if Germany fell to the Allies. Detection of underground Nazi groups, therefore, became a high-priority task.

Most of these investigations were conducted by the Army Counterintelligence Corps. This agency worked closely with CROW-CASS and served as a political police, in effect, in the U.S.-occupied zone of Germany during the first few years after the war.

CIC investigations into underground Nazi activity became some of the first Nazi recruitment operations. This paradox is similar in many respects to the situation often faced in more conventional police work; destruction of a ring of criminals sometimes requires enlistment of one of them as an informer against the others. This enrollment of criminals, which is the daily bread of most civilian detectives and district attorneys, is typically carried out through harsh threats of punishment, followed by soothing offers of protection if a suspect cooperates. The object, at least ideally, is to bring an entire group of suspects to justice, even if that entails special leniency for a few of them. Not surprisingly, U.S. investigators frequently cut deals with some Nazis in order to land more important fugitives.

As the cold war congealed, however, the targets of the investigations shifted from underground Nazis to underground Communists and to persons viewed as sympathetic to the USSR. Many CIC investigators filed away their dossiers on war crimes suspects or let such cases slip to the bottom of the list of high-priority projects that never seemed to get any shorter. On an administrative level, the leadership and drive needed to trace and prosecute war crimes suspects were eroded.

Meanwhile, the CIC's networks of recruited informants and contract agents consisting of former Nazis and so-called minor war criminals largely remained in place. In several documented cases the CIC undertook efforts to enlist the help of the Nazis' own experts like Gestapo veteran Klaus Barbie in tracking down Communist intrigue.

But it is at that point that the similarity between conventional police work and the security efforts of the CIC ended. No longer were the CIC's Nazis used primarily to trace war criminals, nor were those informers enjoying CIC protection forced to pay some sort of penalty for their role in war crimes and crimes against humanity. As the cold war became an institution, the Nazis were simply turned loose.

The great majority of early (i.e., 1944 to 1947) recruitment and protection of Nazis by the U.S. government was the product of what many people would term "police informer" types of relationships. Gene Bramel, a young CIC agent who worked with SS man Klaus Barbie after the war, summarizes the CIC's point of view neatly: "They say, '[W]hy did you use Nazis?' That is a stupid question. It would have been impossible for us to operate in southern Germany without using Nazis. We were Americans. I spoke pretty good German, but by the time I got through ordering dinner they would have suspected I was American. And who knew Germany better than anyone else? Who were the most organized? Who were the most anti-Communist? Former Nazis. Not to use them would mean complete emasculation. And we used them, the British used them, the French used them, and the Russians used them."[4]

"You deal all the cards and play them as they come," reflects Herb Brucher, a former special agent with the 970th CIC detachment, which handled thousands of former Nazis as informers and contract agents between 1945 and 1949. "We dealt with Communists; we dealt with Nazis. . . . I never held that against the guy—though if you had something you could hold over a guy's head, then you could use that like a form of blackmail to get information." Brucher, like most CIC veterans, has few regrets about his work, which included efforts to locate German scientists for transfer to U.S. laboratories as well as a major campaign utilizing ex-Nazis to penetrate the German Communist party. Use of ex-SS men in such circumstances "never bothered me at all," he comments. "I guess it was all that training, but I personally took to it like a duck to water."[5]

It is clear that a Catch-22, rather than some vast conspiracy, is what accounts for the army's policy toward most Nazi fugitives, at least in the early years. Protecting war crimes suspects from arrest was, of course, banned; one important function of the CIC was, after all, the pursuit and arrest of underground Nazis. There was one hitch, however. A few selected Nazis could be protected or even paid off if doing so led to the arrest of more important fugitives.

At the same time the main type of payment available for the Nazis the 970th had recruited was "an allowance of soap, razors, chewing gum, and a little tobacco," as Brucher puts it, "and who the hell wants to work for that?" Many American agents turned to trading these items on the black market to obtain German currency for paying their informers. But when that failed to yield enough money, the Americans offered their wards the only thing the CIC had that was cheap and plentiful: protection. The more protection the American agents offered, the bigger the network of subagents they could run. The bigger the net, the more information that came in. And the more information that came in, the more successful the American agent was considered. No matter if the information the Nazis were providing was little more than clippings from Czech or Polish newspapers; there was no way to check it anyway, at least not at first. What mattered was volume, and protection equaled volume.[6]

The dusty, sprawling U.S. interrogation center at Camp King, near Oberusel, was apparently the most active recruiting center for ex-Nazis interested in throwing in their lot with the Americans. Commanded by Colonel William R. Philp and later by Colonel Roy M. Thoroughman, Camp King was a striking example of the blurring of the lines between the hunter and the prey.

Camp King had been the Luftwaffe's primary interrogation center for captured American and British fliers during the war, and it was there that the Germans developed highly effective interrogation techniques utilizing the latest breakthroughs in human psychology. Contrary to the stereotyped Nazi use of rubber hoses, the Luftwaffe's approach combined meticulous cross-referencing of every known fact about any given Allied air force unit, on the one hand, with subtle attempts to gain the respect of their prisoners, on the other. The results had been spectacular: Virtually every Allied airman let slip some fragment of information that, when combined with what the Germans already knew, proved to be of intelligence value. "Poker-faced Scharff," by all accounts the best German interrogator, testified later that "all but about 20 out of more than 500 I interviewed did talk, and told me exactly the things I was trying to find out."*[7]

In mid-1945 the United States seized the Luftwaffe center and

---

*The brutality of nazism was masked at the interrogation center but was present nonetheless. One wartime escape ended in the roundup and summary execution of some fifty Allied prisoners of war, mainly British. Consistently uncooperative or escape-prone prisoners were sent to their deaths in concentration camps.

transformed it into a holding tank for a number of the highest-ranking Nazis in captivity, including General Gehlen, Hermann Goering, Albert Speer, and Julius Streicher, as well as military leaders such as Field Marshal Albert Kesselring; Hitler's successor, Grand Admiral Karl Doenitz; and scores of others. Some trusted Luftwaffe interrogators who had once translated English into German for the Nazis were even put back to work translating German into English for the Allies.

Camp King, however, was not simply a high-level POW camp. Its unique mission was, as an internal history of the camp puts it, to "utilize the knowledge and abilities of the former German intelligence personnel to collect information of interest to the United States." About 200 SS, SD, and Abwehr men were assigned to write "histories" of their wartime experiences. Some of these studies concerned Nazi command structures and were subsequently used in connection with postwar trials. But the majority of the studies, even in 1945, were designed to produce information about the USSR, not Nazi Germany, and the authors of such studies were in many cases quietly let out of prison and placed on U.S. or British intelligence payrolls.

The activities at Camp King, although approved by the army's chief of intelligence in Europe, General Sibert, often ran directly counter to the publicly announced policy of the United States. Once, for example, the American zone provost marshal rejected a proposal from Colonel Philp that a systematic screening and interrogation of German POWs released from Russian custody be undertaken to gather intelligence on potential military targets in the Soviet-occupied zone. The provost marshal objected to the fact that Abwehr and SS officers were to be employed as interrogators and analysts in the effort. (Philp's proposal, in fact, had originated with Reinhard Gehlen, who had, as noted earlier, begun his secret spy organization under Philp's patronage at Camp King.) Despite the prohibition, Colonel Philp remained convinced that unless this information was collected at the time the POWs returned to Germany it would be lost forever. Philp, therefore, secretly obtained permission from General Sibert and proceeded. "Screening teams were established within the German refugee processing camps at Hersfeld, Hof, Ulm and Giessen," according to the unpublished history of Camp King.[8] "[A]pproximately 300,000 POWs were screened and carded. In many cases, exploitation [i.e., use as an informer or contract agent] was made at the processing camps."

This two-tier American policy in Germany occurred again and again throughout the cold war and was not so different, in fact, from the practice of the French, British, and Soviet governments. It combined a public condemnation and pursuit of fugitive Nazi criminals, on the one hand, with secret protection and utilization of some of the same men, on the other. Leaks were everywhere, however, and such protection did not remain truly secret for long. As the contradictory two-tier system gradually matured during the late 1940s, it became routine for U.S. intelligence agencies to defy the announced policies of the American government concerning Nazi fugitives. Public leaders in Germany (including newspaper reporters, for example, as well as political officials) tacitly cooperated with the intelligence agencies. "Well-informed people knew that this had to be done," says a former State Department political affairs officer who prefers anonymity, "and it was better to avoid any fuss."

By the end of 1947 the U.S. Army had begun at least a half dozen large-scale programs designed to tap the talents of SS and German military intelligence veterans. Operation Pajamas, for example, organized "exploitation of German personnel used in forecasting European political trends." Birchwood did the same with "economic experts," in this context clearly suggesting men who had worked for the SS and for Goering. Project Dwindle collected Nazi cryptographic experts and equipment. Apple Pie, a joint U.S.-British operation, recruited "certain key personnel of [SS] RSHA Amt VI" who were expert in Soviet industrial and economic matters, according to the U.S. orders that established the code word designators for the program. Project Panhandle undertook "operational exploitation"—in other words, recruitment for pay—"of German ex-Military Intelligence personnel for collecting military intelligence on the USSR and its satellites." Project Credulity traced German scientists wanted for the JIOA Paperclip project. These efforts, though highly secret from the general public, were nevertheless approved and managed through regular intelligence channels. They received conventional code names and were financed in the normal army intelligence budget.[9] These were not a conspiracy within the intelligence community to defy the rest of the government; these exploitation programs were the official, though secret, U.S. policy.

* * *

Virtually all U.S.-Soviet cooperation in the pursuit of war criminals had collapsed by mid-1946, with the important exception of the International Tribunal at Nuremberg. It is possible to debate endlessly over who exactly was to blame for the deterioration of the earlier efforts to bring Nazi criminals to justice. The competition over scientists and industrial laboratories was clearly a factor. So was the larger and more fundamental struggle over spheres of influence in France, Central Europe, and the Middle East. Any way one looks at it, however, it is clear that the failure of East and West to work together to prosecute war crimes suspects provided tickets to freedom, in effect, for thousands of the men and women who were responsible for the Holocaust and other outrages.

Belligerent confrontations began between East and West over just what did, and did not, constitute prosecutable war crimes as early as the summer of 1945. This conflict was particularly sharp in the cases of prominent members of Catholic political parties from Eastern Europe. The Soviets argued that many of these conservative Christian Democratic politicians had carried their countries into an open alliance with the Nazis, that they then had served as responsible officials in Axis regimes and had helped establish or administer laws for registration of Jews, creation of concentration camps, and the rest. Therefore, the Soviet reasoning went, these officials had contributed to the persecution of innocent people—or were at least suspects—and should be delivered to postwar Eastern European governments for trial.

Many American and other Western officials, on the other hand, preferred to concentrate on the role that the same religious parties had played on the eve of Germany's defeat, when much of the Christian Democratic establishment in Eastern Europe had turned against the Nazis. Although the United States had formally agreed as early as 1943 to turn over war criminals to the country where they had committed crimes, by 1945 U.S. policymakers were viewing anti-Communist Catholic leaders as an essential part of postwar coalition governments in Eastern Europe. The United States interpreted many Soviet war crimes accusations as basically political charges tailored to undermine Western influence in the region.

The question of how to handle suspected war criminals was further complicated by serious East-West disputes over repatriation of refugees. At least 8 million displaced people from Eastern Europe were living in hovels in occupied Germany and Austria in 1945. The United States, Britain, and the USSR had agreed at the Yalta Conference that these people were to be returned to their various homelands, where it was hoped they would be reintegrated into postwar society. Contrary to the lurid accounts that appeared in the West during the cold war, the overwhelming majority of these refugees voluntarily returned to their countries of origin without incident.

But the fact remained that between 1 and 2 million of the refugees did not wish to go back. Many of those who refused to return viewed themselves as heroes, of a sort, who had rebelled against Stalin even though that had entailed working with the Nazis. The Soviets, however, regarded most of the remaining refugees as people who had committed serious acts of treason, and Stalin insisted that they be returned. This harsh judgment was not entirely without justification, because a substantial number of the émigrés were, in fact, the former soldiers, SS volunteers, or quisling officials of the Nazis. "Treason" to the Soviets, however, also included acts such as public criticism of the Communist party, which was hardly considered a crime in the West.

The American and British authorities cooperated in the repatriation programs for a time, but with increasing reluctance. The prospect of driving an innocent person into Stalin's USSR against his or her will was distasteful to most Westerners, for obvious reasons. The majority of the remaining displaced persons appeared to be political or economic émigrés, by Western standards, not war criminals.

Western reluctance to turn over refugees—and criminal suspects—to the Soviets was reinforced as word trickled back from the East concerning the fates of some of those who had been delivered during the first months after the war. Trials of suspect quislings and native-born SS men in the East were generally a mere formality in those days and often dispensed with altogether. Thousands of summary executions were carried out in the USSR, Poland, and other areas under Red Army control. Modern historians in Yugoslavia concede that "tens of thousands" of Nazi collaborators were killed, often without trial, in that small country alone during 1945.[10] And millions of men and women from throughout Eastern Europe were deported to forced labor camps deep inside the USSR, many never to return.

Soviet suspicions that the West was intentionally harboring persons they considered traitors and war criminals expanded side by side with the West's growing reluctance to repatriate refugees. The already tense relations between the superpowers further deteriorated. The USSR refused to participate in the CROWCASS identification project or in most other war crimes inquiries sponsored by the Western Allies. Western investigators were generally barred from gathering evidence concerning incidents that had taken place inside Eastern Europe, and the bulk of evidence concerning Fascist crimes collected by the USSR was kept sealed off from the outside world in carefully restricted archives.

The Soviet position on such matters, stated briefly, was that if the West was holding a war crimes suspect, it should simply turn him or her over to the NKVD, which would conduct an investigation. No outside examiners were needed or wanted. Although the USSR did make a vital contribution to the prosecutions at Nuremberg, the fact remains that the unmistakable priority of Soviet investigators during the first years after the war was to lay hands upon any refugee or POW who might conceivably pose a political threat to regions under Russian control and only secondarily to collect evidence of crimes against humanity.

Why did the Soviets refuse to cooperate more fully with the admittedly imperfect and limited efforts that the United States did make to bring war criminals to justice? The people of the Soviet Union, after all, had suffered far more terribly at the hands of the Nazis than those of the United States. And the USSR did undertake a massive (but usually completely independent) effort to locate and punish Nazis and collaborators inside the Soviet-occupied territories.

The reasons for the Soviets' intransigence on this point are open to speculation. The U.S. use of CROWCASS to locate promising Nazi intelligence recruits was no doubt part of the reason. But that cannot be taken as a complete explanation; recruiting defectors from the enemy is, after all, a standard intelligence practice in wartime, one which the Soviets themselves regularly employed.

A more persuasive argument is that especially during the period of the Hitler-Stalin pact, the NKVD had committed a number of atrocities of its own that would have been impossible to conceal if Western investigators were permitted access to the Soviet zone. Public proof of these crimes would likely have been a major setback for the USSR at the time, threatening the Soviets' still-fragile hold over Eastern Europe and undermining the USSR's attempts at expanded political and trade relations with the West.

One notable example of the politically explosive nature of the NKVD's crimes was the Katyn Forest massacre, which remains a bitter problem in Soviet-Polish relations to this day. The preponderance of available evidence in this still-controversial episode points to the conclusion that Soviet security troops executed approximately 5,000 nationalist Polish army officers taken prisoner during 1939, then stacked the bodies like cordwood in mass graves at an isolated outpost. Similar NKVD mass killings of unarmed Ukrainian prisoners took place at Lvov, Dubno, and Vinnitsa, near the present Soviet-Polish border.

Other examples include the NKVD's forced deportation of some 35,000 to 50,000 "suspect" Latvians, Lithuanians, and Estonians to Siberian exile in 1940 and 1941, which has remained a rigidly enforced secret inside the USSR ever since.[11] Soviet security troops also seized approximately 1 million politically suspect Poles during the course of the war and shipped them in railroad cars to gulag prisons and labor camps in Central Asia and Siberia. There tens of thousands of them, perhaps hundreds of thousands were worked to death.

Nor did these practices end with the termination of the Hitler-Stalin pact. By the end of the war Stalin had developed a deeply rooted hatred of several minority groups in the USSR that he regarded as disloyal. As the Red Army reclaimed Soviet territory from the Nazis during 1943 and 1944, special police troops moved in behind the front to secure the ethnic minority regions of the USSR. In some parts of the country all the men, women, and children of entire Soviet nationality groups—the Crimean Tatars, Kalmyks, Chechens, and Volga Germans, among others—were rounded up at gunpoint and exiled to remote settlements deep inside the country for alleged collaboration with the Nazis. Indeed, as Nikita Khrushchev himself later commented, the entire Ukrainian ethnic group "avoided meeting this fate only because there were too many of them and there was no place to which to deport them. Otherwise," Khrushchev continued, Stalin "would have deported them also."[12]

The political price involved in admitting such disgraces was clearly higher than Stalin was willing to pay, and none of this could have been concealed for long had the USSR fully cooperated with war crimes investigations. Instead, the Soviets chose to solicit whatever CROWCASS information they could obtain through the various joint Allied control commissions and committees, at the same time undertaking on their own a vast criminal investigation that was kept carefully sealed off from Western eyes. Only in this way was it possible to maintain the "security" of the USSR—and the NKVD—throughout the purges of Nazi criminals.

It is also clear that the Soviets, like the Western Allies, were engaged in their own recruiting of selected Nazi agents whom they believed to be useful for intelligence or political purposes. The history of that recruitment has been suppressed in the East and is unlikely to be made public anytime soon. A number of documented cases have come to light, however, largely as a result of splits among Eastern Europe's Communist parties during the last thirty years.

Some measure of the scope of the Soviet's Nazi recruitment efforts may be found in Romania. There the country's Communist party, which was thoroughly dominated by a Muscovite clique in the first years after the war, swelled from about 1,000 old-timers in 1945 to some 714,000 members by the end of 1947. Several years later, however, a much more nationalistic faction of Romania's Communist party took control and purged many Muscovite leaders, including the party chief Ana Pauker and secret police chief Teohari Georgescu. That, in turn, led to public revelations of the extent to which Georgescu had relied on recruitment of Fascist Iron Guard veterans for his police apparatus during the first years after the war. According to Nicolae Ceauşescu, the Romanian party's present chairman, the new ruling group purged more than 300,000 "alien careerist elements, including Iron Guardists and hostile persons" who had entered the party's ranks during the height of Stalin's influence in that country.[13] Somewhat similar situations have been reported in both East Germany and Hungary, where Soviet occupation authorities permitted so-called little Nazis to remain in the police apparatus as a means of stabilizing power.

Yugoslavia's split with the USSR in 1948 also brought forth reliable information concerning the extent to which Stalin's secret police chief Lavrenti Beria relied on Nazi collaborators for clandestine operations. According to an official Yugoslav government statement to the United Nations, Beria's police "created a vast network of spies . . . [trained] in the USSR and composed mainly of fascists who had enlisted in the one and only regiment which the Croatian [Ustachi] traitor Pavelić had been able to place at Hitler's disposal." The purpose of the Soviet maneuver, the Yugoslavs charged, was seizure of the government of their country.

Other examples along these lines may be cited. In the Middle East top German espionage agent Fritz Grobba turned himself and his entire spy net over to the Russians at least as early as 1945; in the Balkans Nazi finance expert Carl Clodius, who had built his reputation in part by applying slave labor to Germany's economic problems, went on to become the economics chief in the Cominform's Balkans division; in East Germany SS General Hans Rattenhuber, formerly commander of Hitler's personal SS guard, re-emerged after the war as a senior East German political police official in East Berlin; and so on.*[14] Clearly the Soviets, too, were willing to forgive past Nazi indiscretions when it was in their interest to do so.

*Examples of SS and Gestapo veterans who ended up in police work in East Germany include Abwehr Lieutenant General Rudolph Bamler, who collaborated with Soviet military intelligence following his capture by the Russians and eventually became a department head at state security headquarters in East Berlin; Johann Sanitzer, once in charge of the Gestapo's anti-Jewish work in Vienna and later an East German police major in Erfurt; and SS Captain Louis Hagemeister, who had once handled counterespionage for the SS and later became chief police interrogator in Schwerin. Ex-SS Sturmbannführer Heidenreich became the official liaison between the East German political police and the Central Committee of the country's Communist party after the war. Dimitry and Nina Erdely, a husband-and-wife team specializing in émigré affairs for the Gestapo, ended up with the Soviet United Nations delegation in New York. It is likely that they had been Soviet double agents during the war. Maintaining their wartime cover, however, required that they "help . . . send many Soviet citizens to concentration camps," as a declassified U.S. State Department report on their activities puts it.

At least two former SS officers found their way onto the Central Committee of East Germany's Communist party, the Sozialistische Einheitspartei Deutschlands. They are Ernst Grossmann (a former Sachsenhausen concentration camp guard) and Waffen SS veteran Karlheinz Bartsch. Both were quickly purged when word of their wartime careers was published in the West.

CHAPTER SEVEN

"I . . . Prefer to Remain Ignorant"

The emerging East-West conflict had entered a new and clearly more hostile phase early in 1947. The British government, exhausted by war and deeply in debt, had abruptly announced that January that it was withdrawing from its earlier guarantees to stabilize power in Greece, where a bitter civil war was raging between left-wing rebels and British-backed Greek monarchist forces. President Truman blamed the Soviets for the crisis and stepped in with a multimillion-dollar aid program for the "democratic" forces in Greece—though there is considerable dispute over just how democratic they actually were—and with a series of campaigns to restrict the activities of pro-Communist movements in both the Middle East and Europe.

Truman claimed that the Soviets were underwriting the Greek insurgency and asserted that this justified a major U.S. commitment in that country. In fact, however, the Greek left was primarily an indigenous force. What outside aid the Greek rebels did enjoy came primarily from Tito's Yugoslavia, which was already having serious problems of its own with Stalin.[1]

Be that as it may, it was clear to the Americans that communism was to be regarded as the main enemy in Greece. After liberation in 1944, political power in that country had teetered uneasily between a nationalist-Communist alliance dominated by the Greek Communist party (EAM), on the one hand, and the weakened Greek monarchist forces. Both groups had fought the Nazi occupation during the war, though with varying degrees of dedication. When the British announced in early 1947 that they were withdrawing their sponsorship of the monarchists, almost every observer concluded that a leftist victory was at hand.

There was, however, another force in Greece, and it is to them that U.S. Intelligence turned. This was known as the Holy Bond of Greek Officers, or IDEA, by its Greek initials. This organization was made up in large part of Nazi collaborators. The Greek army and police were well known to have been controlled by rightists since the 1930s, and the bulk of those forces had collaborated with the Nazis during the German occupation. These sympathizers created "security battalions" during the war to hunt down anti-Nazi partisans and to execute Jews who had escaped from the ghetto at Salonika. These detachments were responsible for the murders of tens of thousands of Greeks during the occupation, according to all accounts, and directly assisted the Nazis in the liquidation of about 70,000 Greek Jews. After the Nazis had been driven out of the country, however, the security battalions and their officers were in deep disgrace. Colonel George Papadopoulos helped create IDEA shortly after the Nazis had been driven out of Greece, ostensibly to protect the Greek population from Communist attack. "In reality," however, the *Times* of London later reported, "a principal activity of IDEA was to secure rehabilitation of those officers who had been initially purged by the post-liberation coalition government because of their activities in the collaborationist 'security battalions' of the occupation years."[2]

Secret Pentagon papers now in the U.S. National Archives show that the United States poured millions of dollars into IDEA during the U.S. intervention in Greece in order to create what it termed "Secret Army Reserve" made up of selected Greek military, police, and anti-Communist militia officers. Sufficient money, arms, and supplies to equip a fighting force of at least 15,000 men were shipped to Greece in connection with this program alone. This semiclandestine army soon emerged with American backing as the central "democratic" force in Greece, and a long line of latter-day Greek strongmen such as Colonel Papadopoulos* (who eventually

---

*Greek central intelligence agency liaison chief Papadopoulos and several of his top lieutenants have repeatedly been accused of being Nazi collaborators. After Papadopoulos had

took control of the CIA-supported Greek central intelligence agency, KYP) and military leaders General Alexander Natsinas and General Nicolaos Gogoussis have been drawn from IDEA's ranks.[3]

American arms and money had a powerful impact in Greece. Many Greek nationalist forces abandoned their former EAM allies—in part because of the brutality of the EAM in its execution of an attempted guerrilla war against the U.S.-backed forces—and within two years a strongly pro-American government had achieved control of the country.

Truman's decisive action in Greece had wider ramifications. It helped crystallize sentiment inside the U.S. government, which up to that point had often been divided over just how harshly to deal with the USSR, into a new and much more obdurate approach to U.S.-Soviet relations. This new strategy marked an important watershed in the development of U.S. efforts to make use of Nazis and Nazi sympathizers, eventually creating the administrative structure and bureaucratic rationale for their utilization on an even wider scale than before.

The thinking behind this strategy was perhaps best articulated by George F. Kennan, the State Department expert on Soviet affairs who at the time had recently been appointed chief of the department's Policy Planning Staff. Kennan had served several tours of diplomatic duty in Moscow over the previous two decades, and his experience there had left him deeply bitter about both Stalin's dictatorship and the prospects for East-West cooperation. His antipathy toward Stalin had kept him isolated from the policy process during the Roosevelt administration, when relatively close U.S.-USSR ties were backed by the White House. He had come into his own, however, in the Truman years. His famous 1946 "Long Telegram" from Moscow (as it has since come to be known) became a rallying cry for those at State, the War Department, and the White House who were determined to get tough with the Russians. That message read, as Kennan himself later recalled, "exactly like one of those primers put out by alarmed congressional committees or by the Daughters of the American Revolution, designed to arouse the citizenry to the dangers of the Communist conspiracy." Even so,

---

seized total power in Greece in a bloody coup in 1967, U.S. Senator Lee Metcalf denounced him from the floor of the U.S. Senate, calling his junta "a military regime of collaborators and Nazi sympathizers . . . [who are] receiving American aid."

"its effect . . . was nothing less than sensational," he writes. "It was one that changed my career and my life in very basic ways. . . . My reputation was made. My voice now carried."[4]

By the time the United States intervened in Greece, Kennan enjoyed the direct sponsorship of Secretary of the Navy (soon to be Secretary of Defense) James Forrestal and of Secretary of State George Marshall. Acting on Forrestal's behalf, Kennan prepared a pivotal analysis of the USSR that has since come to be called the "containment doctrine" and is generally recognized as one of the basic programmatic statements of the cold war. In it, Kennan succeeded in reconciling many of the inchoate and conflicting perspectives on how to deal with the Soviets that had characterized Truman's administration up to that point. He argued that U.S.-Soviet relations were a fundamentally hostile, protracted conflict that had been initiated by the USSR—not the United States—and that normal relations between the two states would be impossible as long as a Soviet type government was in power in the USSR. Their "ideology," he wrote, ". . . has taught them that the outside world was hostile and that it was their duty eventually to overthrow the political forces beyond their borders. . . . [This] means that there can never be on Moscow's side any sincere assumption of a community of aims between the Soviet Union and powers which are regarded as capitalist."

The USSR was an imperial empire, Kennan continued, but the modern-day East-West clash could be managed through measures short of all-out war through what he termed "long term, patient but firm and vigilant containment of Russian expansive tendencies" and the "adroit and vigilant application of counterforce at a series of constantly shifting geographical and political points." As originally formulated, the containment doctrine envisioned bottling up internal pressures inside the USSR until they forced the Soviet Union to "cooperate or collapse," as *Newsweek* summarized it, a process that was expected to take about ten to fifteen years. "Soviet power," Kennan concluded, ". . . bears within it the seeds of its own decay, and . . . the sprouting of these seeds is well advanced."[5]

Kennan was later to assert that his intention at the time he prepared his analysis was to say that the "counterforce" and "containment" that gave the doctrine its name should employ political, not military, tactics. The phrases quoted above, he said, were misinterpreted by Secretary of Defense Forrestal and others when they used Kennan's formulations to promote NATO, a giant arms budget, the permanent division of Germany, and a number of other policies that the diplomat opposed.[6]

Regardless of Kennan's reservations, it was precisely these more aggressive aspects of containment that attracted Forrestal and other hard-liners in the Truman administration. In their hands, containment became the theoretical framework for U.S.-Soviet relations under which a wide variety of clandestine warfare tactics, ranging from radio propaganda to sabotage and murder, was chosen to counteract—"contain"—left-wing initiatives virtually anywhere in the world.

Although it was rarely mentioned in the public discussions, it is clear that covert operations aimed at harassing (and, if possible, overthrowing) hostile governments were an integral part of the containment strategy from the beginning. A new breed of realpolitik advocates among the government's national security specialists embraced containment as a rationale for what has since come to be called "destabilization" of the USSR and its satellites. Put briefly, destabilization is a type of psychological or political warfare that is calculated to undermine a target government, to destroy its popular support or credibility, to create economic problems, or to draw it into crisis through some other means. U.S. security planners of the late 1940s became fascinated with the prospect of destabilizing the Soviet Union's satellite states while simultaneously harassing the USSR. They were anxious to capitalize on the spontaneous rebellions against Soviet rule then rumbling through the Ukraine and parts of Eastern Europe, some of which were approaching civil wars in intensity.

As is well known, Kennan's public work during this period concentrated on development of the Marshall Plan for the economic recovery of Europe and on U.S. policy in the Far East, both of which were tasks with far-reaching implications that have enjoyed lengthy treatment in cold war historiography ever since. Less understood, however, is the role he played in development of American covert operations abroad. Kennan was deeply involved in preparations for several large-scale clandestine propaganda and guerrilla warfare projects aimed at Eastern Europe at the same time he was preparing the containment paper for Forrestal.[7]

Use of former Nazi collaborators became interwoven with these clandestine destabilization efforts and with the containment doctrine in general from 1947 on. According to Pentagon records, at the same time that Kennan was publicly promulgating containment, he and his close colleague Charles Thayer were lobbying with top Department of State and military officials for a revival of the remnants of the Nazi collaborationist Vlasov Army for use against the USSR. Kennan and Thayer pushed for the creation of a new school for anti-Communist guerrilla warfare training designed to bring together U.S. military specialists, Vlasov veterans, and other Eastern European exiles from Soviet satellite states. Several such schools were eventually established in Germany and in the United States and served not only as a training ground for insurgents but also as a source of highly skilled recruits for a variety of other American clandestine operations as well.[8]

The story of how Kennan and Thayer developed their attitudes toward revitalization of the Vlasov Army and similar organizations of former Nazi collaborators is worth examining as an illustration of a broader shift in opinion that was under way in American national security circles as the cold war deepened. Kennan, Thayer, and a number of other latter-day U.S. experts on Soviet affairs had first encountered one another at the U.S. Embassy in Moscow during the mid-1930s. The outpost where the young men worked was, as Kennan put it later, "in many respects a pioneer enterprise—a wholly new type of American [diplomatic] mission—the model and the precursor of a great many missions of a later day." Following more than a century of relative isolationism in American foreign policy, the U.S. center in Moscow was "the first to cope seriously . . . with the problems of security—of protection of codes and files and the privacy of intra-office discussion—in a hostile environment," according to the diplomat.[9]

The intelligence work of the Moscow staff was much more sophisticated than that under way at other U.S. embassies of the prewar period. The Russian embassy staff (particularly Kennan and his colleague Charles Bohlen) developed a technique that was then new for the Americans and that later became the intelligence analysis backbone of the wartime OSS and still later of the CIA. Unlike more traditional consular reports of foreign trade regulations, court intrigues, and similar diplomatic chitchat, this new approach included the systematic collection of published materials concerning a given country, then the supplementing of those data with information gleaned from secret sources and espionage, and finally the interpretation of the lot by researchers with extensive backgrounds in the subject area. This method has more in common with good scholarship or journalism than it does with James Bond types of affairs, though there was room for those, too. By late 1936, according to Kennan, use of these techniques had made the U.S. Embassy one of the best informed and most highly respected diplomatic missions in Moscow. There was only one rival when it came to collection of information on the USSR. That contender was the embassy of Nazi Germany, whose inside knowledge of Soviet affairs was, as Kennan puts it, "at all times excellent."[10]

Kennan, Thayer, Bohlen, and a number of the other U.S. diplomatic personnel in Moscow established enduring friendships with several top German diplomats during this period, including senior Konsul Gustav Hilger, Military Attaché Ernst Köstring, and Second Secretary Hans Heinrich Herwarth. Such men were at the core of Germany's diplomatic expertise on the USSR, and they shared both professional and personal interests with their American colleagues.[11]

These bonds survived the war. Thayer, as it turned out, in 1945 became chief of the OSS in Austria. There he rediscovered Herwarth—who, it will be recalled, had served as a senior political officer of the Wehrmacht's *Osttruppen* (eastern troops) program for recruiting collaborators during the conflict—when Herwarth turned himself in after Germany's formal surrender.

Their 1945 reunion was warm and mutually profitable. Thayer regarded Herwarth as "an old friend who happened to be a captain in the German Army," as he put it later, and used the power of his OSS office to intervene on the German's behalf. Thayer considered Herwarth to be an anti-Nazi and an excellent source of information on Soviet affairs. Thayer remembered from his embassy days, for example, that Herwarth had in 1939 leaked secret information to the Americans concerning the Hitler-Stalin Pact. He knew that Herwarth had been a friend of Claus von Stauffenberg (who had organized the July 20, 1944, attempted assassination of Hitler) and that Herwarth, like a number of other German political warfare experts, had been critical of Hitler's policies in the East prior to the war.

Thayer also knew that Herwarth had been involved in the defector troops' antipartisan warfare in Yugoslavia in 1944, for he has admitted this himself, and it was his responsibility as OSS chief in Austria to know that those campaigns had been marked by thousands of mass executions of civilian hostages, looting of villages, and other crimes. Even so, Thayer quickly arranged for Herwarth to be demobilized from the Wehrmacht, kept out of U.S. POW camps, and freed from American custody without even the cursory investigation of wartime activities given to noncommisioned officers.

"None of us had as yet any inkling of what really hapened on the Russian front since June 22, 1941 [when the Germans invaded]," Thayer explained later. "There were a lot of questions that he [Herwarth] could answer, and from my experience with him before the war I was sure those answers would not be only reliable but expert."[12]

"For about nine weeks I remained with Charlie," Herwarth writes. "He asked me to write down my experiences in the war with the Soviet Union, and especially to describe the activities of the *Freiwilliganverbande* [the Germans' collaborationist troops in the East]. Every day, I went with Charlie [to] his office, which was in the old monastery of St. Peter. . . . In late summer I was assigned to the American historical research group [at Camp King]. . . ."[13]

Thayer credits Herwarth, more than anyone else, for educating him about German political warfare efforts in the East and about the anti-Communist potential of the collaborationist troops that had served under German command. With Thayer's help, Herwarth emerged as one of the first, and certainly one of the most influential, German advocates of resurrecting the Vlasov Army and similar collaborators for use against the USSR. Herwarth was uniquely qualified for the task. In addition to having served as Köstring's political officer, he had also represented the Wehrmacht at the official founding of the Komitet Osvobozhdeniia Narodov Rossii (KONR), the political arm of the Vlasov Army that had been created under Nazi auspices.

Herwarth's value to the OSS at the time of his work for Thayer lay in his ability to identify useful Germans with expertise on the USSR and Eastern Europe. Among the first such experts to be plucked out of the squalid U.S. POW camps in Germany were Gustav Hilger; Herwarth's commandant, Köstring; and many of the surviving members of the German Embassy's prewar staff in Moscow. Some, like Köstring and Herwarth, were immediately put to work writing intelligence reports for the Americans on what they knew about the Red Army and the Germans' use of collaborators. Others, like Hilger, received the full VIP treatment, complete with secret trips to the United States for debriefing at the special army facility for senior German POWs at Fort Hunt, Virginia.[14]

Through these channels and others like them Kennan, Thayer,

and other American specialists on Soviet affairs learned of the details of German political warfare in the East. The Americans' later acts strongly suggest that they also accepted the basic features of Herwarth's version of what had taken place there: that the eastern troops were idealistic volunteers who had been motivated by a desire to overthrow Stalin's dictatorship; that they had not been involved in—and indeed had not even heard of—Nazi war crimes until the conflict was over; and that the collaborators were really pro-Western and prodemocracy at heart.

George Kennan's perspective on Nazi war crimes is relevant here because it bears on the question of how closely he was willing to look at the wartime careers of those in the Vlasov Army and similar groups during his service as a senior U.S. national security strategist. He has written that he viewed the Nuremberg war crimes tribunal with "horror," not because of the evidence of Nazi criminality presented there but rather because the trial and judgment of the Nazis themselves may have impeded improving U.S.-German relations in the wake of the war.

As Kennan saw it, a thorough purging of Nazis and even of war criminals from postwar German governments was undesirable for several reasons. He summed up his views on this topic in a wartime memo prepared for Henry P. Leverich, a senior State Department official specializing in U.S. planning for post-war Germany. First, he argued, "it is impracticable," because the Allies could never cooperate efficiently enough to do the job. "Second . . . whether we like it or not," the diplomat wrote, "nine tenths of what is strong, able and respected in Germany has been poured into those very categories which we have in mind" for purging from the German government—namely, those who had been "more than nominal members of the Nazi Party." Rather than remove the "present ruling class of Germany," as he put it, it would be better to "hold it [that class] strictly to its task and teach it the lessons we wish it to learn."[15]

The actions of the Nazis and their collaborators reflected the "customs of warfare which have prevailed generally in Eastern Europe and Asia for centuries in the past," Kennan wrote to Ambassador John G. Winant at that time, "they are not the peculiar property of the Germans. . . . If others wish, in the face of this situation, to pursue the illumination of those sinister recesses in which the brutalities of this war find their record, they may do so," he concluded. But "the degree of relative guilt which such inquiries may bring to light is something of which I, as an American, prefer to remain ignorant."[16]

By 1947, then, a bold perspective on how to wage the cold war had begun to take shape in the minds of Kennan, Thayer (who by that time had been appointed director of the Voice of America), and most other national security strategists in Washington. As Thayer sums it up, this theory held that Hitler's wartime offensive in the East had failed primarily because of his failure to follow the advice of political warfare experts such as Herwarth. The German experience, however, had "proved" that the population of the USSR was eager for life without Stalin and that millions of people in the Soviet Union and its satellites could be rallied against communism through new promises of democracy, religious freedom, and an end to police state rule.

Not all the clandestine containment programs were aimed at the USSR and its satellites. Some of the most important early applications of these tactics began in Western Europe. The Italian elections of early 1948 marked another important milestone in the development of U.S. covert operations and in high-level U.S. support for use of former Nazi collaborators. Two developments of far-reaching importance for these programs took place during this election campaign. First, U.S. security agencies successfully tested a series of propaganda and political manipulation techniques that were later to come into widespread use around the world, including inside the United States itself. Secondly, the CIA established much deeper and broader ties with the hierarchy of the Roman Catholic Church in Rome than had previously been the case. This not only had a powerful impact on the Italian political scene but also—as is discussed in a later chapter—laid the foundation for the agency's relationship with Intermarium, an influential Catholic lay organization made up primarily of Eastern European exiles that operated under the protection of the Vatican. At least a half dozen senior leaders of Intermarium and its member groups can be readily identified as Nazi collaborators. Some were fugitive war criminals. However, Intermarium was later to emerge as one of the mainstays of Radio Free Europe, Radio Liberation from Bolshevism (later renamed Radio Liberty), and scores of other CIA-sponsored clandestine operations during the next two decades.

The Italian Communist party was favored to score heavily in the 1948 elections, and many analysts said that the party might democratically win control of the country's government. This prospect created such alarm in Washington that George Kennan—by then the foremost long-range strategist for the U.S. government—went so far as to advocate direct U.S. military occupation of the Foggia oil fields if the voting results went wrong from the point of view of the United States.[17]

Washington's apprehension was shared—indeed, was enthusiastically fueled—by the Holy See. The church's hierarchy, which was already under severe economic and political pressure in Eastern Europe, feared a Communist takeover of the very heart of its institution, or at least of its worldly resources. The prospect of a Communist electoral victory in Italy coming close on the heels of Communist gains in Yugoslavia, Hungary, Czechoslovakia, and Poland was viewed by many of the hierarchy as the most profound material crisis the church had seen in centuries. Prochurch Italian officials were "positively desperate and almost immobilized by the fear which hangs over them," Bishop James Griffiths, an American emissary to the Vatican, wrote at the time. They were afraid, the bishop said, of a "disastrous failure at the polls which will put Italy behind the Iron Curtain."[18]

The election campaign became a major test of containment and of its accompanying clandestine political warfare strategy. Allen Dulles, Frank Wisner, James Angleton, William Colby, and a team of other top-ranked U.S. intelligence officials put together a crash program of propaganda, sabotage, and secret funding of Christian Democratic candidates designed to frustrate the Italian Communist party's ambitions. The CIA was a young organization in those days and was primarily limited (until June 1948) to simple information gathering and analysis. Therefore, much of this campaign was handled on an ad hoc basis out of the offices of Allen and John Foster Dulles at the Sullivan & Cromwell law firm in New York. Kennan watched events unfold from his vantage point at State Department headquarters in Washington, while Thayer kept up a steady cannonade of pro-West and anti-Communist broadcasts over the Voice of America.

Working in close coordination with the Vatican and with prominent Americans of Italian or Catholic heritage, the CIA found that its effort in Italy succeeded well beyond its expectations. On a public level the United States dumped $350 million in announced civil and military aid into the country during this campaign alone. Bing Crosby, Frank Sinatra, Gary Cooper, and a score of other prominent Americans were enlisted to make radio broadcasts to Italy warning against the Communist electoral menace.* A CIA-financed media blitz showered Italian newspapers with articles and photographs expressing American munificence and Communist atrocities, both real and manufactured. The archbishops of Milan and Palermo announced that anyone who voted for the Communist party's candidates was prohibited from receiving absolution or confession. Eugène Cardinal Tisserant went further. Communists "may not have a Christian burial or be buried in holy grounds," he pronounced.

Francis Cardinal Spellman of New York served as a crucial go-between in CIA-Vatican negotiations. "The Vatican [has] been promised that American funds would be made available to assist in the presentation of the anti-Communist appeal to the Italian public," Spellman wrote following a meeting with U.S. Secretary of State Marshall. The U.S. government, the cardinal said, had secretly "released large sums in 'black currency' in Italy to the Catholic Church."[19] This "black currency" did not come from the American taxpayers. Rather, a substantial part of the funding for clandestine activities in Italy came from captured Nazi German assets, including money and gold that the Nazis had looted from the Jews.

The trail of this tainted money dates back to 1941, when the War Powers Act authorized the U.S. Treasury's Exchange Stabilization Fund to serve as a holding pool for captured Nazi valuables—currency, gold, precious metals, and even stocks and bonds—seized as the Germans or other Axis governments attempted to smuggle them out of Europe. The captured wealth, which eventually totaled tens of millions of dollars, included substantial amounts of blood money that the Nazis had pillaged from their victims. Indeed, it was precisely this type of criminal booty that overeager Nazis had most frequently attempted to export from Europe.

The Exchange Stabilization Fund was authorized to safeguard the portion of the Nazi hoard that had been uncovered and confiscated by the United States in the Safehaven program, which sought to interdict the German smuggling efforts. The official purpose of the fund was to serve as a hedge against inflation and as a bankers' tool to dampen the effects of currency speculation in the fragile economies of postwar Europe and Latin America. In

*There is no evidence that Crosby, Sinatra, and Cooper were aware of the seamier aspects of the U.S. government's campaign in Italy or that they knew that U.S. intelligence was underwriting the publicity campaign to which they lent their names.

reality, this pool of money became a secret source of financing for U.S. clandestine operations in the early days of the CIA.[20]

The first known payments from the Exchange Stabilization accounts for covert work were made during the hotly contested Italian election. The CIA withdrew about $10 million from the fund in late 1947, laundered it through a myriad of bank accounts, then used that money to finance sensitive Italian operations. This was the "black currency" that Cardinal Spellman asserted was given to the Vatican for anti-Communist agitation.

Much of the CIA's $10 million Italian war chest was delivered through clandestine campaign contributions to Christian Democratic candidates. The agency, it is true, refused to fund openly Fascist candidates. A "conscious policy was made both in Washington and Rome," former CIA Director William Colby writes, "that no help of any kind was to go to the Neo-Fascists or Monarchists." Instead, the center parties were to be strengthened to form what Colby terms a "stable, viable and truly democratic governing majority." The reasons for this strategy were both ideological and pragmatic: "Any strengthening of the Neo-Fascists and Monarchists, we recognized, would inevitably weaken the Liberals and Christian Democrats [the CIA's favored parties in this case], for that was the only place from which added strength could come to them, not from the Communists."[21]

Colby's comment is correct. What it fails to reveal, however, is the fact that many of the remnants of the Fascists' wartime ruling apparatus, as well as most of the police, had joined Christian Democratic ranks after 1945. The CIA's "black currency" in Italy may not have gone to the discredited diehard Fascist groups, but it did go to clerics and other leaders who were themselves closely tied to Fascist rule.

The curious events surrounding Monsignor Don Giuseppe Bicchierai of Milan are disturbing. Bicchierai had served during the closing months of the war as an intermediary in surrender negotiations between Allen Dulles of the OSS, on the one hand, and Walter Rauff of the SS and SD. Rauff, in turn, was representing SS General Karl Wolff and Field Marshal Albert Kesselring, who were the senior German police and military officials in Italy. The OSS called these negotiations "Operation Sunrise." They played a large role in establishing the reputation of Allen Dulles as a consummate spy master, though a strong argument may be made for the contention that they failed to shorten the war in Italy by a single day. Be that as it may, it is clear that Sunrise established a close working relationship between Dulles and Bicchierai that was to flower in the years ahead.

But first there is the matter of Walter Rauff. Rauff was a major war criminal. He had personally developed and administered the notorious gas truck execution program which took the lives of approximately 250,000 people, most of them Jewish women and children who died in unspeakable filth and agony. Rauff escaped from Europe in 1948, traveling first to Syria and later to South America.

An extensive study of Rauff's life by the Simon Wiesenthal Center suggests that Monsignor Bicchierai may have helped Rauff and other Nazi fugitives escape from war crimes charges by aiding their flight from Europe. According to the Wiesenthal report, Rauff was interned at the Rimini POW camp for about eighteen months after the war but succeeded in slipping away under mysterious circumstances in December 1946. Wiesenthal believes that it was Bicchierai who sheltered Rauff after this escape and arranged for him to stay secretly "in the convents of the Holy See," as Rauff himself testified years later. Rauff hid in Rome for more than a year, then used false passports to travel to Syria and South America. Wiesenthal has repeatedly asked Pope John Paul II to open an investigation into Bicchierai's role in this affair. So far these requests have been ignored.*[22]

*What Allen Dulles knew, if anything, of the circumstances of Rauff's escape from Europe is open to question. He fails to comment on the matter at all in his own history of the 1945 negotiations, *The Secret Surrender.* State Department files, however, contain an intriguing top secret memorandum dated September 17, 1947, that casts some new light on the department's attitude concerning war criminals who participated in the Sunrise negotiations.

Sometime shortly before that date, the U.S. political adviser's office in Germany cabled Washington requesting information on how to handle war criminals who claimed that they had been involved with Sunrise. The text of this message is missing from State's archives, but the answer to the query has been located. It reads: "Officials concerned with Operation Sunrise report no, repeat no, promises furnished," State's head of security Jack Neal wired back to Germany. "However, these officials are of the opinion . . . that allies owe some moral obligation in return for aid performed and risks taken, therefore, definite consideration should be given to those favorable aspects when weighing any war crimes with which they are charged."

Each of the SS officers involved in Operation Sunrise managed to escape serious punishment after the war despite the fact that each was a major war criminal. A U.S. military tribunal tried Walter Schellenberg, who had helped trap and exterminate the Jews of France. He was convicted but freed shortly thereafter under a clemency from the U.S. high commissioner for Germany, John McCloy. Schellenberg became an adviser to the British intelligence service. The gas truck commander Rauff, as noted in the text, escaped under mysterious circumstances to South America. SS Obersturmbannführer Eugen Dollman, who had been instrumental in the killing programs directed at Italian Jews, was in American hands in 1947 yet managed to escape to Switzerland in the early 1950s.

Walter Rauff was still hiding in the "convents of the Holy See," as he put it, when the CIA provided his sponsor Monsignor Bicchierai with enough money to buy Jeeps, bedding, and guns for an underground squadron of some 300 anti-Communist Italian youths for use during the 1948 elections.[23] The job of this band was beatings of left-wing candidates and activists, breaking up political meetings, and intimidating voters. Bicchierai's troops became the forerunners of a number of other similar paramilitary gangs funded by the CIA in Germany, Greece, Turkey, and several other countries over the next decade.

The CIA's strategy in Italy, including Monsignor Bicchierai's strong-arm squad, was a great success. The Italian Communists lost by a comfortable margin, and the American intelligence services emerged with the Catholic Church as a powerful new ally. Perhaps most important of all, the strategy of using covert operations to achieve political goals in peacetime was firmly implanted in the minds of Washington's foreign policy elite as a powerful weapon in an increasingly dangerous cold war.

The utility of the new covert operations apparatus seemed clear at the time: It permitted the White House to circumvent the cumbersome bureaucracy of Congress and the Department of State in the field of foreign affairs; it extended the reach of the United States with what appeared to be relatively little risk; and it permitted the president secretly to carry out actions that would discredit the United States if they were undertaken openly. Covert action was also relatively cheap, at least compared with the costs involved in maintaining a permanent military presence throughout the world.

George Kennan, in particular, "was deeply impressed by the results achieved in Italy," according to Sig Mickelson, the longtime chief of Radio Free Europe. "And [Kennan] foresaw similar crises arising in the future." Kennan was "directly concerned with the refugee problem and worried about the weakness of the nation's intelligence apparatus," Mickelson writes. "[He] advocated the creation of a covert action capability designed to complement covert

---

Himmler's personal adjutant SS Gruppenführer Karl Wolff was sentenced to "time served" in a denazification proceeding in 1949, then released altogether without any objection from the U.S. occupation authorities. Fifteen years later a West German court tried Wolff a second time. Then, he was convicted of administering the murder of 300,000 persons, most of them Jews, and of overseeing SS participation in slave labor programs at I. G. Farben and other major German companies. Wolff served seven years of a life sentence, then was released again.

psychological operations somewhere in the governmental structure. . . . His intention was to create a mechanism for direct intervention in the electoral processes of foreign governments," the former Radio Free Europe president continues. "It would be under the control of the Department of State, specifically [Kennan's own] policy planning staff, but it would not be formally associated with the department. State was still skittish about dealing openly with foreign governments on the one hand [while] carrying out covert destabilizing efforts on the other."[24]

Greece in 1947 and Italy in 1948 also taught the CIA that it could employ former Nazi collaborators on a large scale in clandestine operations and get away with it. U.S. national security planners appear to have concluded that extreme-right-wing groups that had once collaborated with the Nazis should be included in U.S.-sponsored anti-Communist coalitions, for the participation of such groups became a regular feature of U.S. covert operations in Europe in the wake of the Greek and Italian events.

A case may be made for the idea that doing so was simply realpolitik. Former collaborators were, after all, a substantial organized force, so why not make use of them? At the time the benefits of using former Nazi collaborators appeared to outweigh any drawbacks. The American media—and the American people, for the most part—warmly welcomed the victories of European center parties over their Communist rivals. There were few public questions concerning exactly how these successes had been brought about. The long-range implications for this policy were, as shall be seen, more problematic.

CHAPTER EIGHT

Bloodstone

The Greek and Italian campaigns revealed something else as well: Covert action was largely out of the control of the established foreign policy apparatus in Washington. Although the Italian operation had been endorsed by all the appropriate government committees, not one of them had really known what was under way. The ease with which Republican activists Allen and John Foster Dulles had commandeered control of America's largest postwar secret campaign to date was bound to raise eyebrows at Truman's National Security Council. The closely contested 1948 Truman-Dewey U.S. presidential election was only months away, and John Foster Dulles was, after all, among the Republican challengers' most influential foreign affairs strategists. The implications of conceding this much power to the political opposition—or, equally dangerous, to the military—were not lost on the White House.

Serious blunders in secret U.S. political warfare operations involving Eastern European nationals had already taken place. Most notable of these was a bungled U.S.-backed coup plot in Romania in March 1947. Circumstantial evidence suggests that a still-active splinter of the old OSS was behind the operation, though the full story has yet to be told. It is clear, however, that the Romanian affair was undertaken without the knowledge of the secretary of state, who had directly forbidden such meddling because of sensitive ongoing negotiations over U.S. investments in the Ploesti oil fields. The attempted coup took place with such amateurishness that the conspirators took "stenographic notes . . . of the [clandestine] proceedings . . . and placed [them] on file with other persons," according to Robert Bishop, a longtime American intelligence agent in Romania. This, Bishop notes blandly, "was a foolhardy procedure."[1] The conspirators were soon rounded up by Romanian police, tried, and sent to jail for many years. U.S.-Romanian relations, already tense, further soured. The Ploesti oil field negotiations failed.

Secretary of State George Marshall counted on George Kennan to make sure that obvious blunders like the Romanian affair did not occur again. By the summer of 1948 Truman and Marshall had delegated personal responsibility for political oversight of all peacetime clandestine operations to George Kennan, according to a later Senate investigation of U.S. foreign intelligence activities. (Control of espionage and counterintelligence, however, remained outside the diplomat's purview.) Key members of Kennan's Policy Planning Staff—officially a somewhat egg-headed institution dedicated to planning U.S. strategy for ten or twenty years in the future—were detailed to help him with this task.

Two forces, then, converged to thrust the covert operations weapon into Kennan's hands. First, there was President Truman's desire—strongly backed up by Secretary of Defense Forrestal—to make use of this powerful tool in what appeared to be a deteriorating situation in Europe. Secondly, there was the determination, especially by Secretary of State Marshall as well as by Kennan himself, to make sure that no one else in the U.S. government seized political control of this prize before the State Department did.

A new stage in the American effort to use ex-Nazis began. The early "tactical" or short-term utilization of former Fascists and collaborators—techniques somewhat akin to the exploitation of prisoners of war by intelligence agents—gradually came to an end. American agencies and policymakers replaced the tactical approach with a deeper "strategic" appreciation of the usefulness that émigré groups might have in large-scale clandestine operations against the USSR. The U.S. government increasingly accepted the exiles' organizations as legitimate and began to pour substantial amounts of money into them—at least $5 million in 1948 alone, and probably considerably more.

The spring and summer of 1948 were a period of extraordinary activity in U.S. national security circles. The East-West conflict over administration of occupied Germany finally pushed past the breaking point. The collapse of the Czech government in February, the spring war scare, spy scandals at home, and setbacks for Chiang Kai-shek's Chinese nationalists at the hands of Mao Zedong's People's Liberation Army accelerated the deterioration of U.S.-Soviet relations. By June a relatively minor dispute over German currency reform had prompted the Soviets to shut off Western access to Berlin, and this in turn precipitated the Berlin airlift. There was a real possibility that any further escalation—especially a major military mobilization by either side—could lead to all-out war.

The strategic thinking behind the United States tactics during this period is best summarized in a top secret National Security Council directive and a group of supporting policy papers which are known collectively as NSC 20. These documents, which were drawn up primarily by Kennan and his Policy Planning Staff (PPS), were formally adopted by Truman's NSC in August 1948.[2] They deserve quotation at some length because they provided the basic policy framework for U.S. clandestine operations against the Soviets, including the use of former Nazi collaborators, for the remainder of Truman's term.

Kennan sought, as the preamble of his policy statement states, "to define our present peacetime objectives and our hypothetical wartime objectives with relation to Russia, and to reduce as far as possible the gap between them." The objectives, he writes, were really only two:

> a. To reduce the power and influence of Moscow. . . . b. To bring about a basic change in the theory and practice of international relations observed by the government in power in Russia.
>
> Adoption of these concepts in Moscow [however] would be equivalent to saying that it was our objective to overthrow Soviet power. Proceeding from that point, it could be argued that this is in turn an objective unrealizable by means short of war, and that we are therefore admitting that our objective with respect to the Soviet Union is eventual war and the violent overthrow of Soviet power.

But actual warfare is *not* what he had in mind. The idea, rather, was to encourage every split and crisis inside the USSR and the Soviet camp that could lead to the collapse of the USSR from within, while at the same time maintaining an official stance of nonintervention in Soviet internal affairs. "It is not our peacetime aim to overthrow the Soviet Government," NSC 20 continued. "Admittedly, we are aiming at the creation of circumstances and situations which would be difficult for the present Soviet leaders to stomach, and which they would not like. It is possible that they might not be able, in the face of these circumstances and situations, to retain their power in Russia. But it must be reiterated: that is their business, not ours. . . ."

Anti-Communist exile organizations are cited as one of the primary vehicles for the creation of the desired domestic crisis. "At the present time," Kennan continues, "there are a number of interesting and powerful Russian political groupings among the Russian exiles . . . any of which would probably be preferable to the Soviet Government, from our standpoint, as rulers of Russia." At the same time it is decided that both the Soviet internal problems and the official "hands-off" posture that the United States desires could be more effectively achieved by promoting *all* the exile organizations more or less equally rather than by sponsoring only one favored group. "We must make a determined effort to avoid taking responsibility for deciding who would rule Russia in the wake of a disintegration of the Soviet regime. Our best course would be to permit all of the exiled elements to return to Russia as rapidly as possible and to see to it, in so far as this depends on us, that they are all given roughly equal opportunity to establish their bids for power. . . ."[3]

The policy framework for clandestine operations involving exiles from the USSR, in short, was to encourage each of them to attempt to seize power in his or her homeland but to attempt to decline responsibility for having done so. Most interesting in the present context, no distinctions were to be made in the extension of aid to the various exile groups. The practical implication of this decision in the world of 1948 is clear: The United States would indeed support the veterans of the Vlasov Army, the eastern SS collaborators, and other groups that had permitted themselves to become pawns of Berlin during the war.

The State Department began the first known major clandestine effort recruiting Soviet émigrés at the same time its drafts of NSC 20 were working their way through the policy process. This project was known as Operation Bloodstone, and it became one of the department's most important covert projects from 1948 until approximately 1950, when it was superseded by similar programs under direct CIA sponsorship.

Bloodstone proved to be an open door through which scores of leaders of Nazi collaborationist organizations thought to be useful for political warfare in Eastern Europe entered the United States. The project's usual cover, even in top secret correspondence, was an innocuous effort to utilize "socialist, labor union, intellectual, moderate right-wing groups and others" for distribution of anti-Communist "handbills, publications, magazines or use of . . . radio" that was secretly financed by the U.S. government.[4] This all was true enough.

But there was much more to Bloodstone than its cover story. In reality, many of Bloodstone's recruits had once been Nazi collaborators who were now being brought to the United States for use as intelligence and covert operations experts. Some of them eventually became U.S. agent spotters for sabotage and assassination missions. The men and women enlisted under Bloodstone were not low-level thugs, concentration camp guards, or brutal hoodlums, at least not in the usual sense of those words. Quite the contrary, they were the cream of the Nazis and collaborators, the leaders, the intelligence specialists, and the scholars who had put their skills to work for the Nazi cause.

Bloodstone's primary sponsors were a circle of political warfare specialists in the PPS and the Office of the Assistant Secretary of State for Occupied Areas, joined in this effort by Undersecretary of State (later Secretary of Defense) Robert Lovett. Frank Wisner spearheaded the lobbying effort in favor of Bloodstone inside the top-level U.S. interagency security committee known as SANACC* and the National Security Council.[5]

According to Wisner's 1948 records of the affair, a portion of which has now been declassified, the official object of the program was to "increase defection among the elite of the Soviet World and to utilize refugees from the Soviet World in the National interests of the U.S." Anti-Communist experts including social scientists and propagandists were recruited to "fill the gaps in our current official intelligence, in public information and in politico-psychological operations," the last of which is a euphemism for covert destabilization and propaganda operations. Wisner proposed that some 250

---

*SANACC stands for "State, Army, Navy, Air Force Coordinating Committee." As its name suggests, SANACC attempted to provide high-level coordination to U.S. security policies overseas, particularly in occupied Europe and Japan. SANACC was originally founded in 1944 as SWNCC ("State, War, Navy Coordinating Committee"), then changed its name with the reorganization of the War Department in 1947. The NSC coexisted with SANACC from 1947 through 1949, then eventually absorbed it.

such experts be brought into the United States during the first phase of the operation; 100 of them were to work for the Department of State, primarily at Thayer's Voice of America, and 50 at each of the armed forces.[6]

In June of that year Wisner expanded on his theme. "There are native anti-Communist elements in non-Western hemisphere countries outside the Soviet orbit which have shown extreme fortitude in the face of the Communist menace, and which have demonstrated the "know-how" to counter Communist propaganda and in techniques to obtain control of mass movements," a Bloodstone briefing paper notes. However, "because of lack of funds, of material, and until recently, of a coordinated international movement, these natural antidotes to Communism have practically been immobilized." The paper continues:

> Unvouchered funds in the amount of $5,000,000 should be made available by Congress for the fiscal year 1949 to a component of the National Military Establishment. Upon receipt, the component should immediately transfer [the] funds to the Department of State . . . [which] should be responsible for the secret disbursement of these funds in view of the fact that the problem is essentially one of a political nature. . . . Disbursements should be handled in such a manner as to conceal the fact that their source is the U.S. government.

The Bloodstone proposal was approved by SANACC, the special interagency intelligence coordinating committee, on June 10, 1948.[7]

A month later the JCS approved a second, interlocking plan for the recruitment and training of guerrilla leaders from among Soviet émigré groups. This initiative was a slightly modified version of the revived Vlasov Army plan, which had originally been promoted by Kennan, Thayer and Franklin Lindsay,* who later worked with many of these same guerrillas on behalf of the CIA. In their report on this second proposal the Joint Chiefs reveal that Bloodstone was part of a covert warfare, sabotage, and assassination operation—not simply an innocuous leaflet distribution plan. According to the Pentagon records, the recruitment of foreign mercenaries for political

---

*Lindsay had served during the war as OSS liaison to Tito's guerrillas in Yugoslavia. He later became deputy chief of the Office for Policy Coordination in charge of behind-the-lines guerrilla actions in Eastern Europe between 1949 and 1951. He joined the Ford Foundation in 1953 and was named president of the Itek Corporation in 1962. In 1968 President-elect Nixon named Lindsay head of a secret task force on CIA reorganization.

murder missions was a specific part of Operation Bloodstone from the beginning.

The real purpose of Bloodstone, the top secret JCS documents say, was the "extraction of favorably disposed foreigners for the purposes of special operations and other uses. . . . Special operations," the JCS writes, "comprise those activities against the enemy which are conducted by allied or friendly forces behind enemy lines. . . . [They] include psychological warfare (black), clandestine warfare, subversion, sabotage and miscellaneous operations such as assassination, target capture and rescue of downed airmen."[8]

In September 1948 a new Joint Chiefs order amplified the plan. "A psychological offensive to subvert the Red Army is considered a primary objective," it states. "This type of offensive, as attempted by the German Army in World War II, was known as the 'Vlasov Movement.' It resulted in a resistance movement of approximately one million people." This new order went on to make a country-by-country survey of the prospects for special operations and appears to link the Gehlen Organization to the plan implicitly. The survey ranks Poland and Lithuania as "excellent prospects" with dissident groups already well established. Hungary and Romania were rated "unpromising . . . [but] with German help and leadership, limited results for underground operations might be expected."[9]

The National Security Council had delivered President Truman's official go-ahead for the special operations segment of Bloodstone and other U.S. covert warfare plans in a June 1948 decision known in national security parlance as NSC 10/2 ("NSC ten-slash-two"). The decision marked a crucial turning point in the history of U.S. intelligence, in the cold war, and, indeed, in the entire U.S.-Soviet relationship. It dealt with the types of clandestine operations the U.S. government was willing to undertake and how they were to be administered.

Through NSC 10/2, the National Security Council authorized a program of clandestine "propaganda, economic warfare, preventative direct action including sabotage, anti-sabotage, demolition and evacuation measures," according to the top secret text. It went on to call for "subversion against hostile states, including assistance to underground resistance movements, guerrillas and refugee liberation groups, and support of indigenous anti-Communist elements in threatened countries of the free world." All this was to be carried out in such a way that "any U.S. government responsibility for them is not evident to unauthorized persons and that if [they are] uncovered the U.S. government can plausibly disclaim any responsibility for them." No longer would the CIA and other spy agencies be limited primarily to gathering and processing information about foreign rivals. The administrative hobbles that had limited U.S. covert activities since the end of World War II were about to come off.[10]

A new Office of Special Projects (soon to be renamed Office for Policy Coordination, or OPC) was created within the Central Intelligence Agency to "plan and conduct" these operations. Secretary of State Marshall gave Kennan the job of selecting OPC's chief, and the man Kennan chose was Frank Wisner, the intense, dynamic OSS veteran who had helped engineer the Bloodstone project.[11]

The creation of OPC as a specialized clandestine warfare and propaganda agency "was a very natural development," John Paton Davies, one of Kennan's top aides in State at the time, commented in an interview years later. "During the war we had used these techniques against the Nazis. After the war, a number of [U.S.] military operators had come over to the civilian side [i.e., to the CIA and State Department], and we became interested in using these techniques to counter Soviet attacks. The job couldn't be done using formal warfare. . . . We had the problem of the Communist-led labor unions in France, for example. The AFL [American Federation of Labor] was working with their people, trying to combat this large subversive force in France. We couldn't just send in the Eighty-second Airborne, you know, [to help them], nor could we do it with diplomatic means. So we did what worked at the time." According to Davies, "the backing for it [clandestine operations] existed in [Kennan's] Policy Planning Staff . . . [and] there was no opposition within the government that I can recall."[12]

Nor was there any known resistance outside the government either. This is for the simple reason that the NSC 10/2 decision was shrouded in such secrecy that only a tiny group of men and women at the most senior levels of the emerging national security complex even knew that this form of war had been declared. Indeed, had it not been for the congressional investigations into U.S. intelligence practices that followed the Watergate affair almost thirty years later, the very existence of this decision would still be secret.

While NSC 10/2 authorized a significant expansion of U.S. covert warfare operations, it simultaneously attempted to do something else as well: to control U.S. subversion operations overseas by institutionalizing them and subjecting them to central civilian authority. This type of coordination, which tended to benefit the Department of State, had been an important aspect of the reorganization of the Pentagon, the creation of the NSC and the CIA in 1947, and most other "national security" reforms of the period.

Secretary of State Marshall gave George Kennan responsibility for policy guidance of the entire NSC 10/2 effort. According to a still-secret internal history of the CIA, fragments of which were published by the U.S. Congress in 1976,[13] Kennan insisted at the time the OPC was created that he had to have "specific knowledge of the objectives of every operation and also of the procedure and methods employed in all cases where those procedures and methods involved political decisions." Kennan would, he said, "assume responsibility for stating whether or not individual projects are politically desirable." This broad grant of authority was directly endorsed by CIA Director Rear Admiral Roscoe Hillenkoetter and NSC Executive Director Sidney Souers.

During the months that followed NSC 10/2, subordinate operational responsibility for Bloodstone was divided up among State Department intelligence (then headed by W. Park Armstrong*), the military services, and Frank Wisner's new team. Wisner's OPC was given responsibility for "politico-psychological" operations as well as for preparing two policy statements on utilization of refugees from the Soviet bloc. The State Department, on the other hand, continued to lay claim to jurisdiction over recruitment of émigrés for use at the Voice of America and in intelligence analysis programs, as distinguished from the secret propaganda and covert warfare missions run by Wisner.[14]

Once 10/2 had been approved, the Bloodstone team at the State Department moved quickly to enlist the support of a handful of powerful senators and representatives in what appears to have been a conscious evasion of immigration law. Undersecretary of State Lovett ordered Charles Bohlen, then chief counselor of the Department of State, to meet secretly with influential congressional leaders so that, as Lovett's aide Charles Saltzman noted, "when the inevitable undesirable alien brought in under these programs appears in the U.S., Congress will have been forewarned and undue

---

*W. Park Armstrong, one of the most powerful and least known figures in the U.S. intelligence community of the period, claimed in an interview with the author that he had "no recollection" and had "never heard" of Bloodstone or of any other effort to import Nazi collaborators into the United States for intelligence purposes. However, memos discussing the division of assignments under Bloodstone that were drafted and signed by Armstrong are now a matter of public record.

criticism of the Departments of State and Justice should be thereby minimized."

According to Bohlen's notes, Leslie Biffle (the secretary of the Senate and executive director of the Democratic Party Policy Committee), Texas Congressman Sam Rayburn (later to be speaker of the House), New Jersey Representative Charles Eaton (chair of the House Foreign Affairs Committee), Senate Minority Leader Alben Barkley (later to be Truman's vice president), and Republican foreign affairs expert Senator H. Alexander Smith of New Jersey were approached with the proposal during July and August 1948. Arthur Vandenberg, the chair of the Senate Foreign Relations Committee, was apparently consulted later. "In each case," Bohlen noted, the senator or congressman said he thought the project seemed "sensible." Rayburn underlined the conspiratorial atmosphere of the encounter. "Congressman Rayburn was particularly insistent," according to Bohlen, "that the members of Congress who had been inclined to make difficulties should this project become public were not those with whom it could be discussed in confidence with any assurance that it would be kept confidential."[15]

Kennan was later to testify before Congress that the entire NSC 10/2 effort, of which Bloodstone was but one part, was very limited in scope. "We had thought that this would be a facility which could be used when and if the occasion arose, when it might be needed," he said in 1975 congressional hearings[16] on the origins of U.S. covert operations. "There might be years when we wouldn't have to do anything like this."

But Kennan's comments in those latter-day hearings were something of an understatement. In fact, the Bloodstone record makes clear that the OPC and its associated émigré projects were actually major projects with multimillion-dollar budgets from the beginning. But no matter; Kennan was surely telling the truth as he perceived it. He had only wanted, he declared in his testimony, someone in the government who had the funds and the experience to do things "in a proper way . . . if an occasion arose."

Kennan's anticommunism was far more sophisticated than that of many of his colleagues, and he wanted to use clandestine warfare techniques carefully. He viewed as unrealistic and dangerous demands for a quick "liberation" of Eastern Europe from Soviet influence, which were beginning to make themselves heard from the political right. Kennan had long been suspicious of popular participation in the formulation of foreign policy, and he considered the

U.S. Congress, for example, too mercurial, too ill informed, and too much subject to domestic pressures to serve the country well when it came to foreign affairs. These attitudes made him aware of the dangerous impact that yahoo-style reaction was beginning to have on American policy overseas. "I personally look with some dismay and concern at many of the things we are now experiencing in our public life," Kennan had written in the spring of 1947.[17] "In particular I deplore the hysterical sort of anti-Communism which, it seems to me, is gaining currency in our country."

Whatever the reason, Kennan made common cause in those years with other men who were soon to commandeer the work he had begun and take it places the diplomat apparently never expected. NSC 10/2 failed to bring covert operations under close civilian control. Instead, the clandestine service metastasized through the government at an extraordinary rate. Regardless of what Kennan may have intended, as NSC 10/2, NSC 20, and other programs he had helped design became institutionalized, they transformed themselves into an unrelentingly hostile effort to "roll back communism" in Eastern Europe, an effort that eventually consumed millions of dollars, thousands of lives, and considerable national prestige. As the political temperature between the superpowers inevitably got more frigid, the forces that Kennan had once ridden to power overwhelmed him and his program. By 1950 his erstwhile allies in secret work—men like Allen and John Foster Dulles, Paul Nitze, and Arthur Bliss Lane—were grasping for more power and depreciating Kennan's policies for being "soft on communism."

In the end, Kennan testified many years later, "it did not work out at all the way I had conceived it."[18]

CHAPTER NINE

"See That He Is Sent to the U.S. . . ."

The men and women who created and administered Operation Bloodstone for the U.S. government had no sympathy for nazism as such, nor any desire to protect Nazis and collaborators in general from prosecution. They brought Bloodstone recruits into this country for three specific and sensitive purposes. First, there was the collection and analysis of intelligence on the USSR and its Eastern European satellites that the program's backers claimed were unavailable from any other source. Secondly, Bloodstone recruits trained U.S. intelligence, propaganda, and covert warfare specialists. And finally, some Bloodstone leaders were used for recruiting other émigrés for large-scale clandestine warfare, including sabotage and assassination missions.

By 1948, when the program began, the U.S. officials responsible for the approval and administration of Bloodstone were already senior, trusted officials with top security clearances. The names of more than three dozen of these officials are today found in a slender file of declassified Bloodstone records. They include Tom Clark, for example, the attorney general of the United States, who authorized the program on behalf of the Department of Justice; W. Park Armstrong, the director of the State Department's Office of Intelligence and Research; and John S. Earman, Jr., the CIA observer on the Bloodstone team who later became inspector general of the agency.

Another notable Bloodstone veteran is Boris Pash, a career intelligence officer identified in the *Final Report* of the U.S. Senate's 1975–1976 investigation into U.S. intelligence activities as the retired director of the CIA unit responsible for planning assassinations.

Also found in the Bloodstone record are the names of more than twenty senior State Department officials concerned with Soviet or Eastern European affairs. This select crew went on to become the top officials in virtually every phase of U.S.-Soviet relations during the 1940s and 1950s and included, for example, three future U.S. ambassadors to Moscow; a director of the Voice of America; a director of Radio Free Europe; and two future directors of the State Department Intelligence section specializing in East bloc affairs.[1] In a very real sense, the men and women who engineered Bloodstone were the same ones who designed U.S. cold war strategy for every administration from 1945 to 1963.

The officials who handled the day-to-day mechanics of the program are also of interest. John P. Boyd was the deputy commissioner, the number two man, at the Immigration and Naturalization Service in 1948. He was appointed to represent the Department of Justice on the Bloodstone team (then known as the SANACC 395 Committee) on April 15, 1948, and was named chairman of the entire effort two months later. He signed the Justice Department's formal approval for the project and asserted that the "Attorney General himself" had reviewed and approved the program. The Justice Department's approval was subject to only one proviso: that the recruits be "brought in under the Displaced Persons Act, if practicable."[2]

The phrase is significant, and it appears several times in Justice Department correspondence concerning Bloodstone. Under the Displaced Persons Act, there are two main categories of persons barred from entry into the United States. The first category is "war criminals, quislings and traitors . . . [including] persons who can be shown to have assisted the enemy in persecuting civil populations . . . [or who] have voluntarily assisted the enemy forces since the outbreak of the second world war," and the second is "ordinary criminals who are extraditable by treaty." True, the act did set limits ("quotas") on the numbers of immigrants from each country, but it also permitted the federal government to move special immigrants to the head of the entry list, so that favored immigrants need not be excluded from entering under it for quota reasons. In short, the only ones not "practicable" to be brought in under the Displaced Persons Act were Nazis and Nazi collaborators, on the one hand, and common criminals, on the other.[3]

It is worth noting that Communists were *not* barred from entry into the United States under the Displaced Persons Act until amendments were passed by the Congress in June 1950, after the period that Boyd spent as head of the Bloodstone project. In any event, it is clear that few of the Bloodstone recruits had ever been Communists. Some of them, however, should have been excluded under the laws then on the books, as fugitives from charges of crimes against humanity.

The actual issuance of visas for Bloodstone recruits was handled by Robert C. Alexander, then second-in-command of the State Department Visa Division. Alexander was appointed the State Department representative to the interagency Bloodstone committee as the project moved into its implementation stage in June 1948.*[4]

Many of the crucial intelligence analysis aspects of Bloodstone, however, were handled by another man: Evron M. Kirkpatrick, then chief† of the State Department's External Research Staff, a

---

*Alexander's highly publicized activities during 1948 are another indication that Bloodstone was geared to bring in Nazi collaborators, not Communists. In July of that year Alexander defied Secretary of State Marshall by testifying in Congress that "Communist agents" were entering the United States under cover of United Nations agencies. The United Nations Relief and Rehabilitation Administration "was the greatest offender," he said, adding that some of the Communists had been trained as spies and terrorists. Alexander's testimony, in short, stressed the need to keep Communists, former Communists, and anyone who might be sympathetic to them out of the country at all costs.

Secretary Marshall was concerned that conservatives in Congress would use the "UN spy" testimony, as it came to be known, to derail a $65 million U.S. loan to the United Nations that was being strongly backed by the administration. The secretary rejected Alexander's charges, and a variety of follow-up studies concluded that Alexander's "irresponsible statements produced serious repercussions on the foreign policy of the United States."

Alexander was eventually appointed deputy administrator for all U.S. refugee programs under the Refugee Relief Act. He publicly recommended that the "free nations of the world . . . undertake a concerted effort to solve the refugee problem" by organizing military retaliation against governments—particularly Communist ones—that were producing too many refugees. In the meantime, he cautioned, accepting more exiles from socialist countries "even for humanitarian reasons" only "drain[ed] off the properly discordant and recalcitrant elements" of their populations, thus propping up Soviet rule.

†Kirkpatrick is today an irrepressibly cheerful man with a comfortable girth and a goatee that makes him resemble, of all people, an aging Leon Trotsky. He is also husband to Jeane Kirkpatrick, the former U.S. ambassador to the United Nations during the Reagan administration. Mr. and Mrs. Kirkpatrick share ownership in Operations and Policy Research, Inc. (also known as OPR, Inc.), which has benefited over the years from government contracts for studies in psychological warfare, defense policy, and political behavior. Critics have alleged that the company served as a funding conduit between U.S. intelligence agencies and promising scholars.

special team of scholars operating under the auspices of the Office of Intelligence and Research.

Kirkpatrick had come up with the idea for systematic use of scholarly defectors based on his wartime experience in the OSS. "The [State] Department and foreign policy in general did not make as much use as they should have of scholars and foundations on the outside," Kirkpatrick remembered during an interview with the author. "So we [the External Research Staff] would pull in two or three people at a time for discussions for the benefit of Department of State and other foreign policy organizations such as Defense, intelligence, et cetera." Émigré scholars and former Eastern European political leaders were hired as consultants or given funding for study of U.S. foreign policy objectives.

According to Kirkpatrick's former assistant and longtime colleague Howard Penniman, "my job was to find out what the agencies wanted in the way of information. Then I would retail that to [Frederick] Barghoorn and [Francis] Stevens," who worked for the External Research Staff at the time. They, in turn, would comb the displaced persons camps for émigrés who might be able to answer sensitive questions about the USSR and Eastern Europe. "During 1948, '49, and '50 there were some interesting people coming out of the USSR and Eastern Europe. We were responsible for two things as far as they were concerned," according to Kirkpatrick. "Number one, to learn as much as we could. Number two, to find them places, find them jobs at universities." Kirkpatrick mentioned Nikolai N. Poppe in particular as one such scholar whom he assisted in placing.

It is difficult to determine today just what Kirkpatrick did or didn't know about the defectors and émigrés placed under his care in the early days. "I don't think I had any cases of those who had cooperated with the Germans," he commented in an interview. "But of course, you always heard about that. After all, you even had Jews that cooperated with the Nazis."

Kirkpatrick's recollection of the Poppe case is intriguing. As he remembered it, Poppe was the "Soviets' head of intelligence for the whole Asiatic USSR" before he came to the United States, and he had supposedly defected directly from the USSR to the United States. In reality, however, Poppe had been one of the *Nazis'* senior intelligence analysts "for the whole Asiatic USSR," and he had spent considerable time working for them in Berlin before striking a deal with the Americans.[5]

Who, then, entered the United States under Operation Bloodstone? Which specific Nazis or Nazi collaborators? And where are they today?

The Immigration and Naturalization Service was ordered to keep detailed monthly reports on each person brought to the United States under the program. Unfortunately the agency claims it is unable to locate those records, thus making it impossible, at least for the moment, to construct a comprehensive list of persons with Nazi or Nazi collaborationist backgrounds who were brought to the United States under Bloodstone.

But just as it is sometimes possible to assemble a jigsaw puzzle despite a missing piece, so it is possible to discover a number of Bloodstone's recruits from other government documentation without an official list of their names. A careful examination of the surviving file of Bloodstone records makes it clear that candidates for the program had to meet at least five restrictive criteria that set them apart from the thousands of other refugees who entered the United States following World War II. With those criteria as a guide, it is possible to uncover a number of high-level Nazi collaborators, including some responsible for serious crimes against humanity, who entered the United States under Bloodstone. The criteria used to identify Bloodstone recruits in the pages that follow may be summarized as follows:

First, the recruits had to be leaders of anti-Communist organizations or scholars (especially linguists and social scientists), or skilled propagandists.

Second, they had to have specialized or unique knowledge about the Soviet bloc or skills as an organizer of refugees from countries in the bloc.

Third, they had to have entered the United States between June 1948, when the program was approved, and mid-1950, when changes in U.S. immigration law superseded the effort.

Fourth, they had to have actively cooperated with, or been employed by, U.S. intelligence agencies or the Department of State, particularly in programs such as Radio Free Europe, the Defense Language School at Monterey, California, or the recruitment of émigrés for covert warfare operations.

Fifth—and very important—they had to have enjoyed a direct and documented intervention on their behalf during the immigration process by the political warfare specialists at the State Department who were in charge of the Bloodstone program.[6]

It was *not* necessary that every person brought in under Bloodstone be a former Nazi or Nazi collaborator. Indeed, there is every reason to believe that the cover story of importing "socialist, labor union, intellectual, moderate right-wing groups and others" was, like most cover stories, at least partially true. Bloodstone's ability to circumvent U.S. immigration law, however, appears to have only one reasonable explanation: to permit immigration of former Nazis and Nazi collaborators who would otherwise be barred by the Displaced Persons Act.

The German diplomat Gustav Hilger was only one of many Bloodstone beneficiaries, but he deserves special mention here because of his close friendship with the Americans from the old Moscow embassy circle and the influential (but until now secret) role he played in formulation of U.S. foreign policy toward Germany and the Soviets in the late 1940s and early 1950s.

During the war Hilger had gone directly from the German Embassy in Moscow to service in the personal secretariat of Nazi Foreign Minister Joachim von Ribbentrop, becoming the chief political officer for eastern front questions in the German Foreign Ministry. There Hilger led the Russland Gremium, a group of senior experts on Soviet affairs. Hilger, it is true, had initially opposed the German invasion of the USSR in 1941 and had mentioned this to Hitler during a private conference on the eve of the blitzkrieg. Hilger's advice was rejected, however, and he continued to serve the Reich dutifully throughout the war.

Among his duties at the Nazi Foreign Office was liaison with the SS concerning the Nazi occupation of the USSR, a job which included the processing of SS *Einsatzgruppen* reports on the mobile killing operations in the East. The following is a translated excerpt from one such SS report that was entered into evidence at Nuremberg. The processing marks on the cover letter of this document indicate that it crossed Hilger's desk in April 1942. Similar bulletins followed throughout the war.

OPERATIONAL SITUATION REPORT USSR NO. 11
TOP SECRET

C. JEWS
   In Riga, among others, three Jews who had been transferred from the Reich to the ghetto and who had escaped were recaptured and publicly hanged in the ghetto.

In the course of the greater action against Jews, 3,412 Jews were shot in Minsk, 302 in Vileika and 2,007 in Baranovichi. . . .

Besides the measures taken against individual Jews operating in a criminal or political manner, the tasks of the security police and the SD in the other areas of the Eastern Front consisted in a general purging of larger localities. Alone in Rakov, e.g., 15,000 Jews were shot, and 1224 in Artenovsk, so that these places are now free of Jews.

In the Crimea 1,000 Jews and gypsies were executed.[7]

Clearly, these SS communiqués left no question about the scale of the Holocaust that was taking place on the eastern front, yet Hilger took no action to protest or to remove himself from the bureaucratic machinery of destruction in which he found himself entangled. The diplomat had a small, but direct, role in the murder programs in Hungary. There he helped coordinate the Foreign Office's successful efforts to obtain sanctuary in Germany for several Hungarian army officers responsible for the 1942 murder of 6,000 Serbs and 4,000 Jews. Asylum for the Hungarian killers had been decreed by Hitler himself as a message to every Axis country that Germany would protect those who carried out anti-Semitic murders on behalf of the Reich.[8]

Finally, Hilger played a significant part in SS efforts to capture and exterminate Italian Jews. The Nazis had considerable difficulty deporting Italian Jews to the death camps throughout the war, largely because Italy's early status as a full Axis partner somewhat restricted the power of the Nazis in that country. In December 1943, however, Hilger led the German Foreign Office's effort to convince the Italian government to force that country's Jewish community into work camps, on the condition that no further measures would be taken against Italy's Jews. The Italian government cooperated with Hilger's work camp plan, and many Jews were driven into barracks during the winter of 1943–1944. In reality, however, the Nazis had planned all along to deport to the extermination centers in the East any Italian Jews who entered these camps regardless of what the Italians tried to say about it, and during the spring of 1944 several trainloads of these Jews were shipped to Auschwitz.[9] The exact number of victims of this joint Foreign Office-SS program in Italy is unknown, but it certainly totals several thousand innocent people.

Hilger was also a central figure in the German political warfare faction. The Nazi Foreign Office assigned him to be its chief liaison with Vlasov within a few days of the Russian general's surrender in 1942, and Hilger participated in the various psychological warfare and intelligence schemes that swirled around the Vlasov headquarters throughout the war. By 1944 Hilger had completely integrated himself into the command structure of the Vlasov group.[10]

After the war Hilger was officially being sought by U.S. war crimes investigators for "Torture" (as his wanted notice reads),[11] a catchall charge sometimes used for people sought in connection with the administration of crimes against humanity, as distinct from the actual murders themselves. Officially Hilger remained a fugitive from these charges until the day he died.

Hilger's work in Germany's political warfare program, along with his great expertise in Soviet affairs, won him asylum in the United States after the war. He surrendered to U.S. forces in May 1945 and was briefly interned in the Mannheim POW camp. Charles Thayer, apparently acting on a tip from Hans Heinrich Herwarth, intervened on Hilger's behalf, and the Americans quietly shipped the former diplomatic official to Washington, D.C., for debriefing at Fort Hunt (as Gehlen had been) and for secret employment as a high-level analyst of captured German records on the USSR. Hilger resurfaced briefly in the spring of 1946, when former Nazi Foreign Minister von Ribbentrop, then on trial for his life at Nuremberg, called on him as a defense witness during the war crimes proceedings. After considerable wrangling, the United States conceded that Hilger was indeed in Washington but was "too ill to travel."[12]

Hilger's legal status at that point is foggy. He had technically been a prisoner of war since his surrender in May 1945, but his wanted notice on the war crimes charge remained on the books as an open case. It is certain, however, that he was never actually arrested on the war crimes charges, nor was he forced to face a trial for his wartime activities.

For the next several years Hilger shuttled back and forth between the United States and Germany under the sponsorship of the U.S. State Department, and he is known to have been in Berlin during the spring crisis of 1948. As the East-West tension that led to the famous Berlin airlift heated up during the summer and fall of that year, the State Department was faced with the tricky problem of evacuating a number of ex-Nazis and collaborators, including fugitives such as Hilger, who were working under U.S. sponsorship in Germany at the time.

George Kennan intervened with the U.S. political adviser in Germany, Robert Murphy, on Hilger's behalf in late September 1948. In a series of telegrams marked "Personal for Kennan" and carrying Kennan's hand-scrawled initials, Murphy's and Kennan's deputies proceeded to argue over the best method to bring Hilger into the United States. Murphy noted that the army intelligence men in Germany wanted "visas for five persons [Hilger and his family] and travel arrangements . . . made under assumed names"—an apparent violation of U.S. law.* State Department headquarters favored bringing him in under his real name aboard a U.S. military aircraft, then providing him later with a false identity if necessary. That was the alternative backed by Kennan, and it was eventually implemented.[13] It is worth noting that the arrangements for Hilger were handled directly by Kennan's Policy Planning Staff,† while the Visa Division, which is ordinarily responsible for issuing entry documents to the United States, was provided with only vague verbal reports. All of Hilger's travel expenses were paid by the U.S. government.

Hilger soon became an unofficial ambassador to the United States from Konrad Adenauer's Christian Democratic party in West Germany. "Hilger was negotiating with the U.S. government and was instrumental in the creation of the Adenauer regime," says Nikolai Poppe, a Bloodstone recruit with whom Hilger worked in Washington. "In the very beginning, when Adenauer wished to become head [of the new Federal Republic of Germany], some American officials did not regard him as suitable. . . . But Adenauer was eventually permitted to form a government in 1949. This was due in part to Hilger's contacts with the U.S. State Department. Hilger had great influence there."[14] Of course, Poppe is overstating the

---

*A special Bloodstone subcommittee had, in fact, been created to supply false identities, government cover jobs, and secret police protection to selected Bloodstone immigrants because "the activities in which some of the aliens concerned are to be engaged may result in jeopardizing their safety from foreign agents [inside] the United States."

†The PPS was simultaneously engaged in a second project employing Nazi collaborators through a U.S.-financed "think tank" named the Eurasian Institute. According to declassified State Department records bearing George Kennan's handwritten initials, the Eurasian Institute enlisted such men as Saldh Ulus, who was described in U.S. cables as an "important member of [the] German espionage network in Central Asia from 1931 to 1945," and Mehmet Sunsh, who was said to have been "employed by the German Propaganda Bureau [in] Istanbul 1942."

Eurasian Institute work was handled in large part by Bloodstone specialists John Paton Davies and Carmel Offie, according to declassified State Department records. Many of its recruits were eventually integrated into the Munich-based (and CIA-financed) Institute for the Study of the USSR during the early 1950s.

case: U.S. government support for Adenauer was built upon the chancellor's cooperation with U.S. strategic plans in West Germany, not simply on Hilger's personal influence. Even so, Hilger did play a role in securing support for Adenauer among the Americans.

Hilger met frequently in Washington, D.C., with Kennan and Bohlen, who were then considered the United States' preeminent experts on U.S.-Soviet relations. Kennan personally intervened on Hilger's behalf to obtain him a high-level security clearance, and he listened closely to Hilger's advice before making recommendations on East-West policy to President Truman. In 1950, for example, Bohlen remembers that he, Hilger, and Kennan formed an analysis team specializing in interpretation of Soviet geopolitical strategy following the outbreak of the Korean War. The group was given access to highly classified information and reported directly to the Office of National Estimates, the country's most senior intelligence evaluation group, which in turn reported directly to the director of Central Intelligence and to President Truman. Hilger, the former Nazi Foreign Office executive who had once made his reports to Hitler, emerged in Washington as a highly influential expert on the USSR.[15]

George Kennan has declined several requests for an interview, thus making it impossible to obtain his comments on the memos bearing his name and initials that discuss bringing Hilger into the United States. He did, however, write in 1982: "I do not recall seeing him [Gustav Hilger], or having any contact with him, in the period between the end of the war and his arrival in this country. I do not recall having had anything to do with, or any responsibility for, bringing him to this country; nor do I recall knowing, at the time, by what arrangements he was brought here." He noted at that time, however, that he was "pleased that this had been done, considering that his [Hilger's] knowledge of Russia . . . would be useful to our government and public" and that without his being brought to this country there was a danger that he might have fallen into Soviet hands. Kennan also asserted that he had never seen any signs of Nazi sympathies on Hilger's part.[16]

Kennan must have been aware that Gustav Hilger had been a senior member of the Nazi Foreign Office and an executive in Ribbentrop's personal secretariat during the war. The knowledge gained through that work was, after all, one of the main reasons why Hilger was brought to Washington. Whether or not Kennan knew of Hilger's role in the Holocaust in the USSR, Hungary, and Italy is unknown. It can be said with certainty, however, that the Nazi Foreign Office records documenting Hilger's role in the murder of innocent people were in American hands in 1948 and that the tedious work of analyzing and cataloging that material was well under way. Had George Kennan, or any other member of the U.S. government of his stature, requested a dossier on Hilger's wartime career, those records could have been readily located. There is no indication among the available evidence that Kennan or anyone else ever inquired into Hilger's role in the Holocaust. It is clear, however, that Kennan, then one of the most powerful men in Washington, served as Hilger's personal reference during army and State Department security clearance inquiries.

The aura of respectability that surrounded Hilger seems to have deterred people who would have otherwise had a logical interest in his background. Alfred Meyer, an American expert on communism who coauthored a book with Hilger during the early 1950s, for example, has recalled that he never asked the German whether or not he had ever been a Nazi party member. "It would have been an indiscreet question," Meyer said during an interview with the author. "To have been a Nazi, well, after the war that would have been a stigma."

In fact, Hilger never was a member of the Nazi party. "He was somewhat of a coward politically," as Meyer put it. "He didn't want to stick his neck out." U.S. Army intelligence reports of the period reflect a belief that Hilger was basically a conservative who had found it convenient to join, rather than resist, the Nazi juggernaut. "He was a weak man," Meyer said.

While in the United States, Hilger enjoyed "a generous grant," according to Meyer, from the Carnegie Corporation. Most of his work during this period revolved around the Center for Russian Research at Harvard University and a similar post at Johns Hopkins University, which served as cover, in effect, for his CIA Office of National Estimates consulting assignment.[17]

The only known protest to Hilger's presence in the United States during the 1950s came from Dr. Raul Hilberg, who was at the time a young historian working on a top secret analysis of captured German wartime records code-named Project Alexander. Hilberg, who is today better known as the author of the internationally acclaimed history of the Holocaust *The Destruction of the European Jews,* objected when Hilger was invited to speak at the Federal

Records Center in Virginia, where Project Alexander was then under way. Hilberg told the project's director that he would walk out in protest if the former Nazi diplomat was honored at the center, and shortly thereafter Hilger's invitation to speak was quietly canceled.

This incident did not become public, however, and Hilger remained in the United States until 1953, when he returned to Germany to become a senior adviser on foreign affairs to the Adenauer government. He retired in 1956 but continued to travel frequently between the United States and Europe.

In 1962 journalist and Nazi hunter Charles Allen located Hilger at a residence the German diplomat continued to maintain in Washington, D.C. According to Allen, the seventy-six-year-old Hilger still enjoyed enough clout at the State Department to have it maintain a telephone contact service ("extension 11") on his behalf. Allen has also convincingly documented the State Department's consistent use of falsehoods to conceal its relationship with Hilger over the years.[18] The former member of the Nazi Foreign Office died in Munich on July 27, 1965.

Hilger's colleague Nikolai N. Poppe, a world-renowned scholar on Mongolia and the minority groups of the USSR, was also a Bloodstone recruit. Poppe's life illustrates the complexity and moral ambiguity of the Bloodstone program and of the broader U.S. enlistment of émigrés who had collaborated with the Nazis. Poppe is now ninety years old and living in comfortable retirement in Washington State.

Poppe defected to the Germans in August 1942, the day the Nazis arrived in Mikoyan-Shakhar, where he was teaching in the Pedagogical Institute. He actively collaborated in the creation of the quisling government in the Karachai minority region of the country. Among the first acts of that administration was expropriation of Jewish property, followed shortly by roundups and gassing of all the Jews who could be located in the area. Poppe also, according to his own account, assisted German military intelligence in identifying the rugged mountain passes through which German army and police troops could drive deeper into the country.[19]

After the war Poppe condemned the actions of the SS in the Karachai region, particularly the massacres of Jews. He has written that he personally helped save the lives of a small group of mountain tribesmen known as the Tats from extermination. The Tats were Jewish by religion, but Iranian by ethnic heritage, and the

Wehrmacht and the SS were divided over the question of whether or not they should be massacred. Poppe asserts that he helped convince the Nazis that the Tats should be classed as non-Jewish and thus be allowed to live. There is no known proof other than Poppe's own statement that he took this action. It is a fact, however, that Poppe was an expert on the races of the region, that he was collaborating with the Germans at the time, and that the Tats were indeed spared.[20]

Whatever his reservations about the SS may have been, Poppe nonetheless volunteered to work for it for the remainder of the war. The SS installed him at the Wannsee Institute in 1943 as one of its most important intelligence experts on the USSR. The team of collaborators at Wannsee prepared reliable studies for the SS and the German high command describing the location of promising targets inside the Soviet Union, including concentrations of Jews and other minority groups.[21] This intelligence was of value to the SS for guiding the deployment of killing squads and to the Wehrmacht for planning military operations. While the SS would certainly have destroyed many innocent people without the help of the team of defectors at Wannsee, it is nevertheless true that their research permitted them to do the job more quickly and efficiently than would have otherwise been the case. The Wannsee collaborators did not sign orders for executions; they just told the killers where to find their prey.

Poppe says today that the personnel of the Wannsee Institute did not commit war crimes. In reality, however, Poppe's immediate superior at the institute ordered the murder of Jewish bookdealers throughout Eastern Europe and organized SS looting teams that seized the libraries of universities and scholarly institutes throughout German-occupied territory in order to improve Wannsee's collection of restricted books on the USSR.[22]

Poppe also asserts that his work for the SS consisted exclusively of monographs on Mongolian religious customs and on Siberia. This claim is difficult to take at face value, however, in light of his strong expertise on the Caucasus region of the USSR, one of the most important focal points of the war at the time he was employed by the SS.[23]

After the war Poppe worked briefly for British intelligence, then for the United States in the "historical study group" at Camp King. Before long he approached U.S. intelligence officials seeking permission to emigrate to the United States. U.S. officials knew exactly whom they were getting when they imported Dr. Poppe. Among the now-declassified records of the U.S. Army Counterintelligence Corps is the following memo, which is reproduced here in full:

TOP SECRET

22 May 1947

SUBJECT: Personnel of Possible Intelligence Interest

TO: Deputy Director of Intelligence, Headquarters, European Command, Frankfurt
APO 757 US Army

1. At the present time there is residing in the British Zone a Soviet citizen by the name of Nicolai Nicolovitch [*sic*] Poppe. He is living under an assumed name. Mr. Poppe is an authority on and a professor of Far Eastern languages.

2. His presence in the British Zone is a source of embarrassment to British Military Government, as the Soviet authorities are continually asking for his return as a war criminal. The British feel that Mr. Poppe is valuable as an intelligence source and have asked me if it is possible for U.S. intelligence authorities *to take him off their hands and see that he is sent to the U.S. where he can be "lost."* [Emphasis added.]

3. For my information will you advise me as to what you may be able to do in this matter or in similar cases which may arise in the future.

[signed]

PETER P. RODES
Colonel GSC
Director of Intelligence[24]

Poppe was indeed "lost" by the Americans. Despite U.S. knowledge of Poppe's work for Nazi intelligence and Soviet efforts to capture him—indeed, probably precisely because of that knowledge—he was given a false name (Joseph Alexandris) while in Germany and was brought to the United States in 1949. Sanitized State Department telegraphic correspondence between Berlin and Washington, D.C., released under the Freedom of Information Act reveal that Poppe's immigration to the United States was directly overseen by George Kennan and John Paton Davies, at the time senior executives in the political warfare unit at the State Department.[25]

According to Poppe's own account, he was flown to Westover

Field in Massachusetts aboard a U.S. Military Air Transport plane in May 1949. The following day he was flown to Washington, D.C., "where a man sent by the State Department was standing on the airfield to meet me."[26] While Poppe was in Washington, his work was coordinated by Carmel Offie, the OPC officer working under State Department cover who was responsible for the care and feeding of a number of Bloodstone émigrés.

Nikolai N. Poppe has since emerged as one of America's most prominent authorities on Soviet Mongolia, and he has helped train a generation of U.S. intelligence officers on the politics and culture of minority nationalities inside the USSR. Following a brief sojourn with Gustav Hilger at the State Department, Poppe was employed as a professor of Far Eastern languages at the University of Washington at Seattle. He remained there until his retirement and is a professor emeritus at that institution today. He is also a well-known scholar on Tibetan Buddhism and the author of more than 200 scholarly books, articles, and reviews concerning the history and languages of Central Asian peoples.[27]

An incident during Poppe's career in the 1950s illustrates the delicate influence that certain former Nazi collaborators have had on domestic politics in the United States. Early in the McCarthy era Professor Owen Lattimore, the director of the Walter Hines Page School of International Relations at Johns Hopkins University and a longtime adviser on Asian affairs to the State Department, was brought before a congressional investigating committee to face accusations of espionage and running a "Communist cell" in the Institute for Pacific Relations. McCarthy, whose allegations were already drawing criticism from Democrats and even a few Republicans, had pledged that his entire anti-Communist crusade would "stand or fall" on the supposed proof he had in the Lattimore case. As it turned out, McCarthy did not have evidence, and the committee ended up clearing Professor Lattimore. McCarthy had, in the language of a Senate committee's report on the case, perpetrated a "fraud and a hoax . . . on the Senate" and had "stooped to a new low in his cavalier disregard of the facts."

Poppe's testimony, however, proved to be an important element in the resurrection of McCarthy's case against Lattimore. Poppe had (and has) a personal grievance against Lattimore, who he claims used his influence to block Poppe's immigration to the United States prior to 1949. In 1952 McCarthy and his ally Senator William Jenner organized a series of highly publicized, uncorroborated allegations from former Communist Party, USA, official Louis Budenz claiming that Lattimore had been a party member. Those asser-tions covered Lattimore's domestic activities in the United States. It was left to Poppe, who was also a rival of Lattimore's in the field of Central Asia studies, to suggest that Lattimore's supposed loyalty to Stalin might be even more direct. Much of Lattimore's work on Mongolia was "very superficial," Poppe testified as an expert wit-ness, "and give[s] a distorted picture of the realities. . . . [Lattimore] had read all of this in various Soviet papers, and had taken these statements from them."[28] Poppe also says that he told Senate Inter-nal Security Subcommittee investigators that he knew that Lat-timore had conspired with "important Communist party bosses" during a trip to Moscow in the 1930s, although this latter claim was not published in the committee's testimony. The fact that Poppe had worked for the SS during the war was not brought out at the hearings, nor was the issue of Poppe's personal reason for disliking Lattimore.[29]

Lattimore was hounded by McCarthy and his allies for the rest of his professional career. He was repeatedly called before congres-sional investigating committees, publicly denounced (in part as the result of Poppe's testimony) as a "conscious, articulate instrument of the Soviet conspiracy . . . since the 1930s," and indicted for perjury. The charges were eventually dropped for lack of evidence, but that was a Pyrrhic victory for Lattimore. He left the country at age sixty-three to take a teaching assignment at Leeds University in England.

Today Poppe openly discusses many aspects of his work for the Nazis and insists that he shares no responsibility for war crimes. In 1948, Poppe says, "the Americans who wanted me to come to the U.S. interrogated me. I told them everything about Wannsee and about [SS RSHA] Amt VI. They said that this was not regarded as a war crimes organization. They said, 'All right, you have not to fear anything.'* "[SS Standartenführer] Augsburg and [Wannsee Direc-

---

*In 1985 the U.S. General Accounting Office reported that U.S. intelligence agencies considered Poppe to have been a "traitor" during the war, as the GAO put it, but not a "war criminal" at the time they sponsored his immigration into the United States in 1948.

More recently the U.S. Department of Justice's Office of Special Investigations (OSI), which is responsible for prosecuting Nazis and collaborators alleged to have entered this country illegally, closed out an investigation of Poppe's immigration to the United States without bringing any charges against him. This action was taken in part because the OSI determined that Poppe had disclosed his relationship with the SS to U.S. intelligence prior to his immigra-tion, thus making it highly unlikely that the OSI could successfully prosecute Poppe for illegal entry into the United States.

tor] Akhmeteli," according to Poppe, "also did not have to fear anything. We were just doing research, and any nation does that in wartime." Poppe is philosophical about his defection to the Nazis. "Things do not always go by a straight line," he says, referring to his journey from the USSR to the United States. "There are also breaks, and zigs and zags."[30]

While Poppe was an intelligence expert and Hilger a high-ranking diplomat, a large number of Bloodstone recruits appear to have been leaders of pro-Axis émigré organizations. One example of this type of Bloodstone profile will have to suffice. In this case, which actually involves not just one but at least six high-ranking Albanian émigrés, we again see that certain Bloodstone recruits had backgrounds as leading Nazi collaborators.

Midhat Frasheri had been head of the Albanian Nazi collaborationist organization Balli Kombetar during the war. Frasheri first approached the U.S. ambassador in Rome in 1947 with a plan to import fifty Albanian refugee leaders into the United States to counteract what he called Communist "intrigues" among Albanians living in this country, according to Stanford University doctoral candidate Marc Truitt, who first uncovered the incident.[31]

Among the men proposed by Frasheri were Xhafer Deva, the former minister of interior of the Italian Fascist occupation regime in Albania, who had been responsible for deportation of "Jews, Communists, partisans and suspicious persons" (as a captured SS report put it) to extermination camps in Poland as well as for punitive raids by the Nazi-organized Albanian SS Skanderbeg Division; Hasan Dosti, the former minister of justice in the pro-Fascist government; Mustafa Merlika-Kruja, the Albanian premier from 1941 to 1943; and, of course, Frasheri himself. Frasheri's crew had been responsible for the administration of Albania under Fascist sponsorship. The small mountain territory had relatively few Jews, so relatively few were captured and killed, but not for lack of trying by the Balli Kombetar organization, and the Albanian SS. Surviving reports implicate the Albanian SS division in a series of anti-Semitic purges that rounded up about 800 people, the majority of whom were deported and murdered.

The U.S. State Department initially rejected Frasheri's plan because of what it termed the "somewhat checkered" background of his wards. But his plan later came to the attention of Robert Joyce, the State Department's liaison officer with the CIA and OPC, who was active in Bloodstone and other political warfare programs. On

May 12, 1949, Joyce took steps to obtain a U.S. visa for Frasheri. The Albanian collaborator's entry into the United States "is considered in the national interest" by "our friends," Joyce wrote in an apparent reference to Wisner's OPC division at the CIA. The visa was issued, and Frasheri entered the United States later that year, followed shortly by his team of Albanian leaders.[32]

Once inside the country, Frasheri, Deva, Dosti, and several others established the National Committee for a Free Albania, which was substantially financed by the CIA with funds laundered through foundations and through Radio Free Europe. The committee subsequently played an important role in recruiting Albanian refugees for a series of abortive invasions of their homeland sponsored by the OPC under NSC 10/2. It is now known, however, that those invasion attempts were betrayed by British double agent Kim Philby and by Soviet spies among the émigrés in Europe. The unfortunate Albanian rebels attempting to overthrow the Albanian Communist Enver Hoxha's regime in their homeland were quickly rounded up and shot.

Frasheri's senior lieutenants were safely in the United States and able to avoid that fate, however. Most of them went on to long careers in right-wing politics in the United States and were active in the Assembly of Captive European Nations, which was also financed by the CIA, according to a study by the Congressional Research Service. Deva lived comfortably in Palo Alto, California, until he died in 1978; Merlika-Kruja, the former quisling premier, died in New York in 1958; and Hasan Dosti, the former minister of justice, is at this writing in his eighties and living in Los Angeles. All of them served as senior officers in the National Committee for a Free Albania and on a long list of Albanian fraternal groups in the United States.[33] Dosti dismisses charges that Albanian war criminals entered the United States as nothing more than "Communist propaganda."

CHAPTER TEN

Bare Fists and Brass Knuckles

Many of the Bloodstone recruits—both Nazi collaborators and anti-Nazis—were passed along to two heavily funded CIA psychological warfare projects that are still in operation. These two enterprises were authorized under the "subversion against hostile states" and "propaganda" sections of NSC 10/2 and are probably the largest and most expensive political warfare efforts ever undertaken by the United States. They are certainly the longest-running and best-publicized "secret" operations ever. Their names are Radio Free Europe and Radio Liberation from Bolshevism, the latter of which is better known as Radio Liberation or Radio Liberty.

Radio Free Europe and Radio Liberty (usually abbreviated RFE/RL) began in 1948 as a corporation named the National Committee for a Free Europe, a supposedly private charitable organization dedicated to aiding exiles from Soviet-occupied Eastern Europe. The roots of the RFE/RL effort, in an administrative sense, are the same political warfare programs that gave birth to Bloodstone and NSC 10/2.

George Kennan, Allen Dulles, and a handful of other foreign affairs specialists came up with the National Committee for a Free Europe (NCFE) as a unique solution to a knotty problem. The U.S. government found it advantageous to maintain conventional, albeit frosty, diplomatic relations with the Communist-dominated governments of the USSR, Poland, Hungary, and the other satellite states. However, the Department of State and the intelligence community also wished to underwrite the anti-Communist work of the numerous émigré organizations that claimed to represent "governments-in-exile" of the same countries. It was impossible to have diplomatic relations with both the official governments of Eastern Europe and the "governments-in-exile" at the same time, for obvious reasons. The NCFE was therefore launched to serve as a thinly veiled "private-sector" cover through which clandestine U.S. funds for the exile committees could be passed.[1]

The seed money for the National Committee for a Free Europe was drawn from the same pool of captured German assets that had earlier financed clandestine operations during the Italian election. At least $2 million left over from that affair found its way first into the hands of Frank Wisner's OPC and then into the accounts of the NCFE, according to former RFE/RL president Sig Mickelson, who helped administer Radio Free Europe money for many years. Printing presses, radio transmitters, and other equipment salvaged from the Italian campaign were also transferred to the OPC and from there on to the NCFE.[2]

Allen Dulles and Frank Wisner combined their talents to line up an all-star board of directors for the NCFE that served as a cover, in effect, to explain where all the money was coming from. Early corporate notables who served on the board or as members of the NCFE include (to name only a few) J. Peter Grace of W. R. Grace & Company and the National City Bank; H. J. Heinz of the Mellon Bank and Heinz tomato ketchup fame; Texas oilman George C. McGhee; auto magnate Henry Ford II; film directors Darryl Zanuck and Cecil B. De Mille; and so many Wall Street lawyers that NCFE board meetings could have resembled a gathering of the New York State Bar Association. The intelligence community's contingent featured former OSS chief William J. Donovan, Russian émigré Bernard Yarrow, and Allen Dulles himself, among others. Labor was represented in the person of James B. Carey, a self-described CIO "labor executive" who played a leading role in the trade union movement's purge of Communists during the late 1940s. Carey was outspoken in his attitude concerning communism. "In the last war we joined with the Communists to fight the Fascists," he told the *New York Herald Tribune*. "In another war we will join the Fascists to defeat the Communists."[3]

From the beginning the National Committee for a Free Europe depended upon the voluntary silence of powerful media personalities in the United States to cloak its true operations in secrecy. "Representatives of some of the nation's most influential media giants were involved early on as members of the corporation [NCFE]," Mickelson notes in a relatively frank history of its activities. This board included "magazine publishers Henry Luce [of Time-Life] and DeWitt Wallace [of *Reader's Digest*]," he writes, "but not a word of the government involvement appeared in print or on the air." Luce and Wallace were not the only ones: C. D. Jackson, editor in chief of *Fortune* magazine, came on board in 1951 as president of the entire Radio Free Europe effort, while *Reader's Digest* senior editor Eugene Lyons headed the American Committee for the Liberation of the Peoples of Russia Inc., a corporate parent of Radio Liberation. Still, "sources of financing," Mickelson writes, were "never mentioned" in the press.[4]

The practical effect of this arrangement was the creation of a powerful lobby inside American media that tended to suppress critical news concerning the CIA's propaganda projects. This was not simply a matter of declining to mention the fact that the agency was behind these programs, as Mickelson implies. Actually the media falsified their reports to the public concerning the government's role in Radio Free Europe and Radio Liberation for years, actively promoting the myth—which most sophisticated editors knew perfectly well was false—that these projects were financed through nickel-and-dime contributions from concerned citizens. Writers soon learned that exposés concerning the NCFE and RFE/RL were simply not welcome at mainstream publications. No corporate officers needed to issue any memorandums to enforce this silence: with C. D. Jackson as RFE/RL's president and Luce himself on the group's board of directors, for example, *Time*'s and *Life*'s authors were no more likely to delve into the darker side of RFE/RL than they were to attack the American flag.

CIA-funded psychological warfare projects employing Eastern European émigrés became major operations during the 1950s, consuming tens and even hundreds of millions of dollars. Noted conservative author (and OPC psychological warfare consultant) James Burnham estimated in 1953 that the United States was spending "well over a billion dollars yearly" on a wide variety of psychological warfare projects, and that was in preinflation dollars.[5] This included underwriting most of the French Paix et Liberté movement, paying the bills of the German League for Struggle Against Inhumanity, and financing a half dozen free jurists associations, a variety of European federalist groups, the Congress for Cultural Freedom, magazines, news services, book publishers, and much more.

These were very broad programs designed to influence world public opinion at virtually every level, from illiterate peasants in the fields to the most sophisticated scholars in prestigious universities. They drew on a wide range of resources: labor unions, advertising agencies, college professors, journalists, and student leaders, to name a few. The political analysis they promoted varied from case to case, but taken as a whole, this was prodemocracy, pro-West, and anti-Communist thinking, with a frequent "tilt" toward liberal or European-style Social Democratic ideals. They were not "Nazi" propaganda efforts, nor were many of the men and women engaged in them former Nazi collaborators or sympathizers. In Europe, at least, the Central Intelligence Agency has historically been the clandestine promoter of the parties of the political center, not the extreme right.

Contrary to Soviet propaganda, "anti-Communist" and "pro-Nazi" are not the same thing among the exiled politicians and émigré organizations from Eastern Europe, including those that were sponsored by the CIA in the 1950s. The large majority of these exile politicians and scholars who accepted covert U.S. aid during the cold war had not been Nazi collaborators. Many of them, especially the anti-Communist Czechs and Poles, themselves had suffered grievously at the hands of the Nazis.

But the American policy expressed in NSC 20 and similar high-level decisions set the stage for U.S. enlistment of some exiles who had been Nazi collaborators. By refusing to make distinctions among the various anti-Communist exile groups, the CIA soon found itself with a substantial number of former Nazis and collaborators on its payroll. These recruitments were not "accidental" if the word implies that the CIA did not know what those groups had done during the war, nor were they as rare as most people assume. The how and why of some of those cases are the focus of the story in the pages that follow.

Beginning as early as 1948 and picking up speed in the decade that followed, the National Committee for a Free Europe and its sister project, the American Committee for Liberation from Bolshevism, became the single most important pipeline through which the CIA passed money for émigré leaders. Although both were supposedly private, voluntary organizations, the political control of these projects and virtually all their funding was actually provided by Wisner's OPC division at the CIA.

Contrary to popular impression, the well-known radio transmissions of Radio Free Europe and Radio Liberation were added only as something of an afterthought several years after the CIA's funding of émigré projects had begun. Radio transmissions into Central and Eastern Europe began in 1950 under Radio Free Europe's auspices, then expanded to include programs beamed into the USSR itself through RFE's sister project, Radio Liberation from Bolshevism, in early 1953. Radio Liberation from Bolshevism was renamed Radio Liberty during a thaw in the cold war in 1963. The CIA's direct sponsorship of these programs continued until 1973, when a new (and somewhat more public) Board for International Broadcasting was established to fund and administer the radio propaganda effort. The corporate names and details of organizational structure of these projects went through a number of changes in those years, which are summarized in the source notes.[6] For simplicity's sake, the text that follows uses RFE/RL to refer to these projects.

By the early 1970s the U.S. government had poured at least $100 million into support of political activities of the Eastern European exile groups through the RFE/RL conduit alone, according to an unclassified study by the government's General Accounting Office.[7] That money, however, was only the beginning. An unknown sum clearly totaling many tens of millions of dollars more found its way into CIA-sponsored émigré programs by way of European Recovery Act (Marshall Plan) funds, displaced persons assistance, foreign aid to West Germany, and donations of U.S. military surplus goods.

Nazi collaborators' links to the U.S. political warfare effort became particularly pronounced in the governments-in-exile divisions of Radio Free Europe and Radio Liberation, which were the main administrative channels for CIA money flowing to a number of Eastern European émigré groups. The RFE division funded the "governments-in-exile" or "national committees" (as they were often called) for most of the countries occupied by the USSR at the end of the war, while a similar structure inside Radio Liberation performed much the same job for exiles from a dozen different nationalities within the Soviet Union itself.[8]

During World War II both the Axis and the Allies had financed such national committees as a means of mobilizing resistance, keeping an eye on refugees from occupied territories, and creating behind-the-lines spy networks. The intelligence services or foreign ministries of the belligerents passed money to favored exile leaders, who in turn distributed patronage and favors to followers they considered loyal.

RFE/RL recruiters wanted to re-create these governments-in-exile for propaganda use against the USSR and its satellite countries. They were faced with a difficult problem in the early years, however, because many of their more promising volunteers turned out to have been willing Nazi collaborators. Often the national committees that had been sponsored by Berlin remained well organized and relatively powerful even after the German defeat, and these groups sometimes controlled the displaced persons camps where refugees of their nationality had been dumped by the Allies. The quisling national committees included men whom the Nazis had sponsored as mayors, government officials, newspaper editors, and police chiefs during the German occupation. They were experienced in working together, and their organizations were often backed up by gangs of thugs made up of Waffen SS and Vlasov Army veterans who made sure that things ran smoothly inside the camps.

These formerly pro-Nazi national committees had, almost without exception, jettisoned their Fascist rhetoric and Iron Cross awards following the collapse of Berlin. They took to presenting themselves as democrats, freedom fighters, and even anti-Nazis. These false stories should have been transparent, considering that the United States had captured enough of the German intelligence archives to document the activities of thousands of the more prominent collaborators, had it been a priority to dig their names out of Nazi correspondence. But no one in the Western intelligence agencies, it seems, was willing to look critically at the wartime careers of the émigrés who were eager to help the United States in the cold war. Instead, the intense secrecy that surrounded Wisner's OPC and similar psychological warfare projects protected many ex-Nazis and collaborators by putting a top secret stamp on their activities.

RFE recruiters generally attempted to shun Nazi collaborators when it was possible to do so, and they often favored democrats and moderate socialists for their ability to present an alternative to the USSR, on the one hand, and to the old monarchist or Nazi power structures, on the other. This liberal, anti-Communist approach was successful in recruiting agents from some of the wartime exile governments that had been founded under British auspices in London or from among certain Czech and Hungarian political groups which had established some measure of democratic power between World Wars I and II. The left-leaning Council for a Free Czechoslovakia under Peter Zenkl, to name one example, was usually favored over the more reactionary Slovak Liberation Committee under Ferdinand Durcansky, which openly pledged its allegiance to the genocidal wartime regime of Monsignor Jozef Tiso.[9] RFE's sympathy for the Zenkl committee over its rivals led to endless, bitter attacks on both Radio Free Europe and Zenkl, many of which appeared in rightist émigré journals that were themselves receiving U.S. government subsidies.

Even among exiles from the more democratic countries, however, the Nazi collaborationist influence remained substantial. The Americans sometimes ended up hiring former quislings and collaborators because it seemed there were few other choices available. Men such as Ladislav Nižňanský and Emil Csonka (to name only two examples among many), both of whom had played well-publicized roles in the Nazi occupation of Eastern Europe, found themselves jobs and influence under RFE sponsorship.*

The problem of finding anti-Communist liberals was far more difficult among refugees from the USSR. "There were no significant 'democratic elements' in Russia," Kennan was to admit later. "Thirty years of Communist terror had seen to that."[10] That was an overstatement, perhaps, but not by much. No "democratic" committees had been established among these groups by the British during the war. Stalin's government, after all, had been a crucial ally. Indeed, the only organizations of any strength among the exiles from Belorussia (White Russia), the Ukraine, Turkestan, Azer-

---

*Nižňanský is reported to have participated in the special SS Kommando "Edelweiss" and to have won the German Iron Cross, second class, for his efforts. A Czechoslovakian court tried him in absentia and condemned him to death for war crimes, including four massacres of civilians by troops under his personal command which took place in late 1944 and early 1945 in Nazi-occupied Czechoslovakia. Many of the victims were women and children. In addition, evidence was offered at his trial that he had participated in the December 12, 1944, murder of Anglo-American military mission officers that took place near Polomka. Nižňanský went to work for the CIC at least as early as 1948, when he was an interpreter and interrogator at Braunau. He was hired by RFE at least as early as 1955, and he served for many years as a specialist in work among Czechoslovakians who were visiting or who had emigrated to the West.

Csonka is alleged to have been a member of the Fascist Hungarian Arrow Cross party during the war and to have served as both a youth leader in that organization and, for a time, secretary to Ferenc Szalasi, the organization's leader, who was executed for war crimes in 1946. Following the war Csonka worked for French intelligence. He joined RFE at least as early as 1954 as a political editor specializing in Hungarian questions. He has often used the pseudonym Gergely Vasvari.

baijan, and several other Soviet nationalities were precisely those that had enthusiastically collaborated during the Nazi occupation. Whether out of cynicism or the pressures of the cold war, or both, these organizations and the men who ran them were recruited, financed, and protected by Radio Liberation.

In a number of cases RL recruiters did not even bother to change the names, much less the leadership, of the nationality committees that had served the Nazis. The North Caucasian National Committee, the Georgian Government in Exile, and the Belorussian Central Rada, for example, all of which had been founded or administered under Berlin's watchful eye, retained their names, memberships, and most of their central committees intact under U.S. sponsorship. In a revealing act of indiscretion, even the U.S. cover organization for the Radio Liberation operation, the American Committee for the Liberation of the Peoples of Russia, took its name directly from Vlasov's Komitet Osvobozhdeniia Narodov Rossii (KONR), which had been created under joint SS and Nazi Foreign Office sponsorship in Prague in 1944.[11]

Frank Wisner's Office for Policy Coordination, backed up strongly on this issue by Kennan, established the American Committee for the Liberation of the Peoples of Russia (usually abbreviated as AMCOMLIB). AMCOMLIB was both an implementation and a development of NSC 20. Now, as Wisner envisioned it, the OPC would use its considerable financial resources to induce all the various Soviet émigré organizations, including those that had been most active on behalf of the Nazis, to unite into a single anti-Communist federation. This movement was to include not only people of Russian nationality but those of the Ukrainian, Belorussian, Cossack, Turkic, and other minority groups as well. This was to be a united anti-Stalin movement in which all non-Communist exiles from the USSR could participate.

But the same problems that had once plagued the Germans reappeared almost immediately. Each of the minority groups demanded equality within the envisioned federation. Ukrainian leaders insisted on the right to secede from any government created after the planned overthrow of Stalin. The ethnic Russian nationalists, on the other hand, refused to accept the Ukrainians' conditions because they regarded the Ukraine as a component part of the Russian empire. The battle among the émigré groups escalated from there.

The first concession demanded by the Ukrainians was a change in the name of the federation; a committee for the liberation of the peoples of *Russia* implied that they considered themselves part of Russia, as they emphatically did not. So the name was changed to American Committee for Liberation from Bolshevism, a term which had been favored by Nazi propagandists in the Ukraine. In the end, however, this attempt at unity also failed, and the émigré groups continued bitter factional fighting.

Even the federation's name eventually turned into an embarrassment. The American organizers of the committee, former RFE/RL President Sig Mickelson notes, "seem to have been unaware that 'Bolshevism' had been Hitler's favorite term of disparagement for the Soviet Union." The Soviet government lost no time in pointing out the rhetorical similarity between Radio Liberation's broadcasts and those of the Nazis as well as the fact that a number of easily identified Nazi collaborators were working for the station. According to Mickelson, Radio Free Europe and Radio Liberation were eventually forced to ban the use of the term *Bolshevism* in their news broadcasts because of its unmistakable association with Nazi propaganda in the minds of European listeners.[12]

Wisner's OPC division of the CIA appears to have lost control of many of its émigré assets as their factional conflicts expanded. Exile leaders fought bitterly among themselves, split coalitions they had been instructed to support, and undertook murders and other paramilitary operations that they concealed from their American sponsors. Several leaders of the Russian nationalists are now known to have been simultaneously on several other payrolls, including that of the USSR, and were providing false information to each of their patrons. Double, triple, and quadruple agents were the rule, not an exception. Political murders and kidnappings became commonplace.

One U.S.-financed exile group, known as TsOPE by its Russian initials, even went so far as to blow up its own headquarters, then blame the deed on the Soviet security police. The idea was to prove that its organization must be the most effective anti-Communist force, and thus worthy of increased funding, because the Soviets had singled it out for sabotage. TsOPE's inspired plan unraveled, however, when its office staff was brought in for questioning by American investigators.[13]

The well-known radio broadcasting operations of RFE/RL were secondary to the National Committee for a Free Europe's funding of exile political action committees during the late 1940s. The radios were only added as something of an afterthought as the weaknesses in Thayer's work at the Voice of America became apparent. Thayer's radio propaganda efforts at the VOA—which were, it will be recalled, one of the impetuses for Bloodstone—had been shown to be counterproductive relatively quickly. His vitriolic attacks on Eastern European regimes, the State Department soon discovered, were taken by their targets as official policy statements of the U.S. government because they were broadcast on the official radio voice of the United States. The Policy Planning Staff concluded that use of an official mouthpiece for the more virulent anti-Communist propaganda actually ended up restricting the U.S. government's ability to deal effectively with the complex political rivalries in the region. Instead, it argued, the government should secretly expand the supposedly "private" NCFE to handle radio broadcasting aimed at the USSR and its satellites. This would permit some measure of "deniability" for the broadcasts and personalities associated with RFE/RL.

Unlike the relative moderation of the present-day RFE/RL broadcasts, the cold war operations of these stations were hardhitting. It was "bare fists and brass knuckles," as Sig Mickelson puts it. Their work was, as National Committee for a Free Europe President Dewitt Poole noted in one 1950 directive, "to take up the individual Bolshevik rulers and their quislings and tear them apart, exposing their motivations, laying bare their private lives, pointing at their meannesses, pillorying their evil deeds, holding them up to ridicule and contumely."[14] Further, the radio broadcasting operations were themselves used as covers for a much broader range of political warfare activities, including printing and distributing black propaganda,* intelligence gathering, and the maintenance of agent networks behind the Iron Curtain.

This tough agitation drew its ideological vigor from a variety of sources. Thomas Jefferson and Abraham Lincoln were often quoted and praised in RFE/RL broadcasts, as were Eastern European national heroes like the Hungarian Lajos Kossuth and the Pole Thaddeus Kosciuszko. At the same time, however, RFE/RL sometimes

---

*"Black" propaganda is a standard covert operations technique in which the CIA—or any other intelligence agency—employs agents with no provable ties to the U.S. government to disseminate false information that is designed to discredit hostile foreign states. This includes spreading rumors of impending food shortages in order to precipitate hoarding and economic crises, for example, or leaking forged documents that might undermine the targeted government.

produced a dull undertone of Nazi-like propaganda in its early years. At times material that had been directly created by the Nazi security service SD found its way into RFE/RL broadcasts and publications. The NCFE often distributed the highly publicized— but fraudulent—"Document on Terror," for example, as a means of crystallizing public anger in the West against communism during Radio Free Europe fund-raising campaigns. The "Document" purported to be a translation of a captured Soviet secret police directive encouraging the use of terror against civilian populations. It included sections on "general terror" (murders, hangings, etc.), "creating the psychosis of white fear," "enlightened terror" (use of agents provocateurs), "disintegrating operations," and others. The CIA aggressively promoted the text of the "Document" both directly through RFE/RL and indirectly through coverage planted in a wide variety of sympathetic newspapers, magazines, and television broadcasts to audiences around the world.

The NCFE announced that it had obtained the "Document" from "a former Baltic cabinet minister, favorably known to us," who in turn had gotten it from a Ukrainian refugee, who in turn had "found it on the body of a dead NKVD officer" in Poland in 1948. The committee acknowledged in small type that it had "no means of conclusively establishing the authenticity" of the "Document," but it insisted that it was a "genuine product of Communist theory" whose recommendations "did . . . take place." This low-key caveat concerning the questionable authenticity of the "Document" was soon forgotten in the media storm that followed publication of the item.[15]

The "Document" became a staple of anti-Communist propaganda and continues to show up occasionally in extreme-right-wing publications to this day. Recycled extensively through congressional hearings, *Reader's Digest* articles, and newspaper accounts, this "captured report" emerged as one of the frequently cited sources of "documentary evidence" of Communist terror during the cold war. It was not until 1956, with the publication of Khrushchev's extraordinary report detailing Stalin's crimes, that the "Document" began to fade from view.

In fact, however, the "Document" was a forgery, whose origins can be traced to the wartime Nazi intelligence service. The true source of the "Document" was, according to American psychological warfare expert Paul Blackstock, "one of the Nazi secret police or related terrorist organizations such as the *Sicherheitsdienst* or one of the notorious *SD* or *SS* 'action groups' "—that is, the *Einsatzgruppen* (mobile murder squads). Blackstock uses an etymological investigation to track the origins of phrases used in the "Document" back to their sources.[16] He concludes that the section concerning "disintegrating operations," for example, originated in a Nazi manual used for indoctrinating Eastern European collaborationist troops, including the Ukrainian Waffen SS.

RFE/RL broadcasts sometimes featured well-known Nazi collaborators and even outright war criminals. Officially, of course, the political slant of those stations was nondenominational support for "freedom" and "democracy." The large majority of RFE/RL employees were not Nazi collaborators, and the two stations often quoted anti-Nazi European politicians with approval. RFE/RL's broadcasts of European Social Democrats, in fact, occasionally led to complaints from hard-core anti-Communist congressmen in the United States, who found such ideas dangerously close to communism.

Even so, certain war criminals found a comfortable roost at RFE/RL. Radio Free Europe repeatedly featured Romanian Fascist leader (and Archbishop of the Romanian Orthodox Church in America) Valerian Trifa, for example, in Romanian-language broadcasts, particularly during the 1950s. Vilis Hazners, who was accused in a CBS-TV *60 Minutes* broadcast of spearheading a Nazi gang that "force[d] a number of Jews into a synagogue [which was] then set on fire," emerged as a prominent Latvian personality in Radio Liberation transmissions. Hazners, at last report, was still broadcasting for RL in the 1980s. Belorussian quisling and mass murderer Stanislaw Stankievich also frequently free-lanced programs for the radios.[17]

The Pentagon was gradually coming to grips with using former Nazi collaborators at about the same time that the State Department and CIA were. General Lucius Clay's war scare of early 1948, together with the deepening cold war, convinced many Americans in and out of government that there was at least an even chance of an all-out U.S.-USSR war over Europe before the decade was out.

As the final arbiter of U.S. security the Pentagon considers it part of its job to assume the worst about Soviet intentions in order to be adequately prepared for any eventuality. By 1948 that the United States would increasingly rely on atomic weapons to deter any Soviet military moves against the West had already become a foregone conclusion among most U.S. military strategists. The American perception that the Soviets enjoyed overwhelming superiority in troops and conventional arms in Europe seemed to leave few other choices.

The Pentagon was evolving a strategy of exactly how to go about using atomic weapons in a war with the USSR at about the same time that Kennan, Dulles, and Wisner were hammering together the National Committee for a Free Europe and the NSC 10/2 clandestine warfare authorization. By the time the decade was out, the military's preparations for waging nuclear war—if that proved necesssary—had merged with many of the ongoing CIA and State Department political warfare operations that have been discussed thus far. As those two streams came together, Nazi collaborators became entwined with some of America's most sensitive military affairs.

CHAPTER ELEVEN

Guerrillas for World War III

The Vlasov Army and Waffen SS veterans from Eastern Europe worked hard to integrate themselves into the evolving U.S. nuclear weapons strategy during the cold war years. Colonel Philp and General Gehlen, it will be recalled, began as early as the winter of 1945–1946 to use German officers and refugees from the East to gather information about military construction behind Soviet lines. Each time the location of a new Soviet military site was confirmed, word of its location was passed to a special U.S. Air Force office at the Pentagon whose job was the selection of targets slated for atomic annihilation.

As U.S. atomic planning grew more sophisticated, the role of émigrés in America's nuclear war-fighting strategy expanded quickly. By late 1948 paramilitary expert General Robert McClure had won the U.S. Joint Chiefs of Staff to approval of a full-scale program of guerrilla warfare that was to follow any U.S. nuclear strike on the USSR. From then until at least 1956, when this strategy was at the height of its popularity in U.S. command circles, preparations for post-World War III guerrilla insurgencies employed thousands of émigrés from the USSR. Pentagon documents show that Vlasov veterans and Waffen SS men played a major role in these underground armies. Considering the wartime record of these forces, there is reason to suspect that a number of these enlistees may have been war criminals.

These émigrés did not, of course, create U.S. nuclear strategy. The advent of atomic weapons and their impact on international affairs would have taken place with or without the use of former Nazis and collaborators in U.S. war planning. The exile soldiers simply rode the coattails of the movement toward reliance on nuclear weapons during the late 1940s and early 1950s. In many cases they themselves were not aware of what the Pentagon had in mind for them. The integration of these groups into even the most humble levels of U.S. nuclear planning, however, gave the military and intelligence agencies a powerful reason to conceal the Nazi pasts of their unusual troops.

The process of integrating ex-Nazi émigré groups into U.S. nuclear operations may be traced at least to early 1947, when General Hoyt Vandenberg became the first chief of staff of the newly independent U.S. Air Force. Vandenberg had commanded the Ninth Air Force in Europe during World War II, then been tapped to head the Central Intelligence Group, the immediate predecessor to the CIA, in 1946. Among the general's responsibilities at the air force was the development of written plans describing strategies and tactics for the use of America's new nuclear weapons in the event of war.

"Vandenberg had a clear idea about just how he thought a nuclear war was going to be fought," argues retired Colonel Fletcher Prouty, who was a senior aide to the air force chief of staff in the 1940s and later the top liaison man between the Pentagon and the CIA. "[He] knew that if there was a nuclear exchange in those days—and we are talking about atomic bombs, now, not H-bombs—you would destroy the communications and lifeblood of a country, but the country would still exist. It would just be rubble. People would be wandering around wanting to know who was boss and where the food was coming from and so forth, but the country would still *be there.*" Therefore, the U.S. thinking went, "we must begin to create independent communications centers inside the Soviet Union [after the nuclear blast] and begin to pull it together for our ends."[1]

The army, air force, and CIA all began competing programs to prepare for the post-nuclear battlefield. This included creation of what eventually came to be called the Special Forces—better known today as the Green Berets—in the army and the air resupply and communications wings in the air force. The job of these units, Prouty explains, was to set up anti-Communist political leaders backed up by guerrilla armies inside the USSR and Eastern Europe in the wake of an atomic war, capture political power in strategic sections of the country, choke off any remaining Communist resistance, and ensure that the Red Army could not regroup for a counterattack. "Somebody had to bring order back into the country, and before the Communists could do it we were going to come flying in there and do it," Prouty says.

"The Eastern European and Russian émigré groups we had picked up from the Germans were the center of this; they were the personnel," according to the retired colonel. "The CIA was to prepare these forces in peacetime; stockpile weapons, radios, and Jeeps for them to use; and keep them ready in the event of war. A lot of this equipment came from military surplus. The CIA was also supposed to have some contacts inside [the USSR] worked out ahead of time for use when we got there, and that was also the job of the émigré groups on the agency payroll. In the meantime, they [the émigré troops] were useful for espionage or covert action." Both the army and the CIA laid claim to the authority to control the guerrilla foot soldiers after war had actually been declared.[2]

A recently declassified top secret document from the JCS to President Truman confirms Prouty's assertion that the émigré armies enjoyed an important role in the eyes of nuclear planners of the time. The 1949 study begins with a summary of what was then the current atomic strategy. Seventy atomic bombs, along with an unspecified amount of conventional explosives, were slated to be dropped from long-range planes on selected Soviet targets over a thirty-day period. The impact of the attack had been carefully calculated, according to the JCS memo: About 40 percent of the Soviets' industrial capacity would be destroyed, including most of the militarily crucial petroleum industry.

But this, the chiefs contended, would not guarantee victory. The thirty-day atomic assault, the Pentagon concluded with considerable understatement, "might stimulate resentment against the United States" among the people of the USSR, thus increasing their will to fight. A major program of political warfare following the attack was therefore essential, the JCS determined. In fact, the effectiveness of the atomic attack itself was "dependent upon the adequacy and promptness of [the] associated military and psychological operations. . . . Failing prompt and effective exploitation, the opportunity would be lost and subsequent Soviet psychological reactions would adversely affect the accomplishment of Allied objectives."[3]

The commitment of five wings of B-29 bombers to the émigré guerrilla army project is a practical measure of the importance that the Pentagon attached to it. The B-29 was the largest, most sophisticated, and most expensive heavy bomber in the U.S. inventory at the time. According to Prouty, General Vandenberg originally conceived of the air force's role in psychological and guerrilla warfare as a third branch of his service, equal, at least in administrative status, to the Strategic Air Command and the Tactical Air Command. Special Forces visionaries in the army such as General McClure had similar plans for that service as well.

The Vlasov Army guerrilla training proposals earlier initiated by Kennan, Thayer, and Lindsay fitted neatly into the military's nuclear strike force plans. By the beginning of 1949 the two projects were gradually merging into a single strategy combining preconflagration psychological warfare and clandestine action under the control of the CIA and State Department with postnuclear guerrilla armies under military command.

Extreme secrecy cloaked every aspect of U.S. atomic policy, and the fact that the United States was training an émigré army for use following an atomic attack on the USSR was among the most closely held details. Even the foot soldiers who were destined to be dropped into the radioactive ruins of the USSR were not to be informed of the details of their mission until the final moments before their departure. The secrecy was designed to conceal the military strategy, not the fact that a number of recruits had Nazi backgrounds. But the sensitivity of the mission guaranteed that newspaper reporters and academics could usually be tactfully deterred from probing too deeply into the origins of the Special Forces. Anyone who refused to take the hint was met with a stone wall of government silence.*

It was up to the U.S. Army to devise a program for the day-to-day

---

*Once, in 1952, a reporter strayed too close to the truth, and the following single sentence appeared in *Newsweek:* "The Army will soon open a secret guerrilla warfare and sabotage school for military personnel and CIA agents at Ft. Bragg, N.C." Army psychological warfare chief General Robert McClure was enraged by the security lapse and demanded a full field investigation into the reporter's activities in order to trace the leak to its source. Army intelligence had its hands full with the Korean War at the time, however, and is said to have declined to follow up on McClure's request. Even so, the incident reveals how closely the Special Forces secret was being held.

maintenance of several thousand of the CIA's émigré guerrillas until "the balloon goes up," as a nuclear crisis has come to be called in national security circles. The stockpiling of military equipment was fairly simple in those days, when warehouses full of World War II surplus material were available. But how does even the U.S. Army go about hiding an armed force of several thousand enthusiastic anti-Communists in the European heartland? The answer was simple, in a way: The émigré soldiers were hidden inside another army. Those covers were known as Labor Service companies, and these U.S.-financed paramilitary units are a story in themselves.

These organizations began shortly after the war as U.S. Army-sponsored Labor Service units or Industrial Police corps inside occupied Germany. They were U.S. Army-financed semimilitary corps of about 40,000 displaced persons and refugees set up to guard POW camps, clear rubble from bombed-out cities, locate graves of casualties, and carry out similar tasks. The U.S. government's rationale for the program was that the labor companies provided a cheap and relatively reliable source of workers for the army, navy, and occupation government at a time when the military was struggling against budget cutting and a demobilization mood in the Congress. The units offered employment, housing, and respectability to their recruits at a time when much of Europe was a shattered wasteland, so thousands of displaced persons flocked to enlist.* Former Nazis or members of armies that had taken up arms

---

*The United States' postwar labor service units were known at various times as Labor Service Guard Companies, Labor Service Companies (Guard), Technical Labor Service Units, Labor Service Technical Units, Industrial Police, Civilian Guard Companies, Military Labor Service, and a half dozen other similar names. All, however, were under the nominal command of the U.S. Army European Command's Labor Service Division. The names Labor Service companies and Labor Service units are used throughout this discussion for simplicity's sake.

The use of such Labor Service companies for arms training and as cover for clandestine paramilitary brigades is a well-established practice in Europe. The Nazis, for example, created similar brigades of Ukrainians and foreign-born Germans for use during the invasions of Poland and the Baltic states. These Nazi Labor Service squads often did double duty as triggermen and goons during the Holocaust.

After the war the USSR also organized its own labor companies out of the German POWs it had captured. "Former German military personnel, both officers and other ranks, held in the USSR as prisoners of war have been organized into labor battalions," the CIA reported in 1947. "[They] have been given Soviet training for administration posts, and police work, and in some instances been organized into small combat units for use against Baltic partisans." These men, the CIA continued, were "available for service with whatever regime the Kremlin elect[s] to establish in Germany." The Soviets also created labor units from among captured Poles, Yugoslavs, and Romanians who had fought on the German side during the war, according to the agency.

against the United States were strictly barred from participating in the Labor Service units, at least officially, and U.S. occupation authorities announced that they would undertake a reasonably thorough screening process for new recruits.[4]

Despite the official ban on hiring ex-Nazis, however, the Labor Service divisions began recruiting Waffen SS volunteers at least as early as 1946. Before long many members of Latvian, Lithuanian, and Estonian labor units found themselves serving under the same officers in Labor Service companies as they had earlier in the SS. An examination of several of the Latvian companies provides a clearcut example of the penetration of ex-Nazis into the Labor Service units, and the same pattern held true for Albanian, Lithuanian, and some Estonian units.

The first Latvian labor company, for example, was created on June 27, 1946, under the command of Voldemars Skaistlauks, a former Latvian SS general. All six of his top lieutenants in the U.S.-sponsored unit were Latvian SS veterans. The next Latvian labor unit was the 8850th Engineer Construction Company headquartered at Frankfurt, which officially consisted mainly of truck drivers and heavy equipment operators. The senior Latvian officer there was Talivaldis Karklins, who had been a top officer of the Madonna concentration camp during the war. Karklins was accused in sworn testimony by former inmates of Madonna of leading torture and murder at that camp. He emigrated to the United States in 1956.* His chief lieutenant in the 8850th, according to the unit's roster, was Eduards Kalinovskis, also a veteran of a Latvian police death squad. The senior Latvian officer of the 8361st Company of Engineers was Janis L. Zegners, who had once been the top

*Karklins concealed his wartime career at the time he entered the United States. Detailed charges concerning Karklins's role at the Madonna camp were published in English by a Latvian state publishing house as early as 1963 and had been available in the Latvian language for several years before that. Unfortunately, however, no action was taken against Karklins by American authorities for more than fifteen years.

Finally, in 1981, the Office of Special Investigations (which had been forced to fight a tough bureaucratic battle simply to establish itself within the Department of Justice) succeeded in bringing charges against Karklins. In its complaint the OSI alleged that Karklins had "assisted in the persecution and murder of unarmed Jewish civilians and committed crimes including murder.... During [Karklins's] tenure as Commandant of this camp, unarmed inmates were starved, beaten, tortured, murdered and otherwise brutalized by the defendant and/or by persons acting under his direction. . . ."

Complex litigation ensued, depositions were gathered in Latvia, and thousands of hours of court and attorney time were consumed. Karklins, however, died peacefully on February 9, 1983, in Monterey, California, before a decision concerning his deportation from the United States could be reached.

aide to the inspector general (i.e., commanding officer) of the Latvian SS Legion and deputy warden of the notorious Riga security police during the war. At least half a dozen similar cases have come to light.[5]

The American recruiters for the Labor Service units knew that these highly motivated groups of Eastern European volunteers had earlier served in the Nazi Waffen SS, and they knew, at least in general terms, what the SS had done in Latvia. At the same time, however, the Americans apparently rejected or ignored indications that their enlistees had personally committed atrocities, even though evidence was readily available. "The Russians had their own spies inside the groups who stole the unit rosters and anything else they could get their hands on," states a retired American colonel who once headed a Ukrainian-Polish Labor Service unit. "So the Russians made plenty of denunciations of my guys. But in those days to get denounced by the Communists, well, it probably meant they were doing something right for our side."[6]

Before long the pretense of careful anti-Nazi screening of recruits had been dropped, even in official correspondence. Following a routine revision of Labor Service company orders in 1950, Colonel C. M. Busbee, the chief of the operation, noticed that the wording of a subparagraph in the new orders that barred recruitment of ex-Nazis had been tightened. Busbee wrote to Lieutenant General Daniel Noce, chief of staff of the European command, pointing out that under the new order, "all former SS officers [would be] prohibited from joining labor service units. This policy, if continued, would deprive labor services of a considerable number of these personnel," Busbee argued, "who were previously employed in the Industrial Police and labor service units, and who have proved their dependability through efficient service. . . . [I] request authority to hire former Waffen-SS officer personnel provided they have been properly screened." The reply, interestingly, came back through civilian rather than military channels. Chauncey G. Parker, a senior assistant to U.S. High Commissioner for Germany John McCloy, approved Busbee's request a few weeks later.[7]

There were at least three layers of secrecy surrounding the Labor Service companies and their nuclear mission. The army was reluctant to talk about these units at all, but when questioned about the camps full of Latvian-speaking troops marching in close order drill, it had to provide some sort of explanation. Officially the recruits were nothing more than laborers, truck drivers, and warehouse guards hired to offset the declining number of U.S. troops in Europe.

The next cover story was known to the Labor Service recruits themselves but was kept secret from the general public. This was that the companies were trained and armed for counterinsurgency work inside Germany in the event of a rebellion or an attack by the USSR. "They were," according to a secret Pentagon study obtained through the Freedom of Information Act, "carefully instructed in the suppression of civil disturbances . . . [and] specifically . . . trained to secure military installations, such as ammunition dumps, warehouses, and food depots, or were schooled in interior guard duty, marksmanship, and riot control." Some 30,000 Labor Service recruits, including those supposedly limited to driving trucks, had been fully trained and armed with light infantry weapons and chemical warfare gear by 1950.[8]

Finally, there was the highly classified postnuclear strike mission, which was generally kept secret from the recruits themselves. Approximately 5,000 selected volunteers were trained for the postnuclear guerrilla force. As natives of the USSR and Soviet-occupied countries, these cold war minutemen spoke the language, knew the customs, had military training, and, in some cases, maintained underground contacts that made them seem perfect for guerrilla warfare. Before the decade of the 1940s was out, the recruitment of Labor Service men, including Waffen SS veterans, for behind-the-lines missions into Soviet-occupied Eastern Europe had become commonplace.

In the meantime, the Labor Service militias became a convenient holding tank for a variety of émigré agents attached to the Gehlen Organization, the CIA, or U.S. military intelligence. They were a military reserve, in short, for the ongoing political warfare programs under the OPC. The 4000th Labor Service Company, for example, served as an incubator for 250 Albanian guerrillas engaged in Frank Wisner's Bay of Pigs-style raids on their homeland during 1949 and the early 1950s.[9] These operations were portrayed at the time as spontaneous rebellions led on a political level by Hasan Dosti and the other Albanian Bloodstone recruits in the Committee for a Free Albania. Unfortunately for these émigré soldiers, however, both the 4000th Labor Service Company (Guards) and British intelligence were thoroughly infiltrated by Soviet and Albanian Communist agents. The raids were failures.

In 1950 CIC and CIA agents used the Labor Services cover to begin guerrilla training of at least 100 members of the far-right-wing League of Young Germans (Bund Deutscher Jungen, or BDJ). These "Young Germans" were no Boy Scouts; most were Waffen SS and Wehrmacht veterans, according to a later West German government investigation, and a considerable part of the leadership of the group had been enthusiastic "Jew baiters" in the Goebbels ministry during the Nazis' rule.

The budget for the clandestine group was 50,000 deutsche marks per month, according to records seized by German police in 1952, plus an ample supply of free arms, ammunition, and explosives cached in the Odenwald Hills south of Frankfurt. American and German advisers provided BDJ agents with extensive military instruction, including, as a report in the West German parliament later revealed, "use of Russian, United States and German weapons, including machine guns, grenades, and knives . . . [as well as] light infantry weapons and explosives." The underground group called itself a U.S. "Technical Service" unit.[10]

But the training program was only the beginning. BDJ Technical Service leaders decided that the best thing they could do for Germany following a Soviet attack was to liquidate certain German leaders they regarded as insufficiently anti-Communist. German Communists were, of course, at the top of the Technical Service assassination list. Next in line for elimination were leaders of West Germany's Social Democratic party, the country's loyal opposition during the Adenauer administration. The Technical Service group planned to murder more than forty top Social Democratic officials, including the party's national chief, Erich Ollenhauer; the interior minister of the state of Hesse, Heinrich Zinnkann; and the mayors of Hamburg and Bremen. BDJ's U.S.-trained underground infiltrated the Social Democrats to shadow individual party leaders so as to kill them more efficiently when the day to act arrived.

The plot unraveled in late 1952, however, when a chance arrest by local police led to discovery of the hit list of Social Democratic officials. The CIC's behavior following this accidental exposure was so compromising that it raised serious questions in the German parliament whether the U.S. government was aware of the Technical Service unit's assassination plans all along. Then again, perhaps the CIC response to the arrests was just stupid, not a conspiratorial cover-up. Either way, American CIC officers took custody of the arrested BDJ members and proceeded to hide them from the German civil police, who intended to charge the "Young Germans" with numerous weapons violations and conspiracy to commit murder. The German chief of the Technical Service unit, an ex-Luftwaffe man named Gerhard Peters, was placed under wraps for almost two weeks in a U.S.-requisitioned building that was off-limits to German civil authorities. U.S. CIC agents also seized all the remaining Technical Service records that they could lay their hands on, then refused to turn the dossiers over to the German equivalent of the FBI.[11]

But the cat was out of the bag. Soon Social Democratic deputies were demanding investigations and pounding the lecterns in state and federal parliaments all over West Germany. Unfortunately for the Americans and for the Technical Service, their blunder had been discovered in the midst of a closely fought election, and the Social Democrats made the most of it. In the end, U.S. authorities were forced to confirm, as the *New York Times* reported,[12] that they had "sponsored and helped finance the secret training of young Germans, many of them former soldiers, to become guerrilla fighters in the event of a war with the Soviet Union." The unnamed American officials told the *Times* that they had been unaware of the group's "political activities," including the plan to assassinate selected German leaders. All funding or other support of the BDJ group was said to have been abandoned following the arrests.

In fact, however, the CIC handlers were well aware of at least some BDJ "political activities," like the infiltration of Social Democratic party conventions, and had been all along. According to the later German parliament report on the affair, the American agencies were actually paying the plotters an additional 12,000 deutsche marks per month for these espionage services.[13]

But the assertions of U.S. ignorance concerning the hit list of Social Democratic leaders are probably true. American clandestine policy toward Social Democratic parties in Europe at the time appears to have consisted of the collection of espionage information on their activities, plus a carrot-and-stick type of patronage along the lines of the Italian election model—not the wholesale assassination of their leaders.[14] Indeed, the very amateurishness of compiling a written list of forty prominent targets suggests that Technical

Service chief Peters may very well have kept that activity secret from the Americans.

In a certain sense, that is just the problem. U.S. intelligence was financing, training, and arming a squadron of former Waffen SS and Wehrmacht soldiers with about $500,000 per year—and that's in 1951 dollars—and they *still* could credibly claim that they did not know what their own contract agents were up to. This, moreover, was inside West Germany, where U.S. officials enjoyed enormous influence within the government, where telephones could be tapped with impunity, and where U.S. agents moved without restraint. This "command breakdown" is a clear indication of just how little real control U.S. intelligence had over many of its far-flung paramilitary operations and how carelessly it was willing to spend money.

The question of U.S. use of former Nazi collaborators in assassinations is important, and not just because of the obvious damage that the Technical Service imbroglio did to U.S. relations with Germany's influential Social Democrats. Few subjects are more deeply clothed in mystery than this one, and the evidence concerning how U.S. assassination operations worked during the cold war and who was responsible for them is inevitably scattered and fragmentary. All that can be said with certainty is that such murders did take place and that in some cases former Nazi collaborators were instrumental in carrying them out.

To put the case most bluntly, many American clandestine warfare specialists believed that the most "productive"—and least compromising—method of killing foreign officials was to underwrite the discontent of indigenous groups and let *them* take the risks.[15] American intelligence agencies' use of this technique appears to have originated in operations during World War II, when the OSS supplied thousands of cheap pistols to partisans in France and Yugoslavia specifically for assassination of collaborators and German officials. (According to Pentagon records,[16] the OSS also air-dropped these weapons in areas where there were no significant rebel forces so that the Nazis, upon finding the guns, would tighten the screws on local populations and thereby produce new anti-Nazi partisans.)

The concepts of maintaining "plausible deniability" for the actual murder and of the expendability of the killers themselves are a key to understanding U.S. assassination techniques. In most cases, it appears to have been neither necessary nor practical for U.S. intelligence officers to give precise instructions for murder. Instead, the OPC gave directions to commit assassinations to guerrilla movements in the same simple, sweeping terms that had been used in wartime Yugoslavia. U.S. intelligence encouraged insurgents to "eliminat[e] the command and other dangerous personnel of the MVD and the MGB [the Soviet secret police]," as the psychological warfare appendix to a Pentagon war plan put it in 1948. Other assigned tasks under the Halfmoon war plan, as it was known, included "organiz[ing] for the destruction of industry, communications and other factors in Soviet war-making capacity"; "engag[ing] in sabotage wherever and whenever it disrupts enemy action"; and "creat[ing] panic and terror."[17]

Several organizations of former Nazi collaborators were ready to undertake such slayings on a major scale. Covert operations chief Wisner estimated in 1951 that some 35,000 Soviet police troops and Communist party cadres had been eliminated by guerrillas connected with the Nazi collaborationist OUN/UPA in the Ukraine since the end of the war,[18] and that does not include casualties from other insurgencies in Lithuania and the Muslim regions of the USSR that were also receiving aid from the United States and Britain.

These shotgun-style killings and guerrilla actions account for the large majority of murders carried out with U.S. assistance in Europe during the cold war. It is inappropriate, of course, to lay responsibility for all these deaths at the feet of the CIA. The rebellions against Soviet rule were not initiated by the agency; they exploded inside the country out of discontents that were bound to give rise to violent resistance. Still, it is clear that CIA aid sustained such rebellions longer and made them more deadly to all concerned than they might otherwise have been. Moreover, these widespread shotgun-style slayings served as cover for a smaller number of specific individual assassinations that appear to have been directly ordered by U.S. intelligence officers.

Former Nazi collaborators made excellent executioners in such instances, because of both their wartime training and the fact that the U.S. government could plausibly deny any knowledge of their activities. Suspected double agents were the most common targets for execution. "In the international clandestine operations business, it was part of the code that *the one and only remedy for the un-*

frocked double agent was to kill him" (emphasis added), the CIA's director of operations planning during the Truman administration testified before Congress in 1976, "and all double agents knew that. That was part of the occupational hazard of the job." The former director, whom the government declines to identify, also claimed, however, that he didn't recall any executions of double agents actually occurring during his tenure there.[19] It is understandable that he might fail to remember any executions; for admitting a role in such killings could well lead to arrest and prosecution for conspiracy to commit murder in Europe, if not in the United States itself.*

"We kept personnel at several air bases around the world for these types of missions," says Colonel Prouty, who was responsible for U.S. Air Force air support of CIA missions overseas, including the delivery of agents to their targets and subsequent evacuation measures. "Some of these guys were the best commercial hit men you have ever heard of. [They were] mechanics, killers. They were Ukrainians, mainly, and Eastern Europeans, Greeks, and some Scotsmen. I don't know how the Scotsmen got in there, but there they were. None of them were American citizens." Prouty asserts that teams of such "mechanics" were used in cross-border infiltrations, in highly dangerous rescues of American agents inside the USSR and China, and in special murders. According to Prouty, there was no clear policy concerning the use of killing. "It was an ad hoc event, and it [the actual assassination] was done by third parties. If it had to be done in Yugoslavia, for example, it was set up with exile Yugoslavians or the [émigré] Polish groups. The [U.S.]

---

*Unfrocked double agents were also tortured—there is no other word for it—in so-called terminal medical experiments sponsored by the army, navy, and CIA. These tests fed massive quantities of convulsant and psychedelic drugs to foreign prisoners in an attempt to make them talk, according to CIA records obtained under the Freedom of Information Act by author John Marks. The CIA also explored use of psychosurgery and repeated electric shocks directly into the brain.

Then CIA Director Richard Helms ordered the destruction of all records of these "experiments" in the midst of Watergate and congressional investigations that threatened to bring to light the agency's practices in this field. A cache of papers that he accidentally missed was found some years later, however, and the agency has since been forced to make public sanitized versions of some of those records. It is now known that similar agency tests with LSD led to the suicide of an army employee, Frank Olson, and are alleged to have permanently damaged a group of unsuspecting psychiatric patients at a Canadian clinic whose director was working under CIA contract. The agency unit that administered this program was the same Directorate of Scientific Research that developed the exotic poisons used in attempted assassinations of Fidel Castro and Patrice Lumumba.

Army had by far the best assets" for this type of thing, he states, but "on the operational level there was good cooperation with the air force, CIA, and army." Many of the Eastern Europeans, he says, were Nazi collaborators during the war.[20]

Several such killings did take place during the late 1940s under Operations Hagberry and Lithia, both of which were approved at senior levels of the Pentagon. These two instances, furthermore, must be considered only the documented examples of a more widespread practice. Hagberry required, according to army records, the "liquidation of the Chikalov Ring, a possible Soviet intelligence net operating within the U.S. zone of Germany." And Lithia, which began under army auspices in November 1947, authorized "liquidation in [the] United States Zone [of Germany] of the Kundermann Ring, a large scale Czechoslovakian intelligence net."[21] Army intelligence believed that the Chikalov Ring and the Kundermann organization had managed to plant double agents in certain émigré espionage networks that were being jointly managed by the United States and Britain under still another code-named project, Operation Rusty, and it is those agents who were marked for "liquidation." Army spokesmen today claim with shrugs of their shoulders that all further files concerning Hagberry and Lithia have simply disappeared. No further information is available, they say, and there is no indication of who withdrew the Hagberry and Lithia files or when they vanished.

Other people were murdered gangland-style during Operation Ohio, according to published reports in the United States.[22] Ohio employed a squad of Ukrainian ex-Nazis to carry out at least twenty murders in a displaced persons camp at Mittenwald, south of Munich. The Army CIC and later the CIA are reported to have financed this squad for strong-arm work against double agents, Soviet spies, and similar undesirables. The fragmentary evidence still available suggests that most of the squad's victims were double agents whose deaths—when they became public at all—were attributed to factional violence among rival right-wing Ukrainian émigré groups.

"We were just out of World War Two, and we were using those [wartime] tactics," says Franklin Lindsay, the former CIA/OPC paramilitary expert. "In my case, I had operated only in wartime conditions. Given the feeling that we were very near war at that time, one tended to operate in the same way as in wartime."[23]

Lindsay, however, rejects the term *assassination* as a description of CIA/OPC practice during his tenure there.*

The records of Operation Bloodstone add an important new piece of information to one of the most explosive public issues of today: the role of the U.S. government—specifically the CIA—in assassinations and attempted assassinations of foreign officials. According to a 1976 Senate investigation, a key official of Operation Bloodstone is the OPC officer who was specifically delegated responsibility for planning the agency's assassinations, kidnappings, and similar "wet work."[24]

Colonel Boris Pash, one of the most extraordinary and least known characters in American intelligence history, completes the circle of U.S. agents, Nazi collaborators, and "mechanics" involved in these highly sensitive affairs. Pash is not a Nazi, nor is there any evidence that he is sympathetic to Nazis. But his work for U.S. intelligence agencies places him in the critical office given the responsibility for planning postwar assassination operations.

Pash, now in his eighties, looks much like a bespectacled retired high school teacher. That's not surprising. He taught gym at Hollywood High School for a decade prior to World War II. He is modest—even shy, some might say—with a gravelly voice and a cautious manner born of a lifetime of keeping secrets. Politically Pash remains loyal to the legacy of General Douglas MacArthur, with whom he served in occupied Japan. Colonel Pash is one of the few remaining originals of U.S. intelligence, and his experience in "fighting the Communists" goes back to the 1917 Russian Revolution. He was in Moscow and Eastern Europe in those days with his father, a missionary of Russian extraction, and the young Pash spent much of the Soviet civil war working on the side of the White armies, then with czarist refugees who had fled their country. In the 1920s Pash signed on as a reserve officer with the U.S. military intelligence service, and he maintained the affiliation throughout his years at Hollywood High. He was called to active duty in the first

---

*The USSR, too, made substantial use of assassination as a political tool during the cold war. To name only one example, KGB agent Bogdan Stashinsky murdered émigré OUN leaders Lev Rebet (in October 1957) and Stepan Bandera (in October 1959) with poisonous chemical gas guns. Soviet president Kliment Y. Voroshilov awarded Stashinsky the Red Banner Combat Order for his efforts.

Stashinsky defected to the West after the Bandera murder, bringing with him the Voroshilov award and the chemical pistol as proof of the deed. The assassin, interestingly enough, claimed he had been recruited by the Soviet security police on the basis of threats against family members who had once collaborated with the Nazis.

days of the Second World War, played a role in the internment of Japanese civilians in California, and was soon assigned as chief counterintelligence officer on the Manhattan Project, the supersecret U.S. effort to develop the atomic bomb. (More than a decade later it was Colonel Pash's testimony that helped seal the fate of scientist Robert Oppenheimer in the well-known 1954 security case.) Before the war was out, it will be recalled, Colonel Pash led the series of celebrated special operations known as the Alsos Mission that were designed to capture the best atomic and chemical warfare experts that the Nazis had to offer.[25]

After the war Colonel Pash served as the army's representative on Bloodstone in the spring of 1948, when the tasks of that project, including recruiting defectors, smuggling refugees out from behind the Iron Curtain, and assassinations, were established. Bloodstone's "special operations," as defined by the Pentagon, could "include clandestine warfare, subversion, sabotage and . . . assassination," according to the 1948 Joint Chiefs of Staff records.[26] In March 1949, Pash was assigned by the army to the OPC division of the CIA. There, according to State Department records, his responsibilities included many of the functions originally approved under the Bloodstone program.

At the CIA Boris Pash became an administrator and organizer, as distinct from a field operative. His five-man CIA unit, known as PB/7, was given a written charter that read in part that "PB/7 will be responsible for assassinations, kidnapping, and such other functions as from time to time may be given it . . . by higher authority."[27] Pash's fluency in Russian, his skill in dealing with Bloodstone émigrés, and his solid connections in anti-Communist exile circles were valuable assets in that job. Indeed, those qualifications—along with his sterling record as a counterintelligence officer—may well have been what led to his selection as PB/7 chief.

As with so many other aspects of the history of U.S. intelligence, the evidence here must be carefully sifted. Pash himself denies involvement in the Bloodstone program, asserting that he has "no recollection" of Bloodstone or of "anything like that."[28] However, documents establishing his participation in Bloodstone and PB/7 are now a matter of public record.[29]

Pash did testify before Congress in 1976 that his responsibilities at the CIA included planning for defections from Communist countries, facilitating the escape of prominent political refugees, and disseminating anti-Communist propaganda behind the Iron Curtain—all of which were clearly Bloodstone activities. Pash's supervisor at the CIA (who is not identified in the hearing record) offered further details concerning some of the less savory aspects of émigré operations during the 1940s that coincide with what is known of Bloodstone. Pash's PB/7, the supervisor said, was responsible for "kidnapping personages from behind the Iron Curtain . . . [including] kidnapping people whose interests were inimicable to ours."[30]

Much of the documentary evidence concerning what PB/7 did during the first years of the CIA has disappeared, leaving both Congress and the general public with many unanswered questions concerning U.S. operations among émigrés during the cold war. The CIA claimed in 1976 that it had "no record of documents which deal with this aspect [i.e., assassinations] of Pash's unit" and that even the office's charter was missing. Colonel Pash himself insisted in congressional testimony that he did not "believe" that he had any involvement in or responsibility for planning or conducting assassinations. He also testified that he had no recollection of the language of the charter of PB/7, the CIA office of which he had been in charge.[31]

Despite the mysterious disappearance of the PB/7 records while in the hands of the CIA, the chain of circumstantial evidence concerning some Bloodstone émigrés' roles in paramilitary, kidnapping, and assassination operations abroad is too strong to be easily dismissed. First, there is the incriminating Pentagon document, quoted above, which indicates that paramilitary operations, assassinations, and kidnappings were an explicit mission of the Bloodstone program from its beginning.

Secondly, at least one key Bloodstone official, Boris Pash, was active in Bloodstone's early phases in mid-1948, then became chief of the OPC office responsible for planning paramilitary operations, assassinations, and kidnappings at about the time that control of "politico-psychological" and paramilitary operations was passed from the Bloodstone committee to the OPC.

Thirdly, at least some Bloodstone émigrés with backgrounds as Nazi collaborators—former Albanian Minister of Justice Hasan Dosti, for example—went on to become deeply involved in clandestine operations that did indeed involve paramilitary operations, murders, and unconsummated plans for assassinations, such as the 1949 and 1950 secret raids on Albania designed to overthrow the government. (Dosti did not participate in the actual field operations. But the organization he led, the Committee for a Free Albania, served as a "private" cover for the Albanian guerrillas, who were, in fact, organized and financed by the OPC.)

Fourthly—and perhaps coincidentally—certain Soviet spies, double agents, and "people whose interests were inimicable" to those of the CIA were marked for death by the agency. Pash's immediate superiors in the OPC acknowledge that the "one and only remedy" for Communist double agents was to murder them. According to published reports in the United States,[32] persons accused of being Soviet or East bloc agents were in fact killed during this period by former Nazi collaborators at Mittenwald and in other displaced persons camps, though under mysterious circumstances that have never been clearly traced back to the OPC.

In the opinion of the author, the early Bloodstone operations played a significant role in laying the groundwork for what one Senate investigator later called "a procedure [within the CIA] which, although not spelled out in so many words, was generally understood and served as the basis to plan or otherwise contemplate political assassination."[33] The killings of minor double agents in German DP camps were murders and deserve to be investigated as such. More significant, however, is what these otherwise obscure crimes appear to have foreshadowed: Before the decade of the 1950s was out, the CIA is known to have established mechanisms for using "deniable" assets and émigrés for the execution of heads of state and other international leaders. These later killings, which are arguably the most serious blunders ever made by the CIA, have created blowback problems on an international scale and have had a significant and generally negative effect on the lives of millions of people.

CHAPTER TWELVE

"Any Bastard as Long as He's Anti-Communist"

The more deeply American agencies became involved in relations with the exile groups, the more rapidly myths grew up around those organizations concerning what they had actually done during the war. The common theme of those stories is the tragic heroism of the defectors from the Ukraine, the Baltic states, and Eastern Europe who chose to fight Stalin by joining the Nazis. That proposition was (and is) often accompanied by the assertion that damaging statements about these émigrés are nothing more than Soviet propaganda.

The standard version of that saga and the political use to which it was put during the cold war is perhaps best illustrated by a 1949 *Life* magazine article by noted journalist and psychological warfare expert Wallace Carroll, who argued that during the war "the Germans had millions of eager accomplices in Russia . . . [who] welcomed them as liberators and offered their cooperation." Unfortunately the Nazis let "this chance slip through their hands" because of Hitler's racial policy and the German government's refusal to implement fully a political warfare program when the time was ripe. Hans Heinrich Herwarth and Ernst Köstring's political warfare tactics, when attempted, were "a phenomenal success," according to Carroll. "There was no Partisan movement in their area . . . [and] no sabotage, and the peasants fulfilled the German requisitions of farm products on schedule." The attribution of atrocities to these troops, as well as the numerous pro-Nazi and anti-Semitic periodicals published by the Vlasov organization during the war, were "forgeries [which] Soviet propagandists shrewdly attributed to Vlasov's forces." These "facts," Carroll writes, had been "known for a long time to the Russian experts of the State Department and to a small number of American officers" and were now a "lesson which we must learn without delay."[1] Carroll's 1949 conclusion was, in part, that America needed to embrace the former Nazi collaborators as a central tactic in a comprehensive strategy of political warfare against the Soviets.

The fact that Carroll was a psychological warfare consultant to the U.S. Army at the time he penned this narrative was acknowledged by *Life*'s editors. Indeed, they even included a special introduction that billed Carroll's work for the army as a "perceptive and fresh standpoint from which to re-examine U.S. strategic planning."[2]

The 1949 publication of Carroll's article marked a new stage in the development of U.S. political warfare tactics and in the blowback effect that these operations were beginning to have at home. Up until then every effort had been made to keep secret the increasingly warm relations between U.S. intelligence agencies and émigrés who had once collaborated with the Nazis. The U.S. press had frequently presented heroic accounts of anti-Communist and anti-Nazi émigrés, such as deposed Hungarian leader Ferenc Nagy or Polish anti-Nazi underground chief Stefan Korbonski, who had fled from Eastern Europe after the Soviet occupation of the region. Carroll's article took this publicity an important step further: Nazi collaborators could be considered heroes of a sort, too, as long as they had fought against Stalin. Though not stated directly, the implication of Carroll's thesis was that the United States should encourage wide participation of Vlasov Army and Eastern Waffen SS veterans in U.S.-sponsored anti-Communist coalitions and political warfare projects.

Wallace Carroll was certainly not the first American to advocate these ideas. George Kennan, Charles Thayer, and other national security experts had been promoting them inside the government for several years by the time his article was published. The prominent endorsement given to these theories by the mass circulation *Life* magazine, however, is an indication of the degree to which revisionist theories on the character of the Nazis' eastern legions were already entering the mainstream of American political thought.

Noted American scholars picked up much of the same theme during the intense cold war years of the late 1940s and early 1950s. This trend can be seen even in the work of careful scholars such as Alexander Dallin, who has produced some of the most sophisticated analyses of Soviet affairs available. During the cold war years he prepared a massive study titled *German Rule in Russia* with the cooperation of U.S. intelligence agencies. This work has been considered the classic presentation of the Nazis' use of collaborators in the East practically from the day it was published, yet it mentions the role of Nazi collaborators in crimes against humanity and the Holocaust only in passing. Dallin acknowledges that this was an important oversight. Were he to write the text today, he has commented, he would "dwell at greater length on the 'Final Solution' to the Jewish Question, not only because it sealed the fate of substantial numbers of Soviet citizens but more generally because it was part of the context in which decisions relating to the 'East' were being made in Nazi Germany."[3] Overall, the role of the German political warfare group and their collaborators in crimes against humanity was generally either denounced as Soviet propaganda (as by Carroll) or largely passed over (Dallin). The German political warriors themselves, who produced a flood of memoirs and histories after the war blaming Hitler for the German defeat, consistently denied any knowledge of the atrocities of the war.

A review of the more popular histories of the war published in the West during those years, with a few lonely exceptions, leaves the distinct impression that the savageries of the Holocaust were strictly the SS's responsibility, and not all of the SS at that. The defector troops of World War II—the Russian Vlasov Army, the Ukrainian OUN/UPA, even the nazified SS volunteers from Latvia and other Baltic countries—were frequently portrayed as anti-Communist patriots despite their German uniforms. The SS and Wehrmacht officers who commanded them (despite their Nazi party memberships and their steady advances up the career ladder in the German government) were really anti-Nazis or even just plain democrats who had somehow wound up in uniform through an unfortunate quirk of fate—or so the story went.

This bogus history is important because it became, as Carroll's article illustrates, the basic cover story for the Nazi utilization programs of the U.S. government as well as for many of the individual Germans and Eastern European defectors employed in these programs. Like any good propaganda, there is some truth to the version of events presented by those authors. But a review of the evidence presented at war crimes trials in Nuremberg, from captured war records and interrogation of POWs, would lead most people to quite a different conclusion concerning the role of the Nazis' political warfare specialists in the Holocaust and about the actual character of some of the men who were enlisted by the United States after the war.

The postwar myths of anti-Stalin, anti-Hitler nationalism among the Nazis' armies of defectors had a distinct utilitarian value for the American government during the cold war. These stories permitted more or less satisfying answers to nagging questions concerning the character of certain émigré political organizations whose American sponsorship could not always be successfully disguised. Rewriting the history of the Vlasov Army and other defector troops into a tale of idealistic (though tragic) opposition to Stalin made it easier for U.S. policymakers and intelligence officers to avoid coming to grips with the fact that there were war criminals among America's new recruits.

But those U.S. officers who were sufficiently honest with themselves—and sufficiently well informed about covert CIA and military intelligence operations—did know that former Nazis and collaborators were at the heart of many American clandestine warfare efforts of the period.

"We knew what we were doing," says Harry Rositzke, the CIA's former head of secret operations inside the USSR. "It was a visceral business of using any bastard as long as he was anti-Communist . . . [and] the eagerness or desire to enlist collaborators meant that sure, you didn't look at their credentials too closely."[4]

Franklin Lindsay, who headed CIA paramilitary and guerrilla operations in Eastern Europe in the early 1950s, also acknowledges that a substantial number of the émigrés trained and financed by the CIA during those years had been Nazi collaborators. "Was it right?" he asked during an interview with the author. "That depends on your time horizon. We thought war could be six months away. You have to remember that in those days even men such as George Kennan believed that there was a fifty-fifty chance of war with the Soviets within six months. We did a lot of things in the short term that might not look wise from a long-term point of view. . . . We were under tremendous pressure," he continued, "to do something, do anything to prepare for war."[5]

An important example of these preparations for an all-out war with the USSR was the U.S. role in a guerrilla war that was then simmering in the Ukraine, an ethnically distinct region near the present Soviet-Polish border. Anti-Communist guerrillas led by the Ukrainian nationalist organization OUN were particularly strong in the western Ukraine, which is also known as Galicia.

The western Ukraine is a long-disputed territory that has changed hands among the Russians, Germans, Poles, and—briefly— the Ukrainians themselves at least a dozen times over the last few centuries. Most of the region had been controlled by Poland between World Wars I and II, but the Soviets claimed it as their own following the Russian invasion of eastern Poland under the 1939 Hitler-Stalin pact. The Nazis occupied the area for most of the war; but once the conflict was over, the Soviets moved the borders of the USSR westward into Poland, and the Galician territory was again abruptly incorporated into the USSR itself.

That development seriously threatened wealthy peasants, landlords, and church leaders in the region, for obvious reasons. At the same time much of the ethnic Ukrainian population resented the authority of the new Russian-dominated power structure. These forces combined to provide a narrow but real base of support for a continuing rebellion led by the extreme-right-wing Organization of Ukrainian Nationalists (OUN) and its militia force, UPA, which had frequently collaborated with the Nazis during the German occupation. The small circle of U.S. policymakers responsible for guidance of U.S. clandestine operations during the late 1940s became fascinated by the scope of this postwar Ukrainian rebellion. Here, at last, it seemed, was a movement that was really standing up to the Russians.

The relationship between the Ukrainian nationalists and the Nazis had been complex, and most postwar commentators have chosen to emphasize the aspect that best suits their own point of view. To Soviet commentators, the OUN and the UPA were Nazi collaborators, period.[6] Many Western commentators, on the other hand, contend that they were instead a "third force" during World War II that had actually favored democracy, national independence, and other Western-style values.[7] Both these positions obscure the truth.

The roots of the OUN/UPA may be traced to the militantly anti-Communist and nationalist Ukrainian underground founded by Colonel Eugen Konovalets in the 1920s, when much of the region was under the Polish flag. Its program consisted primarily of a demand for independence for the Ukraine, frequently supplemented by a virulent anti-Russian and anti-Semitic racism. Although certainly opposed to Stalinism, the group was itself totalitarian and Fascist in character, with strong links to the German intelligence service of Admiral Wilhelm Canaris.[8]

OUN activists had been in the business of assassination and terror since the earliest days of the group and were responsible for the 1934 murder of Polish Interior Minister General Bronislav Pieracki, among others. The League of Nations had publicly condemned the OUN as a terrorist syndicate for organizing that killing, and Polish courts had handed down death sentences (later commuted to life imprisonment) to OUN leaders Mykola Lebed and Stepan Bandera for their roles in that crime. Both men were freed, however, in the confusion that followed the German and Soviet invasions of Poland in 1939. Once out of prison, Lebed entered a Gestapo police school near Krakow, while Bandera organized OUN sympathizers into armed squadrons under an Abwehr program code-named *Nachtigall,*[9] or Nightingale.

The Nazis poured money and arms into the OUN during the two years leading up to the Germans' 1941 invasion of the USSR. Specially trained OUN police troops traveled with the German forces during the opening months of the invasion, providing intelligence, creating local quisling administrations in areas under Nazi occupation, and playing an active role in the roundups and murders of Jews. Captured German records make clear that the Nazis considered the OUN their pawn.

But the OUN itself had bigger ambitions. It wished to be the government of the Ukraine, which it envisioned as an ally of Germany, equal in status to Hungary or Romania. This was to be an independent Fascist country whose program included, as the OUN's chief political officer Wolodymyr Stachiw wrote to Adolf Hitler in the midst of the German invasion, the "consolidation of the new ethnic order in Eastern Europe [*völkische Neuordnung in Osteuropa*]" and the "destruction of the seditious Jewish-Bolshevist influence." Writing directly on behalf of the OUN chief Stepan

Bandera, Stachliw appealed to Hitler (the "champion of the ethnic principle," in Stachiw's words) to "support our ethnic struggle [*völkischen Kampf*]."[10]

But Hitler had no intention of accepting an alliance of equals with persons he considered Slavic "subhumans." He double-crossed and arrested a number of OUN leaders who insisted on more autonomy than he was willing to give. At this point a still more complicated relationship between the Nazis and the OUN emerged. OUN activists continued to play major roles in local quisling governments and in Nazi-sponsored police and militia groups, although the OUN organization as such was banned. These German-sponsored police and militia formations, in turn, were deeply involved in thousands of instances of mass murders of Jews and of families suspected of aiding Red Army partisans. Meanwhile, the then underground OUN leadership organized an anti-Communist guerrilla force known as the Ukrainska Povstancha Armia (Ukrainian Insurgent Army), or UPA, in order to continue to pursue its plan for an independent Ukraine. The UPA, according to its own account, did much of its recruiting among the genocidal Nazi-sponsored police groups, on the theory that those already armed and trained men would make the best soldiers. While the UPA insurgents did occasionally clash with the Germans, their true target was the Red Army, which was viewed as the greater danger to Ukrainian independence.[11]

Late in the war the Germans became sufficiently desperate that they reestablished a more or less formal "alliance" with a quisling Ukrainian national committee headed by Pavlo Shandruk, an aging Ukrainian-Polish general who had been a war hero during World War I.[12] This propaganda gesture was accompanied by accelerated German recruitment of Ukrainians from the police groups into the Waffen SS, and by increased cooperation with the underground OUN/UPA leadership in a secret program that the SS-designated Operation *Sonnenblume* (Sunflower). According to U.S. interrogations of SS RSHA Amt VI clandestine operations chief Otto Skorzeny and his adjutant Karl Radl, Amt VI organized *Sonnenblume* in 1944 to coordinate German and OUN efforts during the Nazis' retreat from Russia.[13]

Thousands of tons of arms, ammunition, and other war matériel abandoned by the Nazis were consigned to underground OUN-led troops, Skorzeny told the Americans. The deal proved to be an astute investment for the Germans. The OUN/UPA succeeded in tying down some 200,000 Red Army troops and killing more than

7,000 Soviet officers[14] during the Wehrmacht's disordered flight across Europe during 1944 and 1945.

The case of the OUN illustrates the complexity of the real-world relationships between Berlin and its collaborators on the eastern front. The OUN was not a puppet of the Germans in the same sense that the Vlasov Army was, but it did knowingly ally itself with the Nazis whenever it could. Whatever its conflicts with the Nazis may have been, the OUN's own role in anti-Semitic pogroms—such as the mass murders in Lvov in 1941—and in the Lidice-style exterminations of entire villages accused of cooperating with Soviet partisans has been well established. Many OUN members committed serious crimes during the war, and the primary victims of their excesses were their own countrymen.

As the Germans were driven out of the Ukraine in 1944, many OUN members who had served the Nazis in local militias, police departments, and execution squads fled with them. At least 40,000 other OUN-led partisans, however, retreated to the craggy Carpathian Mountains, where they hid out, waiting for the Red Army front to pass. It was this group that served as the backbone of the Ukrainian rebellion that fascinated the American security experts during the late 1940s.

The convicted assassin Mykola Lebed emerged after the war as one of the United States' most important agents inside the OUN/UPA. His case is of interest here, because it illustrates the manner in which the CIA recruited Nazi collaborators after the war and how it smuggled a number of the top leaders of the OUN/UPA into the United States.

As noted above, Lebed entered the Gestapo's training school in Krakow in 1939. The Yad Vashem archives in Jerusalem contain a detailed description of Lebed's activities at that center that was provided by Mykyta Kosakivs'kyy, a former OUN functionary who worked under Lebed's command at Krakow but who broke with him after the war. As Kosakivs'kyy tells it, Lebed personally led the torture and murder of captured Jews at Krakow as a means of "hardening" his men against bloodshed.[15] (Lebed himself acknowledges that he was active in the Gestapo center but denies he took part in torture or murder.)

According to U.S. Army intelligence records obtained through the Freedom of Information Act, the OUN appointed Lebed "Home Secretary and Police Minister" in the Nazi quisling government in Lvov, the temporary capital of the Ukraine during the German invasion in 1941.[16] There OUN police and militia made a horrifying discovery in the first days of the invasion. The retreating Soviet secret police, they learned, had massacred more than 2,000 unarmed Ukrainian nationalist prisoners in cold blood in Lvov jails, then sealed up the rotting corpses in underground chambers while the NKVD agents made their escape.

The Soviets, for their part, have long claimed that the murders of the nationalists in Lvov were actually committed by the Nazis. Eyewitness testimony, however, refutes that contention. Either way, the atrocity provided a convenient pretext for an OUN-led pogrom against local Jews, who were accused of aiding the Soviets during the arrests of Ukrainians prior to the Nazi invasion. Ukrainian nationalist propaganda whipped the population into a fury against Jews and anyone suspected of Communist sympathies. Police and militia forces presumably under the command of the Police Minister, Mykola Lebed, remained busy day and night with mass roundups of unarmed men and women, public hangings, beatings, and other abuse. Lvov's Jews were arrested, tortured, and shot in large numbers by both OUN troops and Nazi *Einsatzkommando* murder squads. "Long Live Adolf Hitler and [OUN leader] Stepan Bandera!" was among the most popular slogans, according to eyewitnesses. "Death to the Jews and the Communists!"[17]

The killings of these people during these first weeks after the German invasion must have seemed almost carnivallike to some; they were a drunken orgy of violence and a celebration of newly seized power. Resistance was crushed through open terror. OUN police and militiamen raped Polish and Jewish women with impunity; Polish professors were rounded up, beaten, then executed; and Ukrainian nationalist extremists assisted in mass executions of Jews near the gasworks on the outskirts of town. At least 7,000 unarmed Jewish men and women were rounded up and executed in the weeks that followed, according to Nazi *Einsatzgruppen* reports, and this number does not include those who were shot or beaten to death during civilian pogroms.*[18]

---

*Lebed's version of these events is considerably different. In a series of interviews with the author Lebed contended that he arrived in Lvov on July 3, several days after the German invasion. He was not police minister, he says, but instead was "responsible to help transfer members of our organization further east, in march groups." He acknowledges that he was "number three" in the Ukrainian government but denies that he had any official title. He attributes any slayings of Jews that took place during that period to the Soviet NKVD and says that the hangings of Polish intellectuals was the work of the German SD, not Ukrainian

But these "exhilarating days," as they were later described in OUN publications, were soon over. The nationalist government was double-crossed and disbanded by the Germans as soon as its propaganda value for illustrating the supposed "warm welcome" enjoyed by Wehrmacht troops in their invasion of the USSR had passed. Several OUN leaders, including Stetsko and Bandera, were placed under house arrest. One kingpin the Nazis missed, however, was the OUN's ambitious secret police chief, Mykola Lebed.

U.S. Army intelligence reports[19] that Lebed organized the police and militia from the underground, where he forged them into the Slushba Bespiekie (SB), the elite terror arm of the Ukrainian nationalist forces. The specialty of Lebed's SB teams was the hunting down of Red partisan leaders, torture, and interrogation, as well as gathering military intelligence for barter with the Germans. A number of right-wing Ukrainian groups have also accused the SB of murdering competing nationalist leaders who declined to join "united fronts" organized by Lebed and his colleagues—a perception that led to considerable bitterness about Lebed among rival Ukrainian nationalist factions after the war. By 1944 the OUN's SB had proved its effectiveness as an intelligence agency equal to those of both the Nazis and the Soviets. Its experience with the use of assassination as a political tool, in particular, was second to none.

Lebed fled from the Ukraine shortly after the Nazis had left. In early 1945 he escaped to Rome, where he established himself as "foreign minister" of the Supreme Ukrainian Liberation Council, an anti-Communist united front organization dominated by OUN chieftains. He brought with him a treasure of great value: records of the Liberation Council and the SB, including lists of nationalist and Communist agents still in the Ukraine, names of strong-arm specialists, and enough compromising information on personalities of the Ukrainian movement to give whoever enlisted his help a handle on thousands of prominent exiles.

---

nationalists. He also flatly denies that he was ever a leader of the SB, the OUN's secret intelligence organization. "Even the KGB, who often accuse me of all kinds of 'crimes,' " Lebed says, "state that the leader of the SB was Mykola Arsenych, who committed suicide when he was finally surrounded by KGB forces so that he would not fall into their hands alive."

Lebed's assertions on this last point contradict those in contemporary U.S. Army intelligence records, which state that Lebed "became chief of the SB, which is the intelligence organization" and that, according to a second U.S. study, he "organized a strong, underground executive corps of SB security service, which by terrorist methods kept under control the Bandera party [the OUN], as well as later [its army, the] UPA."

Lebed immediately began public and private appeals on behalf of the Ukrainian guerrillas still behind Soviet lines. At first the Americans spurned him. Army CIC reports on Lebed dating from 1945 and 1946 state claims that the nationalist leader was "a well known sadist and collaborator of the Germans,"[20] accuse him of several murders, and assert that he looted money from nationalist organizations.

Sometime during the spring or summer of 1947, however, Lebed made an offer to U.S. Army intelligence that it failed to resist: exchange of his experience and his file collection for the patronage and protection of the U.S. government. The United States "wanted to know what Russia, what the Soviet Union was," Lebed acknowledged in an interview with the author. "They wanted to know what was the [Soviet secret police] MVD, who was who and how things fit together. That was why they wanted me."[21]

A certain Captain Hale of the Rome U.S. Army Counterintelligence Corps office notified CIC headquarters in Munich and recommended that the U.S. Army smuggle the Ukrainian out of Rome and into Germany, where he could be put to better use by American agencies. Munich CIC HQ was pleased with the plan, and the operation was carried out smoothly later that year. Captain Hale—and everyone else involved in the recruitment and transfer of Mykola Lebed—were given letters of commendation. Lebed's new handlers in Munich, it is worth noting, were the same group of American CIC agents who were at that time running Klaus Barbie and Emil Augsburg's network of fugitive SS men.

Lebed's relationship with the CIC in Munich worked well. By mid-1948 his "Liberation Council" was receiving a substantial income from American sources, probably through army intelligence. His handlers liked him; his "political standpoint is positive," reported the CIC in a study of personalities recommended for a Ukrainian government in exile—"i.e., reliable from the point of view of the Western Powers."[22]

But Lebed's life in Germany was fraught with danger. His pseudonym, "Mykola Ruban," was becoming well known in exile circles. Soviet and Polish secret police agents had a blood debt to settle with him, and their attempts to capture him and ship him back to the USSR on war crimes charges were only the edge of a much larger tempest that was headed toward Lebed. Perhaps worst of all, the OUN had undergone another factional split during the summer of 1948, and some of his erstwhile comrades, men who knew his habits, hideouts, and contacts, were now after him as well. His new enemies—a rival OUN faction under Stepan Bandera that included a number of SB men—had a well-deserved reputation for murdering their opponents.

The CIA saved Lebed. Fortunately for him, the agency's OPC division had committed itself to building governments-in-exile for Eastern Europe, and the agency's authority within the American national security complex was on the rise. An innocuous piece of agency-sponsored legislation was winding its way through the U.S. Congress just as Lebed's personal crisis took hold. Most provisions of the proposed new law were routine housekeeping; they authorized the CIA director to commission an official seal for the CIA, for example, and permitted the agency to pay "association and library dues" on behalf of overseas agents.

The 1949 law also contained a provision that eventually rescued Mykola Lebed. It reads: "Whenever the Director [of the CIA], the Attorney General and the Commissioner of Immigration shall determine that the entry of a particular alien into the United States . . . is in the interests of national security or essential to the furtherance of the national intelligence mission, such alien and his immediate family shall be given entry to the United States . . . *without regard to their inadmissibility under their immigration or any other laws and regulations. . . .* [emphasis added]."[23] Up to 100 persons per year, plus their families, could be brought into the United States under this statute with no questions asked.*

Since 1949 nearly everything about this so-called 100 Persons Act has been kept strictly secret by the government. Both the Office of the Attorney General and the commissioner of immigration have claimed—in reply to Freedom of Information Act requests filed by the author—that they have no records whatsoever concerning their activities under the act for any time during the last thirty-five years.[24] The CIA, for its part, defied a congressional committee's request for an accounting—even a secret accounting—of the

---

*Buried in the text of the CIA-sponsored law, and mentioned almost in passing, was legal authorization for the CIA to ignore public accountability for its budget, its personnel policy, or its procurement practices. That one-sentence-long subsection exempted the agency from complying with any *other* law that might disclose "intelligence sources and methods."

A second phrase directs the CIA to "perform such other functions and duties . . . as the National Security Council may from time to time direct." Agency lawyers have long interpreted that passage to mean that secret orders from the NSC or the president carry greater weight than any "ordinary" law passed by Congress. These two brief sections of the law have proved to be the legal foundation upon which most of the modern CIA has been built.

agency's activity under this law. A few things are known, however, as a result of leaks over the years. One is that Gustav Hilger, the former Nazi Foreign Office expert who had entered the country under Operation Bloodstone, became one of the first beneficiaries of the act. Hilger was rewarded for his services with a permanent resident alien status in the United States.

Despite all the secrecy, it is clear that the intent of Congress was in part to limit the CIA's importation of questionable aliens, at the same time giving the agency a legal means of handling the tricky sorts of immigration cases that an espionage agency inevitably faces. Congress put a cap—100 persons per year, plus families—on the number of people the CIA could legally import who would otherwise be excluded from entering the United States. The law also established that senior government officials—namely, the director of the CIA, the attorney general, and the commissioner of the INS—would have to take personal responsibility for stating that the favored immigrant was vital to national security.

The CIA, in short, had a legal avenue to bring Mykola Lebed, or, indeed, anyone else it chose, into the United States if that person was truly needed for national security reasons. In Lebed's case, however, the agency chose intentionally to break the law which the agency itself had sponsored.

In an apparent violation of immigration law and of its own charter, the CIA smuggled Lebed into the country under a false name in October 1949. Officially Lebed was just another immigrant entering the United States under the Displaced Persons Act. An internal U.S. government investigation later found, however, that in reality CIA agents had helped him obtain false identification, a false police clearance form, and false references.[25] The fraudulent identity was necessary, at least in part, because members of the OUN and the "Ukrainian Intelligence Service" were recognized as Nazi collaborators who had persecuted and murdered innocent people during the war and were therefore specifically barred from entry into the United States.[26] The agency was well aware of Lebed's wartime record when they brought him into the country; interrogations dated 1946 and 1947 concerning these activities are found today in Lebed's CIC file, copies of which were undoubtedly provided to the CIA prior to his entry.

The agency followed Bloodstone procedures and notified the INS of some aspects of Lebed's career including the fact that he had once been sentenced to death for his role in an assassination. The CIA concealed Lebed's true name, however, as well as the evidence that he had served as police minister during the Nazi occupation of the Ukraine. Lebed was briefly employed at the Pentagon following his entrance to the United States, and much of the file collection of the "Liberation Council" may still be found among army intelligence records.[27]

Once in this country, Mykola Lebed used his government connections to expand his influence in Ukrainian communities. He embarked on a major speaking tour aimed at boosting U.S. support for guerrilla warfare in the Ukraine. His propaganda efforts caught the media's interest; his dramatically highlighted photograph plugging him as an "underground" leader appeared in *Newsweek,* and his speech at the Yale University Political Union enjoyed front-page treatment in *Vital Speeches of the Day.*[28]

Word of Lebed's true name—and of his notoriety—inevitably reached INS field agents in New York. Not realizing that he had been sponsored by the CIA, the INS men opened an investigation into what appeared at first to be a clear-cut violation of American immigration law. By the time INS headquarters in Washington learned of the inquest, there was already enough evidence on hand in New York to compel Lebed's immediate expulsion from the United States.

It was only at that point—after Lebed had been, in effect, "caught"—that the CIA chose to "legalize" his immigration status under the 100 Persons Act. First, the agency convinced the INS to suppress the results of its own investigation. Then the necessary correspondence was exchanged among Director Walter Bedell Smith, Attorney General James P. McGranery, and INS Commissioner Argyle Mackey. Lebed—the former police minister in Nazi-occupied Ukraine—was formally declared to be a legal permanent resident of the United States "for national security reasons."[29] This was about two years *after* the CIA had smuggled him into the country in the first place.

Since that time, Lebed has made himself a fixture at Ukrainian conferences and gatherings, where his political faction continues to advertise him as the foreign minister of the supposed Ukrainian government-in-exile. He lives today in Yonkers, New York, and it is unlikely he will ever be forced to leave the United States against his wishes.

*   *   *

The CIA's decision to legalize Lebed's status only *after* he had been detected is one of the most disturbing aspects of the entire affair. The obvious question is just how many other Mykola Lebeds did the agency secretly sponsor who were not accidentally caught by INS field investigators?

One other such "illegal" is clearly General Pavlo Shandruk, the chief of the Ukrainian quisling "government-in-exile" created by the Nazi Rosenberg ministry in 1944. Shandruk had actively collaborated with the Nazis since at least 1941, and his role in pro-Nazi, anti-Semitic activities clearly barred him from legal entry into the United States.

But Shandruk had apparently won the CIA's favor by working for both British and U.S. intelligence after the war. He is known to have been paid at least 50,000 deutsche marks by the United States in 1947 (the equivalent of about $150,000 in today's currency) "to organize an intelligence net,"[30] according to his Army CIC file.

Shandruk traveled to America only days before Lebed, also arriving in October 1949. It is likely that Shandruk entered the United States under a false name, as Lebed had. The INS, at least, claims that it has no record of anyone named Pavlo Shandruk (or the various other transliterations of that name) ever entering the United States. But Shandruk did in fact arrive, and he lived openly in New York under his own name during the 1950s. He even eventually published his war memoirs in this country through Robert Speller & Sons, a well-known outlet for right-wing literature. It is clear from the CIC's dossier on Shandruk that that agency, at least, knew of his activities, address, and ambiguous immigration status. Yet no one moved to deport Shandruk, and he remained influential in Ukrainian émigré circles in the United States until his death.[31]

By the time Mykola Lebed arrived in the United States in 1949, the CIA and OPC appear to have discarded any lingering reservations about employment of Nazi collaborators for behind-the-lines missions into the USSR. Who was better suited, after all, to lead an insurgency in the Ukraine than the men who had shared their weal and woe during the war? The OUN/UPA's Nazi collaborators, in short, were not accidentally involved in U.S. efforts in the region through an oversight. In reality, the United States systematically sought out Ukrainian SS and militia veterans because they were thought to be well suited for rejoining their former comrades still holed up in the Carpathian Mountains. The Americans kept careful registers, in fact, of the names, addresses, and careers of thousands of such Ukrainian SS veterans well into the 1950s so that they might be quickly mobilized in the event of a nuclear conflict with the USSR.[32]

Meanwhile, inside the Ukraine many OUN/UPA insurgents continued to employ the same terror and anti-Semitism during the postwar guerrilla conflict that they had during the Nazi occupation. At Lutsk in the western Ukraine, for instance, OUN/UPA guerrillas concentrated on halting Soviet efforts to establish collective farms. Their practice, according to a U.S. intelligence report dispatched from Moscow, was to identify peasant farmers who agreed to join the state-sponsored farms. "That same night," the U.S. military attaché cabled to Washington, OUN guerrillas "appeared in the homes of these individuals and chopped off the arms which the peasants had raised at the [collective farm] meeting to signify assent." Similarly, according to a second American report,[33] "prosperous Jews" were "singled out" for attack along with Communists during the insurgency in much the same way they had been during the Nazi occupation.

The fact that some of the OUN/UPA insurgents had been responsible for atrocities—the looting, the rape, and the destruction of villages that refused to provide them with supplies, for example— does not appear to have entered U.S. policymakers' deliberations of the day to any significant degree. That was a serious blunder for strictly practical reasons, even if one disregards the ethical considerations involved in employing these agents.

The OUN's collaboration with the Nazis during the war, as well as the organization's own bloody history, had fatally severed the insurgents from the large majority of the Ukrainian people they claimed to represent. This was apparently true even among villagers who were opposed to the new Soviet regime. By the time the Americans decided to extend clandestine aid to the guerrillas in 1949, the insurgency was already in serious decline. War weariness, popular disgust with the naked terrorism of OUN/UPA guerrillas, and the Soviets' use of large-scale forced relocations of the indigenous population combined to isolate the guerrillas and cut them off from grass-roots support.

The CIA itself was divided over how to handle the OUN. Allen Dulles, Frank Wisner, and other clandestine warfare enthusiasts advocated extending substantial military aid to the guerrillas. This would rekindle the rebellion, they reasoned, and the insurgents' example might spred to the rest of Eastern Europe. Among Wisner's first maneuvers on behalf of the Ukrainian rebels was a November 1949 agreement with the army for clandestine procurement of "demolition blocks, M4 [plastique explosive] and blasting accessories" for use in sabotage programs, according to Pentagon summaries of CIA correspondence. Less than two months after that Wisner struck a second deal with the military for the off-the-books acquisition of a stockpile of arms and explosives that eventually totaled hundreds of millions of dollars' worth of guns, helicopters, Jeeps, grenades, uniforms, and everything else necessary to equip several small armies.[34]

Even so, a substantial faction of the agency did not favor a full-scale guerrilla conflict in the Ukraine, at least not at that time. The military and political reality of the situation, these men and women argued, was that the United States could harass the USSR in the region but not seriously challenge Soviet rule. CIA executives like Franklin Lindsay and Harry Rositzke, both of whom worked closely with the Ukrainian guerrillas, agreed that underground warfare in the Carpathian Mountains was premature and likely to lead to the complete obliteration of the rebels. As Rositzke tells the story today, some CIA analysts concluded as early as 1950 that the OUN/UPA guerrillas "could play no serious paramilitary role"[35] in the event of a Soviet military move against the West. Rositzke's group instead favored using the guerrillas as a temporary base inside the USSR for espionage and for gathering "early warning" types of intelligence concerning possible Soviet military mobilization.

But significant pressures from the State Department and the Pentagon pushed for a vastly expanded paramilitary effort, and this arm twisting grew stronger after the outbreak of the Korean War. One Pentagon plan confidently predicted that a 370,000-man guerrilla army could be assembled in a matter of months by parachuting in some 1,200 U.S.-trained insurgency specialists, plus supplies.[36] This extensive underground force was supposed to wait patiently for an American order to move once World War III had broken out. "A view was held in both the State Department and the Pentagon," says Lindsay, "that said, 'Go build an organization, and then put it on standby in case we need it.' I remember saying that it just doesn't work that way" when it comes to guerrilla warfare, Lindsay recalls.[37]

In practice, these contradictory forces within the U.S. national security community produced a situation in which some CIA and OPC agents promised nearly unlimited military support to the insurgency but actually delivered relatively little. In the end, U.S. aid was given to the rebels only insofar as it served short-term American intelligence-gathering objectives, no more.

What this meant in strategic terms was that the guerrillas received neither the military support they needed to survive as an insurgent movement nor the patient camouflaging that might have permitted them to exist as spies. Instead, they were used as martyrs—some of whom died bravely; some pathetically—and grist for the propaganda mills of both East and West.

Beginning in late 1949, the agency parachuted U.S.-trained émigré agents into the Ukraine, infiltrating perhaps as many as seventy-five guerrilla leaders into the region over a four-year period. A related American program dropped agents near Soviet airfields and rail junctions farther north, near Orsha and Smolensk, where Gehlen's spy networks left behind during the Nazi occupation maintained a fragile existence. Britain also parachuted exile agents into the Ukraine, dropping in at least three teams of six men each in the spring of 1951 alone, all within about fifty miles of the nationalist stronghold at Lvov.[38]

Despite the heavy secrecy still surrounding Western paramilitary activities in the Ukraine, it is clear that former Nazi collaborators were integral to this effort. In one documented example, the Soviets captured four U.S.-trained exiles within days of one of the first parachute drops of agents into the region. According to a formal complaint later filed by the USSR at the United Nations,[39] the four had been trained for their mission in an American intelligence school at Bad Wiessee, near Munich, then parachuted into the country by an American aircraft stripped of all identification markings. Three of the four captured men—Aleksandr Lakhno, Aleksandr Makov, and Sergei Gorbunov—had worked closely with the Nazis during the occupation of the USSR, the Soviets charged. Lahkno was reported to have betrayed five Red partisans to the Gestapo, while Makov had been a member of the Nazis' "Black Sea" punitive battalion. All four of the captured men were interrogated by Soviet police until they yielded everything they knew of U.S. espionage and covert warfare missions. Then they were shot.

The handful of exiles who survived the harrowing parachute missions were given new identities and safe passage to the United

States. Not too many men lived long enough to take advantage of that program, however. Unfortunately for the U.S. agents, a Soviet spy named Kim Philby had wormed his way into the highest echelons of the British Secret Intelligence Service. Philby used his post aggressively to stir up factional conflicts among the various Ukrainian exile groups and then to betray every American and British agent he could identify to the Soviets. The large majority of the U.S.-trained agents who parachuted into the Ukraine were captured and executed.

In hindsight, it is clear that the Ukrainian guerrilla option became the prototype for hundreds of CIA operations worldwide that have attempted to exploit indigenous discontent in order to make political gains for the United States. Basically similar CIA programs have since been attempted among the Meo and Hmong peoples of Southeast Asia, anti-Castro Cubans, and, most recently, the Nicaraguan contras, to name only a few. Part of the U.S. rationale for these operations has always been that the American money and arms for the rebel groups will somehow provide a spark that will ignite popular support for democracy, civil liberties, and resistance to totalitarian—read Communist—rule. There is every indication, however, that such affairs have often produced serious blowback problems because their actual results have almost always been the exact opposite of what was originally intended, even in instances where the U.S.-backed faction has succeeded in taking power.

In the case of the Ukrainian civil war the detail that it was now the "good" Americans, rather than the Nazis, who were backing the OUN failed to change the brutal, anti-Semitic tactics that this group had historically employed. Instead of rallying to the new "democratic" movement, there is every indication that many of the ordinary people of the Ukraine gave increased credence to the Soviet government's message that the United States, too, was really Nazi at heart and capable of using any sort of deceit and violence to achieve its ends. The fact that this misperception of U.S. intent has taken root and sometimes flourished among native Ukrainians is a bitter pill for most Americans to swallow. But, indeed, how could it be otherwise? If former Nazis and terrorists were the vehicle through which America chose to spread the doctrine of freedom among people who had no other direct contact with the Western world, it is entirely understandable that these types of ideas about the United States seem reasonable to them. The Soviet government, not surprisingly, has long made every effort to reinforce such conceptions of the United States among its population, and with some success. Today, more than forty years after the end of the war, Soviet propaganda still tags virtually any type of nonconformist in the Ukraine with the label of "nationalist" or "OUN," producing a popular fear and hatred of dissenters that are not entirely unlike the effect created by labeling a protester a "Communist" in American political discourse.

The Ukrainian exile leader Lebed's entry into the United States and his high-profile political agitation once he had arrived provide an example of a second type of blowback as well, one which was to become much more widespread in the years to come. To put it most bluntly, former Nazis and collaborators on the U.S. payroll who were also fugitives from war crimes charges began to demand U.S. help in escaping abroad in return for their cooperation with—and continuing silence about—American clandestine operations. Some such fugitives pressed for entry into the United States itself, while others were content to find safe havens in South America, Australia, or Canada. Before the decade of the 1940s was out, some American intelligence agents found themselves deeply embroiled in underground Nazi escape networks responsible for smuggling thousands of Nazi criminals to safety in the New World.

CHAPTER THIRTEEN

Ratlines

Ratlines, in espionage jargon, are networks of agents who smuggle fugitives or undercover operatives in and out of hostile foreign territories. These escape and evasion routes, as they are sometimes called, are a standard part of the clandestine operations of every major power, and there were hundreds of such ratlines snaking out of the Soviet-occupied territories in Eastern Europe in the wake of World War II.

The story of one of these ratlines is of special interest here because it reveals the manner in which the United States became entangled in the escape of large numbers of Nazi and Axis criminals, many of whom remained ardent Fascists as contemptuous of American democracy as of Soviet-style communism. In hindsight it is clear that many of the ratlines used by the United States during the cold war began as independent, unsanctioned Nazi escape organizations that later turned to selling their specialized services to U.S. intelligence agencies as a means of making money and protecting their own ongoing Nazi smuggling efforts. Some of the exiles involved in this dangerous work did it for money; some, for ideological reasons; some, for both.

The most important Western ratlines that have come to light thus far, including those that smuggled Nazis, operated in and through the Vatican in Rome.[1] Unraveling the reasons why and how the Catholic Church became involved in Nazi smuggling is an important step in understanding the broader evolution of the postwar alliances between former Nazis and U.S. intelligence agencies. One organization is worthy of close scrutiny. It is the prominent Catholic lay group known as Intermarium. During its heyday in the 1940s and early 1950s leading members of this organization were deeply involved in smuggling Nazi fugitives out of Eastern Europe to safety in the West. Later Intermarium also became one of the single most important sources of recruits for the CIA's exile committees. This can be said with some certainty because about a score of Intermarium leaders ended up as activists or officials in Radio Free Europe, Radio Liberation, and the Assembly of Captive European Nations (ACEN), each of which the U.S. government has since admitted as having been a CIA-financed and -controlled organization.[2]

For much of the Catholic Church's leadership, it will be recalled, World War II had been an interlude in a deeper and more important struggle against "atheistic communism" that had been raging for decades. This more fundamental struggle had closely aligned the Vatican hierarchy with a half dozen conservative Christian Democratic and clerical-Fascist political parties that were willing Nazi pawns during the war, even when the Church of Rome was itself under ideological attack from the German Nazi party. The majority of the Nazis' Axis partners in Eastern Europe, as well as Vichy France, had been led by Catholic political parties during the war. The puppet government in Slovakia, for example, was run by a Catholic priest, Monsignor Jozef Tiso. Croatia, a terrorist breakaway state from Yugoslavia, described itself as a "pure Catholic state" whose leader, Ante Pavelic, had been personally received by the pope, while clerics in Admiral Nicholas Horthy's Hungary enjoyed a more profound influence in that country's wartime government than did its own parliament. It is well established, of course, that some Catholic Church leaders bravely resisted Nazi crimes, sometimes at the cost of their lives. Even so, it is also true that the church-based political parties mentioned above played a central role in Axis military aggression. These organizations used the mantle and the moral authority of the church to help carry out the preparations for, and in some cases the actual execution of, the Nazi genocide of the Jews.*[3]

*According to a 1941 diplomatic report by Vichy France's representative to the Vatican (which has never been disavowed by the Holy See), the proper Christian attitude toward Jews at that time was summarized as follows:

As Nazi Germany collapsed during late 1944 and early 1945, many senior church officials helped organize a massive campaign of refugee relief for millions of Catholics fleeing from Eastern Europe. Once this was under way, few distinctions were made between the Catholics responsible for the crimes against humanity committed in the Axis states and those being persecuted simply for opposition to the Soviets. The vast majority of the refugees who swept through Rome in the wake of the war had left their homelands for reasons

---

We know by history that the Church has often protected Jews against the violence and injustice of their persecutors, and that at the same time it has relegated them to the ghettos. One of the greatest of churchmen, St. Thomas Aquinas, has left teachings that cast light on this attitude. . . . The Jews must be tolerated in the exercise of their religion; they must be protected from religious coercion; their children must not be baptized by force. . . . On the other hand, while proscribing any policy of repression of the Jews, St. Thomas nevertheless recommends that suitable measures be taken to limit their activities and restrict their influence. It would be unreasonable in a Christian state to allow the Jews to participate in the government. . . . *It is legitimate to forbid them access to public office, and it is also legitimate to admit them to the universities and the liberal professions only on the basis of a fixed proportion.* As a matter of fact, this practice was strictly adhered to in the Middle Ages, and to [the enforcement of] that end a Lateran Council prescribed that Jews should distinguish themselves from Christians by *a peculiarity of dress.* . . . The precepts of justice and charity [should] be taken into account in . . . the liquidation of businesses in which Jews own interests [emphases in the original].

This policy, in practice, led to Catholic political parties' carrying out many of the preparatory steps for the Holocaust, such as registering Jews and expelling them from public life, legislating seizure of Jewish property, and compelling Jews to display yellow Stars of David. But several of the same Catholic parties responsible for this persecution—Horthy's Hungary being the best-known case—hung back from the actual mass murder of Jews, much to the annoyance of Hitler Germany.

Regardless of the intentions of the Catholic collaborators in Eastern Europe, the fact remains that in the end the executions of Jews went ahead anyhow. Monsignor Tiso's Slovakia, for example, had murdered about 75,000 Jews, including children, by the end of the war. In Hungary Germany installed a more cooperative prime minister in 1944 and succeeded in deporting about 70 percent of the country's Jewish population—more than 400,000 people—to death camps in a matter of weeks. In the Baltic countries of Latvia and Lithuania, the subtleties of St. Thomas's distinction between restricting Jews and killing them seems to have gotten lost in the chaos of war. There leaders of Catholic political parties, in some cases accompanied by priests, actively instigated pogroms in which thousands of people lost their lives.

The Vatican did not condone these killings. Indeed, Pope Pius XII and some of his senior lieutenants moved discreetly—too discreetly, some say—to try to bring them to an end. Official letters were secretly dispatched, Jews were given shelter in church buildings, and the pope himself is said to have spent the bulk of his personal fortune on relief work. In Italy and France, in particular, many thousands of Jews owed their survival to the church's efforts on their behalf. There were also individual prelates who acted with great heroism to save innocent people. These include Father Maximilian Kolbe, who gave up his life at Auschwitz so that another man might live. Despite such efforts, however, the results of the "Final Solution to the Jewish Question" are well known.

that had nothing to do with war crimes, obviously; they had simply been in the wrong place at the wrong time when the German or Soviet armies had stormed through their villages.

At the same time, however, these refugee routes became the most important pipelines out of Europe for Nazis and collaborators fleeing war crimes charges. Factions within the church that had long been sympathetic to the Nazis' extreme anti-Communist stand organized large-scale programs to facilitate the escapes of tens of thousands of Nazis and collaborators from Germany, Austria, Croatia, Slovakia, the Ukraine, and a number of other Eastern European states. The pivotal role of the church in the escape of the Nazis has been emphasized by Luftwaffe Colonel Hans Ulrich Rudel, the highly decorated German air ace who became an international spokesman for the neo-Nazi movement after the war. "One may otherwise view Catholicism as one wishes. But what the Church, especially certain towering personalities within the Church, undertook in those years [immediately after the war] to save the best of our nation, often from certain death, must never be forgotten!" Colonel Rudel exclaimed in a speech at Kufstein in 1970. "In Rome itself, the transit point of the escape routes, a vast amount was done. With its own immense resources, the Church helped many of us to go overseas. In this manner, in quiet and secrecy, the demented victors' mad craving for revenge and retribution could be effectively counteracted."[4]

The Vatican's principal agencies for handling refugees were a group of relief agencies in Rome that divided the assistance work according to the nationality of the refugee. Lithuanians went to see Reverend Jatulevicius at No. 6 on the Via Lucullo, for example, while Padre Gallov at 33 Via dei Parione aided Hungarians and Monsignors Dragonovic and Magjerec at the Istituto di St. Jeronimus were in charge of Croatian relief, and so forth.[5]

According to a top secret U.S. State Department intelligence report of May 1947, "the Vatican . . . is the largest single organization involved in the illegal movement of emigrants . . . [and] the justification . . . for its participation in this illegal traffic is simply the propagation of the Faith. It is the Vatican's desire to assist any person, regardless of nationality or political beliefs, as long as that person can prove himself to be a Catholic." The classified study confirmed that Nazis and their collaborators were not excluded from the effort: "[I]n those Latin American countries where the Church is a controlling or dominating factor, the Vatican has brought pressure to bear which has resulted in the foreign missions of those countries taking an attitude almost favoring the entry into their country of former Nazis and former Fascists or other political groups, so long as they are anti-Communist. That, in fact, is the practice in effect in the Latin American Consulates and Missions in Rome at the present time."[6]

Leaders of the Intermarium organization became coordinators of much of the Nazi escape effort, and many of the men who controlled the Vatican's relief campaign simultaneously became the top leadership of Intermarium. Monsignor Krunoslov Dragonovic, who ran escape routes for Ustachi (Croatian Fascist) fugitives, for example, served as the chief Croatian representative on the self-appointed Intermarium ruling council. Archbishop Ivan Buchko of the Ukraine, who successfully intervened with Pope Pius XII himself to win freedom for a Ukrainian Waffen SS legion,* became the

---

*Perhaps the most dramatic single escape through church channels was the 1946 deliverance of an entire Ukrainian Waffen SS division—some 11,000 men, plus many of their families—with the personal assistance of Pope Pius XII. Most of the rescued men, it is true, were no more than simple soldiers caught in a compromising position by events beyond their control. Many of the men in the division, however, were veterans of Ukrainian collaborationist police and militia units that had enthusiastically participated in anti-Semitic and anti-Communist pogroms in their homeland. Some of them—a smaller number—had served as guards in the Nazis' death camps at Treblinka, Belsen, and Sobibor. Many of these men were destined eventually to serve in political warfare projects underwritten by the CIA. Hundreds of them are known to live in the United States and Canada today.

The Ukrainian SS division surrendered to British troops in early 1945 and was interned at the Rimini POW camp north of Rome. Most of them were facing forced repatriation to the USSR under a clause of the Yalta agreements governing return of POWs who had been captured in enemy uniform. If they returned, they would almost certainly be executed for treason or serve long prison sentences in gulag labor camps.

But that spring General Pavlo Shandruk, the leader of a Ukrainian liberation committee that had been founded under Nazi auspices, contacted Archbishop Ivan Buchko, a high-ranking prelate in Rome specializing in Ukrainian matters for the Holy See. Shandruk pleaded with Buchko by letter to intervene on behalf of the Ukrainian soldiers who had served in SS units, particularly what Shandruk termed the "1st Ukrainian Division," which was in fact the 14th Waffen SS division "Galicia." Shandruk hoped that Archbishop Buchko might reach the pope himself with the general's plea for mercy on behalf of his men.

"Archbishop Ivan [Buchko] answered my letter very soon informing me that he had already visited the Division," Shandruk recalled later. "In a special audience (at night) the Archbishop had pleaded with His Holiness Pope Pius XII to intercede for the soldiers of the Division, who are the flower of the Ukrainian nation. . . . I learned from the Archbishop . . . that as a result of the intercession by His Holiness, the soldiers of the Division were reclassified merely as confinees [rather than as prisoners of war], and Bolshevik agents were prohibited to visit their camps [sic]." Although the troops were still confined to the POW camp at Rimini, they were, according to Shandruk, "out of reach of Communist hands" and no longer subject to repatriation to the USSR. By the spring of 1946 Shandruk, backed by Archbishop Buchko and the Ukrainian Relief Committee of Great Britain, had arranged with the British government to extend "free settler" emigration status to the Ukrainian Waffen

senior Ukrainian Intermarium representative, according to U.S. Army investigative records obtained through the Freedom of Information Act. The onetime Führer of the openly Nazi Latvian Perkonkrusts, Gustav Celmins, was tapped as secretary of the headquarters branch in Rome.[7]

Declassified U.S. State Department and army intelligence records trace the roots of Intermarium back to an alliance of militantly anti-Communist Catholic lay organizations from Eastern Europe established in the mid-1930s. The Abwehr (German military intelligence service) used Intermarium contacts as prewar "agents of influence" abroad as well as reasonably reliable sources of information on the large émigré communities of Europe. By the time the Nazis marched across the Continent, Intermarium had become, in the words of a U.S. Army intelligence report, "an instrument of the German intelligence."[8]

The name of the group means "between the seas," and the announced purpose of the coalition was to unite nations "from the Baltic to the Aegean" in a common front against the USSR. Intermarium was also to be the name of a new, unified Catholic federation of all the countries bordering Russia—a new Holy Roman Empire, in effect—that was to be created in order to hasten the overthrow of the USSR. Although never a Fascist or National Socialist group as such, Intermarium was far to the right of the political spectrum, and a number of its leaders actively collaborated with the Nazis. Their strategy was congruent in many important respects with that of Nazi "philosopher" Alfred Rosenberg, and Intermarium leaders established a close working relationship with the Rosenberg ministry at least as early as 1940. Centuries-old Catholic anti-Semitism was rife in the organization, and Jews were excluded from Intermarium's federation plan.

After the war Intermarium became one of the first organizations to campaign openly for freedom for Waffen SS POWs and for permission to establish a volunteer anti-Communist army for use in a supposedly imminent war against the USSR. The group's multilingual *Bulletin*, for example, argued as early as January 1947 that "it does not matter whether it is [now] between a second and a third world war, or else in the middle of a non-finished second world war . . . [but] events should not take us unprepared, like in 1939."

SS veterans at Rimini and to assist them in resettling in Canada, Australia, and other Commonwealth countries.

Organizing must begin immediately, the official publication asserted, for an "amalgamated common armed forces of the Intermarium," built out of exiles who had fought on either side between 1939 and 1945.

The function of this exile army, in Intermarium's vision, was to deal with the USSR as the Allies had with Germany: by "crushing her military strength and partitioning her," as a key manifesto puts it, "into . . . free states in their ethnical borders"[9]—in other words, by dividing up the Soviet Union into smaller ethnic units in much the same way as had been proposed by the Rosenberg group inside the German high command. Not surprisingly, the USSR remained deeply hostile to Intermarium, and Soviet agents arrested the group's leaders whenever they could lay hands on them.

U.S. intelligence became aware at least as early as 1947 that Intermarium had become deeply involved in arranging escapes for a wide variety of Nazis and collaborators from Eastern Europe. In June of that year, for example, U.S. CIC Special Agent William Gowen notified his headquarters in Rome of a curious incident in which a fugitive Hungarian Fascist who had been a part-time informer for him had "escaped" from Italian custody with Intermarium's assistance. According to Agent Gowen, Intermarium enjoyed enough clout inside the Italian police administration that it was able to arrange for the release of his informant through official channels. Following Intermarium's intervention on behalf of the former Fascist, Gowen said, the Italian Ministry of the Interior cabled the prison camp where the informant was interned and ordered it to turn him loose. The freed suspect was then listed as "escaped" in official files.[10]

Gowen and other CIC agents established a working relationship with a number of Intermarium officials that same year. Their immediate goal was to create trouble for the Soviet-aligned government in Hungary, which had deposed a pro-Western prime minister in mid-1947. Not long after the Intermarium escape incident Agent Gowen arranged with intelligence specialists at the U.S. Department of State to provide a U.S. diplomatic visa to a leading Intermarium spokesman, Ferenc Vajda, so that he might travel to America. Vajda's mission for Intermarium (and for the CIC) was to convince the deposed prime minister, Ferenc Nagy, to join with former Axis quislings in a new U.S.-sponsored alliance against Communist power in Hungary.

Vajda, as it turns out, was himself a fugitive from war crimes and treason charges at the time he entered the United States. He had made a career out of extreme-right-wing politics in Hungary and had been a leading anti-Semitic propagandist for the clerical-Fascist Arrow Cross party. In the last months of the war Vajda had helped strip millions of dollars' worth of Hungarian art treasures and industrial equipment from Budapest. This booty then became one of Intermarium's primary sources of funding during the first years after the war.

Vajda had been arrested on war crimes charges in Italy in April 1947. But according to American counterintelligence records which have never before been made public, he soon escaped from Italian police custody in much the same way as Gowen's earlier informant had and fled to Pope Pius's summer estate at Castel Gandolfo, where he was given refuge. U.S. CIC Agent Gowen then helped Vajda secretly exit the country and even provided him with a reference letter that asserted that Vajda "had been of great assistance to Counterintelligence Corps in Rome [by] giving information on immigrants from Russian satellite states."[11] The Hungarian then traveled to Spain, where he succeeded in winning State Department and CIC support for his trip to the States.

Unfortunately for Vajda and Special Agent Gowen, columnist Drew Pearson was in Rome shortly after the Hungarian fled Italy. He was approached by unknown persons—"probably Communists or Communist inspired," Gowen said—who leaked many of the details of Vajda's history and plans to him. Pearson soon discovered that the fugitive war criminal—and Intermarium representative—Ferenc Vajda had actually entered the United States at taxpayer expense and with special State Department clearance. The columnist publicized the incident, and Vajda was soon arrested and held at Ellis Island in New York Harbor. Former Hungarian Prime Minister Nagy, who had been the object of Vajda's mission, denounced the Intermarium envoy as a "Nazi."[12] There followed a brief congressional investigation, the records of which have remained sealed for more than thirty-five years. Vajda was soon deported and found his way to refuge in Colombia. He eventually ended up as Bogotá correspondent for *Time* magazine (though he was fired when his past became public) and as a teacher at an international university whose board, interestingly enough, included Adolf A. Berle, Jr., who is well known today to have served as a conduit for CIA funds throughout this period.[13]

The Vajda affair was a disappointment for the alliance between

U.S. intelligence and Intermarium, but it certainly did not end the relationship. In case after case, a clear continuity of personnel can be established, beginning with the Vatican refugee-smuggling networks in 1945, continuing into Intermarium, and winding up in a variety of CIA-financed political warfare projects during the early 1950s. A number of Intermarium activists, including some who are war criminals by even the strictest definition of the term, followed this pipeline into the United States.

A handful of examples will have to suffice to illustrate this process. The Latvian component of Intermarium was among the most deeply compromised by its service to the Nazi war machine, yet a number of its most prominent members entered the United States. They went on to play leading roles in what are now known to have been CIA-funded émigré projects inside this country.

The Latvian Fascist Perkonkrust Führer Gustav Celmins, for example, had organized a Latvian SS unit in 1941 and served as a Nazi agent inside nationalist circles throughout the war. He went on to become an officer in the powerful Rome branch of Intermarium. Celmins entered the United States as a displaced person in 1950 and was quickly hired as a teacher in a Russian studies program at Syracuse, New York, with a history of ties to American intelligence agencies. Celmins eventually fled to Mexico following a newspaper series that exposed his efforts to organize anti-Semitic activities among Latvian exiles in the United States.[14]

Other Latvian émigrés in Intermarium include Alfreds Berzins and Boleslavs Maikovskis, both of whom were wanted on war crimes charges and both of whom ended up on the payroll of CIA-financed organizations during the 1950s. They served as leaders of the Committee for a Free Latvia and the International Peasant Union, respectively, which were bankrolled with agency funds laundered through RFE/RL and the related Assembly of Captive European Nations (ACEN).[15]

As will be seen in a later chapter, CIA money paid for the ACEN's political congresses, provided substantial personal stipends to émigré leaders like Berzins, and in some cases published transcripts of their speeches in book form. Many Intermarium activists became guests on RFE/RL broadcasts, and the radio stations aggressively promoted the organizations they represented throughout the 1950s. CIA money laundered through Radio Free Europe, it is worth noting, also financed the publication of the book *The Assembly of Captive European Nations,* which presented the proceedings of the first ACEN congress in New York and included commentaries by Berzins and the Albanian Bloodstone émigré Hasan Dosti, among others.[16] This text was distributed free of charge to virtually every library, newspaper, and radio station in the United States and Europe. The propaganda effort was so thorough that this tract continues to turn up regularly in used bookstores and garage sales to this day.

The United States became ensnarled in Intermarium's large-scale underground railroads for Nazis when the CIC hired Croatian Intermarium leader Monsignor Krunoslav Dragonovic to run special ratlines out of Europe for U.S.-sponsored intelligence assets who were too "hot" to have any official connection with the U.S. government. Dragonovic, a high-ranking prelate within the Croatian Catholic Church, was running one of the largest and single most important Nazi escape services at the time the United States hired him. According to a later U.S. Justice Department report, Dragonovic himself was a war criminal who had been a "relocation" official involved in the deportation of Serbians and Jews by the Croatian Fascist Ustachi regime that had been set up inside Yugoslavia during the war. In 1944 he had fled to the Vatican, where he used the auspices of the church to create underground escape routes out of his home country for thousands of senior Ustachi leaders. According to Ivo Omrcanin, a former Ustachi government emissary and senior aide to Dragonovic now living in Washington, D.C., his mentor used church resources to arrange safe passage for "many thousands of our people," as Omrcanin puts it. "He helped as much of the government as he could, not excepting the security officials." These "refugees" included men such as Ustachi chieftain Ante Pavelic and his police minister, Andrija Artukovic, who between them had organized the murder of at least 400,000 Serbians and Jews.[17]

The later U.S. Justice Department investigation into the escape of Gestapo officer Klaus Barbie made public dozens of pages of official records concerning Dragonovic's work for U.S. intelligence that would have otherwise probably never seen the light of day. The Justice Department directly admits that Dragonovic went to work for the Americans in smuggling U.S.-sponsored fugitives, and that—whether the United States liked it or not—this provided a source of financing and shield of protection, in effect, for the priest's independent Nazi smuggling work.[18]

The deal with Dragonovic was a product of the perceived intelligence needs of the period. According to CIC Agent Paul Lyon, the senior officer of the 430th CIC in Vienna, Major James Milano, ordered him to "establish a means of disposition of visitors"—Lyon means exiles from Eastern Europe—in the summer of 1947. These "visitors" were men and women "who had been in the custody of the 430th CIC," Lyon writes, "and whose continued residence in Austria constituted a security threat as well as a source of possible embarrassment to the Commanding General." The CIC man traveled to Rome, where, with the assistance of an exiled Slovakian diplomat, he struck a deal for mutual assistance with Monsignor Dragonovic, who already had "several clandestine evacuation channels to the various South American countries for various types of European refugees" in operation.

Under the agreement the priest·obtained false identifications, visas, secret safe houses, and transportation for émigrés whose flights were sponsored by the CIC. Lyon and CIC Special Agent Charles Crawford, in exchange, helped special refugees *selected by Dragonovic* to escape from the U.S.-occupied zone of Germany. These were almost certainly fugitive Ustachi (Croatian Fascist) war criminals, even according to the Justice Department's version of events.[19]

Officially, of course, the United States was still committed to the capture and punishment of Ustachi criminals. But the CIC-Dragonovic agreement inevitably entailed providing de facto protection not only to the fugitives sponsored by the United States but to the Croatian criminals known to be in the monsignor's care as well. The CIC knew that its arrangement with Dragonovic was facilitating the escape of Fascist fugitives. CIC Special Agent Robert Mudd, for example, reported at the time of the first CIC-Dragonovic contacts that "many of the more prominent Ustachi war criminals and Quislings are living in Rome illegally. . . . Their cells are still maintained, their papers still published, and their intelligence agencies still in operation. Chief among the intelligence operatives . . . appear to be Dragonovic and Monsignor Madjerec," he wrote. "Ustachi Ministers are either living in [Dragonovic's] monastery, or living in the Vatican and attending meetings several times a week at San Geronimo [i.e., the Istituto di St. Jeronimos, of which Dragonovic was in charge.]"[20] Agent Mudd went on to name ten major Ustachi leaders then in Dragonovic's keeping, several of whom had appeared on Allied lists of war crimes suspects. Despite Mudd's report, however, the CIC did not arrest any of the Ustachis in Drago-novic's care, nor did it report where they were hiding to the United Nations War Crimes Commission or the Yugoslav government.

The best known of the U.S.-sponsored passengers on Drago-novic's ratline to come to light so far is Klaus Barbie, the wartime chief of the Gestapo in Lyons, France, who later went to work for U.S. intelligence in Germany. During the war, Barbie had deported Jews to death camps, tortured and murdered the resistance fighters who fell into his hands, and served as the political police in Nazi-occupied Lyons. At war's end Barbie fled back to Germany, where he first came to the attention of the U.S. Army CIC as a target in a hunt. He happened to fall into the sights of Operation Selection Board, a series of joint U.S.-British raids in February 1947, which were designed to round up about seventy Germans who had orga-nized an underground pro-Nazi political party. Barbie was believed to be in charge of intelligence for the group—obtaining false papers and printing equipment, smuggling fugitives, and the like—and as such was high on the arrest list.

He escaped apprehension, however, by climbing out the bath-room window as CIC agents were kicking in the front door. Barbie fled to Memmingen, a small town west of Munich, and there his relationship with the CIC began in earnest. The CIC in Region IV (which included Memmingen) knew that the CIC in Stuttgart, Hei-delberg, and Frankfurt (Regions I, II, and III) had arrest warrants out for Barbie in connection with his escape from Operation Selec-tion Board. But Barbie went to his friend Kurt Merk—a former Abwehr officer who was running his own spy network for CIC Region IV—and volunteered for service in the CIC, the same orga-nization that was attempting to capture him. Merk, himself a fugi-tive from French war crimes charges, convinced his American con-troller, Robert Taylor, that Barbie could be useful. CIC Region IV then hired Barbie and kept him hidden from the *rest* of the CIC.[21]

Agent Taylor and the CIC in Region IV had every opportunity to know before they recruited Klaus Barbie that he had been chief of the Gestapo in Lyons, France, during the war. The CIC's "Cen-tral Personalities Index Card" identifying him as such had been distributed throughout the agency during Operation Selection Board. Barbie's name, moreover, had been listed in the CROW-CASS directories since 1945 as a suspect in the murder and torture of civilians. Barbie himself admitted to his handlers, furthermore, that he had been an SD and a Gestapo officer (though he claimed he had not been involved in torture or crimes against humanity), and passing references to Barbie's background and rank in the Nazi intelligence service are found scattered throughout his CIC file. This self-admitted status as a former SD and SS officer placed Barbie in the "automatic arrest" category under occupation law in Germany at the time. The CIC, if it had felt itself bound by the written laws, should have arrested Barbie without further ado. It was not necessary for the CIC to know the specific crimes Barbie may have committed when it made the arrest, though obviously a full investigation should follow. It was enough that Barbie was an SD man.[22]

Instead, however, Agent Taylor and his successors went out of their way to keep Barbie on the payroll. Barbie's "value as an informant infinitely outweighs any use he may have in prison," Taylor noted in one of several internal CIC recommendations on behalf of his agent, and CIC headquarters in Germany eventually officially approved his recruitment of the former SS officer. Barbie was soon running several separate spy networks that penetrated the French intelligence service and stretched into Romania and into right-wing Ukrainian émigré organizations in Germany. Barbie's subagents also performed undercover work inside the KPD (German Communist party) in Region IV and enjoyed a bonus of 100 deutsche marks when he came up with the "complete KPD membership list of Stadt Augsburg," his security file indicates.[23]

Accounts of Barbie's wartime deeds gradually leaked out through gossip from other Nazis on the U.S. intelligence payroll. U.S. CIC Agent Erhard Dabringhaus, who was Barbie's controller for a short time during the late 1940s, remembers that Barbie's erstwhile friend Kurt Merk informed on Barbie after having been short-changed in his spy pay. Merk "told me these stories about Klaus Barbie having tortured French resistance fighters," Dabringhaus says. "He told me that [Barbie] used to hang them by their thumbs until they were dead . . . [and that] if the French ever found out how many mass graves Barbie was responsible for, even Eisenhower would not be able to protect him."[24] Dabringhaus asserts that he reported all this to CIC headquarters but was met with only silence.

The fact that Barbie may have been a war criminal simply was not of interest at CIC headquarters. There were clearly hundreds of SS men working for the United States at the time, and hundreds more working for the French, British, and Soviets. Why worry about a *Hauptsturmführer* who had served in France? The rumors concerning Barbie were not startling; they were routine. Even Dabringhaus, who today expresses shock at the use of Barbie as an agent, concedes that his other work for the CIC consisted in large part of running still another network of SS men, that one in the Stuttgart area.

But Barbie was different from most of the other Nazis. By coincidence, one of the men whom Barbie had tortured and murdered was Jean Moulin, a French resistance hero. Many French veterans were determined to see René Hardy, who they believed had betrayed Moulin to the Nazis, hang for his role in this murder, and Barbie was the one man who might have the evidence they needed. Thus, there was a powerful constituency for bringing pressure to bear on the CIC in the Barbie case, while other Nazis working for the CIC were, well, just "other Nazis."

Rumors concerning Barbie's employment (and protection) by the Americans began to reach French newspapers and politicians at least as early as 1948. They, in turn, brought increasing pressure to bear on the U.S. government through publicity and eventually through official notes requesting Barbie's extradition from Germany. That, in the final analysis, is why the CIC chose to provide Barbie with a new identity and safe passage to Argentina in 1951, while thousands of other ex-Nazis who had been "of interest" to the CIC at one time or another have simply lived out their lives in Germany. If the CIC had dumped Barbie when the French government began requesting his extradition, he would have had plenty of compromising things to say about the CIC, his handlers agreed at the time. If he talked to the British, it would be "an embarrassing situation" (one internal memo argued) because the Americans had hidden Barbie from them in the wake of Operation Selection Board. If the French got him it would be even worse: CIC headquarters believed that the French Sûreté (security service) had been "thoroughly penetrated by Communist elements," as the U.S. Justice Department's later report on the affair put it, who wanted to "kidnap Barbie, reveal his CIC connections, and thus embarrass the United States."[25]

CIC headquarters' response to France's extradition request was a bureaucratic maneuver of breathtaking simplicity. Barbie, according to headquarters, should be immediately "dropped as an informant." At the same time, however, it was "desired that subject [Barbie] *not be made aware* that his status within this organization has been altered."[26] The only way that Barbie could remain unaware of his "altered status" was for the CIC to continue to pay him, accept his reports, and provide him with new assignments; and that is exactly what happened. Barbie, in short, was employed by the CIC in order to conceal the fact that he had actually been dismissed.

In December 1950 the CIC helped arrange new false identification for Barbie ("Klaus Altmann"), then paid Monsignor Dragonovic to arrange visas and travel to South America for the Nazi fugitive. Agent George Neagoy (who took over the ratline operation from Agent Lyon) handled the affair for the CIC. Barbie's departure from Europe was calm, even routine, according to the army's postmortem of the events.[27]

It is valuable to pause for a moment here to place Barbie's escape in a broader historical perspective. The intense apprehension in Washington created by the outbreak of the Korean War in June 1950 became an important factor in shaping relations between U.S. security agencies and many former Nazis in Europe, of whom Klaus Barbie was only one. U.S.-led United Nations forces scored some impressive early gains against the North Koreans that summer, but the Chinese Communist People's Liberation Army entered the conflict in the fall and inflicted heavy casualties on the UN troops. Communist forces took South Korea's capital, Seoul, during the first week of January 1951. Washington's morale plummeted, and senior officers at the Pentagon and National Security Council began serious discussions of tactics for using atomic weapons against the Chinese.

The Korean crisis precipitated an incident halfway around the world that starkly revealed the extent to which the U.S. security policy of the period depended upon obscuring Nazi criminality. The Americans wanted West Germany's military muscle and steel mills as a linchpin for Western European defense against what many feared was an imminent invasion from the USSR. The West German military and much of that country's political establishment balked, however, arguing that America's treatment of Nazi war criminals thus far had been too harsh and had besmirched the honor of the German officer corps.

The price the new German administration wanted for its cooperation in an alliance with the United States was freedom for the convicted Nazi war criminals imprisoned in Landsberg Prison, near Munich. Many West German leaders were insistent that the fifteen Nazi inmates facing death sentences—most of whom were murder squad leaders—be saved from hanging. Chancellor Konrad Adenauer himself publicly contended that continuing incarceration of these convicts posed what he called a "psychological problem" for the West Germans because imprisonment of certain convicts popular with the West German officer corps "would . . . put obstacles in the way of future [military] recruitment if people against whom no war crimes have been proved continue to be held in jail."[28] The chancellor's bland comment was misleading—the Landsberg inmates had, in fact, been tried and found guilty of the murder of at least 2 million people, profiteering from slave labor, massacring American POWs, and thousands of other specific acts of terror—but it is an indication of what the attitudes of high-level West German government officials were at the time.

Following the outbreak of the Korean War, U.S. High Commissioner for Germany John McCloy moved rapidly to resolve the U.S.-West German dispute over the Landsberg prisoners. He hand-picked a legal review commission to advise him on clemency for the inmates, and the group then spent the next six months poring over the various appeals and requests for mercy filed on behalf of the convicts. McCloy's commission refrained from any contact with the U.S. Nuremberg prosecutors, however, and declined to review documentary evidence of specific acts of Nazi criminality that had been brought to light during the prisoners' trials.[29]

McCloy announced the recommendations of this task force in January 1951, only a few days after Seoul had fallen to Communist forces. He began by acknowledging the "enormity of the crimes" committed by the prisoners at Landsberg and called for stern measures against them. But he then went on to argue that in some cases there was a "legitimate basis for clemency," as he put it, for example, when the Landsberg prisoner's sentence "was out of line with sentences for crimes of similar gravity in other cases" or when the convict had had "relatively subordinate authority" during the war, or when other mitigating factors were present.[30]

McCloy ruled that five of the criminals, including *Einsatzgruppen* commander Otto Ohlendorf and concentration camp chieftain Oswald Pohl, had to hang. He then substantially reduced the prison sentences of seventy-nine other major Nazi war criminals, most of whom were set free within a few months of McCloy's ruling. The beneficiaries of this act included, for example, all of the convicted concentration camp doctors; all of the top judges who had administered the Nazis' "special courts" and similar machinery of repression; fourteen of fifteen convicted criminals from the first *Einsatzgruppen* and concentration camp administration trial, seven of whom were released immediately; sixteen of twenty defendants in the second *Einsatzgruppen* mass murder case; and all of the convicted criminals in the Krupp corporation slave labor case, each of whom was released immediately.[31]

Equally important, McCloy's clemency decisions for the Landsberg inmates set in motion a much broader process that eventually freed hundreds of other convicted Nazi criminals over the next five years. Convicted I. G. Farben executive Fritz Ter Meer put the matter succinctly upon his release from Landsberg a few days after McCloy's clemency. "Now that they have Korea on their hands," he quipped, "the Americans are a lot more friendly."[32]

Klaus Barbie was only a small part of these much larger events. But his U.S.-sponsored escape, when taken together with McCloy's clemency of major war criminals and the Nazi utilization programs discussed thus far, points to an important conclusion. By the winter of 1950–1951 the most senior levels of the U.S. government had decided to abrogate their wartime pledge to bring Nazi criminals to justice. The atrocities of the Holocaust had been reduced to just another uncomfortable fact of history that had to be sidestepped in the interests of preserving West German military support for American leadership in the cold war. While nazism and Hitler's inner circle continued to be publicly condemned throughout the West, the actual investigation and prosecution of specific Nazi crimes came to a standstill.

More than thirty years later the maturing of public opinion and a change of government in both France and Bolivia, where Barbie had ended up, led to the capture of Klaus Barbie by Bolivian authorities and his shipment to France to stand trial for crimes against humanity. This in turn led to a decision by the U.S. Justice Department to open its own investigation into the Barbie matter, a move that was motivated at least in part by the fact that new leaks and rumors concerning the former Nazi's work for U.S. intelligence were now surfacing almost daily and receiving extensive play in the world's press.[33] As noted above, this investigation concluded that the United States had indeed protected Barbie in Europe and engineered his escape but that Barbie was the *only* such Nazi who had been assisted in this fashion.

The U.S. Justice Department's 1983 report on the Barbie escape finessed the inevitable questions concerning just how many other Nazis might have moved through Monsignor Dragonovic's ratline. By limiting its definition of the U.S. responsibility in this affair to only those persons whom the United States directly sponsored for travel through the ratline, the report ignores the role that the CIC's tacit—and at times active—support had in facilitating Dragonovic's *own* Nazi smuggling work. Taking this tack in the report may have some narrow legal justification—this was, after all, an official Department of Justice study. But this approach obscures the fact that the ratline was actually used for mass escapes of Ustachi war criminals throughout the 1940s, and it effectively hides the extent to which the United States' interest in bringing Ustachi war criminals to justice was obstructed by the CIC's pact with Dragonovic.

Then, while addressing the question of just those ratline travelers who were directly sponsored by the CIC, the study concludes: "No other case was found where a suspected Nazi war criminal was placed in the rat line or where the rat line was used to evacuate a person wanted either by the United States Government or any of its post-war allies."[34]

This statement has the ring of being a straightforward declaration, and it was accepted without question by most of the U.S. media to mean "No other Nazis or war criminals were saved through the ratline." The Department of Justice was careful, however, to choose the phrase *post-war allies.* The fact is that Dragonovic and the CIC combined to facilitate the escape of a number of Nazi collaborators sought by the Eastern European governments who were *not* U.S. postwar allies.

The thrust of the Justice Department's presentation on this point is directly contradicted, furthermore, by the very documentation that its own study has made public. Agent Lyon, who is now deceased, wrote a brief report on his ratline activities in 1950. It leaves little doubt that a number of those escapees sponsored by the Americans were, in fact, fugitives from war crimes charges. Obtaining false identification and visas for his "visitors," Lyon states, *"was done illegally in as much as such persons could not possibly qualify for eligibility [for emigration assistance] under the Geneva IRO [International Refugee Organization] charter."*[35] As noted previously, there were two such groups barred by the IRO charter. Nazis and Nazi collaborators, on the one hand, and common criminals, on the other. At least one American agent attached to the 430th CIC in Austria was engaged in moving such "shipments," as the clandestine travelers were called, on a regular basis for more than three years.

Lyon makes it clear that he, Dragonovic, and U.S. officials at least as high as the director of U.S. Army intelligence in Europe were well aware that some of the passengers on the ratline were fugitive war criminals. Dragonovic himself "is known and recorded as a Fascist, war criminal, etc.," Lyon writes, "and his contacts with South American diplomats of a similar class are not generally approved by U.S. State Department officials." In a second report, Lyon says, "some of the persons of interest to Father Dragonovic may be of interest to the DeNazification [*sic*] policy of the Allies"— in other words, they are Nazis. "[H]owever . . . [they] are also of interest to our Russian ally."[36] *Ally* is presumably used sarcastically here, considering this was written at the height of the cold war. According to Lyon, because the Soviets were looking for these Nazis, the program had to go ahead under such secrecy that even most of the CIC had to be kept in the dark about its existence.

Special Agent Lyon went on to recommend expanded U.S. assistance to Intermarium leader Dragonovic. The priest's help was particularly desirable, Lyon writes, because if the smuggling was ever exposed, "we may be able to state, if forced, that turning over of a DP to a Welfare Organization [such as Dragonovic's] falls in line with our democratic way of thinking and that we are not engaged in illegal disposition of war criminals, defectees and the like."[37] Lyon was, in short, offering the "plausible denial" of the very fact that worried the CIC the most: The Austrian branch of the CIC *was* "engaged in the disposition of war criminals, defectees and the like," at least when such persons were believed to be of intelligence value to the United States.

As far as any connections between the Barbie escape and the CIA are concerned, the former Office of Special Investigations director Allan Ryan states flatly in his report on the Barbie affair that "there is no evidence in CIA files that the CIA had any relationship with Barbie prior to 1951 or . . . thereafter." Ryan also told the author shortly after the Barbie study was released: "Frank Wisner had nothing to do with this."[38] Ryan is probably right that the CIA had no operational control over Klaus Barbie. Whether the agency was involved in moving *other* Nazi fugitives with Dragonovic's assistance, however, is another question.

In fact, many of Dragonovic's phony exit papers were arranged through Robert Bishop, an American ex-OSS agent who was then in charge of the eligibility office of the International Refugee Organization (IRO) in Rome, according to CIC records.[39] Bishop was one of the CIA/OPC's most important assets in that city. He had worked with Wisner on a variety of clandestine projects in Istanbul, Bucharest, and Rome since at least 1944. The CIA/OPC's connection to the smuggling operation was through Dragonovic and Bishop, not Barbie.

Bishop and Wisner understood each other well when it came to clandestine operations. They had served together in Bucharest, Romania, in 1944 during what proved to be the first revealing collision between Soviet and American forces in Eastern Europe. Bishop had done truly pioneer work in Bucharest, from Wisner's point of view, by opening up clandestine contacts with the anti-Communist bureau of Axis Romania's wartime secret service in order to gather espionage information on the Soviets. "It was not our job to spy on the Russians [at that time]," Bishop concedes in a 1948 memoir of his Romanian experiences. "But we perceived very early that we were confronted with an even more sinister and potent totalitarian force than the one we were fighting. This realization caused us to spy on the Russians and their Romanian quislings, even though there was an order from the United States War Department that it should not be done."[40]

Bishop went from there to the Italian IRO post. CIC Agent Lyon didn't like Bishop, even though he depended on him for phony identification cards and other refugee paperwork. Robert Bishop "fancied himself a top intelligence operative in Italy," the CIC man sarcastically commented. Bishop drank too much and talked too much, Lyon thought. "After [a] breakdown due to alcoholism, Bishop imagined himself as the savior of Italy," Lyon reported to CIC headquarters in his wrap-up of ratline activities.

During the 1948 Italian election campaign, according to Lyon, Bishop attempted to build the CIC's highly secret underground escape operation into a large-scale paramilitary force. He sought to provide "large numbers of underground troops, military supplies, sea evacuation, air evacuation and the like" for clandestine warfare against Communists, according to CIC records.[41] Bishop's Rome project, in short, was of a piece with Wisner's other insurgency operations in Greece, the Ukraine, and elsewhere. CIC Agent Lyon opposed this grandiose scheme because it would inevitably lead to public exposure of his secret ratline, which Lyon needed for his own purposes. Lyon and the CIC soon began avoiding Bishop when they could, then cut him off altogether in 1950. Dragonovic managed to carry on without Bishop, however, by establishing new sources for false visas and identification through church relief channels.

Considerable evidence suggests that the CIA assumed control of Dragonovic—the "known and recorded . . . Fascist, war criminal, etc.," in Agent Lyon's phrase—in mid-1951, then maintained that relationship for the remainder of the decade. The Justice Department strongly disputes this theory, however, in its report on Barbie. It argues that "the CIA stated . . . that it had no records of such an operation" involving Dragonovic and further notes that CIA officers familiar with the ratline told Justice that the agency "never had any connection with it."

But another look at the evidence made available through the department's own investigation led many people to a different conclusion concerning the CIA's role in Dragonovic's ratline. First of all, Agent John M. Hobbins of the 430th CIC noted in early 1951 that the CIC's budget for running escaping agents through the ratline was scheduled to expire on June 31, 1951. Hobbins should have known, for he was the 430th's specialist in "Informant Disposal" during the early 1950s. The CIA "will assume responsibility for evacuations," according to an order from the head of army intelligence in Austria, Hobbins reported, and the "end of the [CIC] budget and the assumption of control by CIA will roughly coincide."[42]

CIC Agent George Neagoy, the army's principal officer in charge of the ratline after Agent Lyon's departure, transferred from the CIC to the CIA in 1951, at exactly the time the army's ratline "franchise" was to be transferred to the agency. At a minimum, Neagoy brought the CIA a solid working knowledge of the techniques and contacts of Dragonovic's ratline. It is certain that *some* U.S. intelligence group continued to use Dragonovic as a contract agent throughout the 1950s, though not necessarily for smuggling fugitives. The Croatian priest's CIC dossier, for example, leaves no doubt that he was of "operational interest to USI," as the declassified record puts it,[43] at least as late as October 1960. "USI" in this context signifies "U.S. intelligence." The meaning of this phrase is unmistakable: Dragonovic was at the time a contract agent for an unnamed U.S. intelligence agency, most likely the CIA.

Officially Dragonovic remained active in Vatican refugee relief work for much of the 1950s, then gradually drifted into high-profile political activism in the Croatian exile community abroad. He maintained his sympathy for the Ustachis and contributed to publications edited by Ante Bonifacic, an émigré nationalist politician who once served as "director of cultural relations" during the Ustachi regime. Dragonovic also maintained a profitable sideline business of currency smuggling in Italy and Yugoslavia, at least according to testimony in a 1960 trial in which three Yugoslavian Catholic priests confessed to having been used by him for that purpose. They went to prison, but Dragonovic remained free in Rome.

Dragonovic's death was of a piece with his life. The Croatian émigré press proclaimed with alarm in 1967 that the aging priest had been kidnapped by Tito's undercover agents and returned to Yugoslavia. There he was said to have been tortured, tried for war crimes, and executed. This version of events has found its way into a number of otherwise reliable studies of Eastern European affairs.

In reality, however, Dragonovic returned to Yugoslavia voluntarily in 1967, then lived out the remainder of his days in Zagreb, the capital of the Croatian state inside that country. There was no trial for war crimes, no execution, and not even any criticism or harassment in the Yugoslavian press. He died peacefully in July 1983,[44] all of which raises a reasonable doubt about whether Monsignor Dragonovic—war criminal, Ustachi smuggler, and career contract agent for U.S. intelligence—might have been working for the Yugoslav secret service for quite some time prior to his return to his homeland.

Dragonovic's tangled life is an indication of the complexities and contradictions that are an inevitable part of the intelligence business. It is obvious that neither the United States nor any other power limits its operational intelligence contacts to only those persons who might be considered "respectable" at home. But Dragonovic's activities also make it clear that there can be a heavy price to pay for clandestine sponsorship of individuals and groups that have political agendas quite different from those of the United States. The Ustachi criminals saved by Dragonovic did not simply disappear once had they reached the New World. Instead, they established new Ustachi cells in Croatian communities abroad, in some cases headed by the same men who had once led murder squads inside wartime Croatia. The survival of this extremist sect remains one of the more violent examples of the blowback created by the postwar Nazi utilization programs. Ustachis are active to this day in the United States, Australia, and several other countries, and according to reports of FBI investigations, some cells have been responsible for an airplane hijacking, bombings, extortion, numerous murders, and the assassination of several Yugoslavian diplomats over the course of the last two decades.[45]

No doubt the CIC did not anticipate that its support of Dragonovic's ratline would one day contribute, even indirectly, to the creation of terrorist groups inside the United States or other Western countries. But the secrecy that has up to now surrounded U.S. Nazi operations such as the Dragonovic ratline drastically restricted the American public's—and even the intelligence agencies' own—ability to learn from this mistake. Rather than draw back from using Nazis as agents in the wake of the Barbie debacle, the practice expanded and became more flagrant.

CHAPTER FOURTEEN

Pipelines to the United States

American policy on the use of defectors from the East, including those who had been Nazi collaborators, was institutionalized in three National Security Council decisions during late 1949 and 1950. The government still contends that revealing the full text of these orders would "damage national security" if they were published today, more than thirty-five years later. These high-level orders, which were reviewed and approved by both Presidents Truman and Eisenhower, are known as NSC 86, NSCID (pronounced "N-skid" and standing for NSC intelligence directive) 13, and NSCID 14. They are based on recommendations prepared by Frank Wisner's OPC division of the CIA during the Bloodstone program.

These decisions gave the CIA control of several highly secret government interagency committees responsible for handling émigrés and defectors both overseas (NSCID 13) and inside the United States itself (NSCID 14). Like the earlier Bloodstone effort from which these directives sprang, NSCIDs 13 and 14 were not designed to rescue Nazis as such. They were instead aimed at making good use of all sorts of defectors from the East—with few questions asked. The bureaucratic turf remaining after the CIA had taken its share was divided among the FBI, military intelligence, the State Department, and, to a small degree, the Immigration and Naturalization Service (INS).[1]

Most important in the present context, these orders authorized clandestine CIA funding of a variety of ostensibly private refugee relief organizations so as to ensure the cooperation of those agencies in the government's efforts to locate and exploit presumably valuable defectors.*[2] Under the aegis of these secret orders, the CIA assumed the power to bring "temporarily" anyone it wished to the United States (or anywhere else, for that matter), regardless of any other laws on the books in the United States or any other country.

NSCID 14, moreover, dramatically expanded the agency's authority to conduct clandestine operations *inside* the United States—in an apparent violation of the CIA's charter—as long as those affairs were conducted through émigré political organizations that supposedly still had some connection with the old country. The CIA has used that loophole to authorize hidden agency funding for the Committee for a Free Latvia, the Committee for a Free Albania, and other supposedly private exile organizations active in this country. A substantial amount of the agency's money ended up being spent on lobbying the U.S. Congress and on other propaganda efforts inside this country—a clear violation of the law.

When Congress created the CIA, it specifically legislated that the agency be barred from "police, subpoena, law-enforcement powers or internal security functions" in the United States. This was to be a *foreign* intelligence agency, not a still more powerful version of the FBI. Most Americans, including the members of the congressional watchdog committees responsible for oversight of CIA operations, have long contended that this provision banned the agency from involvement in political activities inside this country. Even Senator Leverett Saltonstall, long the ranking Republican on the Senate's intelligence oversight committee, remarked to then CIA Director John McCone (in 1962): "Is it not true, Mr. McCone . . . that any work on ethnic groups in this country would not be within the province of the CIA? . . . Am I correct in that?" (McCone

---

*The CIA maintained at least a half dozen organizational assets involved in immigration of selected Eastern European refugees into the United States, although these groups obviously handled the entire range of exiles, not just former Nazi collaborators. One such group, the International Rescue Committee (IRC), became so intertwined with clandestine CIA affairs that it arguably operated as an adjunct of the agency.

According to Displaced Persons Commission records, the IRC specialized in handling refugee cases that had been recommended by the various "governments-in-exile" and "international organizations" funded by the Free Europe Committee. The favored groups included the International Peasant Union, International Federation of Free Journalists, and International Congress of Free Trade Unions.

replied, "I cannot answer that, Senator," and the matter was dropped.)[3]

But unbeknownst to most of the Congress and the American people, however, the agency has repeatedly chosen to interpret the NSC 86, NSCID 13, and NSCID 14 orders as authorization for substantial political involvement in immigrant communities in America. As early as 1949—only two years after Congress had thoroughly debated keeping the CIA out of American politics—the agency began underwriting several major programs designed to bring favored European exiles into this country. Then, in 1950, this immigration work was coupled with a multimillion-dollar publicity campaign in the United States tailored to win popular approval for cold war measures sponsored by the CIA, including increased funding for Radio Free Europe, Radio Liberation, and the émigré political groups in the governments-in-exile program.

These efforts have left a lasting mark on American political life, especially among the United States' large first-generation Slavic and Eastern European immigrant population. Hundreds of thousands of decent people of Central and Eastern European heritage entered this country legally during the 1950s, often at the price of great personal sacrifice. But the measures undertaken by the CIA in connection with NSC 86, NSCID 13, and NSCID 14 led to the infiltration of thousands of Waffen SS veterans and other Nazi collaborators into their communities in the United States at the same time. This in turn laid the foundation for a revival of extremist right-wing political movements inside immigrant communities in this country that continue to be active.[4]

The CIA, and Frank Wisner's clandestine action shop (the OPC) in particular, were never content with the immigration to the United States of a handful of especially valuable assets. The 100 Persons Act was simply too restrictive, Wisner believed. The agency was running international programs involving thousands of foreign agents, with tens of thousands of subagents. Many of these men and women were risking their lives for the modest paychecks they got from the Americans, as he saw it. The promise of free immigration to the United States was crucial in recruiting new overseas help for the CIA and in retaining the loyalty of many persons already on the U.S. payroll.

According to State Department records, Wisner wanted to grant U.S. citizenship as a reward to not just "100 Persons" per year, but to thousands, even tens of thousands of informants, covert operators, guerrillas and agents of influence. Whatever else might be said of Wisner, he was never one to let sticky legal technicalities stand in the way of what he believed to be the best interests of the country. He set out to create a wide variety of both legal and illegal dodges to bring men and women favored by his organization into the country.

This immigration campaign became an integral part of CIA clandestine strategy of the period. The agency manipulated U.S. immigration laws and procedures on behalf of thousands of favored émigrés, selecting some for entry to this country and rejecting others. While only a fraction of this influx appears to have been Nazis or Nazi collaborators (the true number is impossible to know until the agency opens its files), it is clear that a number of identifiable war criminals were brought to the United States with CIA assistance during this period.[5] Equally important, the security agencies of the government gave tacit support to private refugee relief committees the stated goals of which included assisting thousands of Waffen SS veterans in immigrating to the United States.

Bloodstone had begun this process on a relatively modest scale, with about 250 sponsored immigrants per year. By 1950, however, CIA representatives approached Congress with a plan to authorize special importation of some *15,000* CIA-sponsored refugees per year, in addition to those entering under the Displaced Persons Act and other more conventional immigration channels. They were to be émigrés "whose presence in the U.S. would be deemed in the national interest," according to Department of State documentation,[6] "as a result of the prominent or active part they played in the struggle against Communism." Congress whittled that authorization down to 500 "carefully selected" refugees over a three-year period. Even so, the CIA's professed need for 15,000 annual entrance visas is some measure of its ambitions in this field. Émigrés sponsored under this law came to be known as "2(d)" cases, after the section of the immigration code that provided the legal authorization.

The law established a new category of immigrant, the "Displaced Persons National Interest Case." Officially the departments of State and Defense were supposed to sponsor these immigrants, but in reality this was a CIA program. Agency-funded organizations, "working closely with the National Committee for a Free Europe," like the Committee for a Free Latvia, International Peasant Union, and so on, were singled out for patronage under the new law, according to State Department records. The CIA also sponsored immigrants who had cooperated with U.S. intelligence in espionage or covert operations. Finally, the agency brought survivors of the failed raids on Albania into the United States under the 2(d) program.[7]

Congress's refusal to support fully the agency's 15,000-visa-per-year immigration effort was not the final word on the matter. Indeed, the CIA expanded upon the authority it had been granted by the National Security Council under NSC 86 and NSCIDs 13 and 14. If the agency was barred from directly importing 15,000 exiles annually, it reasoned, it could still employ the NSC's top secret authorization to sponsor indirectly many of the same émigrés through ostensibly private relief organizations. Some U.S.-based refugee assistance groups specializing in aid to Latvian, Lithuanian, Belorussian, and Ukrainian émigrés made no secret of their desire to import precisely the same anti-Communist activists, some of them Waffen SS veterans, in whom the CIA was most interested. Wisner found the solution to his legal problems by secretly underwriting the activities of such organizations, then letting them do the legwork involved in bringing their countrymen to the United States. In this way, the Mykola Lebeds, Gustav Hilgers, and other exiles who entered the country with direct agency assistance soon became only the tip of a much larger iceberg.

Beginning at least as early as 1950, the CIA earmarked money for favored émigrés and passed it through a variety of cutouts—including both private foundations and "overt" governmental programs—to selected refugee relief groups serving Eastern European immigrants. Control of this effort was centralized in the NSC's executive committee responsible for oversight of the NSC 10/2 program and other CIA covert operations.[8] A full accounting of these funds has yet to be made, but the public reports of the National Committee for a Free Europe, the U.S. Displaced Persons Commission, and the fragmentary declassified records of the NSC indicate that major recipients included the International Rescue Committee (IRC), the National Catholic Welfare Conference, the United Lithuanian Relief Fund of America, and a number of similar ethnic and religious-based charities. At least $100 million was spent on such efforts during the decade of the 1950s according to presently available reports,[9] and the true total may well be considerably higher.

The private refugee aid groups were closely monitored by the

CIA. As a later NSC decision on refugee and defector programs puts it, these programs "contribute to the achievement of U.S. national security objectives both toward Communist-dominated areas and the Free World. . . . These contracts, under which the [private] agencies are reimbursed only for services actually performed on behalf of escapees, are carefully supervised to assure that they give maximum support to the objectives of the program."[10]

Yet in several cases Nazi collaborators and sympathizers took control of key aspects of refugee relief agencies serving their nationalities in the United States. Among Latvians a secretive organization known as the Daugavas Vanagi ("Hawks of the Daugava River") gradually built up an influential political machine in Latvian displaced persons camps in Europe and, later, in Latvian communities in this country as well. The Vanagis began as a self-help and welfare society for Latvian SS veterans in Germany in 1945; many of its leaders had been involved in Fascist activity in Latvia since the 1930s. Like the OUN Ukrainian nationalists, some of the Vanagis' leaders had served as the Nazis' most enthusiastic executioners inside their homeland, only to be spurned by the chauvinistic Germans. The Latvian extremists held on tenaciously during the Nazi occupation, however, and many were rewarded with posts as mayors, concentration camp administrators, and—most frequently—officers of the Latvian Waffen SS division sponsored by the Nazis during the last years of the conflict. Most of the Vanagis' leadership fled to Germany with the retreating Nazis at war's end.[11]

In the first five years after the war the Vanagis gradually came to control Latvian displaced persons camps in Germany. The semisecret society also served as an organizing and coordinating force among the Latvian Waffen SS veterans who enlisted in the U.S. Labor Service units. Many Vanagi members found their way to Britain, Canada, and the United States in the guise of displaced persons during this period.

Highly disciplined and organized, the Vanagis maintained their linkages during their diaspora and used their international connections to expand their influence inside Latvian communities abroad. In the United States several Vanagis who had once been high-level Nazi collaborators created interlocking directorships dominated by party members among the American Latvian Association, the Latvian-American Republican National Federation, and the CIA-funded Committee for a Free Latvia.[12] These organizations, which came to be controlled or strongly influenced by the Vanagis, exercised considerable unofficial authority over which potential Latvian immigrants would obtain visas to the United States—and which would not. Not surprisingly, their exercise of this power has consistently tended to reinforce Vanagi authority inside Latvian-American communities.

It is clear today that several of these groups and a number of individual Vanagi Nazi collaborators enjoyed clandestine U.S. government subsidies from the CIA. This money was laundered through the CIA's Radio Free Europe and Assembly of Captive European Nations channels or through private organizations such as the International Rescue Committee, among others.[13] Whether or not the CIA approved of the Vanagis' sometimes openly racist and pro-Fascist political behavior, the fact remains that it helped underwrite the careers of at least three—and probably more— senior Vanagi leaders that the U.S. government itself has accused of Nazi war crimes. The three beneficiaries were Vilis Hazners, Boleslavs Maikovskis, and Alfreds Berzins.

Vilis Hazners is an SS veteran and a winner of the German Iron Cross. The U.S. government has accused him of serving as a senior security police officer in Riga, Latvia, for much of the war. The government records include reports that the men under Hazners's command committed serious atrocities, including herding dozens of Jews into a synagogue and setting it aflame. Hazners successfully defended himself from these charges, however, during a deportation proceeding in the late 1970s.[14]

Hazners entered the United States in the early 1950s. Whether or not the CIA assisted him in this is unknown, but it is clear that it sponsored him and helped pay his salary once he was here. Hazners assumed the chairmanship of the Committee for a Free Latvia and a post as delegate to the ACEN in New York. Both organizations—including the wages of their officials—are now known to have been financed in part by the CIA. (The sponsorship of these groups was secret during the 1950s but was eventually admitted by the government during the series of scandals that rocked the agency during the 1970s.)[15] "Liberation" committee chairmen like Hazners typically received a salary of $12,000 per year in the early 1950s, a pay rate that was better than that of most mid-level State Department employees of the day.

Hazners did not hide his Fascist background. He practically flaunted it. At the same time he was active in ACEN, he served as chairman of the Latvian Officers Association, a thinly disguised self-help group made up in large part of Waffen SS veterans. He also served as an officer of the American branch of the Vanagis and as editor of the group's magazine for many years.[16] He was meanwhile active in a number of more respectable groups like the American Latvian Association, which he served as an officer, specializing in immigration and "refugee relief" work on behalf of favored Latvian émigrés in Europe.

Then there is Boleslavs Maikovskis. Also a Latvian police chief decorated with the Iron Cross, Maikovskis has been charged by the U.S. government with having been instrumental in pogroms at Audrini and Rezekne, Latvia, in which dozens of people were murdered in cold blood. He is a longtime Vanagi activist, former vice-chairman of the American Latvian Association, and a former delegate to the ACEN. The U.S. Justice Department's Nazi hunting unit has been trying to deport Maikovskis from the United States for more than eight years as this book goes to press, but the cumbersome judicial process involved in expulsion of Nazi criminals has permitted him to continue to live in New York State until his appeals are exhausted.[17]

Alfreds Berzins, now deceased, was propaganda minister in the prewar Latvian dictatorship of Karlis Ulmanis. During that time Berzins "help[ed] put people in concentration camps," according to his CROWCASS wanted report, and was "partially responsible for the deaths of hundreds of Latvians and thousands of Jews." The United States asserted that Berzins was "responsible for murder, ill treatment and deportation of 2000 persons." He was, the United States said, "a fanatic Nazi."[18]

After the war Berzins went to great lengths to establish himself as democratically minded. He put his propaganda skills back to work on the ACEN's public relations committee. He simultaneously served as editor of the journal *Baltic Review* and as a leading member of the Committee for a Free Latvia. His books on Latvia are found in most major U.S. libraries (one has an introduction by Senator Thomas Dodd), and he served for years as deputy chairman of the American Latvian Association and the World Latvian Association.[19]

These Vanagis did not hesitate to use their political clout and government contacts to sponsor former SS men and Nazi collaborators for U.S. citizenship. In fact, they waged a successful campaign to reverse U.S. immigration regulations to permit Baltic SS men, who had long been the primary beneficiaries of Vanagi assistance anyway, to enter the United States legally.

The Latvian-language *Daugavas Vanagi Biletens,* for example, helpfully provided its readers with English-language texts to send to U.S. officials protesting exclusion of Baltic SS men from U.S. visas and citizenship. Their argument, in brief, was that the Baltic SS men had not "really" been Nazis, only patriotic Latvians and Lithuanians concerned about protecting their countries from a Soviet invasion. "My [brother] who is already a U.S. soldier," the Vanagis urged their supporters to write to Washington, "is going to defend the Free World against Communist aggression [in Korea]. Whay [*sic*] are those Latvians who did the same in 1944—defend our country Latvia, against Communist aggression—not now admitted to the U.S.?[20] These are not more fascists [*sic*] than those American boys who now die from Soviet manufactured and Chinese Communist fired bullets," the appeal continued.

Their effort bore fruit in late 1950, when Displaced Persons Commissioner Edward M. O'Connor forced through an administrative change that redefined the Baltic SS as *not* being a "movement hostile to the United States." The decision cleared Baltic SS veterans for entry into this country. O'Connor's maneuver was opposed by DP Commissioner Harry N. Rosenfield, but without success.[21] Charitable organizations such as Latvian Relief Incorporated and the United Lithuanian Relief Fund of America made sure that the favored SS veterans were not only permitted entry but often given free passage, board, food, emergency funds, and assistance in finding jobs as well.

Similar events and the use of similar interlocking directorships brought extreme rightists to power in a number of Lithuanian, Ukrainian, Croatian, and Belorussian (White Russian) émigré organizations in this country, just as they had in the Latvian groups mentioned above. Their common wartime experience as Nazi collaborators and, often, as Waffen SS men was the glue that held these groups together. Their members adapted reasonably well to the American political scene, putting themselves forward as militant nationalists and anti-Communists, as was true enough, while declaring their personal innocence of war crimes.

At the same time many Americans preferred to concentrate on the role of those former Nazi collaborators as anti-Communists who had worked with the Germans out of "patriotic" motives—as the

Daugavas Vanagi Biletens letter cited above illustrates—while denying evidence of their role in atrocities and crimes against humanity on the ground that such accusations were Communist propaganda. Not all Eastern European anti-Communists were former Nazi collaborators obviously. But it is true that the intense anticommunism of the cold war gave those who *were* Nazi collaborators a means of rationalizing what they had done during the war and, in effect, a place to hide. Respectable conservatives in this country who had never been Nazi collaborators often turned a blind eye to this process and were sometimes the most articulate advocates for SS veterans and other collaborators.[22]

For example, the United Lithuanian Relief Fund of America (known as BALF, for its Lithuanian initials) was created in 1944 for the specific purpose of excluding leftists from any role in Lithuanian relief assistance programs. BALF was, and remains, closely tied to the pre-World War II Lithuanian Activist Front, an extreme nationalist group whose leaders were similar in many respects to those of the Vanagi.

BALF became instrumental, by its own account, in virtually every aspect of postwar Lithuanian immigration to the United States and enjoyed heavy funding from both U.S. government and Catholic Church agencies. It claimed responsibility for selection of, and assistance to, some 30,000 Lithuanian immigrants to America in the wake of World War II.[23] The organization helped many Lithuanians of many different political persuasions, including some who had been persecuted and imprisoned by the Nazis. Even so, aid to Lithuanian Waffen SS veterans was central to BALF"s relief work during the 1950s. The largest single group of alleged war criminals now facing deportation from the United States by the Department of Justice, in fact, are Lithuanian veterans of the SS who entered the country with BALF assistance during the cold war.[24]

BALF's longtime business manager, the Reverend Lionginas Jankus, was a measure of the political point of view that the organization embraced in its refugee relief work. Testimony taken during a 1964 Lithuanian war crimes trial accused Jankus of leading a series of pogroms in the Jazdai forest region that took the lives of some 1,200 people during the Nazi occupation of his homeland. Jankus himself, who was in the United States at the time of the trial and out of reach of the Lithuanian prosecutors, denied he had been involved in the pogrom, if indeed, it had taken place at all. He said

George F. Kennan. As director of the State Department's Policy Planning Staff during the late 1940s, Kennan played an influential role in the development of early U.S. clandestine operations, including recruitment of Nazi collaborators believed to be useful for intelligence and psychological warfare. TOP: Kennan as a young Foreign Service officer in 1938. His service at the U.S. Embassy in Moscow established lifelong friendships with some of America's—and Nazi Germany's—most prominent experts on the USSR.

America's first chief of clandestine operations Frank Wisner, shown here in a rare photograph as an OSS officer in 1945. Wisner's Office for Policy Coordination and, later, Plans Directorate of the CIA became the headquarters for covert warfare employing Nazi collaborators.

Key figures in postwar recruitment of intelligence specialists who had once been Nazi collaborators. TOP LEFT: Voice of America director and OSS veteran Charles Thayer, one of the first advocates of U.S. guerrilla warfare programs employing Vlasov Army veterans. TOP RIGHT: Kennan's right hand in émigré operations, John Paton Davies. BOTTOM RIGHT: Early CIA/OPC operative Carmel Offie, responsible for the care and feeding of selected émigré nationalists brought to Washington, D.C. BOTTOM LEFT: German diplomat Hans Heinrich Herwarth. Recruited by the Americans as a "source inside the Nazi Embassy" in Moscow in 1939, Herwarth served during the war as a leading political officer of the German army's effort to use émigré troops on the eastern front. Charles Thayer rescued Herwarth from an American POW camp in 1945, setting the stage for the postwar revival of Germany's defector troops under new U.S. sponsorship.

Political and psychological warfare specialists. TOP: Senior German expert on the USSR Gustav Hilger (center, in glasses), seen here as first secretary of Germany's embassy in Moscow during the 1940 meeting on the Hitler-Stalin pact. Soviet minister V. M. Molotov is at the far left; Nazi Foreign Minister Joachim von Ribbentrop is at right. In addition to his work on the eastern front, Hilger participated in SS efforts to deport Italian Jews to concentration camps. George Kennan served as Hilger's reference for high-level U.S. security clearances after the war. BOTTOM LEFT: General Ernst Köstring, leader of the Nazis' program to recruit thousands of defectors from the East into the German army. BOTTOM RIGHT: General Andrei Vlasov, who defected to the Nazis following his capture in 1942, reviews a regiment of the German-sponsored "Russian Liberation Army." Vlasov was eventually hanged by the Soviets for treason, but his troops—many of them veterans of Nazi extermination squads—became foot soldiers in U.S.-sponsored anti-Communist psychological warfare operations of the cold war.

Nazi political warfare in the East. TOP: A cavalry unit of Vlasov's Army on patrol on the eastern front. CENTER: Latvian SS volunteers during a training drill, 1944. BOTTOM LEFT: SS photograph of three generations of Jewish women, seconds before they were murdered. The armed men in the background are Latvian police volunteers. BOTTOM RIGHT: Suspected anti-Nazi partisans were hanged by Latvian collaborators in Minsk as a warning to the population.

BOTTOM LEFT: General Reinhard Gehlen, seen here as commander of the Fremde Heere Ost (Foreign Armies East), Germany's most important intelligence organization on the eastern front. TOP: Gehlen at a 1943 FHO staff Christmas party, as the war was turning decisively against Nazi Germany. CENTER: Gehlen with Wilfried Strik-Strikfeldt (center, facing camera), Gehlen's liaison officer with Vlasov. Gehlen eventually became chief of West Germany's intelligence service, BND; Strik-Strikfeldt became a prominent leader of CIA-financed exile programs at Radio Liberation from Bolshevism, the precursor of today's Radio Liberty. BOTTOM RIGHT: Edwin Sibert, the U.S. Army's chief of intelligence in Europe at war's end, who recruited Gehlen in 1945 and protected the Gehlen Organization during its formative stages. The Org was "my baby," Sibert said.

Despite Gehlen's denials, U.S. funds laundered through Gehlen's Org underwrote careers in intelligence for a number of SS men after the war. TOP LEFT: Nazi racial expert and SS intelligence specialist Franz Six. Convicted of mass murder by an American military tribunal in 1948, Six was nonetheless given clemency in order to return to work for Gehlen's Org. TOP RIGHT: Alois Brunner was accused of murdering more than 120,000 Jews in France, Greece, and Slovakia, but escaped to Syria after the war. There, in Damascus, Brunner became the Gehlen Org's resident— a post similar in authority to a CIA chief of station. U.S. funds also underwrote Brunner's work for Egypt during the 1950s. BOTTOM LEFT: SS clandestine operations specialist Otto Skorzeny, seen here at a Nazi party gathering honoring him in 1943. Skorzeny eventually led CIA-financed recruitment of ex-Nazi SS and Abwehr officers for training of Egyptian security police under Nasser. BOTTOM RIGHT: Skorzeny during his later career as an international arms merchant and neo-Nazi spokesman, about 1959.

TOP: Nazi Germany's wartime rocket chief Walter Dornberger (left), seen here with Wernher von Braun in 1944. Dornberger set the schedule by which 20,000 inmates at the Nordhausen concentration camp were worked to death. BOTTOM LEFT: Nordhausen camp shortly after liberation by U.S. troops in April 1945. BOTTOM RIGHT: Dornberger entered the United States under Project Paperclip and eventually emerged as a senior executive of the Bell Aerosystems Division of Textron. The photo here is from 1954.

Influence on American life. LEFT: Russian extreme nationalist leader Constantine Bold-yreff, shown here during a 1948 speaking tour of the United States aimed at raising $100 million to overthrow Stalin. Boldyreff's work in this country was "well known to American intelligence . . . and vouched for by high officials," press reports said. RIGHT: Former SS intelligence specialist Nikolai N. Poppe testifies against Owen Lattimore during Senate Internal Security Subcommittee hearings, 1952.

Klaus Barbie's passport, bearing the false name of "Altmann," with which he escaped from Europe. The ratline that saved Barbie became integral to dozens of intelligence operations.

FOTOGRAFIAS

DATOS QUE PROPORCIONA EL SOLICITANTE

: alemana   ON: mecánico

'onstadt..alemani.   25-10-1915.

TOP: Charles Bohlen, an early advocate of clandestine U.S. programs employing exiled extreme nationalists, eventually became a target of the radical right for his role in the wartime Yalta Conference. Senator Joseph McCarthy—acting on a tip from a former Goebbels propagandist—argued that Bohlen had delivered Poland to the Soviets at Yalta and was "possibly" a Stalinist agent. Here Bohlen meets the press in 1953 in the midst of a bitterly fought battle over his nomination as U.S. ambassador to the USSR. LEFT: CIA Director Allen Dulles: clandestine warfare as an integral part of U.S.–Soviet relations.

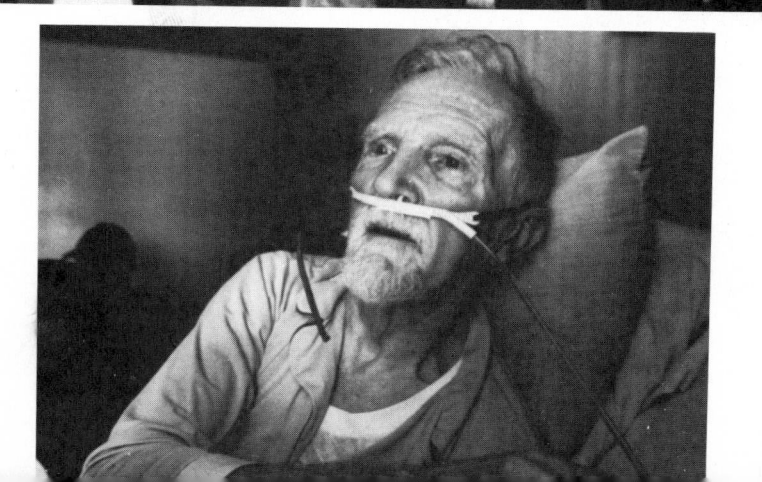

A presumption of innocence: former SS man and CIA contract agent Otto von Bolschwing. TOP: Von Bolschwing as he appeared when he enlisted in the SS. CENTER: With a team of U.S. Army Counterintelligence Corps agents in Austria, 1946. BOTTOM: Von Bolschwing shortly before his death in a California hospital.

Ukrainian extreme nationalist leader Mykola Lebed. Despite Lebed's record as a convicted assassin and security chief in Nazi-occupied Lvov during a 1942 pogrom, the CIA brought him to the United States in October 1949, then intervened to squelch an Immigration and Naturalization Service investigation when word of his background leaked.

TOP LEFT: Wartime Latvian police chief Boleslavs Maikovskis (shown here in uniform in a Nazi propaganda photo) later led a CIA-funded exile organization in the United States. TOP RIGHT: Maikovskis faces deportation during a 1977 trial. He remains in the United States as this book goes to press. BOTTOM LEFT: Former CIA contract agent Edgars Laipenieks walks tight-lipped from the legal hearing room where a witness has identified him as a participant in the hanging of a prisoner at the Riga prison in Nazi-occupied Latvia. The CIA contacted the Immigration and Naturalization Service on Laipenieks's behalf, bringing an early end to the government's first investigation into his past. BOTTOM RIGHT: Former Latvian police official Vilis Hazners, acquitted of charges stemming from the persecution of Jews during the Nazi occupation.

First Captive Nations Day, 1960. Francis Cardinal Spellman (left) blesses Captive Nations Day marchers in native costume at a mass following the parade.

Republican party leaders and Nazi sympathizers meet at a gathering on "organizing ethnics" held in Scranton, Pennsylvania, in 1971. Republican party "ethnics" organizer Laszlo Pasztor (standing, left) and Republican National Committee Cochair Ann Armstrong (seated, right) meet with Austin App (standing, second from left) and Ivan Docheff (standing, fourth from right). App, a leader of the German-American organization DANK, was also a key spokesman for the "Holocaust is a myth" theory and a prominent Captive Nations leader until his death in 1984. Docheff, a longtime director of the extreme-right Bulgarian National Front in the United States, began his political career as a leader of the pro-Fascist political organization in Bulgaria.

Captive Nations Day dinner, 1984. From right in photo: the author; Cossack nationalist and anti-Semitic leader Nicholas Nazarenko; and New York Captive Nations chairman Horst Uhlich.

EASTERN EUROPE UNDER NAZI OCCUPATION—1942

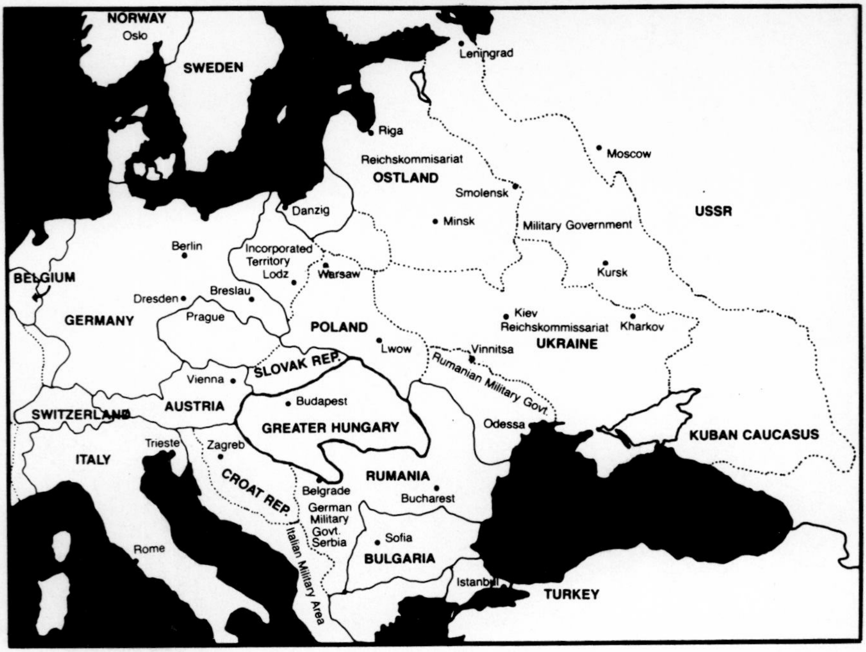

TOP: Nazi-occupied Eastern Europe, 1942. BOTTOM: National and regional boundaries as they appear today.

EASTERN EUROPE TODAY

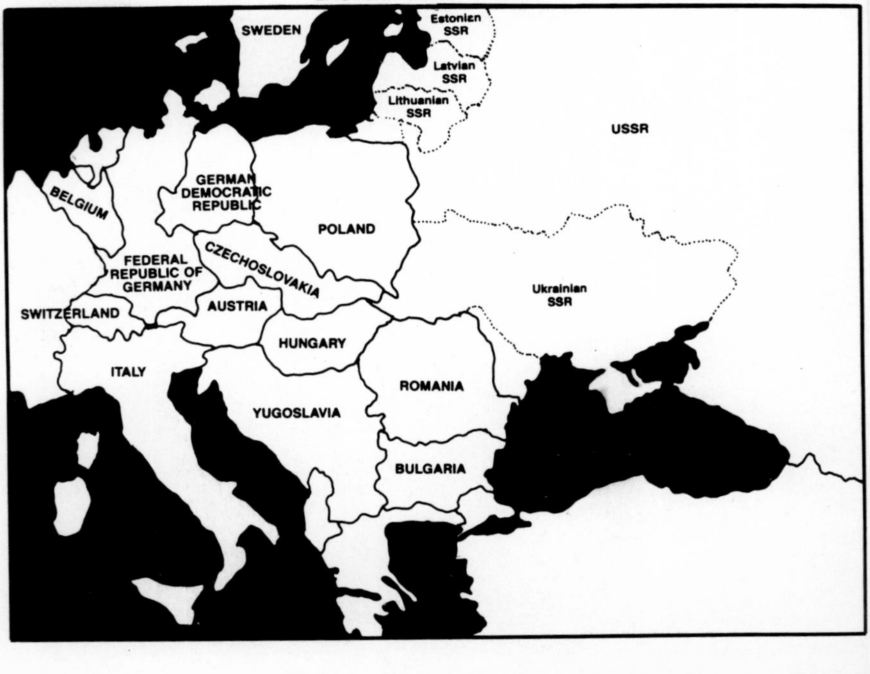

that the whole case was politically motivated propaganda from the USSR designed to discredit Lithuanians.[25]

The preponderance of evidence, however, is that the priest was lying. Prosecutors at the trial introduced physical evidence, including photographs and documents, that they claimed proved Jankus's role in these murders. Dozens of sworn statements from both Lithuanian Jewish survivors and Nazis involved in the pogrom itself were also submitted to the court. An international outcry against Jankus ensued, but BALF kept him on staff as business manager. Jankus died in the late 1960s, and the dispute over his veracity has never been conclusively resolved.

It is evident that the CIA knew that substantial numbers of SS men and former Nazi collaborators were streaming into this country through organizations that were themselves on the CIA's payroll.* Highly competent U.S. intelligence officers followed each

---

*There was also a large program to import former Belorussian (White Russian) Nazis as political warfare operatives, says a former Justice Department Office of Special Investigations staff member, John Loftus. While questions about some aspects of the Belorussian story remain, Loftus has nonetheless used the Freedom of Information Act to bring to light several important records that he asserts establish a prima facie case for the existence of this operation. The Belorussian project is strikingly similar to the Latvian and Lithuanian Waffen SS immigration discussed above.

The first document is simply a chapter on Belorussian Nazis from the U.S. Army's top secret *Consolidated Orientation and Guidance Manual,* which was prepared by the 970th CIC unit in the U.S. zone of Germany in 1948. It shows that U.S. intelligence was well aware of the massacres and pogroms that took place in Belorussia during the war, and it lists scores of Belorussian collaborators who believed to have been involved in those crimes.

The second record is a secret sixteen-page letter from Belorussian Nazi collaborationist leader Radislaw Ostrowsky to Frank Wisner's OPC division of the CIA dated 1952. It details the history of the Belorussian quisling movement and bluntly proposes that the CIA finance and protect Ostrowsky's "government-in-exile" for clandestine operations against the USSR.

In this letter Ostrowsky directly admits that the SS and Gestapo sponsored his organization during the war and states that he personally helped build a large SS unit used in antipartisan warfare. But, Ostrowsky writes, "it is unimportant that we were collaborators during the war, and it is utterly unimportant with who [sic] we collaborated—Germans or devils. What is important is that we were never collaborators with Stalin.

"The intelligence branches of every government must of course have their own agents in the territory of the countries in which they are interested," he continues. "This circumstance led me to turn to the intelligence service of the USA with the proposal that we unite our forces." Ostrowsky then pleads for money from the United States and proposes that the CIA work "in conjunction with our modest forces . . . [in] complete frankness and trust."

The agency appears to have accepted the offer. A few months later, former SS General Franz Kushel (who was Ostrowsky's most bitter political rival and a major Belorussian war criminal in his own right) complained to the FBI that the CIA-financed American Committee for Liberation from Bolshevism had cut off his funding and was instead pouring money into Ostrowsky's coffers.

Less than a year after that more than 100 Belorussian exiles gathered in the United States for a special political congress. The men and women at that gathering, practically without

twist and turn of these émigré organizations and knew exactly who was linked to which political faction in the old countries. The affairs of Eastern European exiles were, after all, a major focus of the CIA's work at the time. Their relief groups and political organizations were thoroughly infiltrated with agency informers. Indeed, if the CIA did *not* know what was taking place in the immigration process, that in itself raises serious questions concerning its ability to collect and analyze information from refugee sources.

But nothing was done by the CIA, so far as can be determined, to stop the influx of ex-Nazis and collaborators during the 1950s. If anything, the government subsidies to their organizations actually increased. Some men and women who had once enlisted as agents for the Nazi occupiers of their homelands put their skills back to work as inside sources for the CIA and FBI once they had arrived here. Federal agencies are, of course, unwilling to release the names of their confidential informants, but a 1978 study by the General Accounting Office[26] clearly establishes that working relations between U.S. police agencies and these former Fascists did exist. The GAO found that of a sample of 111 persons reported to have been war criminals—not simply ex-collaborators—discovered in the United States, some "seventeen were contacted by the CIA in the United States" for use as informants, many of whom had previously been CIA contract agents overseas. Five more cooperated with the agency in a variety of other capacities. Others worked for the FBI. In all, about 20 percent of the GAO's sample of alleged war criminals had worked as informants for U.S. security organizations inside this country.

Meanwhile, a parallel and sometimes overlapping series of events was taking place inside the army's guerrilla warfare training program. The embarrassing incident in Germany with the

---

exception, were the chiefs and staffs of the wartime puppet government that Ostrowsky had pitched to the CIA. The list of delegates is led by Ostrowsky himself and includes at least a half dozen other known war crimes suspects connected with his political faction. Many of them had been specifically named in the earlier army study on Belorussian war criminals.

These records do not necessarily prove that the clandestine action arm of the CIA organized this conference but they do raise obvious questions about exactly what role the agency may have had in obtaining visas to the United States for these exiles. In at least one known case, State Department political officers—a frequently used cover post for OPC and CIA operatives—did directly intervene to obtain a U.S. visa for Emanuel Jasiuk, who had served for much of the war as a Nazi puppet administrator in Kletsk during massacres which took the lives of some 5,000 Jews.

"Young Germans" assassination squads slowly convinced U.S. intelligence that the Labor Service units in Europe were unsuitable for the major guerrilla warfare and espionage projects that the army and CIA were attempting to hide in them. The army command eventually decided that much tighter control would be necessary to ensure the security and effectiveness of postnuclear guerrilla operations. The best of the émigré foot soldiers should be brought to the United States, the army concluded, enlisted in the U.S. Army, and provided with intensive training far beyond what was possible in the Labor Service units. The army reasoned that this more formal recruitment of émigrés would also permit the granting of security clearances to translators with backgrounds in Russian, Ukrainian, and other Eastern European languages. The new enlistees were to remain under U.S. Army control, even though the military was eager to cooperate with the CIA on specific missions.[27]

In 1950 the army convinced Congress to pass an unusual piece of cold war legislation, known as the Lodge Act, that permitted 2,500 alien nationals (later raised to 12,500) residing outside the United States to enlist in the U.S. Army. It guaranteed them U.S. citizenship if they successfully completed five years of service.[28] The overwhelming majority of the Lodge Act recruits who volunteered over the following decade have proved themselves to be loyal citizens. Most are intensely patriotic, many have been decorated for heroism in battle, and some have given their lives in service to their adopted country. It is ironic, then, that the U.S. Army chose to mix Gestapo agents and Nazi collaborators with this group of decent men.

The Labor Service units, which were by that time officially accepting Waffen SS veterans, were identified as the "largest and logical source of alien recruits" for the Lodge Act, according to a 1951 army adjutant general report. Both before and after passage of the bill the military drew up detailed studies that evaluated the number of potential recruits, their health, military training, language skills, and even "political reliability."

Stunning examples of the self-deception and ethnic discrimination that took place during the army's screening of Lodge Act volunteers may be found in the military's studies of the "political reliability" of émigrés during this period. One top secret army study, for example, determined that the *entire population* of displaced persons from Latvia, Lithuania, and Estonia meeting the age and sex requirements* (including, presumably, the thoroughly nazified Latvian officers discussed previously) were "politically acceptable" for enlistment in the U.S. Army.

The Adjutant General's Office, which was ultimately responsible for screening émigré recruits, also determined that such Baltic volunteers were "100 percent" reliable on political grounds. With backing like that, the Latvian Labor Service veterans had little difficulty entering the army and eventually obtaining U.S. citizenship. Other nationalities (Ukrainians and Yugoslavs, for example) were believed to require closer scrutiny. The army considered Jews at the bottom of the list; only "50%" of them were considered politically reliable, according to the adjutant general's study, and in practice Jews were generally excluded from entering the United States under the Lodge Act.[29]

The percentages of "politically reliable" foreign recruits in the Labor Service units were ranked by the army according to nationality, as follows.[30] Ratings of " −100%" mean that something fewer than all the volunteers of that ethnic group were considered politically suitable, while a " +50%" listing means that only about one-half that nationality was believed to be reliable.

Nationality	Political Reliability
Esthonian [sic]	100%
Latvian	100%
Lithuanian	100%
Ukrainian	− 100%
Yugoslav	− 100%
Poles	− 100%
Jews (Poles)	+ 50%
Jews (Hungarian, Romanian, etc.)	+ 50%
Russian	?
Stateless	?
Italians	?

The first known group of Lodge Act recruits arrived by a military airlift at Camp Kilmer, New Jersey, in October 1951. Most were Ukrainians and Poles, but virtually every Eastern European nationality was represented. After an initial orientation at the camp the army shipped these recruits, like most of those who followed, to Fort Dix, New Jersey, for eight to sixteen weeks of basic training. Others were sent directly to a special army intelligence Language

*That is, male, age eighteen to thirty-four, unmarried, and physically fit.

Qualification Unit at Fort Devens, Massachusetts. Following basic training, the recruits were dispersed across the United States and Europe. Substantial numbers were posted to the Defense Language School in Monterey, California; others to the unique Armed Forces Demonstration Unit at Fort Monroe, Virginia, where defectors from Eastern Europe taught Red Army tactics to U.S. strike force teams.

According to declassified orders now found in the National Archives, about 25 percent of the enlistees were channeled into a variety of especially confidential assignments, including slots as atomic, chemical, and biological warfare specialists. Others became translators of captured secret documents and instructors for U.S. intelligence analysts.[31]

Many of the remainder of the Lodge Act recruits underwent special guerrilla training at Fort Bragg, North Carolina, and became the nucleus of the present-day Green Berets. Indeed, the famous green beret itself is in part a legacy of the European military fatigues that so many of America's first Special Forces recruits had worn during their service prior to their arrival in this country. The commander of the program at Fort Bragg, interestingly enough, was Colonel Aaron Bank, an army paramilitary expert who only a few months previously had directed the CIC units responsible for running Klaus Barbie, Mykola Lebed, and similar intelligence assets in Germany.[32]

Colonel Charles M. Simpson, the unofficial historian of the Green Berets and a thirty-year army veteran, leaves little question about the training of army and CIA volunteers placed under Colonel Bank's care at Fort Bragg. The instruction, Simpson writes, began with selection of sites for clandestine airdrops of agents behind enemy lines, then went on to "raids and ambushes [and] guerrilla organization." Particular attention was placed, he says, on "kidnap and assassination operations."[33]

Unfortunately for the army, Lodge Act recruiting went more slowly than expected, and only 211 men (out of 5,272 applicants) had passed screening and actually enlisted by August 1952. Special Forces recruiters responded by easing the language and literacy requirements and by streamlining many of the security checks that had previously slowed the processing of volunteers.

Army Adjutant General Major General Edward Witsell ruled that the civilian immigration laws that barred ex-Nazis and collaborators from obtaining U.S. citizenship would *not* apply to the army's

Lodge Act recruits. "[I]ndividuals enlisted under these regulations are not subject to exclusion from the United States under the provisions of the Internal Security Act or under the Immigration and Nationality Act . . . ," Witsell ordered, taking responsibility for screening émigrés out of the hands of civilian authorities altogether. True, "members . . . of any totalitarian party" were still barred from the United States under the army regulations, but *ex*-members of Fascist organizations were not, nor were veterans of armies that had made war on the United States.[34] Witsell's unusual and probably unconstitutional decision seems to have gone entirely unnoticed at the time, perhaps because of the fact that the very existence of the ruling was withheld from the public under a classification of "Restricted—Security Information."

One result of this policy was that certain racist perspectives bordering on Nazi-style anticommunism persisted in the early Green Berets. As Richard Harwood reported in the *Washington Post* some years later, "during those years, the Special Forces attracted recruits from Eastern Europe and old-line NCOs with single-minded views about 'fighting Communism.' . . . 'We had an awful lot of John Birch types then,' says an officer with several years of experience in the Special Forces," Harwood writes. " 'They thought like Joe McCarthy.' "[35]

The fact that the army's Lodge Act decision encouraged scores of former Nazis and Nazi collaborators to obtain U.S. citizenship with the prior knowledge of U.S. officials can be clearly documented with the army's own records. The army's decision on where to send a recruit depended in part on the answers he gave in an interview at the time he arrived at Camp Kilmer. Each new enlistee was asked a series of simple questions about his background in police security work, guerrilla warfare, or resistance movements; his language skills; and his willingness to volunteer for guerrilla warfare or paratrooper operations on behalf of the United States. Summaries of several hundred of these interviews of Lodge Act recruits were discovered recently in secret files of army archives in Washington, D.C. One group of enlistees processed at Camp Kilmer in March 1954 is fairly typical. Of forty-four new enlistees processed that month, three admitted membership in the Wehrmacht between 1942 and 1945; another was a Gestapo veteran; two more were veterans of other Axis armies who had fought under Nazi leadership against Allied forces during the war. In short, about

14 percent of the recruits in this squad *admitted* past membership in organizations that might have otherwise barred them from obtaining U.S. citizenship.*[36]

As puzzling as it may seem today, there is no question that the American army officers who recruited former Nazis into the Special Forces were motivated primarily by a hatred of totalitarianism. As they saw it, the Special Forces units were something of a creative maverick within the hidebound army; its members disdained shiny boots, army protocol, and just about anything that smacked of brass. The Special Forces motto, *"De Oppresso Liber,"* which the Green Berets translate as "From Oppression We Will Liberate Them," was not chosen for its public relations value; the slogan, like almost everything else about the forces, was generally kept secret in the early days. This catchphrase reflected the beliefs of the officers, or perhaps more accurately, it reflected what the officers thought that their beliefs were. In those simpler days the army staff could argue in complete seriousness that use of former Nazi collaborators as guerrillas behind Soviet lines would "prove . . . that our American way of life is approaching the ideal desired by all mankind."[37]

In sum, the influx of former Nazis, Waffen SS veterans, and other Nazi collaborators into the United States during this period was not simply an oversight or an administrative glitch created by the inefficiencies of the INS. It was, rather, a central, though usually unacknowledged, aspect of U.S. immigration policy of the day, particularly as the program applied to refugees from the USSR and the Soviet-occupied states of Latvia, Lithuania, and Estonia. About 500,000 Eastern European exiles entered the United States under the Displaced Persons Act and the later Refugee Relief Act during this period, and it is obvious that relatively few of these immigrants were former Nazis or Waffen SS men and that of those who did fall into those categories, fewer still were war criminals. But even a small percentage of 500,000 people is a large number. Allan Ryan, the former director of the Justice Department's war criminal investigation unit, estimates that nearly *10,000* Nazi war criminals en-

---

*The past careers of the other recruits in the March 1954 enlistment are also worthy of note. Three were veterans of British-sponsored Polish exile armies in Italy, which were well known to have been thoroughly penetrated by both German and Soviet intelligence. One was a defector from the Czech secret police, and another had defected from the Soviet NKVD. Two were recent defectors from the Czech army and two more were Polish army veterans from an unknown period. Sixteen of them—including the self-acknowledged ex-Gestapo man, Libor Pokorny—volunteered for training as airborne guerrilla warfare experts.

tered the United States during this period, although he rejects the suggestion that U.S. intelligence agencies had anything to do with this.[38]

One of the most important characteristics of the war criminals who did come to the United States is that they did not arrive here as isolated individuals. As has been seen in the cases of the Croatian Ustachis, the Ukrainian OUN, and the Latvian Vanagis, to name only three, many of these immigrants were, in fact, part of experienced, highly organized groups with distinct political agendas that differed little from the Fascist programs they had promoted in their homelands. The anti-Communist paranoia of the McCarthy period gave these groups fertile soil in which to put down roots and to grow. In time they began to play a small but real role in the political life of this country.

CHAPTER FIFTEEN

The Politics of "Liberation"

The Central Intelligence Agency did not sever its ties with the extremist exile organizations once they had arrived in this country. Instead, it continued to use them in clandestine operations both abroad and in the United States itself. Before the middle of the 1950s the agency found itself entangled with dozens—and probably hundreds—of former Nazis and SS men who had fought their way into the leadership of a variety of Eastern European émigré political associations inside this country.

Instead of withdrawing its support for the extremist groups and for the men and women who led them, the CIA went to considerable lengths to portray these leaders as legitimate representatives of the countries they had fled. At about the same time that the agency initiated the immigration programs discussed in the last chapter, it dramatically expanded its publicity and propaganda efforts inside the United States itself. A major theme of this effort was to establish the credibility and legitimacy of exiled Eastern European politicians—former Nazi collaborators and noncollaborators alike—in the eyes of the American public. Through the National Committee for a Free Europe (NCFE) and a new CIA-financed group, the Crusade for Freedom (CFF), the covert operations division of the agency became instrumental in introducing into the American political mainstream many of the right-wing extremist émigré politicians' plans to "liberate" Eastern Europe and to "roll back communism."[1]

The agency's entry into the American political scene was part of a broad escalation of the U.S. conflict with the Soviets that coincided with the outbreak of the Korean War. Coming on the heels of the Communist victory in China, the Soviet atomic bomb tests, and the Alger Hiss spy scandal in Washington, the North Korean attack on the U.S.-backed government in the South seemed to many in the West to prove all of the most alarming predictions about Communist—specifically Soviet—ambitions for world conquest. "Containment," they argued, had only fueled Russia's designs for power in somewhat the same way that "appeasement" at Munich had encouraged Hitler. There was little that the Truman administration could say in reply; it had spent much of the previous four years aggressively promoting the conception that communism was a monolithic criminal conspiracy at work everywhere in the world and that America's job was to "contain" and preferably to stop it altogether.

Truman's failure to achieve that goal became proof in the minds of many that the *tactics* of containment had not been sufficiently aggressive. It would be decades later—after the Sino-Soviet split, the U.S. debacles in Cuba and Vietnam, and the rise of third world nationalism as a major political force—before the fallacies of containment's basic premises, not just its tactics, would begin to find a hearing in American political discourse. At the time, however, it seemed to many that the only possible response to the crisis precipitated by Korea and the Soviet atomic tests was a major escalation of U.S. weapons programs, coupled with intensified clandestine campaigns to undermine Soviet rule everywhere it had been established.

The price tag for the U.S. arms buildup, according to Paul Nitze, who drafted most of the main policy statements on the issue, was some $50 billion—almost three times the then existing U.S. military budget. The real question for U.S. policymakers of the day, write Walter Isaacson and Evan Thomas in their study of American foreign policy formulation *The Wise Men,* "was whether Congress and the Administration would pay for it. The public had to be persuaded. The way to do that, Nitze knew from experience, was to scare them; to tell them that the Soviets were intent on world domination, that they were poised to attack, and that the U.S. had to meet them everywhere."[2]

It was in this context that the CIA launched a major propaganda effort in the United States. Despite a legal prohibition against domestic activities by the agency, it initiated a multimillion-dollar publicity project in this country called the Crusade for Freedom. This new group served as a fund-raising arm for Radio Free Europe, the various Free Europe exile committees, and eventually Radio Liberation from Bolshevism, all of which worked primarily overseas, where the agency had stronger statutory authority to operate. These overseas propaganda programs were posing as private corporations made up solely of individual citizens who wanted to do something about the problem of communism in Europe, it will be recalled, and the CFF's fund-raising efforts in the United States provided a convenient explanation for where all the money that RFE was spending was coming from, the CIA's longtime legislative counsel Walter Pforzheimer has said.[3] Its work permitted the broadcasting operations to claim that they were financed by millions of small contributions from concerned Americans—not by the government.

In reality, one of the most important reasons for the CFF was to bring to America the analysis of foreign affairs that had been developed by the National Committee for a Free Europe—and by the CIA. The CFF became a "gigantic, nationwide drive," as former RFE/RL director Sig Mickelson has put it, "to obtain support for the activities of the Free Europe Committee."[4]

The basic message of that analysis was a more aggressive, hardhitting version of the containment doctrine that would soon come to be known as "Liberation." Liberation, in a nutshell, began at about the point that containment left off, politically speaking. It held, as many containment advocates had argued earlier, that the socialist governments of Eastern Europe were unremittingly despotic regimes, installed by the Red Army and ruled exclusively by Stalin-style terror. Liberation proponents discarded the earlier circumspection about public calls for the overthrow of those states, however, and openly agitated for the "rollback of communism" in Eastern Europe through U.S. instigation of, and support for, counterrevolutionary movements in those countries. "Some day, sooner or later, the Iron Curtain is bound to disintegrate," NCFE Board Chairman Joseph Grew exclaimed at the launching of the Crusade for Freedom. "So let's prepare for that day in advance."[5] The name eventually chosen for the radio broadcasting into the Soviet Union—Radio Liberation from Bolshevism—neatly summed up the political point the group was trying to make every time it identified itself on the air.

Although it was little known in the United States at the time, the genesis of the liberation philosophy can be clearly traced to émigré propagandists who had worked for the Nazis on the Eastern Front during World War II. After the war the various conservative and liberal anti-Communist organizations in the United States that adopted liberation as a rallying cry added new and specifically American elements to the program that altered the earlier German strategy in basic ways. Liberation, in its American version, included an insistence that the anti-Communist revolution be democratic rather than Fascist in character, and it abandoned the racial theories and anti-Semitism of the earlier Nazi propaganda. Liberation, in the United States' hands, was billed as the fulfillment of America's own revolutionary heritage of resistance to tyranny.

It is useful to look at the gradual evolution of how these changes took place. The political rhetoric of the extremist exile groups that had once worked for the Nazis also evolved in a complex interaction with the gradual introduction of liberationist thinking into America. By the late 1940s exiled extremist leaders had learned the rhetoric of this new, more "American" form of liberation. Their adoption of lip service to democracy began to provide former Fascists with a platform to promote their agenda to millions of Americans, and it created a shelter, in effect, that protected them from the exposure of their Nazi pasts. They were no longer seen as the triggermen of Nazi genocide in the public mind but, rather, as fervent anti-Communist patriots. The government's intelligence agencies played a substantial role in this shift.

The changes in the rhetoric of the extreme Russian nationalist organization Natsional'no-Trudovoi Soyuz (NTS), which is still active in today's Russian emigration, are a case in point. This once openly Fascist group was founded in the early 1930s by a congress of younger Russian exiles who had fled their homeland in the wake of the 1917 revolution. During the first decade of its existence the NTS proclaimed the Nazis as models. NTS members were contemptuous of any sort of democratic norms and of the United States, which they viewed as degenerate. Their party program called for an anti-Communist revolution in the USSR, assassination of Soviet leaders, disfranchisement of Jews, and confiscation of Jewish property. When war broke out, the NTS unhesitatingly rallied to the cause of Nazi Germany.[6]

NTS strategy during the conflict centered on an attempt to convince the Germans to sponsor its members as the new rulers of a puppet state inside the Nazi-occupied zone of the USSR. They gradually became a central part of the Germans' Vlasov Army political warfare project, serving as political officers and informers among the Eastern European troops who had defected to the Nazis. As a declassified U.S. State Department study on the group puts it, the NTS "served in the good graces of the Germans . . . [and] it placed its men into the *Kriegsgefangenenkommissionen* [part of the Nazi prisoner of war camp administration frequently used for interrogation and recruitment of defectors]; into the special training camps [for] politically reliable prisoners . . . and, above all, [into] the propagandists' schools at Wustrau and Dabendorf; as well as into Goebbels' *Anti-Komintern,*" a Nazi-sponsored alliance of Fascist parties from around the world. "Graduates of the [NTS] training program," the study continues, "were assigned to positions in German-occupied Russia, such as chiefs of police, deputy mayors [and] propagandists with army units."

Many of the NTS leaders of the 1950s, particularly those who served as police and city administrators in the Nazi occupation zone, are major war criminals who personally helped organize the identification, roundup, and execution of millions of Jewish and Slavic civilians. Insofar as NTS men won control of local administrations in the Nazi-occupied regions of the USSR, the organization became an integral part of the Nazis' propaganda, espionage, and extermination apparatus in the East.[7]

The main theme of NTS propaganda throughout the conflict was a campaign to "liberate" the USSR from Stalin, communism, and the Jews through a mutiny by the Red Army. This became the centerpiece of Vlasov Army recruiting efforts at least as early as 1942 and was elaborated in considerable detail with tactics for counterinsurgency operations in the Nazi occupation zone, behind-the-lines infiltration of NTS agents on espionage and sabotage missions, propaganda themes tailored to appeal to Russian sensibilities and similar specifics. When the Germans were finally driven out of Russia, selected NTS agents were left on "stay-behind" missions in an attempt to organize subversion in Soviet rear areas once the Red Army front had passed. The NTS also served as the dominant force (after the Nazis themselves) in the Russkaja Osvoboditel 'naia Armiia (Russian Army of Liberation, or Vlasov Army) and the Komitet Ozvobozhdeniia Narodov Rossii (German-sponsored Committee for the Liberation of the Peoples of Russia), the Nazis' primary front group for eastern front political warfare operations in the desperate closing months of the war.[8]

It was through the NTS, and through the rival national liberation programs sponsored among Soviet minority groups by the Nazis' Rosenberg ministry, that the strategy and tactics of the "liberation" of the USSR were first hammered out. These were the laboratories, so to speak, used by Hans Heinrich Herwarth, Gustav Hilger, and the other German political warfare officers discussed earlier to develop the propaganda themes and behind-the-lines subversion tactics believed most suitable for reaching people inside the USSR.

Constantine Boldyreff was a founder of NTS and a senior leader of the group throughout the war. His wartime career is shrouded in secrecy today; but it is clear that the CIC believed that in late 1944 he helped administer gangs of Russian laborers for the SS.[9] He is a case in point of the manner in which the intervention of U.S. intelligence agencies shepherded the migration of liberation propaganda out of the fallen wartime ministries of Berlin and into the living rooms of America.

According to U.S. Army intelligence records obtained under the Freedom of Information Act, the mainstream U.S. anti-Communist organization Common Cause—no relation to the present-day liberal organization of the same name—sponsored the NTS spokesman's travel to the United States in 1948, then gave him a media campaign that enabled him to reach into millions of American homes during the late 1940s and early 1950s.[10] Common Cause was a prototype of, and a sister organization to, the CIA-sponsored National Committee for a Free Europe. Its directors included many of the men—Adolf Berle, Arthur Bliss Lane, and Eugene Lyons, among others—who simultaneously led CIA-financed groups such as the NCFE and, later, the American Committee for Liberation from Bolshevism.[11]

Boldyreff's speaking and writing tour in this country became one of the first rallying cries in the United States for a liberationist political agenda. The campaign aimed at winning financial and popular support for the NTS as a weapon in clandestine warfare against the USSR. The NTS, claimed Common Cause chairman Christopher Emmet, controlled a gigantic underground apparatus that had penetrated every major Soviet city. The USSR was on the edge of an anti-Communist revolution, Boldyreff announced, and the NTS could bring Stalin to his knees.[12]

In reality, most of the NTS's supposed "underground network" inside the USSR did not exist. True, the Nazis' SS RSHA Amt VI had helped the NTS create such clandestine cells during the German retreat from the USSR, although the Nazis' connection to this program, needless to say, was not publicized in the United States during Boldyreff's tour. Subsequent events were to show, however, that most of those underground cells had already been mopped up by the NKVD by the time the émigré leader arrived in America.

But that did not deter the publicity campaign. Common Cause arranged well-attended press conferences for the NTS spokesman in New York, Boston, Washington, and Baltimore. A dozen newspapers published prominent interviews or articles about supposed NTS clandestine activities inside the Soviet Union. This revolutionary work was said to include anti-Communist radio broadcasting, use of rockets to distribute airborne leaflets over Red Army ground troops, and a variety of other dramatic psychological warfare techniques. In fact, however, most of these claimed actions either never took place at all or were vastly exaggerated by NTS propagandists. Nevertheless, every article, with the exception of a *Newsweek* piece penned by Ralph de Toledano (who favored a different faction of Soviet émigrés), offered virtually uncritical praise for the NTS and acceptance of Boldyreff's claims. Boldyreff pledged that the NTS would soon mobilize enough dissident Russians to overthrow the Stalin dictatorship, thereby supposedly saving the world from war. The price tag for NTS help in getting rid of communism, he said, was $100 million.[13]

It is impossible to determine today what Common Cause knew, if anything, of the NTS's wartime record at the time it sponsored his speaking tour. It is clear, however, from Boldyreff's own U.S. Army intelligence file that the CIC was well aware that the NTS was a totalitarian and pro-Fascist organization. Instead of making this fact clear, however, U.S. intelligence promoted Boldyreff's propaganda work in this country. "A Common Cause spokesman said that Boldyreff is 'well known to American intelligence,' " the *Boston Herald* reported in its coverage of one of the NTS man's early news conferences. " '[He] is vouched for by high American officials,' and cooperated with the American military government in Germany."[14]

Over the next four years Boldyreff went on to ghostwritten feature stories appearing under his by-line in *Look, Reader's Digest,* and *World Affairs.* "Will Russia's democratic revolution take place in time to keep the Communist plotters from using their atomic bombs against humanity?" he asked readers of the American Federation of Labor's mass circulation *Federationist.*[15] "The answer to this all important question depends on how hard the free world fights to pierce the Iron Curtain and join forces with Russian anti-Communists."

It is clear that Boldyreff was soon enjoying the direct sponsorship of the CIA. British intelligence historian E. H. Cookridge reports that the U.S. agency put Boldyreff on retainer for assistance in recruiting Vlasov Army veterans for espionage missions inside the USSR—a claim that the nationalist leader does not deny. Moreover, several of Boldyreff's ghostwriters—including James Critchlow, who coauthored the article quoted above—have since become known as career executives of the CIA's political warfare projects such as Radio Liberation, a fact that strongly suggests that the agency also had a hand in Boldyreff's publicity tours in the United States.*[16]

*Boldyreff was by no means the only senior NTS leader who enjoyed the sponsorship of Western intelligence agencies in the wake of the war. As early as 1946 Boldyreff created an elaborate plan under U.S., British, and French sponsorship in which NTS-led bands of exiles established construction companies in Morocco. In reality, however, "these were military groups, companies of the Vlasov Army, most of them soldiers together with their officers," Boldyreff remembered during an interview. We "kept them together in order to provide special fighting units in a war with the Soviets." The point of the Boldyreff plan, he says, was to subsidize these Vlasovite colonies, while at the same time preserving their military potential. Boldyreff specifically excluded refugee Jews from this program, although several other Eastern European groups—Latvians, Lithuanians, etc.—were included. Boldyreff blamed this bit of postwar anti-Semitism on the Moroccan authorities.

A brief look at the men mentioned in the declassified State Department study on the NTS referred to in the text is useful as an illustration of how other NTS collaborators found their way into secret employment in the West. The State Department report indicates that Roman Redlich and Vladimir Porensky, for example, led Nazi recruitment and training of Russian defectors at a special school at Wustrau, that Yevgeniy R. Romanov served in Berlin as a leading Vlasov propagandist, and that an NTS man known simply as Tenzerov served as chief of security for the Vlasov Army. Vladimir Porensky (sometimes spelled Poremsky), in particular, enjoyed a reputation as a "200% Nazi," the study asserts.

Of just these men, a RAND Corporation study identifies Redlich as an officer in the notorious Kaminsky SS legion, and Soviet publications have repeatedly charged him with personally committing atrocities during the Nazi occupation of their country. U.S. intelligence nevertheless hired Redlich after the war to train behind-the-lines agents at its school at Regensburg, the Department of State admits. Redlich is also known to have been active at Bad Homburg, where agent training was carried out under cover of a "journalism" program at the CIA-financed Institute for the Study of the USSR. By the late 1950s Redlich had become chief of teams of Russian émigrés responsible for attempting to recruit Soviet tourists, businessmen, and sailors traveling abroad, an intelligence service that eventually became the bread and butter of the NTS's contract with the CIA as the cold war wound down.

Meanwhile, the Berlin propagandist Romanov became chairman of the NTS Executive Bureau and served for years as the broker for NTS agents interested in employment with

According to Boldyreff's CIC dossier, U.S. Army and U.S. Air Force intelligence arranged a job for him at the prestigious Foreign Service Institute at Georgetown University in Washington. There, he taught psychological warfare techniques to pilots engaged in clandestine air missions into the USSR. As Boldyreff himself put it in an interview, the air force assignment involved training "about 120" U.S. pilots responsible for cross-border flights into the USSR. "This was the cold war," he says. "Air force officers were more frequently captured, [because] their planes would be shot down, and they needed to know what to do, how to survive. That sort of thing was much more open then than it is today."[17]

But that was only the beginning. Next came radio interviews, then lucrative speaking engagements at Daughters of the American Revolution and American Legion conventions. The powerful Henry Holt publishing company issued a book made up largely of Boldyreff's commentaries exposing both real and imagined Stalinist assassination plots. Last but not least, Boldyreff made the circuit in Washington of congressional investigating committees, which sought out his advice on fighting communism, psychological warfare, and spotting supposed Red agents inside U.S. government agencies.[18]

Whatever one may think of Boldyreff's politics, none of his personal actions in this country are known to have been illegal. At the same time, however, the actions of the CIA and other intelligence agencies in promoting his entry into American politics were, on their face, an apparent violation of U.S. law and of the CIA's charter. Legal questions aside, it is clear that Boldyreff was only one of a long train of more or less similar ex-Fascist leaders whose publicity work on behalf of "liberation" during the late 1940s and early 1950s was underwritten at least in part by the U.S. government.

Western espionage groups. Romanov's close friend Porensky, the "200% Nazi," was imprisoned as a war criminal in 1945, then released in 1946, with the cooperation of the British secret service. Porensky then went on to run the NTS's Possev publishing house in Munich, where tens of millions of agitative leaflets used among Soviet émigrés outside the USSR were printed at British and American expense. Porensky's Possev eventually became a major funding conduit through which U.S. payments to the NTS were passed, and the CIA's later financial backing permitted the NTS to print millions of newspapers, pamphlets, books, and other literature, a good part of which was used to influence public opinion in Western Europe and the United States. Porensky has also served as NTS chairman.

Finally, Tenzerov, who had been chief of security for the Vlassov Army, was betrayed by other NTS leaders in the last days of the war and left the organization in a fury. Army CIC records indicate that SS veteran Emil Augsburg (of the Gehlen Organization and the Barbie network) later recruited him as an agent.

Ironically, George Kennan and Charles Thayer—who once had helped sponsor the U.S. political warfare programs that had rehabilitated the NTS and similar groups—were among the first men targeted by the radical right once the liberation message started to catch on. What was needed, the far right argued, was a much more aggressive American policy overseas. The United States should underwrite the "revolutionary" activities of anti-Communist émigrés such as the NTS on a much larger scale, they said. The "rollback of communism" in the East should become the touchstone of U.S. efforts on the Continent. America should make a public declaration of its intent to "liberate" Eastern Europe, exiles like Boldyreff and their supporters argued, in order to encourage discontent with Soviet rule. The CIA should then deliver clandestine U.S. arms and money to the rebels to back up that promise. Some even argued that the United States should send in American troops.

Supporters of liberation had no patience for Kennan's ten- to fifteen-year strategy for the containment and eventual collapse of the USSR, even if it actually worked. "The expression in those days was 'We're sitting on our suitcases,' " says Vladimir Petrov, a leading Russian scholar in the United States and a onetime Vlasov Army adviser. "They were ready to go back at any time."[19] Many believed that the sooner a U.S.-USSR war over Europe broke out, the better.

George Kennan became a target within the Truman administration for the radical right. Regardless of what the diplomat may have backed as far as clandestine U.S. policy was concerned, he favored U.S. government recognition of the reality of Soviet power in Eastern Europe, and many extremist émigrés saw that as a sellout of their aspirations to return to power in their former homelands. As the political fortunes of the radical right in the United States rose, Kennan grew increasingly disillusioned with the results of the American foreign policy he had once been instrumental in formulating. He clashed sharply with Truman's new secretary of state, Dean Acheson, over such key issues as the establishment of NATO, the permanent division of Germany, and large-scale U.S. intervention in Asia, all of which Kennan opposed. Soon Acheson's disdain and Kennan's stomach ulcers got the better of Kennan. He was hospitalized briefly, and when he returned to work, he discovered that he had been frozen out of Acheson's inner circle of advisers, then stripped of his oversight authority in clandestine operations as well.[20]

The émigré anti-Communist movement continued to accelerate. Soon there emerged in the United States "one vocal and not uninfluential element that not only wanted war with Russia, but had a very clear idea of the purposes for which, in its own view, such a war should be fought," as Kennan noted later in a discussion of his views on the possibility of war with the USSR during the early 1950s. "I have in mind the escapees and immigrants, mostly recent ones, from the non-Russian portions of the postwar Soviet Union, as well as from some of the Eastern European satellite states.

"Their idea," he writes, "to which they were passionately and sometimes ruthlessly attached, was simply that the United States should, for their benefit, fight a war against the Russian people to achieve the final breakup of the traditional Russian state and the establishment of themselves as the regimes of the various 'liberated' territories." Kennan is referring here to the spokesmen of the so-called "Captive Nations" movement, particularly Ukrainian and Baltic nationalists.

"These recent refugees were by no means without political influence in Washington," Kennan adds. "Connected as they were with the compact voting blocs situated in the big cities, they were able to bring direct influence to bear on individual Congressional figures. They appealed successfully at times to religious feelings, and even more importantly [*sic*] to the prevailing anti-Communist hysteria." Among the countries the Captive Nations movement represented were several that the diplomat admits had been "invented in the Nazi propaganda ministry during the recent war."[21]

Agitation by these émigrés became a part of dozens of CIA-sponsored exile operations in the United States during the early 1950s. Almost all these affairs were sponsored by the CIA covert operations directorate's International Organizations Division, which was then administering the NCFE, the CFF, and similar overlapping projects. This division organized and bankrolled the CFF with an initial grant of $180,000, according to former RFE/RL chief Mickelson. The agency, working through the NCFE, then went on to pour at least $5 million into CFF propaganda work inside the United States over the next five years.[22]

That $5 million figure is only a pale reflection of the true scope of the CFF's effort, however. The campaign arranged with the nonprofit Advertising Council of America for thousands of hours of free radio and television time as well as for countless free magazine and newspaper promotions. The crusade paid only for the actual production of the proliberation political advertising, which was then broadcast or published without charge by media outlets enjoying substantial tax deductions for airing these "public service" announcements. This unique program "made it possible for the American people to read, hear and see The Crusade Story in all media of communications," the National Committee for a Free Europe boasted in an annual report, including "newspapers, magazines, outdoor advertising, radio, television and newsreels."[23]

But the CIA's $5 million direct contribution to anti-Communist education through the CFF can serve, at least, as a yardstick for comparing the scope of the crusade promotion to other political propaganda efforts undertaken in this country at about the same time. That $5 million contribution exceeds, for example, the *combined* total of all the money spent on the Truman/Dewey presidential election campaign of 1948. It establishes the CIA (through the CFF) as the largest single political advertiser on the American scene during the early 1950s,[24] rivaled only by such commercial giants as General Motors and Procter & Gamble in its domination of the airwaves.

The campaign's program began by naming a board of directors headed by General Lucius Clay, the hero of the Berlin airlift, who was falsely given credit for originating the Crusade for Freedom concept in order to enhance the program's patriotic appeal. Next came the casting of a ten-ton bronze "Freedom Bell" (to "let Freedom ring"), and a ticker-tape "Freedom" parade up Broadway in New York City, culminating in a huge rally on the steps of City Hall. The Freedom Bell became the centerpiece of a national promotion tour led by a phalanx of political notables, including many anti-Communist exile leaders. They loaded the bell onto a special "Freedom Train" and shuttled it to propaganda events from coast to coast. There were stops at Pittsburgh, Cleveland, Detroit, Chicago, Denver, Salt Lake City, San Francisco, Los Angeles, and at least thirteen other major cities. Each event came complete with a continuous drumbeat of publicity in radio, newspapers, magazines, churches, and social clubs of every description. Posters, handbills, billboards, commercials, and even fund-raising telethons filled out the picture. (America's first simultaneous coast-to-coast television broadcast, in fact, was a Crusade for Freedom telethon.)[25]

The CFF consistently stressed the leading role of anti-Communist exiles in the liberation campaign. It was "essential to maintain as many [émigré] leaders as we can," said NCFE President Dewitt

Poole, "[to prepare for] the day of their country's liberation."²⁶ Spokesmen for organizations founded and controlled in large part by such Nazi collaborators as the Free Albania Committee and the Committee for a Free Latvia, discussed above, appeared at many of these events side by side with leaders of more respectable associations, such as the Hungarian National Council, Bulgarian National Committee, and the various other groups gathered under NCFE's wing. They testified to their determination to free their homelands from Communist domination.

Similarly, the NCFE used its economic muscle to rent meeting halls and provide the public relations support that puffed up scores of otherwise minor émigré events into major "news" stories that enjoyed extensive play in the American media. Former Nazis did not control such programs, but they were sometimes able to make use of the prevailing anti-Communist hysteria to promote policies that they favored. The NCFE gave the annual Baltic Freedom Day Committee free use of Carnegie Hall once a year for at least three years, according to the organization's annual reports, then used its influence to line up noted speakers, including a half dozen U.S. senators, the president of the NCFE itself, and a leading board member of the U.S. Displaced Persons Commission to grace the event. Most important to the favored Baltic politicians was a flood of endorsements arranged by the NCFE that included a proclamation by the governor of New York and public messages of solidarity from the then president of the United States, Harry Truman, and the man who was soon to be Eisenhower's secretary of state, John Foster Dulles. These were obviously not "Nazi" political gatherings. The major theme was support for democracy and for national independence of the Baltic states of Latvia, Lithuania, and Estonia from the USSR. Even so, the Vanagis among the Latvians and other extreme-right-wing forces within the Baltic immigrant community succeeded in placing speakers at the rostrum at Carnegie Hall to promote the myth that the Baltic Waffen SS legions were simply anti-Communist patriots and to press for changes in U.S. immigration regulations that would permit easy entry of such persons into this country under refugee relief programs.²⁷

The crusade was only one part of a much broader CIA-sponsored effort to shape U.S. (and world) public opinion. Related programs included book publishing, scholarly studies of the USSR by carefully selected researchers, and bankrolling hundreds of rallies, commemorations, and other media events. The principal political point of this program was to provide extensive publicity for all available evidence that the USSR was a dangerous imperial power. The agency went on to emphasize news of the "liberation" movements of the exiles as an important morale booster and an illustration of the resistance to Soviet expansion.

The CIA financed a literary campaign explicitly designed to promote former Nazi collaborators as appropriate leaders of liberation movements among their respective nationalities. The German author Heinz Bongartz (pen name Jürgen Thorwald) recounts how he was approached in 1950 by a CIA officer named Pleasants with a proposal that he write a promotional account of the Vlasov Army for distribution in both the United States and Europe. Pleasants had read an earlier Bongartz tract that was strongly sympathetic to Vlasov and "he thought I would be the 'right fellow'" to write further material on the subject, Bongartz remembers.

The German author accepted Pleasants's offer. The CIA—with the cooperation of Heinz Danko Herre, a senior officer in the Gehlen Organization—provided him with stenographers, translators, travel expenses, a substantial grant, access to secret U.S. records, and assistance in locating SS and Vlasov Army veterans scattered all over Europe. Bongartz's glowing report of Vlasov was published in German and English two years later, and it remains an often-cited work in the field.[28] The book presents a thoroughly whitewashed picture of the Vlasov movement, but Bongartz deserves credit, at least, for openly discussing the sponsors of his book, more than can be said for a number of other scholars of the period.

This broad-based, multifaceted effort legitimized for many Americans what the extreme-right-wing émigré movement had been saying since the end of World War II. The United States could easily liberate Eastern Europe from the Soviet Union and even dismember the USSR, the theory went, by bankrolling stepped-up subversion programs in the East.

"It became an article of faith that the USSR was going to fall apart at any time," notes scholar Vladimir Petrov. "The idea was that communism was a small conspiracy of men sending out the revolution, that it was hated by the people, [and so] naturally they wanted to overthrow it right away. Communists killed people to maintain their power, so the first chance [the people] had there would be a rebellion."[29]

John Foster Dulles articulated this myth neatly in congressional testimony that went entirely unchallenged at the time. "Some

dozen people in the Kremlin," he proclaimed, "are seeking to con-
solidate their imperial rule over some 800,000,000 people, representing what were nearly a score of independent nations."[30] With
those kinds of odds—800 million against 12—the overthrow of communism from within would seem like a fairly simple task.

"That was the theory at the time," Petrov says. "There was a lot
of enthusiasm. Many people thought that communism could be
very simply gotten rid of." But in reality, Petrov reflects with a sigh,
"this just wasn't true."

The liberation message struck an extraordinarily responsive
chord in the United States, one which reverberated far beyond the
relatively narrow community of Eastern European exiles. Its potent
blend of anti-Communist paranoia, American patriotism, and the
self-perceived generosity of doing something practical to aid people seen as suffering from persecution abroad appealed to millions
of Americans.

It is probably impossible today to determine the impact that the
CIA's émigré programs and domestic propaganda efforts had on the
election of 1952 or other mainstream political events of the period
with any degree of scientific certainty. The information detailing
the full extent of the agency's efforts to shape domestic public
opinion remains buried in classified files, if it has not been purged
from the record altogether. The carefully controlled surveys of
public opinion that might enable scholars to disentangle the specific
effects of the CIA's immigration and propaganda programs from
the broader political impact of the media's day-to-day coverage of
international events were not taken at the time, and it would be
pointless to try to take them today, thirty-five years later. It is not
surprising that sociologists and political scientists of the period
failed to make use of surveys and other statistical tools to examine
the impact of CIA clandestine action campaigns in the United
States; after all, the fact that a systematic propaganda effort even
existed was a state secret at the time.

But the anecdotal evidence concerning the significance of these
programs is strong. The role of former Nazi collaborators and U.S.
intelligence agencies in promoting the penetration of liberationist
political thinking into the American body politic may be traced
through several clear steps. First, the rhetoric and the detailed
strategies for the "liberation" of the USSR and Eastern Europe
were originally generated before World War II by pro-Fascist

émigré organizations enjoying direct sponsorship from Nazi Germany's intelligence agencies, which were intent on using these groups as pawns in their plans to exterminate European Jewry and to achieve a military victory in the East. The Nazis significantly developed both the liberation strategies and their exile constituencies during the war, despite the Germans' own internal factional fighting over how to make best use of collaborators.[31] Secondly, after the war U.S. intelligence agencies brought leaders of a number of these pro-Fascist groups—the Ukrainian OUN, the Russian nationalist NTS, the Albanian Balli Kombetar, certain of the Baltic Nazi collaborators, etc.—into the United States through programs the specific purpose of which was, in part, the generation of effective anti-Communist propaganda.[32] Next, these same exile leaders aggressively promoted essentially the same liberation propaganda in the United States that they had advocated under Nazi sponsorship, though now with a new appeal to American values, such as democracy and freedom, rather than the earlier open advocacy of racial politics and fascism. The CIA gave these domestic publicity campaigns multimillion-dollar clandestine backing during the 1950s by providing operating cash, salaries, and logistic and publishing support and—not least—by facilitating endorsements from respected mainstream politicians.

Neither the Eastern European exile community in America nor, still less, the minority of former Nazi collaborators among them had the political muscle to force adoption of a liberation agenda on the American public by themselves. But they could, and did, often serve as catalysts that helped trigger the much bigger political "chemical reaction," so to speak, that was then under way, the primary ingredients of which were East-West disputes over economic and military spheres of influence. The first and in some ways most credible spokesmen in the United States for liberationist thinking were exiled activists who were, like NTS executive Constantine Boldyreff discussed above, "well known to American intelligence [and] vouched for by high American officials."[33] Their message and slogans caught on with millions of Americans during the first half of the 1950s, especially among conservatives and others alarmed by the spread of communism abroad. In 1952 the public support in the United States for threats to liberate Eastern Europe and the USSR from their Communist governments was sufficiently broad that the Republican party adopted an explicit call for liberation as the main foreign policy plank in its party platform and as a central theme in its presidential and congressional election campaigns.

The Republicans' campaign platform demanded "the end of the negative, futile and immoral policy of 'Containment,' " as the *New York Times* reported, "which abandons countless human beings to a despotism and godless terrorism." The GOP pledged to "revive the contagious, liberating influences that are inherent in freedom" and to mark the "beginning of the end" for Communist party rule in Eastern Europe and the USSR.[34] America, the Republicans' primary foreign policy spokesman, John Foster Dulles, wrote in *Life* magazine, "wants and expects liberation to occur." This anti-Communist revolution, he claimed disingenuously, would come about "peacefully."[35] The Republicans used this liberation rhetoric as a means of distinguishing their promises of a new, tougher foreign policy from the program of the Democrats. What exactly Eisenhower intended to do to promote the liberation of Eastern Europe once the election campaign was over, however, was usually left vague.

Arthur Bliss Lane, who had been U.S. ambassador to Poland during the Truman years, became the point man in the Republican party's effort to swing the enthusiasm created by the Crusade for Freedom into the GOP's column during the 1952 election. Lane's inspiration was to attract the large Slavic and Eastern European voting blocs in the United States, which had traditionally voted for Democratic candidates, to the Republican party through demagogic promises to "liberate" their former homelands with American assistance.[36]

Along with his party assignment, Lane, as noted earlier, simultaneously served on the boards of both the NCFE and the CFF, and he was an indefatigable speaker and promoter on behalf of each of his causes. Soon Republican election tactics in ethnic communities paralleled the CIA's Crusade for Freedom campaign so closely that considerable political sophistication was required to distinguish one from the other. The party sponsored Committees of Crusades to Lift the Iron Curtain, Liberation Centers, Liberation Week festivities, and Liberation Rallies, designed to draw ethnic voters into the Republican camp. These campaigns imitated and sometimes overlapped the CFF's Freedom Weeks, Baltic Freedom Days, and Freedom Rallies. Speakers and local activists of the two crusades were frequently the same people.[37]

Several of Lane's top ethnic advisers personified the gradual evolution from World War II collaboration into cold war liberation advocacy that has been seen in the CIA's propaganda programs. Lane's specialist in Republican party appeals to Americans of Russian and Ukrainian ethnic descent, for example, was the scholar and publicist Vladimir Petrov. Petrov, a survivor of Stalin's prison camps in the 1930s, had defected to the Germans early in the war and spent much of the conflict assigned to a Nazi-sponsored propaganda group in Vienna, according to his own account, and as a publicist promoting Vlasov's "Russian Army of Liberation." Petrov also served as a quisling city administrator in Krasnodar, in the USSR, during the Nazi occupation. He insisted in a recent interview that he had no knowledge when he was serving in Krasnodar of the Nazis' gas truck extermination program, which was introduced in Krasnodar during Petrov's tenure as transportation and finance chief. The Germans killed at least 7,000 people in this manner during Petrov's brief time in office, then used collaborationist militia troops to shoot others in tank ditches on the outskirts of town.* During the 1952 election campaign Petrov served both as an adviser to Lane and as a leading Russian-language journalist in the ethnic press in this country.[38]

The gradual merging of the Republicans' election campaign and the Crusade for Freedom reached its logical culmination on the eve of the 1952 election. The party's ethnic division under Lane approved and allocated money for a psychological warfare tactic that had earlier been used by the CIA in Italy and Eastern Europe. Millions of yellow leaflets were slated to be dropped from airplanes "over places such as Hamtramck," the large immigrant community near Detroit, plugging Eisenhower and blaming Democrat Adlai Stevenson for the "betrayal" of the Slavic "Fatherland and relatives" to the Communists. The yellow paper was to dramatize the

---

*In his published memoirs Petrov contradicts the statement that he was unaware of Nazi extermination efforts in Krasnodar. There he says that he *did* know Jews were being systematically murdered in Krasnodar even before he became a city official. In *Escape from the Future* Petrov also writes that he appointed the city's chief of police during the Nazi occupation. Petrov claims that he helped warn Krasnodar's Jews of their danger and even encouraged them to escape.

Whichever version is true, Petrov says today: "I did not make decisions on the basis of massacres. Where I had been [in prison camp] in Siberia," he continues grimly, "there were also massacres, if not of the German style. There were many people done to death against their wishes and without honor. So there were massacres here, massacres on that side, all around. . . . Over here [in the United States] there is a distinction about who is killed," he says, with a trace of irony. "If one is a chosen person, then that means something. But if one is a Russian peasant, then that counts for nothing."

leaflet's conclusion. "If you men and women of Polish and Czech descent can, after reading the above, vote for the Democratic candidate," the handbill proclaimed, "you are as yellow as this paper."[39] Everything was ready to go "within 48 hours," according to correspondence in Lane's archives, but Eisenhower's inner circle of election advisers canceled the plan at the last minute.

Eisenhower's election campaign was successful in any event. Lane's "ethnic" campaign produced mixed results: The Republicans did draw substantially more votes from ethnic districts than they had been able to do previously, according to contemporary reports,[40] although the Democratic party's influence in these wards was by no means extinguished. In any case, the majority of American voters backed Eisenhower, at least in part because of his proliberation, "let's get tough with the Communists" foreign policy stance. In January 1953 the first Republican administration in twenty years entered Washington with a grand inaugural parade and a rhetorical commitment, at least, to a mission to liberate Eastern Europe from Communist rule.

Former Nazis and collaborators combined with right-wing elements within the U.S. intelligence community to bring another sort of pressure to bear on the U.S. political scene. The flood of government and private money flowing into anti-Communist political warfare programs during the early 1950s created a cottage industry, of sorts, for informers, professional ex-Communists of varying degrees of reputability, and "information bureaus" specializing in the blacklisting of Americans viewed as politically suspect. One of the least known but most important of these entrepreneurs was John Valentine ("Frenchy") Grombach. He was, it will be recalled, the former military intelligence agent whose leaks to Congress had led to the purge of Colonel Alfred McCormack and McCormack's team of skeptical intelligence experts back in 1946 and 1947.

During the late 1940s Grombach had become a businessman who specialized in selling political and economic intelligence derived in large part from old boy networks of German SS officers, former Hungarian Axis quislings, and Russian nationalist NTS men to the State Department, the CIA, and corporate customers in the United States and Western Europe. Grombach's espionage network operated through, and was partially financed by, the N. V. Philips Gloeilampenfabrieken corporation of the Netherlands and its American affiliate, Philips North America, according to records found in his CIC dossier.[41] This was the same major electronics manufacturer that had provided a channel for his clandestine wartime operations. One of Grombach's most important assets, according to U.S. naval intelligence records obtained under the Freedom of Information Act, was SS General Karl Wolff, a major war criminal who had gone into the arms trade in Europe after the war.[42] A second primary component of Grombach's private intelligence apparat was a large group of Hungarians loyal to the former royal privy councillor Tibor Eckhardt, according to Ray Ylitalo, who handled liaison with Grombach's undercover service for State Department intelligence.[43]

Grombach worked simultaneously under contract to the Department of State and the CIA. The ex-military intelligence man succeeded in creating "one of the most unusual organizations in the history of the federal government," according to CIA Inspector General Lyman Kirkpatrick.[44] "It was developed completely outside of the normal governmental structure, [but it] used all of the normal cover and communications facilities normally operated by intelligence organizations, and yet never was under any control from Washington." By the early 1950s the U.S. government was bankrolling Grombach's underground activities at more than $1 million annually, Kirkpatrick has said.

As the cold war deepened, Grombach had wheeled and dealed and tried to slide himself into a position where he would have a shot at the top spot in the American intelligence complex. He wanted to be director of the CIA or, better yet, chief of an entirely new U.S. espionage machine built on the ruins of that agency. "Grombach," says Ylitalo,[45] "never could figure out whether he was an employee [of the CIA] or a competitor. That was the problem in a nutshell."

Grombach promoted himself as the most pro-"liberation," most anti-Communist of all of Washington's competing spy chiefs. His organization stood ready, he said, to purge the State Department and the CIA of Communist dupes, homosexuals, and liberals of all stripes. High on the list of his targets were the men who had articulated and implemented Truman's containment strategy: George Kennan, Charles Thayer, Charles Bohlen, and their allies at State and the CIA. In Grombach's eyes, these officials were like his old nemesis Colonel McCormack: too soft on communism and the USSR; too favorable to liberal elements in the CIA; too closely tied to the elitist eastern establishment that had been running the State Department for generations.

Grombach banked on his close connections with Senators Joseph McCarthy, William Jenner, and other members of the extreme Republican right to propel him to national power. He believed that the McCarthyite right was on its way to the White House, and he intended to be there when it arrived. Grombach's outfit effectively became the foreign espionage agency for the far right, often serving as the overseas complement to McCarthy's generally warm relations with J. Edgar Hoover's FBI at home.

Through a quirk of fate Frenchy Grombach found himself in a position where he could exercise enough influence in Washington to help derail the government careers of his rivals. U.S. government contracts bankrolling a network of former Nazis and collaborators gave him much of the ammunition he needed to do the job. Grombach used his networks primarily to gather dirt. This was the American agent's specialty, his true passion: political dirt; sexual dirt; any kind of compromising information at all. "He got into a lot of garbage pails," as Kirkpatrick puts it, "and issued 'dirty linen' reports on Americans."[46] Grombach collected scandal, cataloged it, and used it carefully, just as he had done during the earlier McCormack investigation. He leaked smears to his political allies in Congress and the press when it suited his purposes to do so. Grombach and congressional "internal security" investigators bartered these dossiers with one another almost as though they were boys trading baseball cards.

One of Grombach's most important weapons in his struggle for power was a series of blackmail type of dossiers that his men had compiled on his rivals inside the U.S. intelligence community. He had retailed much of this data piece by piece to the CIA over the years but by 1952 had decided to make use of his network of former SS men and collaborators on behalf of Senator Joseph McCarthy. Grombach's primary targets included a number of current and former U.S. intelligence officials—Charles Thayer, Carmel Offie, William Bundy, Colonel Alfred McCormack, and a half dozen others—whom he regarded as vulnerable liberal targets.

Grombach leaked these "dirty linen" files to Senator McCarthy, according to both Kirkpatrick and Ylitalo. Soon an anonymous letter went the rounds on Capitol Hill, charging Thayer with sexual promiscuity, homosexuality, and a series of vague security violations during Thayer's tenure as chief of the Voice of America, which was a frequent target of McCarthy's attacks.[47] Other charges soon flowed out of McCarthy's offices about William Bundy, then a member of the CIA's elite Office of National Estimates, and John Paton Davies, who had been Kennan's right-hand man in Bloodstone.

Lyman Kirkpatrick handled the matter for the CIA. "As I studied the names [on McCarthy's list of suspects]," Kirkpatrick says, "and particularly the comments made about them, I became more and more convinced that I had read those comments before. . . . We went back and checked the files, and sure enough some of the phrases were identical to the so-called dirty linen reports that the subsidiary organization [Grombach] had fed to us about our own people, and some of the names were identical with those that [he had] regarded as sinister." It was Grombach, Kirkpatrick then knew, who had fed this collection of rumors—some of them gathered at the CIA's own expense—to McCarthy.

Kirkpatrick—by then confined to a wheelchair with a nearly fatal case of polio he had picked up on an inspection tour in Southeast Asia—confronted the burly Grombach in a Washington hotel room a few days later. "I went alone with a copy of Senator McCarthy's report, handed it to [Grombach] . . . and told him that he had given it to Senator McCarthy," Kirkpatrick writes. "After a bit of blustering and blowing, he admitted that he had done this and claimed that it was not only his right, but his responsibility." Grombach "went on to say that he had proposed to Senator McCarthy that his entire organization work for the Senator in doing nothing but investigating employees of the United States government."[48]

McCarthy let it be known that he intended to call Thayer for hearings on his supposed fitness for office, perhaps at the same time that the nomination of Thayer's brother-in-law, Charles Bohlen, as ambassador to the USSR was up for consideration. The hearings, like most McCarthy events, would probably receive live national TV coverage. Thayer resigned a few days later.

A simple resignation was not enough for McCarthy, however. The State Department had permitted Thayer to maintain the fiction that he had voluntarily resigned "to pursue a writing career" and had even put out a press release to that effect. But McCarthy insisted on making Thayer's public humiliation complete. Under intense questioning by the senator, a department spokesman admitted that Thayer had been "separated on the basis of morals charges"—a 1950s euphemism for homosexuality.[49] Newspapers headlined the case from coast to coast.

That was one down. Next on McCarthy's list—and on Grombach's—was John Paton Davies. Davies, a China policy specialist and close friend of George Kennan's, had frequently served as the Policy Planning Staff's point man in Bloodstone cases. He had been instrumental in the immigrations of Nazi Foreign Office specialist Hilger and the SS Wannsee Institute defector Poppe, in the exploitation of former Nazi agents Ulus and Sunsh, and in much of the rest of the clandestine side of State Department affairs during the Truman administration.[50] Davies generally favored a hard-line attitude toward Moscow and even went so far as to advocate a "preventative war against the USSR," as the *New York Times* described it, following the detonation of the first Soviet atomic bomb in 1949. (In a more recent interview, however, Davies denied that he called for war with the Soviets, preferring instead to term his strategy a "showdown.")[51]

Ironically, though, Davies had become the whipping boy of the right-wing China Lobby during the late 1940s because of his controversial opinions on American strategy in the Far East. He had once (in 1945) favored a de facto U.S. alliance with Mao Zedong in order to undermine Soviet influence in Asia. Davies's advice on this matter was largely rejected, but after Mao's victory in 1949, the far right in the United States scapegoated Davies and other State Department China hands as the supposed cause of Chiang Kai-shek's defeat.

The sacrifice of John Paton Davies at McCarthy's hands is a vivid illustration of the influence of the radical right on American political affairs. Davies, as it turns out, had suggested an intelligence project code-named Tawney Pippet to a CIA/OPC liaison officer named Lyle Munson. Tawney Pippet was to be a fairly straightforward variation on the ongoing Nazi utilization projects, but it had a twist. This time Kennan's PPS wanted OPC to fund secretly a think tank of *left*-wing and pro-Communist scholars, who could be tapped without their knowledge as sources of information on China. Some of them might also be available as deep-cover channels for U.S. government communication with the Chinese Communists.

OPC Agent Munson, however, was alarmed over the prospect of the U.S. government's having any contact with left-wing scholars, even those being unwittingly used for ulterior purposes. He leaked word of Tawney Pippet to J. Edgar Hoover, and from there it found its way through unknown channels into the hands of Grombach and eventually McCarthy.[52] Munson billed the Tawney Pippet project as a plan to infiltrate Communists into the CIA.

It was Munson, not Davies, who had spilled CIA secrets and sabotaged Tawney Pippet. But it was Davies who was hounded and dragged before no fewer than eight separate State Department and congressional "loyalty" investigating committees on the basis of Munson's allegations. The radical right in general, and McCarthy in particular, made the dismissal of Davies an acid test of the Eisenhower administration's determination to get rid of supposed subversives in the State Department.

In the end, there was very little that the loyalty inquests could pin on Davies. Grombach had failed to turn up any real dirt on him beyond the Tawney Pippet affair and early China gaffes. Davies had had a reasonably distinguished career, and his loyalty to the United States was clearly strong. His real problem was that he had favored a rapprochement with China twenty-five years before it became politically acceptable to do so, and he refused to grovel about it.

Davies hung on in government for almost twenty months after Thayer fell. Finally, however, John Foster Dulles dismissed the Foreign Service officer for his supposed lapses of judgment and his "personal demeanor," as Dulles called it,[53] under hostile questioning.

Charles Bohlen—a close Kennan ally who, according to his own account, had been instrumental in the original recruitment of German political warfare expert Hans Heinrich Herwarth for U.S. intelligence—was next.[54] Eisenhower had nominated Bohlen as U.S. ambassador to the USSR in February 1953, but the nomination had to be confirmed by the Senate before Bohlen could take his post. Ike liked and respected Chip Bohlen; they had been golf partners in France during the forties. Eisenhower had personally chosen Bohlen for the Moscow assignment, much to the discomfort of his secretary of state, John Foster Dulles.

Arthur Bliss Lane, Joe McCarthy, and the rest of the liberationist stalwarts balked at the Bohlen nomination. Even Secretary of State Dulles was concerned about how Bohlen's earlier leading role in containment and in the 1945 Yalta accords with the USSR might look to voters who had just elected the Republicans on a liberation ticket.

Dulles gingerly testified on Bohlen's behalf anyway, and it seemed for a while as though the nomination might go smoothly. But Dulles had underestimated the strength and virulence of the McCarthyite movement, which up to that time he and most of the rest of the Republican party had openly supported. Dulles's top internal affairs officer at the State Department, it turned out, was a McCarthy man who believed that anyone who had been as deeply involved in the Yalta negotiations as Bohlen had been was a security problem pretty much by definition. The internal affairs chief opposed the diplomat's nomination, and McCarthy used that dissent as a pretext for claiming that Bohlen was a "security risk."

McCarthy marshaled Senators Everett Dirksen, Homer Capehart, and the rest of the far right caucus, then unleashed an emotional floor debate in the Senate in an attempt to block approval of Bohlen's nomination. The tide was against McCarthy; he was, after all, a Republican senator bucking a Republican president on what would ordinarily be a routine appointment. McCarthy's speech during the showdown lasted more than an hour. He rehashed the party's line on containment, lambasted Bohlen's brother-in-law Charles Thayer, then accused Bohlen himself of "cowardice" and of being "so blind that he cannot recognize the enemy."[55]

McCarthy presented his trump card at the climax of his argument. It was an affidavit from Igor Bogolepov, who claimed that he knew that the Soviet secret police had regarded Bohlen as a "possible source of information" and a "friendly diplomat" during a Bohlen tour of duty in Moscow in the 1930s.[56]

Bogolepov was an NTS man who free-lanced as an anti-Communist expert in Washington. In the early 1950s he was on a number of payrolls, including Grombach's, and the State Department's Ylitalo says that it was Grombach who primed Bogolepov for his role in McCarthy's attack on Bohlen. Bogolepov had once been a Soviet Foreign Ministry official, but he defected to the Nazis and spent most of World War II making anti-Semitic propaganda broadcasts for the Goebbels ministry. Bogolepov says that U.S. intelligence brought him to this country in the late 1940s—apparently illegally, considering his work for Goebbels—and that he had worked on and off for the CIA for several years. In time, however, Bogolepov grew discontented with the agency, mainly because it did not pay him as much as he thought he deserved.[57]

The cooler heads on Capitol Hill considered Bogolepov a crackpot. The radical right did not, however, and readily used his statements as "proof" that among other things, Communist fellow travelers were engaged in a campaign to rewrite U.S. Army training manuals and that Charles Bohlen was "possibly" an undercover Stalinist agent.

Even Bogolepov's affidavit failed to bail out McCarthy this time.

The senator was outvoted, and Bohlen's nomination was approved. The *New York Times* carried the entire affair on its front page and prominently quoted the NTS man's affidavit.[58] The Russian defector's stint in the Goebbels ministry, which had been made public in earlier congressional testimony, was not mentioned in the report.

McCarthy succeeded in drawing some blood despite losing the vote on Bohlen. According to columnists Joseph and Stewart Alsop, Republican Majority Leader Robert Taft visited Eisenhower shortly after the vote. Taft insisted that "no more Bohlens" be sent to the Senate as nominees. Eisenhower agreed, the Alsops reported, and Taft "hastened to spread the happy word on Capitol Hill that Senator McCarthy and his ilk would thereafter enjoy a virtual veto on all presidential appointments."[59] The Alsops were overstating the case, perhaps, but it was clear enough that McCarthy had demonstrated his power as a spoiler in the Senate. Eisenhower's diplomatic nominations were screened for their acceptability to the extreme right for much of the rest of his administration.

Bohlen left for Moscow about a week after his confirmation. Shortly before he departed, however, John Foster Dulles implored Bohlen to stay in Washington for just a few more weeks so that the diplomat could travel to Russia together with his wife and family. Traveling alone, Dulles suggested, would only raise an issue of Bohlen's possible "immoral behavior." The diplomat was dumbfounded. He later confided to a friend, historian David Oshinsky recounts,[60] "that it took every ounce of his patience to keep from smashing Dulles in the face."

The role of Grombach's former Nazis and collaborators in gathering political ammunition for Joseph McCarthy is, in many respects, only a short footnote to the history of high politics in Washington. Grombach rapidly lost influence in the State Department and the CIA in the wake of his showdown in the hotel room with Kirkpatrick, and McCarthy, too, discredited himself in the end. Bogolepov returned to Europe, where he is reported to have committed suicide several years later. Bohlen went on to do a workmanlike job as U.S. ambassador to Moscow and eventually ended up as a central player in U.S.-Soviet relations over the next two decades.

But incidents such as the purging of Thayer and Davies and the crisis over Bohlen's nomination can sometimes point to larger historical patterns. The popular support for liberation that was so carefully nurtured during the early 1950s provided fertile ground for entrepreneurs like Grombach to put down roots. Regardless of its "American" and patriotic trappings, liberation's paranoid anticommunism made it easier for some U.S. politicians to make common cause with a former Goebbels propagandist such as Bogolepov or with public spokesmen for prewar anti-Semitic terrorist groups such as NTS leader Boldyreff.

As was seen in the case of the Bogolepov affidavit, private intelligence apparats like John Grombach's organization formed one of the important linkages between the careful politicians in Washington and the former Nazis and collaborators who were occasionally thought to be useful to them. Such unofficial clandestine action groups have long played a sporadic but sometimes important role in American political life; witness G. Gordon Liddy's Watergate burglary team or the more recent scandal surrounding Colonel Oliver North's activities inside the National Security Council. The extralegal status of Grombach's group permitted him to hire and exploit former Nazis and Axis officials for intelligence-gathering purposes, then secretly to put the products of his work to use in partisan political battles in the United States. Perhaps in some other decade John Grombach would have hired persons from other failed regimes as agents; the continuing intrigues among anti-Castro Cubans and the former South Vietnamese police suggest that a new generation of espionage entrepreneurs in the Grombach mold is still at work. But in the early 1950s it was former Nazis and collaborators who were in the most abundant supply for such affairs. It is they who formed much of the heart of Grombach's overseas network and they who gave him much of the ammunition he needed to participate in McCarthy's purges.

At the same time that McCarthy and his allies were battling in the Senate for the dismissals of Thayer, Davies, and Bohlen, the Republicans' election year pledge to liberate Eastern Europe also fueled a rapid expansion of clandestine destabilization operations. A special series of foreign policy conferences code-named Solarium reaffirmed that the new administration would engage in "selected aggressive actions of limited scope, involving moderately increased risks of general war," as Eisenhower's top national security adviser, Robert Cutler, put it, in order "to eliminate Soviet-dominated areas within the free world and to reduce Soviet power in the Satellite periphery." U.S. policy aimed at "a maximum contribution to the increase in internal stresses and conflicts within the Soviet system."[61]

But despite the Republicans' public attacks on Truman's containment policy, Eisenhower's election had been a victory for the Republican establishment, not for the radical right. The Republicans did not have a substantially new strategy for dealing with the Soviets, beyond a tendency to use harsher rhetoric than the Democrats. George Kennan's containment theories may have seemed like part of the problem to most liberation advocates, but his thinking on clandestine political warfare against the Soviets was most welcome to Eisenhower and dominated the scene at the Solarium strategy conferences. Eisenhower himself personally endorsed Kennan's stratagems, his analysis of East-West affairs, and the former diplomat himself.[62]

The president and his advisers decisively renewed the ongoing program of harassment and destabilization inside Eastern Europe that had given birth to the Nazi utilization efforts in the first place. Further efforts to "reduce indigenous Communist power" through clandestine CIA action were approved in both Western Europe and the third world. Guatemala and the Middle East were also singled out for CIA attention, while agency Director Allen Dulles promoted a renewed attempt to overthrow the government in Albania.*

The clandestine action provisions of Solarium were later codified in NSC 5412, a slightly revised version of Truman's NSC 10/2 covert warfare decision. NSC 5412 again affirmed that the United States was fully committed to a broad campaign of political war against the USSR.[63] It again affirmed that "underground resistance movements, guerrillas and refugee liberation groups"—obviously including the various surviving collaborationist organizations from

---

*In 1985 the State Department published a number of key Solarium records in its highly regarded series, *Foreign Relations of the United States.* Unfortunately it chose to delete almost the entire text of the program put forward by Frank Wisner and Admiral Richard L. Connolly's "Team C" concerning clandestine operations.

The deletions in these documents are not easily apparent to the casual reader of the *Foreign Relations* volumes, and that has led to considerable misinterpretation of the Solarium record. The *Washington Post* reported after the new Solarium papers were published, for example, that Eisenhower had flatly rejected Wisner's covert operations plan. In fact, however, the conferences concluded that the United States should selectively integrate stepped-up clandestine action into the broader U.S. security policy.

The State Department's decision to publish only an expurgated version of the Solarium record contributes to the continuing confusion over what U.S. foreign policy actually was during the 1950s. This is particularly unfortunate considering the role the Solarium sessions played in setting the stage for America's clandestine entrance into the Vietnam conflict, the decision to undertake a coup in Guatemala, and other covert operations of the day that have since proved to have had far-reaching implications for U.S. relations abroad.

Eastern Europe—were still at the center of U.S. covert paramilitary programs.

In the meantime, however, the existing threads of clandestine operations, liberation politics, and the abandonment of war crimes investigations and prosecutions were woven together into a new and more disturbing tapestry. By 1953 the CIA was willing to finance and protect not simply former Nazis and Gestapo men but even senior officers of Adolf Eichmann's SS section Amt IV B 4, the central administrative apparatus of the Holocaust.

CHAPTER SIXTEEN

Brunner and von Bolschwing

The tough-guy ethos of most professional intelligence officers has always militated against letting conventional ethical considerations stand in the way of collecting information or carrying out special operations. "We're not in the Boy Scouts," as latter-day CIA Director Richard Helms often said. "If we'd wanted to be in the Boy Scouts we would have *joined* the Boy Scouts."[1]

By the time Allen Dulles became CIA director in 1953, almost all resistance within the CIA to using Nazi criminals to accomplish the agency's mission seems to have evaporated. In the Lebed affair top CIA officials as well as the U.S. attorney general intervened to "legalize" the ex-OUN man's status in the United States after Lebed had been accidentally caught by an overeager INS agent. In a second case, that of former SS officer Otto von Bolschwing, the agency smoothed the former Nazi's entry into the country through consultations with interagency intelligence coordinating committees, then contacted "outsiders" at the INS—in writing—on the ex-Nazi's behalf. In the arcana of espionage etiquette, these acts are unmistakable indicators of high-level consent for von Bolschwing's immigration.[2]

But the key phrase remained "to accomplish the agency's mission." Nazis were never employed or protected for their own sake, but only as a means to achieve some other goal that was presumably in the interests of U.S. national security. Conversely, the fact that a man might have been a mass murderer did not by itself disqualify him from working for the agency if he was believed to be useful. And once such a person *had* worked for U.S. intelligence, there was inevitably pressure to protect him, if only to keep out of the public eye the operations he had been involved in.

There was, it is true, concern inside the CIA about the possible public relations problems involved in employing persons who had been compromised by their earlier service to the Nazis. In the case of Belorussian Nazi leader Stanislaw Stankievich, for example, his CIA case officers fretted during the 1950s and 1960s that Stankievich "has been and perhaps remains ardently Fascist" and that "continued use [of him] might be a source of embarrassment to the Project and/or the Agency."[3] Stankievich, who had once served as the SS-appointed mayor of Borisov during a 1941 pogrom that took the lives of thousands of Jews, was at the time of the CIA officer's comments a leading member of the Institute for the Study of the USSR in Munich, a CIA-financed émigré think tank affiliated with Radio Liberation. The Munich institute is the "Project" to which the quoted CIA records refer.

According to the CIA's own documentation, the agency oversaw Stankievich's recruitment to the institute, then reviewed and passed on his various promotions as he rose through the ranks there. The agency also directly intervened to bring him to the United States, according to a study by the U.S. General Accounting Office, by falsely certifying that it had no derogatory information on Stankievich that would bar him from coming into the country when in fact, it had a record of his role in the Borisov massacre and of his ongoing association with extremist émigré organizations.[4]

The only known internal opposition to this Nazi's repeated professional promotions and eventual U.S. citizenship came from a CIA officer who was clearly disturbed by Stankievich's continuing dedication to Fascist causes. Yet the agency's informal code of conduct impelled the officer to make the only complaint that might have any effect—that is, using the "Butcher of Borisov" (as Stankievich had come to be called) was a mistake not because Stankievich played a role in a pogrom but because he "might be a source of embarrassment."[5] In the end, however, this protest, too, was overridden.

There were occasional internal purges of former Fascists for public relations reasons from time to time during the 1950s. A series of Soviet propaganda broadsides exposing Nazis at RFE and RL in

1954 led to the dismissals or reassignments of thirteen employees. And Eberhardt Taubert, a former Goebbels ministry propagandist with anti-Semitic credentials stretching back to the 1920s, was forced to resign from the directorship of the CIA- and German government-financed Peoples League for Peace and Freedom in 1955 under public pressure, even though Taubert himself claimed to have abandoned Nazi thinking.[6] A handful of other examples along these same lines cropped up in the course of the decade.

But the fundamental decision to exploit anyone who might have something to offer to the struggle against Moscow remained untouched. This is precisely because such "pragmatism" is at the very heart of contemporary clandestine practice. Using Nazis (or the Mafia or, conversely, a church-sponsored organization of college students) was never an aberration in the minds of most intelligence operatives. This is simply the way clandestine wars are fought, they say, whether the general public likes it or not.

Still, public opinion does remain a factor, at least in the West. Gehlen's organization benefited greatly from that fact because the CIA often turned to Gehlen when it wished to bury certain very sensitive operations even more deeply than usual. At those times his contacts among former SS and Gestapo men could be uniquely valuable. One such occasion took place in Egypt in late 1953, shortly after Solarium's renewed approval of large-scale CIA countermeasures aimed at offsetting Soviet influence in the Mideast. There the Central Intelligence Agency bankrolled the activities of SS Sturmbannführer Alois Brunner, a man considered by many to be the most depraved Nazi killer still at large.

Brunner had once been Eichmann's top deportations expert for the entire Reich. He was a skilled administrator who specialized in driving Jews into ghettos, then systematically deporting them to the extermination camps. This was a difficult job, requiring a keen sense of the exact types of terror and psychological manipulation necessary to disarm his victims.

Brunner did not simply administer the deportations. He was a troubleshooter who rushed from Berlin to Gestapo offices throughout occupied Europe to train local Nazi satraps in how to carry out the destruction of Jews quickly and thoroughly. He did not neglect the murder of children because (as he told Berlin lawyer Kurt Schendel, who was pleading on behalf of a group of French orphans) they were "future terrorists." Brunner studied hard for his assignment and is said to have eventually become an expert on the railway systems of Europe so that he could locate enough boxcars to carry out his mission for the fatherland. "He's one of my best men," Eichmann said.[7]

The Simon Wiesenthal Center estimates that Brunner is personally implicated in the murder of 128,500 people. The French government eventually convicted him in absentia of crimes against humanity and sentenced him to death. Instead of facing trial, however, Brunner was in Damascus, Syria, where he had become Gehlen's "resident"—a post similar in authority to the CIA chief of station—shortly after the contract for the Org had been picked up by the Americans in 1946, keeping him safe from the French. His alias was "Georg Fischer."[8] Brunner/Fischer eventually became an important part of a CIA-financed program to train Egyptian security forces.

The Egyptian episode began as an attempt to protect U.S. interests in Egypt as the monarchy of King Farouk crumbled. Frank Wisner had dispatched his top troubleshooter in the Mideast, Kermit ("Kim") Roosevelt, to Cairo as early as 1951 to open secret negotiations with Colonel Gamal Abdel Nasser and his insurgent Society of Free Officers. They found, Roosevelt telegraphed back to Washington, "a large area of agreement."[9] Nasser asked Roosevelt for aid in building up Egypt's military intelligence and internal security squads. Both men agreed that a better-trained security force was in the mutual interest of both Egypt and the United States. But domestic politics in both countries required that the American involvement in this effort be kept very low-profile.

So CIA Director Allen Dulles turned to Gehlen in 1953 for help in the Egyptian situation. Gehlen's men and the contract agents he kept on tap had many of the qualities that Dulles was looking for: They were experienced in police security work, were willing to work cheaply, and were not inclined to call attention to themselves. The committed anti-Semitism of some of Gehlen's men was also a plus, at least in the eyes of some members of the Egyptian secret service. At the same time West Germany's deeply conflicted relationship with Israel during the postwar period ensured that almost any group of German experts who went to Egypt could be easily penetrated and internally monitored by both Gehlen and the CIA as the project went forward.

Gehlen enlisted the help of Otto Skorzeny, a hulking former SS *Sturmbannführer* who had once been dubbed by the wartime German press "Hitler's favorite commando." At six feet four inches and 220 pounds, with appropriately arrogant "Aryan" features and a five-inch dueling scar down his left cheek, Skorzeny had transformed himself during the war from an unknown SS truck driver into a walking symbol of Nazi strength and cunning. He had specialized in training behind-the-lines sabotage and assassination teams for SS RSHA Amt VI during the war as well as in daring commando raids to rescue Mussolini and to kidnap recalcitrant Hungarian politicians and in similar exploits. Hitler loved him and seemed to believe that Skorzeny and his gang of cutthroats would become the secret weapon that could single-handedly reverse Germany's disastrous military losses.[10]

Skorzeny did nothing to reduce his legend after the war. At one point he escaped from American custody under mysterious circumstances while awaiting a denazification trial in 1948, leaving behind a note claiming that he had "only done my duty to my Fatherland" both during the war and after it. Skorzeny pictured himself as something like a latter-day Scarlet Pimpernel fighting for the "honor" of Hitler's Germany and the SS against overwhelming odds.[11] He spent many of the early postwar years deeply involved in running escape operations through Spain and Syria for fugitive Fascists. Both the Odessa and *die Spinne* (the Spider) SS escape organizations revolved in large part around the personality—and the myth—of Otto Skorzeny.

As intelligence veteran Miles Copeland tells the story, Gehlen wanted to subcontract the CIA's Egyptian training mission to Skorzeny in 1953. The former *Sturmbannführer* demurred, however. The Egyptians simply did not pay enough, he argued. Gehlen promised that Skorzeny's salary from Nasser would be subsidized with CIA money laundered through the Org and that the expenses of the operation would also be covered by American funds. Skorzeny's position in Egypt, furthermore, would give him a valuable entrée into the lucrative Middle Eastern arms trade. Copeland, who was personally involved in the affair, reports that "a certain well-known Major General of the American Army" (whom he declines to identify) was enlisted to convince the former Nazi commando that his services were greatly needed in Egypt.[12]

When Skorzeny continued to balk, Gehlen brought pressure to bear on Skorzeny's father-in-law and chief financial sponsor, Dr. Hjalmar Schacht. Schacht, who had been Hitler's financial genius of clandestine rearmament, had only recently avoided an eight-year prison sentence when his conviction under denazification laws had been quashed by John McCloy, the U.S. high commissioner in Germany. When Schacht, too, stressed the usefulness of helping the Americans, Skorzeny came around at last. He agreed to take the Egyptian training mission, on the condition that his stay in Cairo be limited.

Over the next eighteen months Skorzeny used CIA money to recruit for the Egyptian security services about 100 German advisers, many of whom he reached through neo-Nazi organizations and SS escape networks. Among his wards were Hermann Lauterbacher, an SS man and former deputy leader of the Hitler Youth, and Franz Buensch, a Goebbels propagandist best known for his pornographic work *The Sexual Habits of Jews.* Buensch, Gehlen's resident chief in Cairo, was a veteran of Eichmann's SS "Jewish Affairs" office.[13]

This "talented" group was later joined by Alois Brunner. As "Georg Fischer," Brunner moved to Cairo in the midst of the Skorzeny project in Egypt and quickly integrated himself into that effort. He remained in Cairo until 1962, when an exploding Israeli letter bomb tore off several of his fingers. The Israeli intelligence service Mossad has claimed—unofficially, of course—that after Brunner's stint with Skorzeny he enjoyed a second Egyptian contract under which he helped recruit a corps of German rocket experts on behalf of the Egyptian government.[14] Israeli secret agents are said to have undertaken the letter bomb campaign that very nearly killed Brunner.

The *Times* of London reports that Brunner returned to Syria after the bomb attack. He lives today in the prosperous Abu Rumaneh district of Damascus.[15]

What the CIA knew, if anything, of the background of "Georg Fischer" will remain a mystery until its files on the Skorzeny operation are opened. Considering, however, that American tax money was underwriting both Gehlen and the Skorzeny project, and considering Skorzeny's frequent efforts to promote himself as an international neo-Nazi leader and benefactor of SS fugitives, it is reasonable to ask just what steps, if any, the CIA took to determine who it was it had hired to train Nasser's secret service.

A good place to begin such an inquiry is with the former CIA agent Miles Copeland, who worked closely with the German advisers assembled by Gehlen and Skorzeny in Egypt. Copeland's writings do not discuss Brunner, but he confirms that it was Skorzeny who did the contracting for the Egyptian project and that he brought in about 100 German advisers. The hirelings "were not—or in some cases *not quite*—war criminals," Copeland writes.

Copeland insists that the men he worked with were not "unrepentant Nazis." Their rejection of neo-Nazi ideology might actually be considered unfortunate in a certain sense, in Copeland's opinion, "because as mere survivalists rather than men of principle, even wrong principle," he writes, "they find no difficulty in adjusting to Leftish influences in Nasser's government."[16]

Copeland's frank comment is a revealing illustration of a much broader trend of thinking in U.S. government security circles during the 1950s. Because the Soviets were also recruiting selected former Nazis after the war, Copeland argues, "we simply could not bring ourselves to let valuable non-Anglo-American assets (who, as Nazis, were under perfect 'cover') go to waste." He continues: "It was to our advantage to have [Nazi intelligence specialists] absorbed, with a minimum of fuss and embarrassment, by various countries of the world where they could live inconspicuously and earn a living." This policy was the necessary "amorality of power politics," he argues. "Believe it or not"—Copeland approvingly quotes an unidentified U.S. Army intelligence colonel—"some of us are still able to put future American interests ahead of the delights of revenge."[17]

The story of U.S. intelligence relations with criminals such as Brunner is of necessity fragmentary, for both the CIA and Brunner himself have taken extensive measures to keep such affairs hidden. It is clear, however, that Brunner was not an exception to the rule who managed to ingratiate himself with the Americans through guile or through an oversight. There is, in fact, at least one other known case of U.S. recruitment of another SS veteran of Adolf Eichmann's "Jewish Affairs" office, the elite committee that served as the central administrative apparatus of the Nazis' campaign to exterminate the Jews.

That recruit's name is Baron Otto von Bolschwing. Supremely opportunist, von Bolschwing succeeded in traversing the whole evolution of U.S. policy toward Nazi criminals. He had profited during the war from the Nazi confiscation of Jewish property, then later from the defeat of Nazi Germany itself. Von Bolschwing enlisted as a CIC informer for the Americans in the spring of 1945, and before two years were out, CIA agents in Vienna, Austria, had recognized his skills and recruited him for special work on some of the most sensitive missions the agency has ever undertaken. These included running secret agents behind the Iron Curtain and even spying on Gehlen himself on behalf of the Americans.

Von Bolschwing was deeply involved in intelligence work—and in the persecution of innocent people—for most of his adult life. He had joined the Nazi party at the age of twenty-three, in 1932, and had become an SD (party security service) informer almost immediately.[18] In the years leading up to 1939, von Bolschwing became a leading Nazi intelligence agent in the Middle East, where he worked under cover as an importer in Jerusalem. One of his first brushes with Nazi espionage work, according to captured SS records, was a role in creating a covert agreement between the Nazis and Fieval Polkes, a commander of the militant Zionist organization Haganah, whom von Bolschwing had met through business associates in the Mideast. Under the arrangement the Haganah was permitted to run recruiting and training camps for Jewish youth inside Germany. These young people, as well as certain other Jews driven out of Germany by the Nazis, were encouraged to emigrate to Palestine. Polkes and the Haganah, in return, agreed to provide the SS with intelligence about British affairs in Palestine. Captured German records claim that Polkes believed the increasingly brutal Nazi persecution of the Jews could be turned to Zionist advantage—at least temporarily—by compelling Jewish immigration to Palestine, and that the Haganah commander's sole source of income, moreover, was secret funds from the SS.[19]

It was in the course of these negotiations that the young Baron von Bolschwing gained the trust of Adolf Eichmann, who was at the time an obscure SS functionary specializing in intelligence on Freemasonry and Jewish affairs for the Nazi party. The acquaintance was more than a casual one, for von Bolschwing went on to play a central role in arranging conferences between Eichmann and Polkes in Vienna and Cairo, contacts that established Eichmann as the SS's "Jewish affairs expert" and laid the foundation for his later career as the architect of the extermination of European Jewry.

Perhaps it was inevitable that Eichmann—ever the plodding, careful clerk—would have learned about Jewry and Zionism from someone. But as fate would have it, it was Otto von Bolschwing who became Eichmann's teacher. "The first time I was occupied with Jewish matters," Eichmann testified under interrogation prior to his 1962 trial for crimes against humanity, "was when [Nazi agent Theodor von] Mildenstein visited me at my workplace together with von Bolschwing—never before that."

Thereafter "Herr von Bolschwing would often drop in at our office and talk to us about Palestine," Eichmann recalled. "He spoke so knowledgeably of the aims and situation of Zionism in Palestine and elsewhere that I gradually became an authority on Zionism. . . . I kept in touch with Herr von Bolschwing . . . because no one else could give me firsthand information about the country I was most interested in for my work."[20]

Von Bolschwing teamed up with Eichmann in 1936 and 1937 to draw up the SS's first comprehensive program for the systematic robbery of Europe's Jews. "The Jews in the entire world represent a nation which is not bound by a country or by a people but [rather] by money," von Bolschwing argues in a pivotal SS policy study. "Therefore they are and must always be an eternal enemy of National Socialism . . . [and they] are among the most dangerous enemies." The whole point of his plan, he notes, was to "purge Germany of its Jews."[21]

Of course, von Bolschwing was not the only Nazi to come up with schemes for persecution of Europe's Jews, nor was he the first. His techniques, however, were uniquely practical and well suited for implementation by Germany's modern bureaucratic state machine. Within months after von Bolschwing's proposals had circulated through the SS "Jewish affairs" apparatus, the SS implemented a series of aryanization measures in Austria that institutionalized many of the measures that von Bolschwing had outlined. These tactics then became a model for anti-Semitic persecution throughout Nazi-dominated Europe.[22]

The SS soon appointed von Bolschwing to a prestigious post as SS and SD clandestine operations chief in Bucharest, Romania. There, according to captured German war records, he personally helped organize a coup attempt and pogrom led by the Romanian Iron Guard, a Fascist organization that maintained fraternal ties with the German Nazi party.

Iron Guardists stormed into the Jewish sector of Bucharest on January 20, 1941, burning synagogues, looting stores, and destroying residences. Hundreds of innocent people were rounded up for execution. Some victims were actually butchered in a municipal meat-packing plant, hung on meathooks, and branded as "kosher meat" with red-hot irons. Their throats were cut in an intentional desecration of kosher laws. Some were beheaded. "Sixty Jewish corpses [were discovered] on the hooks used for carcasses," U.S. Ambassador to Romania Franklin Mott Gunther wired back to Washington after the pogrom. "They were all skinned . . . [and] the quantity of blood about [was evidence] that they had been skinned alive." Among the victims, according to eyewitnesses, was a girl no more than five years old who was left hanging by her feet like a slaughtered calf, her body bathed in blood.[23]

Von Bolschwing helped arm and instigate the rebels by giving them the secret blessing of the SS, according to German records.[24] Later he smuggled a dozen of their top leaders out of Bucharest when the rebellion was put down by a rival faction of Romanian rightists. About 630 people were killed during the violence, according to contemporary reports, with another 400 reported missing. "In the Bucharest morgue, one can see hundreds of corpses," a Nazi military attaché cabled back to headquarters in Berlin. "But they are mostly Jews."[25]

At the end of the war von Bolschwing abandoned his SS comrades to their fates as soon as it became profitable to do so. He began active—one might even say enthusiastic—collaboration with the Allies at least as early as the spring of 1945, when American troops swept through western Austria. Von Bolschwing's new alliance with U.S. intelligence proved to be deep and abiding. "I agreed to obtain for them information concerning the movements and strengths of the German military, including German rocket research at Camp Schlatt," von Bolschwing explained later. "After the German surrender, I continued working for the U.S. forces, first in the capacity of the military government, and then starting in 1947 in intelligence activities with the U.S. forces. . . . I had continuous service with U.S. intelligence until my departure [for America] in January 1954.[26]

"In 1947, 1948 and early 1949, I was assigned [by the CIA] to the Gehlen Organization . . . primarily in offensive intelligence against the East Bloc," he asserted in a secret interview with investigators from the U.S. Air Force. The CIA provided him with money, a top secret security clearance, and travel privileges throughout Europe.[27]

Officially von Bolschwing worked for Austria Verlag in Vienna, a branch of the Austrian League for the United Nations, according to records found in his archives. He used that position—along with the active intervention of U.S. intelligence agencies—to apply for

Austrian citizenship in 1948 and to win clearance for his Nazi activities from an Austrian denazification court.[28] Otto von Bolschwing became one of the highest-ranking CIA contract employees in Europe after the war. His responsibilities included spotting and recruiting agents, and he specialized in cross-border operations infiltrating spies into Hungary and Romania.

There can be little doubt that the U.S. intelligence agencies that made extensive use of von Bolschwing were aware of his role in the Bucharest pogrom. At the end of the war, the United States had captured the SS and German Foreign Office files in Bucharest nearly intact, including extensive SS files concerning the 1941 pogrom. The seizure of these records was regarded by the OSS as one of the most important intelligence triumphs of the war, and they were rapidly analyzed by a team of American experts. According to the official war report of the OSS, the records permitted the identification of more than 4,000 Axis intelligence agents, about 100 subversive organizations, and some 200 firms used as commercial covers by Nazi spies. The files were transmitted to Allied headquarters, according to the OSS report, and were used in the Nuremberg investigations into Nazi war crimes.[29]

There is another important bit of evidence concerning American awareness of von Bolschwing's relationship with the Iron Guard leadership and the 1941 pogroms. According to a sworn deposition von Bolschwing gave to the U.S. Justice Department in June 1979, he was utilized by U.S. intelligence *precisely because* of his Iron Guard connections. "In the summer of 1948, at the height of the Civil War in Greece, I was asked by my American courier officer to make contact with the Romanians, who might influence the Greek situation," von Bolschwing asserted in the interview. "In the course of that endeavor, I visited with Mr. Constantin Papanace [a top Iron Guard minister whose life von Bolschwing had saved during the war], who was residing under the presumed auspices of the Vatican in or near Rome. . . ." Von Bolschwing's contacts in the Iron Guard, some of whom were still inside Romania at the time, became central figures in the espionage network he was running for the CIA.[30]

Von Bolschwing left the Gehlen Organization in late 1949 but retained his U.S. sponsorship in a new operation under even deeper cover. He managed to convince American authorities for a time that rival powers were using the Nazi and Wehrmacht old boy networks to infiltrate the Org.

"The French, British and also Russians had gotten hold of a large number of [German] General Staff officers," von Bolschwing recalled later. "Each one of them was using them in intelligence work. Recognizing the traditional closeness of most German intelligence personnel and General Staff personnel, I feared that we were being penetrated by the East, rather than penetrating them." He obtained U.S. funding to establish yet another (though much smaller) secret German intelligence organization, which operated parallel to Gehlen's. It continued infiltrations into Eastern Europe, at the same time discreetly keeping an eye on Gehlen's work for his American sponsors.[31]

In 1953, for reasons that are as yet unclear, the CIA decided to bring Otto von Bolschwing to the United States. Von Bolschwing—as a former SS man, Nazi party member, and Nazi SD agent—was clearly ineligible for a visa to the United States or American citizenship, and the CIA knew it. As in the Lebed, Shandruk, and Stankievich cases, the CIA did not attempt to bring von Bolschwing into the country "legally" under the special authority it enjoyed through the 100 Persons Act. Instead, at least two high-ranking CIA officers—including Everett C. O'Neal, who is most recently reported to be CIA chief of station in a plum assignment—engineered a complicated scheme to spirit the former Nazi illegally into this country.[32]

According to the CIA's own records, von Bolschwing's supervisory agents concluded prior to his departure from Europe that they would have to quash the routine character inquiries ordinarily made of prospective U.S. citizens if they expected to get him into the country. The "Department of State's background investigation," the CIA resolved, "would have to be controlled."[33] The agency set out to do just that.

First, it supplied the former Nazi with a false police report and military background check that claimed that no derogatory information was known about him. Next, a senior CIA officer personally accompanied von Bolschwing to the U.S. Consulate in Munich and convinced the visa officer there to provide all the necessary travel paperwork virtually overnight.

Later agency headquarters in Washington directly intervened again, this time with the State Department and the INS, to ensure that von Bolschwing's entry into the United States went smoothly. In its letter to the INS the CIA falsely claimed that it had "conducted a full investigation of the subject [von Bolschwing]" and "had no reason to believe him inadmissible."[34] In reality, of course, the agency knew perfectly well he was inadmissible; that is why it had fabricated the military and police clearance forms for him in the first place.

Von Bolschwing's travel documents at the time he arrived in this country were full of inconsistencies, but the immigration authorities admitted him nonetheless. His passport—actually a "Temporary Travel Document in Lieu of Passport" issued by the U.S. State Department in Berlin—contradicted his immigration visa on at least five points. He did have at least one thing going for him, however. His visa listed his destination as "Washington 25," a Department of State post office known to intelligence insiders as a mail drop for the CIA and other U.S. security agencies. The U.S. sponsor on his visa application was Colonel Roy Goggin, a career U.S. Army Counterintelligence Corps officer who had worked closely with von Bolschwing for almost a decade.[35]

CIA spokesmen will say nothing official about the von Bolschwing affair. Key aspects of the case, however, have been pushed onto the public record by a criminal prosecution of the former Nazi during the late 1970s, a government General Accounting Office study of Nazi immigration to the United States, and investigative reporting by Peter Carey of the *San Jose Mercury News* and by this author.[36] The more that is known about this episode, the more serious its implications become.

To put the most positive possible face on the matter, the CIA's "official" version of events is that yes, it did bring von Bolschwing into the United States in early 1954 and it did know at the time that he was an SS man, a former Nazi party security service (SD) agent, and a Nazi party functionary, among other things. But no, it did not know he was a war criminal. This is the classified account that the CIA provided to U.S. General Accounting Office (GAO) investigator John Tipton on the condition that the GAO keep von Bolschwing's identity secret.

(Tipton was making an official inquiry into von Bolschwing's arrival in the United States following a congressional request for information on Nazis who worked for U.S. intelligence. Tipton respected the CIA's request for confidentiality in his report to the House Judiciary Committee and used an anonymous designation, "Subject C," to refer to von Bolschwing in his account of relations between U.S. intelligence agencies and former Nazis.[37] The CIA even officially cleared Tipton's study before it was released to the public. Despite this attempt to keep von Bolschwing's identity secret, however, it is without doubt that the anonymous man called "Subject C" in Tipton's report to the Congress is, in fact, Otto von Bolschwing.[38])

The CIA's cryptic admission is, by itself, shocking. Since when, it might be asked, was it considered acceptable to smuggle SS men, SD agents, and Nazi party veterans into the United States as long as "we didn't know" that they were war criminals? What exactly was the standard of proof used at the time to determine who was, and who was not, a "suspected" war criminal? Considering that Otto von Bolschwing had spent most of his adult life working full-time as a salaried executive of the Nazi party security service and SS police apparatus, the CIA's refusal even to *suspect* that he might have committed crimes against humanity appears to give him a presumption of innocence of truly munificent proportions.

In reality, however, the agency's assertion that it "didn't know" that von Bolschwing was a criminal at the time he entered the United States is most likely a lie. His involvement in the Bucharest pogrom, for example, would be evident to anyone making a routine check of captured SS files at the Berlin Document Center, not to mention the much more extensive group of records concerning the Bucharest events that were then in CIA hands.

And if the agency had simply missed this evidence through some fluke, why, then, did it set out deliberately to obstruct any *other* investigation into the former SS man's bona fides? Its suppression of the routine visa inquiry into von Bolschwing's affairs clearly suggests that something more than a naïve presumption of innocence was at work here. For one thing, muzzling the State Department's visa examination was itself highly irregular. For another, why would the CIA go out of its way to "control" State's review unless there was some concern about what it might uncover? The implication is inescapable: The CIA believed that von Bolschwing was *guilty* of war crimes, not innocent, and was worried that even a brief study of his visa application might reveal that fact.

The cases of SS veterans like Alois Brunner and Otto von Bolschwing provide a small but documented glimpse into a broad trend of events in U.S. intelligence relations with the former "assets" of Nazi Germany's intelligence services. By the time von Bolschwing entered the United States in 1954, his former patron, Reinhard Gehlen, had parlayed his American backing into de facto recognition as the official intelligence service of the emerging Federal Republic of Germany. CIA Director Allen Dulles liked Gehlen for the simple reason that he seemed to produce useful results. Gehlen's intelligence assets in Eastern Europe appeared to be solid, and his contacts in the German-speaking enclaves in South America, the Middle East, and Africa were second to none. His Org also helped the United States collect signals intelligence, though his work in that area was still not up to the British standard. All these services and more, and all at what seemed a reasonable price.

If there were former SS and Gestapo men at Gehlen's Pullach headquarters, senior members of the American intelligence community didn't want to know enough about them to be forced to do something about it. "I don't know if he's a rascal," Dulles said of Gehlen. "There are few archbishops in espionage. . . . Besides, one needn't ask him to one's club."[39]

One incident vividly illustrates the power of the Gehlen Organization in Washington during Allen Dulles's tenure as director of Central Intelligence. In October 1954 West German Chancellor Konrad Adenauer visited the United States in the midst of sensitive negotiations to enlist West Germany as a full member of the NATO alliance. At a diplomatic reception the then chief of U.S. Army intelligence, General Arthur Trudeau, personally told the chancellor that he did not trust "that spooky Nazi outfit at Pullach."[40] He suggested that it would be wise for the Germans to clean house before they were admitted to NATO. Word of the incident was leaked to the press, infuriating Allen Dulles.

In the ruckus that followed, General Trudeau was backed by the turf-conscious Joint Chiefs of Staff, while Dulles rallied his brother, John Foster Dulles, then secretary of state, to Gehlen's defense. When the dust cleared, Gehlen had been appointed chief of West Germany's new official intelligence agency, the Bundesnachrichtendienst (BND), and Trudeau had abruptly left intelligence work for a less visible command in the Far East. He quietly retired from the military a few years later.[41]

The frailty—from a strictly practical point of view—of Gehlen's heavy reliance on former Nazi intelligence operatives did not become clear until almost a decade later, when the chief of Gehlen's counterespionage division was revealed to be a Soviet spy.

Ironically it was precisely the camaraderie and trust found among the old Nazis in the Gehlen Org that the USSR used to do its penetration job. This particular case stands out because of the far-reaching damage this spy did to Western intelligence, though it is possible to cite many lesser examples. The name of the Soviet double agent—a former SS *Obersturmführer* who had once led Nazi gangs during the 1938 night of looting and temple burnings known as the *Kristallnacht*—is Heinz Felfe.

Felfe never would have gotten into the Gehlen Organization in the first place had he not been a Nazi and an SS man. He was recruited in 1951 by SS veteran Hans Clemens, who in turn had been picked up by ex-SS *Oberführer* Willi Krichbaum, one of the Org's original circle of Nazi officers personally enlisted by Gehlen back in 1946. Krichbaum was at the time Gehlen's chief organizer in Bad Reichenhall, and he relied heavily on references from SS and SD veterans to locate and clear new agents. But SS man Clemens was a Soviet spy, as it turns out, and once Clemens was on board, he recruited Felfe.[42] Felfe's motivation for spying for the Russians appears to have been primarily ideological support for communism combined with a desire for money, although the complex psychological forces at work in any double agent's mind are notoriously hard to discern.

Felfe traded on his Nazi credentials to win the trust of other Gehlen Organization leaders. The Soviets carefully cultivated their inside man and kept him well supplied with doctored information that permitted him to capture supposedly important Russian spies as well as to gather what seemed to be detailed information on East German intelligence. Felfe's sterling performance soon made him one of Gehlen's favorites, and he was promoted to chief of the organization's anti-Russian counterintelligence section. Later Gehlen gave Felfe extensive responsibilities for liaison with the CIA and other Western espionage groups and even placed him in charge of Gehlen's own effort to spot East bloc spies inside the Org itself.

Every aspect of West German intelligence was open to Felfe. If there were any secrets at all that he missed, it was only because there is a human limit to how much spying one man can do in ten years. By the time he was finally exposed through the decoding of an intercepted radio message, Felfe's espionage had destroyed hundreds of the Org's remaining agent networks inside Eastern Europe. His treachery led to the arrest of almost 100 senior Gehlen agents as well as revealed codes, communications, and courier channels on which both Gehlen and the Americans depended, according to evidence brought out at Felfe's espionage trial.[43] Finally, Felfe had funneled so much half-accurate and suspect information concerning Soviet agents into Western hands that significant parts of both West German and American counterintelligence had to be uprooted and begun all over again.

The Felfe case, along with the Philby affair in England, which broke open about a year later, sent a shock wave of panic through the CIA. The internal German damage assessment detailing agents and information Felfe had compromised ran to tens of thousands of pages, and the money necessary to rebuild the networks he had sold out to the Soviets certainly totaled tens of millions of dollars. The supposedly secure brotherhood of German intelligence specialists on which the CIA had spent so much to build turned out to be a house of cards, and the American decision to look the other way when the Gehlen Organization had gone about enlisting SS men was an important part of the blunder. The Felfe affair is an important indicator that even when one leaves aside all questions of morality, the CIA's Nazi utilization programs never did produce the practical benefits to the United States that their sponsors once claimed they would.

By the time Felfe was arrested, however, the CIA's commitment to Gehlen had become a matter of high policy. The skinny German general was ensconced as chieftain of the secret service of one of America's most important allies. There was very little that the CIA could do about the Felfe affair except to ride it through and use whatever revelations it produced to improve U.S. counterintelligence practices. Gehlen himself remained sacrosanct despite the Felfe revelations. He was not removed from office. A brief purge shook out a handful of ex-Nazis who were in on the Felfe affair, along with a few others, like Brunner, whose records as mass murderers were simply too grotesque to ignore.[44]

The purge of certain Nazis in the wake of the Felfe matter and the CIA's ongoing efforts to conceal its relationships with Brunner and von Bolschwing point up another important fact: A substantial segment of the American public has long opposed the use of Nazis and war criminals in clandestine operations. When specific cases of this type have come to light in the past, as they did in the wake of the Felfe trial, public pressure has forced the CIA and even the Gehlen Organization to abandon at least some of the former Nazis on the intelligence payroll. Public condemnation of the CIA's use of Nazis in clandestine operations of questionable morality and uncertain legality is not simply a product of America's present-day reexamination of intelligence practices, nor is it ex post facto moralizing to oppose these affairs today. The use of Nazis has, instead, often been the subject of general opprobrium—at least outside the elite national security circles of the government—and it is for that reason that the government attempts to conceal such practices to this day.

The revelations of the full implications of the Felfe affair were still well in the future back in 1954, however, when President Eisenhower and his National Security Council approved NSC 5412 and the related measures that were intended to guide U.S. covert operations for the remainder of his administration. That decision, it will be recalled, was the latter-day recapitulation of Truman's NSC 10/2 clandestine political warfare directive, and NSC 5412 again affirmed that "underground resistance movements, guerrillas and refugee liberation groups"[45] were the main forces in U.S. covert paramilitary programs of the day. These directives provided the broad strategic outline through which both the Nazi programs and the government's rhetorical commitment to liberating Eastern Europe were supposed to be executed.

The underground forces of NSC 5412 were to be the "bite" behind liberation's "bark," so to speak; they were the armed squads that were to ignite a popular revolt inside the satellite states that would "roll back communism" in Eastern Europe. By mid-1956 the CIA's clandestine operations chief, Frank Wisner, had decided that the time was ripe to act.

CHAPTER SEVENTEEN

The End of "Liberation"

Push came to shove for the "liberation" program that had provided the policy framework for the ex-Nazi recruitment programs in Hungary in November 1956. Under CIA covert operations chief Frank Wisner's guidance, Radio Free Europe and Radio Liberation had hammered away at the liberation theme for Eastern European audiences through the first half of the 1950s. Listeners were told that America strongly supported freedom for the Soviet satellites, that the U.S. government was convinced that this freedom would come "soon," and that the United States was willing to do its part to help bring this about. What exactly this all meant in terms of aid was never stated explicitly in the broadcasts, but the tone of the rhetoric left little doubt that the Americans would do *something*.

The discontent inside the satellite countries that the agency's broadcasts attempted to tap was very real; the subsequent revolts in Poland, Hungary, and eventually Czechoslovakia proved that. But the liberationists had seriously misjudged the balance of international power. To put it most bluntly, the Soviets were willing to undertake a nuclear war to preserve their hold over the satellite states. The Americans, though rhetorically committed to liberation, were not willing to fight World War III to achieve that object.

The tragic story of the Hungarian events has been often told. Tens of thousands of students and workers broke into the streets, burning local Communist party headquarters, seizing radio stations, and erecting barricades. Thousands of Hungarian soldiers and officers joined the strikers. Crack Soviet troops equipped with tanks, machine guns, and even jet fighter aircraft invaded Budapest to suppress the rebellion. They were challenged—and even held off, for a time—by untrained civilian militias armed only with gasoline bombs and a handful of guns seized from local police warehouses.

One of the first things the Soviets did after their invasion was to sever all telephone contact into and out of Budapest, effectively sealing off the rebellion from the outside world. But by a curious oversight they forgot to shut down newspaper teletype lines, and it is through that medium that the epitaph of the liberation policy was written:

RUSSIAN GANGSTERS HAVE BETRAYED US; THEY ARE OPENING FIRE ON ALL OF BUDAPEST. PLEASE INFORM EUROPE AND THE AUSTRIAN GOVERNMENT . . . clattered a message to the Associated Press from rebels who had occupied the offices of the Hungarian state news agency building. WE ARE UNDER HEAVY MACHINE GUN FIRE. . . . HAVE YOU INFORMATION YOU CAN PASS ON . . . TELL ME, URGENT, URGENT.

There was a pause.

ANY NEWS ABOUT HELP? QUICKLY, QUICKLY. WE HAVE NO TIME TO LOSE. NO TIME TO LOSE.

The connection broke. Soon, however, the teletype line between the Vienna AP office and a second Hungarian newspaper came to life.

SOS SOS SOS, was banged out. THE FIGHTING IS VERY CLOSE NOW AND WE HAVEN'T ENOUGH TOMMY GUNS IN THE BUILDING, Budapest cabled. I DON'T KNOW HOW LONG WE CAN RESIST. . . . HEAVY SHELLS ARE EXPLODING NEARBY. . . .

WHAT IS THE UNITED NATIONS DOING? GIVE US A LITTLE ENCOURAGEMENT.

THEY'VE JUST BROUGHT A RUMOR THAT AMERICAN TROOPS WILL BE HERE WITHIN ONE OR TWO HOURS. . . .

Like most rumors in war, the story was wrong. There would be no American soldiers in Hungary.

Moments later this came over the UPI wire: GOODBYE FRIENDS. GOODBYE FRIENDS. GOD SAVE OUR SOULS. THE RUSSIANS ARE TOO NEAR.[1]

The line went dead.

At least 15,000 people, including about 3,000 Soviet soldiers, were killed in the fighting, according to contemporary reports.[2]

The United States huffed and puffed over Radio Free Europe. Wisner and a large crew of CIA agents personally manned the Austrian-Hungarian border, carrying out refugee relief, agent recruitment, and clandestine radio broadcasting. There were the usual protests in the United Nations. But the Western allies were embroiled in the dispute over the Suez Canal at the time of the rebellion, and no one was willing to go nose to nose with the Russians over Hungary. The Republican administration's liberation rhetoric was put to the test—and failed.

The Nazi collaborationist exile organizations on the agency's payroll again played a thoroughly counterproductive role in the Hungarian events. In the wake of the failed rebellion there was considerable controversy over whether or not the United States had misled street fighters in Budapest into believing that U.S. military aid would be delivered to the rebels. Many anti-Communist Hungarian refugees bitterly charged that such promises—supposedly broadcast over Radio Free Europe—had resulted in considerable unnecessary bloodshed when rebels held out to the last man in the false hope that international help was on the way.[3]

An internal inquiry, as well as a German government study, largely cleared RFE of those charges. The CIA then used these clearances to reassure congressional oversight committees—such as they were in those days—that the United States had not unduly interfered in the Hungarian events.[4]

In fact, however, misleading claims that American military aid was on the way *had* been broadcast by radio, though not by Radio Free Europe. According to a special investigation by the parliamentary Council of Europe, the Russian nationalist NTS organization was responsible for beaming the ill-considered pledges into Hungary at the height of the rebellion. The NTS, as it turns out, sporadically operated a clandestine radio station named Radio Free Moscow, aimed at Soviet troops in East Germany, and they decided to send its signal into Hungary at the height of the fighting. As with other NTS projects of the period, Radio Free Moscow was staffed primarily by former Nazi collaborators—for it is they who made up most of the NTS leadership during the 1950s—and was almost entirely financed by the CIA. Whether or not the agency directly authorized broadcasts of the false promises concerning American help during the crisis is unknown.[5]

The practical result of the agency's sponsorship of the NTS extremists in this incident is similar in some important respects to the earlier pattern of events in the Ukraine. In both cases, clandestine U.S. sponsorship of groups dedicated to war on the Soviets enabled them to serve as provocateurs, in effect, triggering further bloodshed and increased repression, the primary victims of which were the ordinary people of those lands whom the United States professed to support. The United States, of course, made full use of the propaganda material provided by the brutal Soviet invasion of Hungary, just as it had earlier in the Ukraine. But neither crisis advanced the longer-term—and more fundamental—U.S. interest in the creation of stable, independent states in Eastern Europe.

The high U.S. policy decisions on clandestine operations that have since leaked into the public domain did not specifically mention the NTS or von Bolschwing, Lebed, Ostrowsky, and the other fugitives from war crimes charges who were entering the United States during the cold war. The thrust of the government's covert operations authorization was, as always, support for pro-Western forces inside Communist countries, not for former Fascists.

But the fact remains that quisling "governments-in-exile" frequently became the primary beneficiaries of the clandestine political warfare strategy. This practice gradually became so open that almost any scholar, journalist, or politician with a reasonably sophisticated knowledge of the events of World War II could have deduced that *somebody* was underwriting the political activities of former Fascists and extreme nationalist exile leaders who had found their way to the United States. The political tenor of the day, however, seems to have ensured that such questions rarely found their way into mainstream political discourse or the media.

A good example of how this self-censorship worked—and the political blowback it produced—may be found in the case of the Assembly of Captive European Nations (ACEN). The ACEN became the showcase of the CIA's numerous exile projects inside the United States beginning in 1954. Although the CIA's direct funding and orchestration of the ACEN remained veiled during the 1950s,* the U.S. government's strong political support for the project was quite open. The ACEN was a miniature United Nations made up

---

*A 1972 Congressional Research Study finally admitted that this effort had been bankrolled by the CIA. That fact had become obvious to many observers much earlier, however, because nonclassified annual reports published by the Committee for a Free Europe had also openly discussed that RFE's funds were underwriting the assembly's activities.

of the best representatives of Eastern European life, the official story went. There "the efforts of the legitimate representatives of these nations, representing all democratic political trends and groups," as the organization's founding documents put it, "could be united on a continuous and enduring basis."[6]

Above all, the ACEN was supposed to be respectable. Its job was to provide a dramatic counterpoint to statements made by Communist UN deputies from Czechoslovakia, Poland, and other satellite countries. It met in parallel with the official United Nations at the elegant Carnegie Endowment International Center on UN Plaza itself, considered many of the same subjects, and sought to discredit Soviet claims of democracy and freedom in the satellite states. The *New York Herald Tribune* welcomed its formation as a "rallying point for the submerged hopes and desires of subjugated populations . . . a voice to command the attention of the outside world." Similar glowing editorial endorsements appeared in the *New York Times, Christian Science Monitor,* and many other newspapers and magazines.[7]

Even in this carefully groomed project, however, former Nazi quislings held dominant positions in several delegations. The Albanian collaborationist Balli Kombetar organization controlled the pivotal ACEN Political Committee for most of the 1950s. Onetime Nazi collaborators also enjoyed substantial influence in the Lithuanian delegation and in the observer group known as the Liberal Democratic Union of Central Eastern Europe, which was still another émigré political association financed primarily by the CIA. Latvia's Alfreds Berzins (the former pro-Nazi propaganda minister) was placed in charge of the ACEN's "Deportations" Committee, though the subject of its interest was Soviet deportations of Latvian nationalists to Siberia, not the Nazis' wartime deportations of Jews. The International Peasant Union, as noted previously, was represented at many ACEN functions by a mass murderer who had once been a Latvian police chief.[8]

It would be a mistake, however, to view the ACEN as a whole as a "Nazi" organization. The influential Czech delegation was controlled by anti-Nazi (and anti-Communist) moderate socialists. The Polish delegation consisted in large part of the old wartime Polish government-in-exile in London combined with a handful of surviving Polish underground fighters, many of whom had risked their lives in the struggle against Germany. Most of the Hungarian emissaries were undisputably conservative but apparently free of culpability for war crimes, and so on.[9]

The relatively mainstream character of those ACEN groups, including the anti-Communist and anti-Nazi credentials of some top ACEN leaders, gave this Captive Nations movement a thoroughly acceptable image in the eyes of the media and the public at large. Furthermore, the ACEN had money and contacts among powerful people. Its support group, American Friends of the Captive Nations, for example, was headed by Christopher Emmet (the onetime sponsor of Constantine Boldyreff) and included such notables as former Ambassador Clare Boothe Luce, IRC Chairman Leo Cherne, and noted attorney Adolf A. Berle, Jr.[10]

But other ACEN member groups, as has been seen, were deeply compromised by their leaders' wartime collaboration with the Nazis. And those organizations, together with some of the more extreme nationalists in the Radio Liberation camp, drew the ACEN into a variety of Captive Nations coalitions with yet another Eastern European émigré coalition, the neo-Nazi Anti-Bolshevik Bloc of Nations (ABN).

The ABN was dominated by Ukrainian nationalist veterans of the OUN/UPA, and it included a half dozen open Nazi collaborators on its executive board. Its newspaper, *ABN Correspondence,* published praises of wartime genocidalists such as Ustachi Führer Ante Pavelic and Slovakian quisling Premier Monsignor Jozef Tiso. Alfreds Berzins, whom the U.S. government once termed a "fanatic Nazi" responsible for sending innocent people to concentration camps, was the president of the ABN "Peoples Council." (Berzins was simultaneously a Latvian leader in the ACEN.) His vice-president at the ABN was the Belorussian quisling Radislaw Ostrowsky.[11]

The ABN nevertheless enjoyed substantial support among radical rightists on Capitol Hill. The powerful China Lobby, together with congressmen such as Senators McCarthy and Jenner, gave open support to the group and sometimes provided a national platform for it to air its views. These congressmen established several highly publicized investigating committees, including the House select Committee on Communist Aggression and Representative Charles Kersten's inquiry into the Soviet role in the Katyn Forest massacre, at which the ABN both set the agenda and provided most of the witnesses.[12]

The single most important American ABN activist was the National Security Council's Dr. Edward M. O'Connor. O'Connor, it will be recalled, had been the U.S. displaced persons commissioner who had spearheaded the legal revisions that permitted Waffen SS veterans from Latvia, Lithuania, and Estonia to enter the United States freely, beginning back in 1951. O'Connor moved that year to a post in the directorship of the NSC's Psychological Strategy Board and spent most of the remainder of the 1950s in a variety of NSC assignments concerned with the administration of clandestine operations in Eastern Europe. He was a specialist in the national security aspects of immigration policy and made no secret of his political affinity for the exiled anti-Communist groups of the ABN. He eventually served as chairman of the private support group American Friends of the Anti-Bolshevik Bloc of Nations and as a founder of the National Captive Nations Committee.*[13]

The government-financed ACEN and its partially interlocked ally, ABN, gradually coalesced into a faction of the far right wing of the Republican and, to a lesser degree, Democratic parties. By 1960 this Captive Nations movement had used the support it enjoyed in the media and in conservative circles to garner a measure of real power. Its annual parade committee in New York that year was endorsed by eighty-four senators and congressmen. Conservative heavyweights such as William F. Buckley, Jr., Sidney Hook, and Fred Schlafly openly promoted the event. Scores of ethnic leaders, including a number of Jewish notables, mobilized for the march. The political tone, of course, was thoroughly patriotic, pro-American, and anti-Communist. Nevertheless, side by side with the careful politicians on the rostrum were open apologists for Nazi genocide.[14] One of the key organizers of the 1960 event, for example, was Austin App, a cheerful American of German descent whose books *History's Most Terrifying Peace* and, later, *The Six Million Swindle* are considered the foundation of the "Holocaust never happened" school of historical revisionism.[15]

---

*Later Dr. O'Connor reemerged as a leading public spokesman on behalf of Ukrainian émigrés in the United States accused of war crimes. O'Connor was announced as a featured speaker at a 1985 rally organized on behalf of Ivan Demjanjuk, for example, who was found by a U.S. federal court to have been a former Treblinka death camp guard responsible for loading prisoners into the gas chambers. O'Connor contended that the KGB had falsified the evidence against Demjanjuk. O'Connor's son Mark, as it turns out, was Demjanjuk's defense attorney.

Edward O'Connor died at age seventy-seven on November 24, 1985.

Captive Nations activists became dedicated foot soldiers in just about every right-wing crusade undertaken in the United States during the 1950s and 1960s. They turned out hundreds of demonstrators to pelt Soviet diplomats with eggs and garbage during the official celebration of the fortieth anniversary of the 1917 revolution, for example; picketed department stores that carried goods made in Eastern Europe; and disrupted local school board meetings with charges that small-town principals and the PTA had gone Communist. Captive Nations activists succeeded in purging libraries in some jurisdictions of books they considered insufficiently hostile to the USSR.

Equally important, Captive Nations lobbyists on Capitol Hill began to play a small but real role in American foreign affairs. They could not, of course, write U.S. policy. But working together with corporate-financed lobbies such as the proarmament American Security Council, Captive Nations leaders have acted as influential spoilers capable of obstructing important East-West peace initiatives undertaken by both Republican and Democratic administrations. They continue, in fact, to play that role today.

"It is a common and long standing phenomenon of American political life," George Kennan wrote some years later of his experience with Captive Nations activists, ". . . that ethnic groups of this nature, representing compact voting groups in large cities, are often able to bring to bear on individual legislators, and through them on the United States government, an influence far greater than an equivalent group of native citizens would be able to exert."[16] As early as July 1959 the U.S. Congress unanimously adopted a resolution calling for an annual Captive Nations Week. The CIA-funded ACEN "strongly promoted" the resolution on Capitol Hill, according to Senator Charles Mathias of Maryland, a member of the Senate Foreign Relations Committee. (The use of CIA funds to lobby Congress, it should be noted, is a specific violation of law.) The openly pro-Axis ABN also backed the bill and succeeded in introducing language into the text of the resolution calling for freedom for such "nations" as Cossackia and Idel-Ural, both of which are fictitious entities created as a propaganda ploy by Hitler's racial theoretician Alfred Rosenberg during World War II. The congressional pronouncement also called for, in effect, the dismemberment of the USSR through "freeing" the Ukraine, Georgia, and Belorussia from Soviet captivity. The resolution was "churned out" of Congress, according to a columnist of the day, "along with casual holiday proclamations, such as National Hot Dog Month."[17]

Yet the timing of the proclamation was significant, and it constituted a major victory for hard-line Captive Nations organizers. Vice President Richard Nixon—hardly a liberal on the question of communism—was then in Moscow on a major Republican effort to improve East-West communication and stabilize the nuclear arms race. Soviet Premier Khrushchev took exception to the unanimously passed congressional statement calling for the disintegration of his country and used the incident to raise questions about American sincerity in the negotiations. Nixon was forced to explain and, in effect, apologize for the U.S. Congress, pointing out that even President Eisenhower did not control the timing of congressional acts. "Neither the President nor I would have deliberately chosen to have a resolution of this type passed," Nixon said soothingly, "just before we were to visit the USSR."[18] The damage, however, had already been done.

According to Senator Mathias, the Captive Nations movement also succeeded in placing obstructions in the path of Kennedy's and Johnson's policy of "building bridges" to Eastern Europe, which those presidents hoped to use as a means of gradually winning some measure of influence in the region. Captive Nations organizers spearheaded appeals to broad cold war constituencies in the United States to force the cancellation of major trade contracts with Yugoslavia, Romania, and Poland that had been approved by Washington. George Kennan, who had returned to government in 1961 as U.S. Ambassador to Yugoslavia under President Kennedy, remembers how this same ethnic coalition succeeded in pressuring Congress to stop the extension of most favored nation trading status to Yugoslavia and then in halting the shipment of obsolete jet fighter parts—for which the Yugoslavs had already paid—to that country altogether. The CIA-funded ACEN's role in banning the export of the fighter parts is ironic because the agency had itself helped arrange the sale of the previous-generation jets to the independent-minded Yugoslavs in the first place as a means of splitting that country away from Moscow.[19] After the Americans' promises for spare parts had collapsed, Marshal Josip Tito of Yugoslavia went back to the USSR for his first reconciliation with the Soviets in almost fifteen years. He was met at Moscow's airport with roses and marching bands.

The Assembly of Captive European Nations, in short, began as what must have appeared to be a clever propaganda project, an appropriate counterpart to the Crusade for Freedom. In the end, however, it became a political force to be reckoned with on the American far right. And the radical right, in turn, remains a very real force in Washington, D.C.

These exiled leaders have by no means disappeared, and some such groups have won the open support of the Reagan administration. The Captive Nations activists have been particularly strong in the National Republican Heritage Groups (Nationalities) Council, led by conservative activist Frank D. Stella.[20] This national GOP organization embraces several score of conservative ethnic organizations and state coalitions that tend to identify with the far right wing of the party. While the large majority of the organizations in the Republican Nationalities Council are thoroughly respectable, it is nonetheless true that the council has become fertile ground for political organizing by certain former Nazi collaborators still active in immigrant communities in this country.

Perhaps part of the reason for this is that the director of the council during the early 1970s was Laszlo Pasztor, a naturalized American of Hungarian descent who served during the war as a junior envoy in Berlin for the genocidal Hungarian Arrow Cross regime of Ferenc Szalasi. Pasztor, in an interview with reporter Les Whitten, insisted that he did not participate in anti-Semitic activities during the war.[21] Furthermore, he says, he has attempted to weed out extreme-right-wing groups from among the GOP's ethnics.

But the record of Pasztor's "housecleaning" leaves much to be desired. The GOP nationalities council has provided an entry into the White House for several self-styled immigrant leaders with records as pro-Nazi extremists. Bulgarian-American Republican party notable Ivan Docheff, for example, who has served as an officer of the Republican party's ethnic council for years, has acknowledged that he was once a leader in the National Legion of Bulgaria, a group that the more moderate Bulgarian National Committee in the United States has described as "Fascist." He also spent twelve years as chair of the influential New York City Captive Nations Committee as well as president of the Bulgarian National Front, an extreme rightist émigré organization long active in the openly pro-Axis Anti-Bolshevik Bloc of Nations (ABN). Docheff, who describes himself as "100 percent anti-Communist, not a

Nazi," was once invited to the White House to share a Captive Nations[22] prayer breakfast with President Richard Nixon.

A half dozen other somewhat similar cases among Republican ethnics may be readily identified. The official Latvian-American organization in the GOP's nationalities council is the Latvian-American Republican National Federation, which was led for years by Davmants Hazners (president) and Ivars Berzins (secretary). During the 1970s the group shared the same office and telephone number in East Brunswick, New Jersey, with the Committee for a Free Latvia. The latter group, it will be recalled, was led for most of the last decade by the by-now familiar Vilis Hazners (president) and Alfreds Berzins (treasurer and secretary) despite accusations aired by *60 Minutes* and other media that both had been responsible for serious crimes during the war. Their associate Ivars Berzins is most recently noted as a leading proponent of the campaign to halt prosecutions of fugitive Nazi war criminals in the United States.[23] There is no indication, it should be stressed, that Ivars Berzins or the other leaders of the Latvian-American Republican party group engaged in any sort of disreputable activity. Even so, the intimate ties between these two organizations and their leaderships raise legitimate questions concerning what the political agenda of the Republican organization may actually be.

Perhaps most disturbing, the GOP ethnic council has passed resolutions on racial and religious questions sponsored by an openly pro-Nazi, anti-Semitic activist in that organization on at least three occasions in recent years. The author of those resolutions is worthy of note, if only as an indication of the degree of racial extremism that the Republican organization has been willing to tolerate in its ranks. His name is Nicholas Nazarenko, and he is the self-styled leader of the World Federation of Cossack National Liberation Movement of Cossackia and the Cossack American Republican National Federation, which is a full organizational member of the Republicans' ethnic council. The Republican party's Cossack organization describes itself as a "division" of the world federation and shares the same leadership, letterhead, and post office box address in Blauwelt, New York, as the world federation group. Nazarenko has admitted in an interview with the author that he spent much of World War II as an interrogator of POWs for the SS in Romania.[24]

Nazarenko's speech at the 1984 Captive Nations ceremonial dinner in New York left little to the imagination about his own point of view or that of his audience. He spoke of what was, in his mind, the heroism of the Eastern European collaborators in the German legions during the war, and he spoke of why, in his mind, the Nazis lost the war. "There is a certain ethnic group that today makes its home in Israel," Nazarenko told the gathering. "This ethnic group works with the Communists all the time. They were the Fifth Column in Germany and in all the Captive Nations. . . . They would spy, sabotage and do any act in the interest of Moscow," he claimed. "Of course there had to be the creation of a natural self defense against this Fifth Column," he said, referring to the Nazi concentration camps. "They had to be isolated. Security was needing [*sic*]. [So] the Fifth Column was arrested and imprisoned.

"This particular ethnic group was responsible for aiding [the] Soviet NKVD," he continued. "A million of our people [were] destroyed as a result of them aiding the NKVD. . . . You hear a lot about the Jewish Holocaust," he exclaimed, his yellowed mustache quivering, "but what about the 140 million Christians, Moslems and Buddhists killed by Communism? That is the real Holocaust, and you never hear about it!"[25] The Captive Nations Committee's crowd responded with excited applause in the most enthusiastic welcome for any speaker of that evening.

There is also substantial overlap between the Captive Nations Committee, the Republicans' ethnic council, and a broad variety of other well-known right-wing organizations, some of which enjoy multimillion-dollar financing and play substantial roles in U.S. elections. About 15 percent of the organizational members of the American Security Council's Coalition for Peace Through Strength—the high-powered lobbying group that led the successful campaign to stop SALT II—are these same Captive Nations groups. The coalition dispenses hundreds of thousands of dollars it has received from major defense contractors to candidates it favors in U.S. congressional campaigns and is generally regarded as one of the most effective proarmament lobby groups in Washington. At least four coalition member organizations still openly support the enemy Axis governments of World War II; one is led by Nazarenko, who has stated publicly that the Coalition for Peace Through Strength has provided him with a mailing list of senior U.S. military officers for use in Captive Nations propaganda work.[26]

More important than any organizational connections, however, is the manner in which "liberation" thinking has again taken hold in Washington, D.C. The Reagan wing of the Republican party has historically maintained extremely close ties with the Captive Nations movement. Many top Reagan activists have spent much of their lives promoting the liberationist cause, even when the theory fell out of fashion after the Hungarian uprising of 1956.

President Reagan himself bestowed a Medal of Freedom, the country's highest civilian honor, on liberation theorist (and former OPC/CIA émigré program consultant) James Burnham in 1983. Burnham's liberation analysis "profoundly affected the way America views itself and the world," Reagan intoned at the awards ceremony. "And I owe him a personal debt," the president continued, "because throughout the years of travelling on the mashed-potato circuit I have quoted [him] widely."[27]

Today the Reagan administration has updated liberationism to apply to 1980s crisis points like Angola and Nicaragua. The CIA, with the president's backing, is now spending in excess of $600 million per year to equip some 80,000 to 100,000 anti-Communist "freedom fighters" with arms, supplies, and even state-of-the-art Stinger antiaircraft missiles. This renewed cold war strategy, sometimes known as the Reagan Doctrine, has also become a litmus test of conservative Republican orthodoxy, writes *Washington Post* political analyst Sidney Blumenthal.[28] Right-wing true believers have taken to using votes on funding for "freedom fighters" like Angolan rebel strongman Jonas Savimbi as a means of extracting concessions from Republican moderates and driving their party farther to the right. The new liberationists' goal, Blumenthal writes, "is to ensure that no Republican will be nominated for president who has not pledged fealty to their ideology."

The liberation ideal—"permanent counterrevolution," in Blumenthal's words, meaning protracted conflict with the USSR, leading to a final showdown in which communism is wiped from the face of the earth—is not simply a "Nazi idea," nor is it appropriate to label people who support it Nazis or Nazi sympathizers. The *Post*'s Blumenthal, for example, attributes many of Burnham's liberationist theories to Burnham's flirtation with Trotskyism in the 1930s.

But the fact remains that ideas and theories have histories, just as nations do. They are the products of particular circumstances and junctures in civilization. Burnham's theories were based on his work with exiles during the early years of the American Committee for Liberation, Radio Liberation from Bolshevism, and similar projects that enlisted numerous Nazi collaborators among that generation of "freedom fighters." Burnham speaks highly of Germany's political warfare in Belorussia and the Ukraine; it was only Hitler's later blunders that made its eastern front policy a mistake, he writes in *Containment or Revolution.* [29] The true origins of liberationism as a coherent philosophy lie in Nazi Germany and in the Nazis' political warfare campaign on the eastern front, nowhere else.

Today liberation activists often have a reasonably sophisticated political agenda and enough clout to arrange annual Captive Nations commemorations hosted directly by the president or vice president of the United States.[30] Their political stands are not entirely unreasonable: Most Captive Nations activists are strong supporters of improved human rights inside the Soviet bloc, for example, although their record on civil rights inside the United States is somewhat less exemplary. The one position they cling to above all, however, is an implacable paranoia toward the USSR that would permit no arms control treaties, no trade and indeed no East-West cooperation of any type, only relentless preparation for war.

The scars that secret émigré anti-Communist programs have left on life in the United States run considerably deeper than the contribution they may have made to the early 1950s purge of former Voice of America Director Charles Thayer or to the escape of certain Nazis from justice. The cold war itself—and, indirectly, much that has flowed from it—should be reconsidered today in the light of what is beginning to be known of clandestine activities during that period.

Many, though obviously not all, U.S. covert operations of the period involved use of Nazi collaborators, and it is that aspect of American secret warfare that has been the focus of attention here. The basic rationale for using Nazis in covert operations has consistently been that doing so was of practical value to the United States in international relations, that it was putting "future American interests" ahead of the "delights of revenge." In reality, however, these affairs have worked to the long-term—and frequently the short-term—detriment of the United States. The negative blowback from U.S. operations employing Nazis and collaborators may be generally grouped into six categories. The first of these, chronologically speaking, stems from the intense West-East competition over recruitment of German scientists and secret agents. The fight over these intelligence assets played a surprisingly large role in the rapid erosion of trust between the superpowers, especially in the first months after the defeat of Hitler Germany.

The mistrust engendered during this race proved to be an important factor in undermining the possibility of superpower peace as early as the Potsdam Conference of July 1945.[31] Both sides at Potsdam read the clandestine campaigns of the other as the "true" policy behind the veils of diplomacy. Yet both also insisted that their own diplomatic initiatives be taken at face value. One practical result of this semiotic clash was an acceleration of the upward spiral of suspicion, hostility, and fear.

The second major type of damaging blowback has been the destructive effect that Western covert operations and political warfare—particularly programs employing Nazi collaborators—has had on provoking the cold war and later crises in East-West relations. These affairs were not only products of the cold war but also catalysts that escalated the conflict. They offer graphic proof that the United States' struggle against the USSR began considerably earlier and was carried out with far more violence than the Western public was led to believe at the time.

The U.S. "national security state," as it has since come to be termed, established itself very quickly in the wake of the showdown at Potsdam. Before three years had passed, the emerging intelligence community had begun undertaking small- and medium-scale campaigns using former Nazis and Axis collaborators as operatives in the coup plot in Romania, the subversion of elections in Greece and Italy, and attempts to manipulate favored political parties throughout the Soviet-occupied zone of Eastern Europe. One can well imagine what the USSR's interpretation of these U.S. initiatives was at the time, considering the Marxist-Leninist dictum that the United States is inherently imperialist in character.

The liberal anti-Communist consensus of the day in the West saw covert operations as a viable "national security" option that was short of open warfare. Such tactics were supposed to be a relatively enlightened and effective means of advancing American interests at the expense of their Soviet rival. George Kennan, Charles Thayer, Brigadier General John Magruder, and other theoreticians of clandestine political warfare contended that the relatively successful experience that the United States had enjoyed in sponsoring an anti-Nazi underground during wartime could be selectively applied to the harassment, "containment," and perhaps the overthrow of the postwar pro-Soviet states in the East.[32]

There was a fundamental difference between the United States' wartime experience, however, and the postwar practice of attempting to bankroll alliances between Eastern European center parties and the remnants of the Axis power structure that still held on in the Soviet-occupied zone. In many cases, the U.S.-backed factions lacked either the moral authority or the simple competence to rule, particularly in the face of Soviet hostility. But instead of urging its proxies to cooperate as junior partners in the early postwar coalition governments dominated by Communists—and thereby to stabilize the situation in Eastern Europe with some measure of democracy, however imperfect—the United States encouraged its sympathizers to attempt to seize total power (as in the Romanian coup plot of 1947) or, that failing, to use clandestine action to disrupt the ability of any other group to govern (as in Poland from 1946 to 1951).[33] Captivated by a vision of the world in which any enemy of the Communists was a friend of ours, the United States' *public* role in Eastern Europe during the cold war consisted in large part of the creation of polarized crises in which East-West cooperation became impossible, while the *clandestine* counterpart to this same policy often created secret alliances with war criminals, Nazis, and extremists. It is clear from the secrecy that surrounded these alliances that many U.S. national security experts recognized at the time such tactics as reprehensible. However necessary such tactics may have seemed in the 1940s and 1950s, in retrospect this policy has proved to have been an ineffective way to deal with Eastern Europe, one which some subsequent U.S. administrations have spent considerable effort trying to correct.

The results of the clandestine policy have set back, not advanced, American efforts to win friends in Eastern Europe, lessen repression, and improve civil liberties in the region. The American sponsorship of Gehlen and other collaborators may have remained largely secret in the United States, but it became a long-running theme in pro-Soviet Eastern European publicity, precisely because such practices tended to discredit America. The hypocrisy of U.S. actions and the CIA's not-so-secret encouragement of disgraced Axis collaborators tended to undermine Eastern European public understanding of Western-style norms and civil liberties, which had never been a strong tradition in the region in the first place. Furthermore, exposure of U.S.-backed campaigns of this type tended to provide satellite states with convenient and surprisingly credible outside scapegoats for the failures of their own governments, especially during the years of extreme economic problems in the immediate aftermath of the war. In many cases—Romania, Poland, and the Ukraine—clandestine campaigns by U.S. intelligence may have ended up actually strengthening the pro-Soviet regimes they were intended to subvert.

Even some of the "success stories" of the postwar Nazi campaigns have rebounded in unpleasant ways for the United States. In Greece the United States backed the reintegration of wartime Nazi collaborators into that country's police agencies as a means of fighting an insurgency, and the strategy did indeed succeed in placing political parties favorable to the United States in power there. At the same time, however, leaders of the CIA-trained and-supported police agency KYP—many with records of Nazi criminality—became the center of a long string of extremist plots, coup attempts, and brutality that eventually culminated in the imposition of neo-Fascist rule in that country under Colonel George Papadopoulos from 1967 to 1974.[34] The role of American multinational corporations and the CIA in the Papadopoulos coup of 1967 continues to undermine U.S.-Greek relations to this day.

Despite the demonstrable lack of success of these clandestine tactics in Europe, especially those involving rehabilitated Nazi collaborators, the United States has expanded and intensified similar émigré subversion programs all over the world during the past three decades. Instead of being discarded, the early émigré operations employing Waffen SS veterans have become a model for thousands of other U.S. clandestine operations. The CIA's present techniques for virtually every type of covert operation from black propaganda to murder were first formulated during the agency's work with the Eastern European collaborationist troops it inherited from the Nazis. True, some types of psychological strategies are as old as warfare itself, and other modern clandestine techniques may be traced to British, German, or Soviet programs initiated during the 1920s and 1930s. The first systematic use of assassinations, coups d'état, ratlines, and subversion began for Americans, though, while working with Axis assets in the wake of World War II. The National Security Council's pivotal NSC 10/2 and later NSC 5412 decisions—the rationales for both of which were intimately tied up with the enlistment of Waffen SS veterans and anti-Communist irregulars left over from the war—have proved to be the foundation upon which more than three decades of multibillion-dollar clandestine activities have been built. The present-day U.S. sponsorship of the Nicaraguan contras, including the well-publicized CIA training of contras in the assassination of medical workers, schoolteachers, and civilian officials,[35] are in many respects a replay of tactics that were tested—and failed—in the Ukraine more than thirty years ago.

The third major type of blowback is insidious and subtle. Former Axis intelligence analysts enlisted by the U.S. Army and the CIA consistently reinforced the existing self-deception among U.S. national security experts concerning the USSR, particularly during the first formative years of the cold war and the emerging U.S. national security apparatus. Examples may be readily identified today in spite of the extreme security measures that still surround the internal intelligence evaluation processes of those years. These include very basic errors that range from misappraisal of the size and war readiness of the USSR's military establishment to fundamental misjudgments about Soviet political intentions in both Western and Eastern Europe.

The information-gathering and analysis divisions of intelligence agencies are intensely political organizations. Instead of the ideal of dispassionate, accurate evaluation of facts, what one actually encounters inside such groups is a sharply competitive business in which final reports are often shaped as much by the policies of the administration in power as they are by the underlying reality of any given situation. Bureaucratic infighting and even domestic partisan debates play a very substantial role in the creation of intelligence analyses.[36] During the cold war years the CIA and army intelligence often selectively enlisted those persons abroad who confirmed those agencies' vision of what U.S. strategy in Europe should be. At the same time they purged other analysts, including highly trained Americans of impeccable reputations, who challenged those assumptions. These personnel decisions seem to have been motivated primarily by a desire for institutional orthodoxy, not by the actuality of Soviet behavior of the day.

Information and analysis that reinforced the dominant preconceptions of the day almost always received a far more sympathetic reception in Washington than news that ran counter to those beliefs. Thus General Clay's (and Gehlen's) alarms about the Red Army in early 1948 counted for more in U.S. national security circles than the reality that the USSR had significantly reduced its troop strength in Europe, in large part because Clay's war scare confirmed the American leaders' worst suspicions concerning the USSR.

Entrepreneurs such as General Gehlen, John Valentine Grombach, and their various rivals have historically been able to manipulate this situation to their own advantage, sometimes for years at a time. Gehlen, above all, proved to be the master at playing to the audience of American national security experts. By shaping the data that shaped global decisions, he played an indirect yet substantial role in world events. His support for a relentlessly hostile cold war against the USSR, together with the success he enjoyed in undermining his critics, has left a durable mark on European history.[37]

The fourth important type of blowback is the long-term corrupting influence that financing the work of men like Alois Brunner, Klaus Barbie, Stanislaw Stankievich, and others has had on the American intelligence agencies themselves. The corrosive effect of recruiting criminals, mercenaries, and torturers as CIA contract operatives extends well beyond the impact of any single incident or operation in which such persons may become involved. The internal logic of clandestine agencies demands that the organization protect its former agents long after their usefulness has passed—or at least to "dispose" of such agents properly, as it is termed in intelligence jargon—in order to retain their loyalty to the institution as long as possible. This can produce compromising personnel problems that last for years, even for decades.

The CIA has historically dealt with its disposal problem by quietly resettling its former contract agents in South America, Canada, or Australia. It has also brought a smaller number of operators to the United States, official reports have finally admitted. (Traitors and suspected double agents present a special sort of disposal problem, of course. Congressional testimony and fragmentary CIA records now in the public domain suggest that some such persons have been murdered.)[38]

Ongoing agent disposal programs create a strong incentive for the government to continue protecting retired Nazis or other criminals for years after their supposed usefulness to this country has expired. The CIA's present determination to protect its agent disposal system remains one of the single greatest obstacles to expulsion of known Nazi criminals hiding in the United States.

As late as 1976 the agency's practices in this regard were still so blatant that the CIA actually wrote an unclassified letter to a former CIA contract agent, Edgars Laipenieks, who was then facing deportation from the United States in connection with allegations that he had committed multiple murders, torture, and other crimes against humanity at the Central Prison in Riga, Latvia, during the war. "We have been corresponding with the Immigration and Naturalization Service about your status," agency spokesman Charles Savage wrote to Laipenieks on official CIA letterhead. "It is our understanding that INS has advised their San Diego office to cease any action against you. If this does not prove [to be] the case, please let us know immediately. Thank you once again for . . . your past assistance to the Agency. Sincerely," etc.[39]

Laipenieks, as it turned out, made the CIA's letter public during his legal defense, and caused something of an uproar, for obvious reasons. Since that time the agency has been more cautious about what it sends out to disposed agents with questionable backgrounds. The practice of tacitly protecting them continues, however, and remains a factor in several cases of Nazi criminals still living in the United States.

The reverse side of this particular type of blowback is the intrinsic weakness, from a strictly practical point of view, of the networks of contract agents who had been compromised by their service to Hitler during the war. As was seen in the case of Heinz Felfe inside the Gehlen Organization, the tight, often cultlike relationships among Nazi veterans actually provided a relatively easy means for Soviet agents to penetrate U.S.-sponsored espionage operations.

Intelligence agencies of both East and West have effectively obstructed prosecution of Nazi criminals on a far broader scale than simply the handful of cases cited above. To put it simply, espionage organizations have long found it more profitable to use the evidence of criminality that has come into their hands as a means of blackmailing or suborning former Nazis (or any other compromised persons) into cooperating with intelligence operations rather than bring such persons to trial in an open forum. In case after case, America's—and the world's—long-term interest in advancing social justice has been subordinated to short-term espionage gains. The full extent of this practice will probably never be known. The successful execution of this sort of blackmail, it is important to remember, requires continuing the cover-up of an individual's criminal past, if only to ensure that the espionage agency can come back for another "bite." But the recent revelations of alleged blackmail of United Nations Secretary-General Kurt Waldheim using charges of wartime crimes against humanity is one more indication that this type of extortion of ex-Nazis for intelligence purposes has reached far more deeply into European life than is generally known.[40]

The fifth and perhaps the most damaging type of blowback from the émigré and Waffen SS utilization programs stems from the CIA's large-scale intervention in domestic American politics during the 1950s. These operations became important elements in the complex process through which U.S. intelligence agencies systematically nurtured persons viewed as useful, while attempting to suppress those deemed dangerous.

The CIA was presumably motivated by a desire to achieve U.S. foreign policy objectives when it promoted the careers of Eastern European liberation activists inside the United States. Foreign affairs, after all, are the CIA's assigned sphere of operations. But the agency's liberation campaigns were never confined to overseas operations or even to immigrant communities in this country. Instead, they became a component of the agency's larger domestic political agenda. The CIA combined the émigrés' liberation efforts with other agency programs of even larger scope, such as the manipulation of mainstream U.S. media, direct propaganda broadcasting in this country through the Crusade for Freedom and other CIA-financed radio shows, surveillance and harassment of opponents, careful sculpting of academic and scholarly research programs, aggressive lobbying on Capitol Hill, and penetration of the senior leadership of trade unions, corporations, religious groups, and even student organizations.[41]

Many details of the CIA's domestic campaigns have gradually leaked into the public domain over the last decade. The synergistic effect that this enormous effort produced on life in this country is still not adequately understood, however, and may not be for many years. The fact is that the CIA's domestic operations had a substantial and lasting impact on political debate in this country during the cold war years, most important of all on foreign policy issues. The agency played a powerful role in setting the general parameters of the foreign policy debate in the United States throughout those years and in drawing the lines that separated "respectable" opinions from those considered beyond the pale.

America's large Eastern European immigrant population was particularly vulnerable to this process. The renewed liberation politics hammered out by compromised exile politicians in the wake of World War II became the only acceptable point of view in many immigrant communities in the 1950s; those with different perspectives learned that it was safer to hold their tongues.[42]

Ironically, even the anti-Communist exiles most favored for their usefulness by the CIA also suffered, though to a lesser degree. Regardless of the rhetoric of the day, the secret councils of the U.S. government never actually determined to liberate any Eastern European territory, at least not if doing so required substantial risks or sacrifices on the part of the United States. The exiled nationalist foot soldiers became mere pawns in the superpower contention over Europe, inexpensive agents whose lives were expended as though they were dollar bills that could be bet and lost without any great consequence to the men who formulated the grand strategies.

The final major type of blowback is the role that these clandestine operations played in the obstruction of justice. U.S. courts assert that they have no jurisdiction to try persons accused of committing Nazi war crimes or crimes against humanity, in large part because the offenses took place in foreign countries and generally did not directly involve U.S. citizens. Therefore, the present U.S. government Nazi hunters who work for the Justice Department's Office of Special Investigations (OSI) are limited to bringing charges against war criminals in this country for violations of U.S. immigration law—not for murder, looting, or other persecution. If the prosecution is successful, the Nazi criminal is expelled from this country.[43]

Although the OSI is loath to admit it, the fact is that its attorneys often have difficulty with war crimes suspects who plead the "CIA defense" in response to OSI charges. Former Nazis and collaborators who once worked for U.S. intelligence agencies are arguing in court that they disclosed their wartime activities, SS membership, or other compromising evidence to their CIA or army controllers back during the cold war. In so doing, defense lawyers claim, their clients satisfied any legal requirement to acknowledge their pasts to the U.S. government during immigration. Therefore, the lawyers say, they cannot be deported today.[44]

In other instances, persons whom some have accused of crimes against humanity like Mykola Lebed are unlikely to be brought to trial in the first place because their immigration to the United States was legally sponsored under the 100 Persons section of the 1949 CIA charter. Similarly, some ex-SS men insist that they entered the country under the Displaced Persons Act waiver for Baltic SS veterans engineered by Displaced Persons Commissioner O'Connor back in 1951. Their U.S. citizenships are perfectly legal despite their SS backgrounds, they say.[45]

Court rulings on such arguments have been mixed. Tscherim

Soobzokov, a onetime Waffen SS and police battalion activist suspected of multiple murders, succeeded in forcing the OSI to drop its deportation case against him when he proved at the eleventh hour that he had in fact disclosed his work for the SS to the CIA prior to his immigration to this country.[46] The agency also intervened in the case of Otto von Bolschwing, the career SS and SD veteran who had once helped organize the Bucharest pogrom, and helped engineer a settlement under which the gravely ill von Bolschwing was forced to give up his U.S. citizenship yet permitted to remain in the country until his death.[47] Edgars Laipenieks, the one who received the written endorsement from the CIA's spokesman, having successfully resisted earlier deportation attempts, remains comfortably in the United States as this book goes to press, more than ten years after the agency's letter. Court decisions are pending concerning CIA defense claims by several other former Nazis.[48]

At the same time a second maneuver, known among war crimes attorneys as the "KGB defense," has become the single most popular plea on behalf of the Nazi criminals facing deportation from the United States today. In a replay of the same cold war arguments that brought many Nazi collaborators to the United States in the first place, lawyers for accused collaborators are arguing that the Soviet KGB, now supposedly working with the tacit cooperation of the U.S. Justice Department, is manufacturing documentary evidence against their clients for political reasons. The Soviets, they say, are really the ones who are behind the evidence that Nazi criminals are hiding in America, and the U.S. Justice Department has somehow been taken in by their scheme. Many Americans feel a deep antipathy toward the USSR and believe the KGB forgery stories just might be true.

The records the defense lawyers are attempting to suppress through the "forgery" claims include captured SS identification cards, for example, and Axis police reports that establish that certain Nazi collaborators had been leaders of genocidal organizations, or that they participated in massacres and other crimes against humanity. Considering the passage of time since the Holocaust took place, these records are often essential to building solid cases against Nazi criminals.

In case after case the defense claim that the Soviets have falsified evidence on behalf of the U.S. Justice Department has itself proved to be false. "When the Red Army advanced westward across Poland

in 1944 it captured massive quantities of German personnel files,"
U.S. Justice Department attorney Eli Rosenbaum pointed out in the
case against Liudas Kairys, a Waffen SS veteran who is facing deportation from this country in connection with his role in atrocities at
Lublin, Poland, and at the Treblinka labor camp. "The Soviet government has routinely made such files available for war crimes trials
in West Germany for many years. None have ever been shown to
be—or even seriously suspected of being—forgeries." Such records
have been introduced by U.S. prosecutors in many deportation
proceedings against Nazi collaborators, he continued, and "in all
cases these documents have been admitted in evidence."[49] None of
the claims of forged evidence has ever stood up in a U.S. court
despite the fact that all questioned evidence is routinely made
available to defense attorneys and trained document examiners in
order to test its authenticity.

The failure of these claims in the courts notwithstanding, the
proponents of KGB/U.S. Justice Department conspiracy theories
have undertaken a major publicity campaign playing on the
"forged evidence" theme, and having as its object the abolition of
the U.S. government's Office of Special Investigations, which inves-
tigates and prosecutes Nazi criminals in America. As documented
in a recent study by the Anti-Defamation League of B'nai B'rith,[50]
this anti-OSI campaign frequently has a distinctly anti-Semitic tone.
Dr. Edward Rubel, a board member of the same New York-based
Captive Nations Committee discussed previously, is a leading
spokesman for the effort. Stalin's Russia was "exclusively ruled by
Marxist Zionist Jews as a ruling class," Rubel argued in a recent
letter to U.S. Secretary of State George Shultz. Now, he continued,
a "Jewish Zionist pressure group in Washington speaks through the
OSI for the U.S. Government." Rubel went on to demand that "the
'Holocaust' propaganda" be "clear[ed] up once and for all" and that
the OSI be abolished for its supposed collusion with the KGB.[51]

Rubel's views are extreme, but he is by no means alone. Reveal-
ingly, many of the same leaders of the old "liberationist" political
coalition have resurfaced in the present campaign to end prosecution of Nazis in America. Prominent among them is former White
House Communications Director Patrick Buchanan, who has publicly characterized the U.S. Justice Department's prosecution of
Treblinka death camp guard Ivan Demjanjuk as "an official lynch-
ing, choreographed by the KGB."[52]

* * *

In the final analysis, the cold war became the means for tens of thousands of Nazi criminals to avoid responsibility for the murders they had committed. The breakdown of East-West cooperation in the prosecution of war criminals—motivated, again, in part by the short-term interests of the intelligence agencies of both sides in protecting their clandestine operations assets—provided both the means for criminals to escape to the West and the alibis for them to use once they arrived here. "Nazi criminals," as Simon Wiesenthal has commented, "were the principal beneficiaries of the Cold War."[53]

Most of the American officials originally involved in the articulation of "liberation" during the 1950s or who played roles in Operation Bloodstone and other programs employing Nazi collaborators have long since died or retired. OPC consultant James Burnham suffered a stroke several years ago and is now hospitalized in Baltimore. Others, like W. Park Armstrong, Edward M. O'Connor, Robert Joyce, and Robert Lovett, died while this book was in preparation. Evron Kirkpatrick, who once ran the State Department's external research program, is today ensconced at the American Enterprise Institute. John Grombach died in 1983; his archrival in CIA internal factional fighting, Lyman Kirkpatrick, is in Middleburg, Virginia, writing a history of the American presidency.[54]

Frank Wisner, the chief of U.S. covert operations throughout the cold war and the driving force behind most of the Nazi utilization operations, began to come unglued at about the time that "liberation" met its Waterloo in Hungary. Wisner worked and drank like a trooper throughout his career, and by late 1956 he was overweight, addicted to alcohol, and given to episodes of severe paranoia and depression. The November 1956 revolt proved to be his breaking point. "That's when he first went nuts," says agency veteran Tom Braden. "Frank may have gone nuts partly because here was this Hungarian thing and we weren't doing anything about it. . . . [T]his was the first time he broke down, and it came about because we didn't do anything."[55]

Wisner's emotional distress was compounded by a serious physical illness. Shortly after the abortive rebellion he picked up a case of hepatitis and suffered profound collapse and a temperature of up to 106 degrees for days at a time. He began to have hysterical episodes in which he screamed at his CIA colleagues that they were "a bunch of Commies."[56]

Wisner partially recovered in early 1957 and returned to work as CIA deputy director in charge of clandestine action. His doctors gave him the usual warnings about getting plenty of rest and giving up alcohol; but the pace of CIA covert operations actually accelerated during this period, and Wisner remained a nightly fixture on Washington's fashionable social circuits. In August 1958 Frank Wisner broke down completely and was dragged screaming from CIA headquarters. His colleagues watched in horrified fascination as he shouted and struggled with the muscular hospital attendants in white coats. He underwent six months of electroshock treatment and emerged from the experience a deeply shaken, shattered man.

CIA Director Dulles gave Wisner a largely titular post as chief of station in London, but even a figurehead's job proved to be beyond him. Wisner returned to Washington after a few months at the London office, then retired altogether. His physical condition stabilized briefly, then began slipping again with the onset of hernia problems, liver ailments, and the gradual toll of age.

His depression returned with a vengeance. In October 1965 Frank Wisner blew off the top of his head with a twenty-gauge shotgun.[57]

The former Voice of America Director Charles Thayer died on the operating table in the midst of heart surgery in 1969. He was only fifty-nine. Thayer had, as he hoped, become a writer after he was hounded out of government, authoring a biography of his mother, a polemic in support of guerrilla warfare, and several books on U.S.-Soviet and U.S.-German relations.[58]

And George Kennan keeps on. Now well over eighty, he maintains a remarkably rigorous schedule of public speaking and writing, a neatly cultivated mustache, and a reputation as a senior statesman. He lectures at length on a multitude of subjects without notes, staring thoughtfully at the ceiling rather than at his audience.

He considers himself "a strange mixture of a reactionary and a liberal," as he put it recently, and favors decidedly hierarchical governments run by an enlightened few regardless of the shifting currents of mass public opinion. Democracy, he once quipped, should be compared to "one of those prehistoric monsters with a body as long as this room and a brain the size of a pin." He views the political left with undisguised contempt and presents the long dictatorship of Portuguese strongman Antonio Salazar as a model of governmental efficiency.[59]

Yet Kennan is today one of the few men of his station who have had the courage to take public issue with the Reagan administration's efforts to renew the cold war in the 1980s. The present American military establishment, he wrote recently, operates on the "assumption not just of the possibility of a Soviet-American war but of its overwhelming *probability* and even imminence." He blames the present administration, together with the media, for creating an "image of the Soviet opponent in his most terrible, desperate and inhuman aspect: an implacable monster, incapable of impulses other than the lust for sheer destruction, and to be dealt with only in a final military struggle." What much of the U.S. government and journalistic establishment says today about the USSR is "so extreme, so subjective, so far removed from what any sober scrutiny of external reality would reveal that it is not only ineffective but dangerous as a guide to political action." He fears, he says, "the cards today are lined up for a war."[60]

That situation may be traced in part to Kennan's own role in the CIA-sponsored anti-Communist exile programs of the 1940s and 1950s, including those that employed Nazi collaborators. True, the problems of the U.S.-Soviet confrontation are far deeper than any clandestine program. But there are moments in history when small events clarify much bigger patterns, and such is the case with the CIA's enlistment of Nazis during the 1940s and 1950s.

Here one sees the extent of the corruption of American ideals that has taken place in the name of fighting communism. No one, it seems, not even Adolf Eichmann's personal staff, was too tainted to be rejected by the CIA's recruiters, at least as long as his relationship with the U.S. government could be kept secret.

The American people deserve better from their government. There is nothing to be gained by permitting U.S. intelligence agencies to continue to conceal the true scope of their association with Nazi criminals in the wake of World War II. The files must be opened; the record must be set right.

Source Notes

Author's note: All source material listed here is now declassified and in the public domain. The security classifications appearing after certain citations (e.g., "secret," "top secret," etc.) are references to the original security status of the document prior to its declassification. The abbreviations RG and NA used in the source notes that follow refer to Record Group and National Archives.

Prologue
1. Interview with Allan Ryan, April 18, 1985. For description of events in this section, see author's notes on August 16, 1983, press conference.
2. For Ryan's report, see: Allan Ryan, *Klaus Barbie and the United States Government* (Washington, D.C.: U.S. Government Printing Office, 1983), hereinafter cited as Ryan, *Barbie Report,* and *Klaus Barbie and the United States Government, Exhibits to the Report* (Washington, D.C.: U.S. Government Printing Office, 1983), hereinafter cited as Ryan, *Barbie Exhibits.* For quotes from Ryan statements at press conference, see author's notes of the event and Ryan, *Barbie Report,* p. 212. For UPI quote, see Barbara Rosewicz, "Prober: Barbie the Exception, Not Rule," UPI ticker, August 17, 1983; for *Nightline* quotes, see *Nightline* broadcast, August 16, 1983, author's notes. See also "No Minor Cases for U.S. Nazi Hunter," *New York Times,* July 16, 1983, p. 4.
3. Von Bolschwing gave the U.S. Air Force Office of Special Investigations an account of his work for U.S. intelligence in connection with a 1970 application for a military security clearance, which he needed because the company he then headed had landed a classified air force contract involving computerized interpretation of surveillance satellite data. The Air Force Office of Special Investigations is not to be confused with the Department of Justice's Office of Special Investigations, with which von Bolschwing also had dealings about a decade later. For the air force records, see U.S. Air Force, Otto Albrecht Alfred von Bolschwing, "Statement of Civilian Suspect," Form 1168a, December 22, 1970 (secret), and Otto Albrecht Alfred von Bolschwing, "Report of Investigation," Form OSI 6, file HQD74(32)–2424/2, September 25, 1970 (secret). For more easily available accounts, see Pete Carey, "Ex-Nazi's Brilliant U.S. Career Strangled in a Web of Lies," *San Jose* (California) *Mercury News,* November 20, 1981; the author's "Not Just Another Nazi," *Penthouse*

291

(August 1983), and Allan Ryan, *Quiet Neighbors* (New York: Harcourt Brace Jovanovich, 1984), pp. 218–45; hereinafter cited as Ryan, *Quiet Neighbors.* Von Bolschwing's case is discussed in more detail in Chapter Sixteen.

4. On Verbelen affair, see Anti-Defamation League of B'nai B'rith press statement of December 20, 1983; Reuters dispatch, "Belgian Ex-Nazi Admits Working for U.S. Intelligence After 1945," *New York Times,* December 23, 1983, p. 7; and Ralph Blumenthal, "New Case of Nazi Criminal Used as Spy by U.S. Is Under Study," *New York Times,* January 9, 1984. Sanitized original documentation concerning Verbelen and Rudolph was released by the U.S. Army Intelligence and Security Command (INSCOM), Fort Meade, Md., in 1984 following Freedom of Information Act requests. On Verbelen, see Dossiers No. AE 502201 and H 8198901, plus accompanying cables; on Rudolph, see INSCOM Dossier No. AE 529655; these records have varying original classification ratings from "confidential" to "top secret." On Blome and Rudolph affairs, see also Linda Hunt, "U.S. Coverup of Nazi Scientists," *Bulletin of the Atomic Scientists* (April 1985), pp. 16ff.

5. For "pragmatic" quote, see Ryan, *Barbie Report,* pp. 193–94. For Barbie CROWCASS, see Ryan, *Barbie Exhibits,* Tab 19. A sanitized version of Barbie's CIC dossier is available in the *Exhibits.*

Chapter One

1. On religious attitudes toward communism, see, for example, *Divini Redemptoris* (often referred to as "On Atheistic Communism"), encyclical letter of Pope Pius XI (1937), and Fulton J. Sheen, *Communism and the Conscience of the West* (1948). For more extended treatments of the complex development of the Catholic Church's perception of communism, see Hansjakob Stehle, *Eastern Politics of the Vatican 1917–1979,* tr. Sandra Smith (Athens, Ohio: Ohio University Press, 1981), Wilfried Daim, *Der Vatikan und der Osten* (Vienna: Europa-Verlag), and John Cooney, *The American Pope: The Life and Times of Francis Cardinal Spellman* (New York: Times Books, 1984).

2. On "underground resistance movements," see NSC 10/2, "Office of Special Projects," June 18, 1948 (top secret), RG 273, NA, Washington, D.C. The designator "NSC 10/2" is used to identify National Security Council decision documents in series in this archival record group.

3. The media's role in the transformation of former Nazi collaborators into anti-Communist "freedom fighters" is discussed in Chapters Twelve, Fourteen, and Fifteen. For an example of this process, see Wallace Carroll, "It Takes a Russian to Beat a Russian," *Life* (December 19, 1949), p. 80ff.

For archival documentation concerning the close relations between senior U.S. media figures and the U.S. intelligence community during the cold war, see JCS 1735/41, "Guidance on Psychological Warfare Matters," February 20, 1950; also letter of Major General Charles Bolté to Brigadier General Robert A. McClure, July 7, 1949, discussing personnel for psychological warfare program and McClure's reply of July 20, 1949, with enclosure and subsequent correspondence, all secret, found in U.S. Army P&O Hot Files 091.412TS through 334WSEGTS, Box 10, Entry 154, RG 319, NA, declassified following author's request. General McClure, commander of all U.S. Army psychological warfare activities during World War II and much of the cold war, referred to

C. D. Jackson (of Time/Life) and William Paley (of CBS) as "my right and left hands [during World War II]. . . . [They] know more of the policy and operational side of psychological warfare than any two individuals I know of." See July 12, 1949, correspondence cited in the Hot Files series.

For a more accessible source on many of the personalities of cold war psychological warfare operations, see Sig Mickelson, *America's Other Voice: The Story of Radio Free Europe and Radio Liberty* (New York: Praeger, 1983).

4. Telegram traffic includes: Berlin to Washington dispatch marked "Personal for Kennan," 862.00/9-2548, September 25, 1948 (top secret); Heidelberg to Washington dispatch marked "For Kennan," 862.00/9-2748, September 27, 1948 (top secret); Washington to Heidelberg, 862.00/9-2848, September 28, 1948 (top secret); Heidelberg to Washington, 862.00/9-3048, September 30, 1948 (top secret), all of which are found in RG 59, NA, Washington, D.C.

5. Hunt, op. cit. The intelligence coordinating center referred to in the text is the Pentagon's Joint Intelligence Objectives Agency (JIOA), which is discussed in Chapter Three; for correspondence concerning suppression of records on Nazi past of scientists, see JIOA Deputy Director Walter Rozamus letter to Intelligence Division, U.S. Army General Staff, November 18, 1947. For Wev quote: JIOA Director Bosquet Wev to General S. J. Chamberlin, director of intelligence for War Department General Staff (G-2), July 2, 1947 (secret), both cited in Hunt, op. cit.

6. E. H. Cookridge (Edward Spiro), *Gehlen* (New York: Random House, 1971), pp. 121–25.

7. Author's interview with Victor Marchetti, June 7, 1984.

8. For discussion of cold war plans for use of Soviet bloc émigrés in guerrilla operations, including George Kennan's role, see Joint Strategic Plans Committee (JSPC), "Proposal for the Establishment of a Guerrilla Warfare School and a Guerrilla Warfare Corps" (JSPC 862/3), August 2, 1948 (top secret), P&O 352 TS (Section 1, Case 1), RG 319, NA; Kennan correspondence with General Alfred Gruenther, April 27, 1948 (secret) in P&O 091.714 TS (Section 1, Case 1), RG 319, NA; and JSPC "Joint Outline War Plans for Determination of Mobilization Requirements for War Beginning 1 July 1949" (JSPC 891/6), September 17, 1948 (top secret), with discussion of Vlasov and psychological warfare at Appendix "E," p. 36, in P&O 370.1 TS (Case 7, Part IA, Sub No. 13), RG 319, NA.

On controversy over Waffen SS discussed in footnote, see Eugene Davidson, *The Trial of the Germans* (New York: Macmillan, 1966), pp. 15–17, 553; or particularly Kurt Tauber, *Beyond Eagle and Swastika* (Middletown, Conn.: Wesleyan University Press, 1967), vol. I, p. 332ff.

9. The CIA's role in propaganda operations in the United States, including those employing former Nazi collaborators, is examined in detail in Chapters Fourteen, Fifteen, and Seventeen. For government records concerning payments to émigré leaders, see James R. Price, *Radio Free Europe: A Survey and Analysis* (Washington, D.C.: Congressional Research Service document no. JX 1710 US B, March 1972), pp. 9–10, and the following correspondence obtained through the Freedom of Information Act: Uldis Grava (American Latvian Association) to President Richard Nixon, January 4, 1972; Lucius D. Clay (Radio Free Europe) to Secretary of State Henry Kissinger, October 7, 1971;

Kissinger's reply to Clay, November 1, 1971, and attached correspondence, Department of State FOIA Case No. 8404249, September 25, 1986.

10. The spearhead of this publicity campaign was known as the Crusade for Freedom, although it also included a number of subordinate efforts detailed in Chapter Fifteen. On the CFF, see Mickelson, op. cit., pp. 41 and 53–58; Larry Collins, "The Free Europe Committee: American Weapon of the Cold War," (1975) Carlton University doctoral thesis, Canadian Thesis on Microfilm Service, call no. TC 20090, p. 256ff.; and Free Europe Committee, Inc., *President's Report* (New York: 1953).

11. For staffing of the Assembly of Captive European Nations (ACEN), see Assembly of Captive European Nations, *First Session: Organization, Resolutions, Reports, Debate* (New York: ACEN publication No. 5, 1955), p. 177ff. Note roles of Hasan Dosti (p. 180), Alfreds Berzins (p. 183), and Boleslavs Maikovskis (p. 186). For information concerning wartime role of these individuals, see Ralph Blumenthal, "Axis Supporters Enlisted by U.S. in Postwar Role: Albanians Said to Have Been Spies in the Balkans," *New York Times,* June 20, 1982 (on Dosti); Central Registry of War Criminals and Security Suspects (CROWCASS), *Wanted List No. 14,* Berlin Command, Office of Military Government-U.S. 11/46, p. 14 (on Berzins); U.S. Department of Justice, Office of Special Investigations, *Digest of Cases in Litigation* July 1, 1984 (Washington, D.C.: 1984), pp. 34–35 (on Maikovskis). Concerning certain Ukrainian fraternal groups, see Ralph Blumenthal, "CIA Accused of Aid to '30s Terrorist," *New York Times,* February 6, 1986, and Joe Conason, "To Catch a Nazi," *Village Voice* (February 11, 1986) both of which concern the case of noted Ukrainian émigré leader Mykola Lebed. On Daugavas Vanagi, see *Daugavas Vanagi Biletens,* no. 4 and no. 10 (1951), (at the New York Public Library, which identifies Berzins as a member of its central committee and editor of its journal; on Berzins's wartime career, see CROWCASS entry cited above. At least three other senior Vanagi leaders have also been accused of war crimes.

12. For Walter Lippmann quote, see Senator Charles Mathias, "Ethnic Groups and Foreign Policy," *Foreign Affairs* (Summer 1981), p. 982.

Chapter Two

1. Control Council Law No. 10 (Berlin, December 20, 1945) is published in Leon Friedman, ed., *The Law of War: A Documentary History* (New York, Random House, 1972), together with considerable other documentation tracing the evolution of these concepts. See also, Morris Greenspan, *The Soldier's Guide to the Laws of War* (Washington, D.C.: Public Affairs Press, 1969).

2. There is an extensive literature on the Nazi war on the eastern front and on the Holocaust in German-occupied territories. For reliable studies used in the preparation of the present text, see Lucy Dawidowiscz, *The War Against the Jews* (New York: Bantam, 1976), pp. 537–41; Martin Gilbert, *The Holocaust* (New York: Holt, Rinehart & Winston, 1985), hereinafter cited as Gilbert, *Holocaust*; Nora Levin, *The Holocaust* (New York: Schocken, 1973), pp. 268–89; Gerald Reitlinger, *The House Built on Sand* (London: Weidenfeld & Nicolson, 1960), pp. 249–56, and Gerald Reitlinger, *The SS: Alibi of a Nation* (Englewood Cliffs, N.J.: Prentice-Hall, 1981), hereinafter cited as Reitlinger,

House, and Reitlinger, *SS;* World Jewish Congress et al., *The Black Book: The Nazi Crime Against the Jewish People* (New York: Nexus Press, 1981; reprint of the 1946 edition). Martin Gilbert's concise *Atlas of the Holocaust* (New York: Macmillan, 1982), is also excellent, and contains an extensive bibliography, hereinafter cited as Gilbert, *Atlas*. The best single documentation of Nazi crimes presently available in English is Raul Hilberg's extraordinary *The Destruction of the European Jews* (New York: Harper & Row, 1961), particularly pp. 177–256. Hilberg's book has recently been revised and expanded; the page number citations to the Hilberg book mentioned in the present text, however, are to the original edition.

On Manstein's order and POW starvation, see Alexander Werth, *Russia at War 1941–1945* (New York: Avon, 1965), p. 646, and Davidson, op. cit., p. 568. Gilbert, *Holocaust*, p. 845, estimates losses of Soviet POWs at about 2,500,000, of whom 1 million were shot and the remainder killed through starvation and exposure. Manstein's postwar career mentioned in footnote is noted in Hilberg, op. cit., pp. 698 and 710. On the "Commissar Decree," see Alexander Dallin, *German Rule in Russia*, 2d ed. (Boulder, Colo.: Westview Press, 1981), pp. 30–31 and, on resettlement, p. 255ff., hereinafter cited as Dallin, *German Rule*. The mass killings at Rasseta and elsewhere are noted in Werth, op. cit., pp. 659–60. The Odessa massacre is described in Gilbert, *Holocaust*, pp. 217–18, and Hilberg, op. cit., pp. 200–01. On "hundreds of Lidices," see Werth, op. cit., p. 658ff.

3. For comment on "humane" methods, see Hilberg, op. cit., p. 210.
4. The seminal work on political warfare on the eastern front—though perhaps the least available—is Friedrich Buchardt's top secret manuscript "Die Behandlung des russichen Problems wahrend der Zeit des national-sozialistischen Regimes in Deutschland" (1946?), originally prepared for British intelligence and later made available to American agencies as well. Based also on author's interview with Mrs. Buchardt, May 17, 1984. Dallin, *German Rule*, devotes almost 200 pages to his study of "political warfare" as utilized on the eastern front; see pp. 497–505 and 660–78 for summaries. Reitlinger, *House*, pp. 248–56, offers valuable insights into the relationship between political warfare and the extermination program; and Matthew Cooper, *The Nazi War Against the Soviet Partisans 1941–1944* (New York: Stein & Day, 1979), presents a useful summary of the *Osttruppen* programs on pp. 109–23.
5. On Pfleiderer, see *Proceedings of the International Tribunal* (at Nuremberg), vol. VIII, pp. 248–249; by Reitlinger, see Reitlinger, *House*, pp. 250 and 256.
6. For SS role of Six and Augsburg, see captured SS Dossiers No. 107480 (Six) and No. 307925 (Augsburg) in the Berlin Document Center.

On Hilger: Alfred Meyer interview, December 30, 1983. See also citations to wartime documentation on Hilger in Chapter Nine.

On Köstring: "Final Interrogation Report: Koestring, Gen D Kav, CG of Volunteer Units," Seventh U.S. Seventh Army Interrogation Center, SAIC/FIR/42, September 11, 1945 (confidential), Box 721 A, Entry 179, Enemy POW Interrogation file (MIS-Y) 1943–1945, AC of 5, G-2 Intelligence Division, RG 165, NA, Washington, D.C.

On Herwarth: Hans Heinrich Herwarth von Bittenfeld, *Zwischen Hitler und Stalin* (Frankfurt: Verlag Ullstein, 1982), and Charles Thayer, *Hands Across the Caviar* (Philadelphia: Lippincott, 1952), pp. 183–200, hereinafter cited as Thayer, *Hands*.

On Gehlen: Cookridge, op. cit., or citations in Chapter Four.

On Strik-Strikfelt: Wilfried Strik-Strikfelt, *Gegen Stalin und Hitler: General Wlassow und die russische Freiheitsbewegung* (Mainz: Hase & Koehler Verlag, 1970); in English, *Against Stalin and Hitler,* tr. David Footman (New York: John Day Co., 1973).

7. Werth, op. cit., p. 646.

For account of Vlasov discussed in footnote, see Strik-Strikfelt, op. cit., with quoted portion at pp. 229–30 in the English-language edition; quote concerning execution of Vlasov is on p. 245. For Thorwald quote in footnote, see Jürgen Thorwald (Heinz Bongartz), *Flight in the Winter* (New York: Pantheon, 1951), p. 293. See also Jürgen Thorwald, *The Illusion: Soviet Soldiers in Hitler's Armies* (New York: Harcourt Brace Jovanovich, 1974), p. 315ff., hereinafter cited as Thorwald, *Illusion.*

For background and documentation on Vlasov and the Vlasov movement, see particularly Boris Dvinov, *Politics of the Russian Emigration* (Santa Monica, Calif.: Rand Corporation study No. P-768, 1955), pp. 54–112, and Boris Dvinov, *Documents on the Russian Emigration: An Appendix to Rand Paper P-768* (Santa Monica, Calif.: Rand Corporation study No. P-865, 1956), hereinafter cited as Dvinov, *Politics of the Russian Emigration* and Dvinov, *Documents*. Also valuable: "Russian Émigré Organizations," United States Political Advisor for Germany, May 10, 1949 (secret), at 861.20262/5-1049 Secret File, State Decimal files, RG 59, NA (this text is based on a U.S. interview with the former chief of Mil Amt "C" of the RSHA, Lieutenant Colonel Werner Ohletz, a senior German Abwehr officer involved in Soviet émigré programs). For data on anti-Semitic activities by Vlasov's movement, see Grigori Aronson, "Pravda o Vlasovtsakh ["The Truth About the Vlasovites"]," New York, 1949. For a typical contemporary U.S. interrogation of a Vlasov leader, see "Preliminary Interrogation Report, Source: Jung, Igor," U.S. Seventh Army Interrogation Center, July 12, 1945 (confidential), Box 721-A, Entry 179, MIS-Y Enemy Interrogation Files, 1943–1945, RG 165, NA.

Dallin, *German Rule,* p. 553ff., and Reitlinger, *House,* p. 371ff., offer probably the best and most accessible summaries of Vlasov and his army. Joachim Hoffmann, *Die Geschichte der Wlassow-Armee* (Freiburg im Breisgau: Verlag Rombach, 1984), presents a pro-Vlasov polemic that nevertheless offers many new details concerning the Vlasov movement's role in the closing months of the war. Although dated, the best single guide to material about Vlasov held in American collections is probably still Michael Schatoff, *Bibliography on [the] Vlasov Movement in World War II* (New York: All Slavic Publishing House, 1961), in Russian and German, with summaries in English, which focuses primarily on Columbia University's archives.

8. Carroll, op. cit.

9. On Kaminsky troops' role in Vlasov Army, see Köstring, "Final Interrogation Report." On this point see also: George H. Stein, *The Waffen SS* (Ithaca, N.Y.: Cornell University Press, 1966), pp. 187–88 and 265. See Alexander Dallin,

The Kaminsky Brigade 1941–1944 (Cambridge, Mass.: Harvard University Russian Research Center, 1956), hereinafter cited as Dallin, *Kaminsky*. On Kaminsky troops' role in antipartisan and anti-Semitic activities in Belorussia, see Werth, op. cit., pp. 651–64 passim and 782–83; and Gilbert, *Holocaust*, p. 298, for discussion of Belorussian police.

For Guderian comment, see Heinz Höhne, *The Order of the Death's Head* (New York: Ballantine, 1971), p. 615. For Kaminsky troops' role in anti-Semitic murders in Warsaw uprising, see Höhne, op. cit., p. 615ff., and Gilbert, *Holocaust*, p. 717.

10. For Bossi-Fedrigotti quote, see Dallin, *German Rule*, p. 519, n. 2. Dallin presents the controversy over Nazi racial politics as it applied to war on the eastern front at length; see pp. 107–304 and 587–636. See also: Dvinov, *Politics of the Russian Emigration*, Dvinov, *Documents*, George Fischer, *Soviet Opposition to Stalin* (Cambridge, Mass.: Harvard University Press, 1952), and John A. Armstrong, *Ukrainian Nationalism 1939–1945* (New York: Columbia University Press, 1955).

11. Heygendorff's comments are drawn from secret studies on use of defectors on the eastern front prepared for U.S. Intelligence by German political warfare experts after the war. Though many such reports remain classified, an important collection of them (including the Heygendorff paper) has been published as part of a twenty-four volume series titled *World War II German Military Studies*, edited by Donald Detweiler, Burdick, and Rohwer. See also Köstring and Seraphim's account titled *MS C-043: Eastern Nationals as Volunteers in the German Army*, in the same series, which reaches much the same conclusion as Heygendorff. For a more extensive collection of the United States' systematic program to tap German military knowledge, see the Foreign Military Studies records of RG 338, NA, Washington, D.C.

12. For quotations from Nuremberg tribunals cited in this section, see *Trials of War Criminals Before the Nuernberg Military Tribunals Under Control Council Law No. 10* (Washington, D.C.: Government Printing Office, 1949–1953), vol. IV, with discussion of the roles of interrogators and *Vorkommandos* on pp. 523–25 and 575–76.

13. Strik-Strikfeldt's post as chief interrogator (under Roenne's command in Abwehr Group III) is noted in Heinz Höhne and Hermann Zolling, *The General Was a Spy* (New York: Bantam, 1972), p. 40. See also Cookridge, op. cit., pp. 50–52, 56–67.

14. Ohlendorf testimony on the *Einsatzgruppen* appears in an affidavit of April 24, 1947, pp. 92–95, in *Trials of War Criminals*, loc. cit.

15. Hilberg's comments on the role of auxiliaries in killing operations is found in Hilberg, op. cit., pp. 205–06 and 243–46, with Biberstein's comment on p. 206.

16. On the CIOS and S Force etc., see: *Report of the Combined Intelligence Objectives Subcommittee*, (Washington, D.C.: Office of Technical Services, U.S. Department of Commerce, 1944), and Doris Canham, *History of AMC Intelligence, T-2* (Wright Field, Ohio, 1948). For more accessible summaries, see Clarence Lasby, *Project Paperclip* (New York: Atheneum, 1975), pp. 18–26; Boris Pash, *The Alsos Mission* (New York: Award House, 1969), pp. 24, 54, 57–59, and 136; and Michel Bar-Zohar, *La Chasse aux Savants Allemands* (Paris: Librairie Arthème Fayard, 1965). See also: "Minutes of Meeting Held

20 December 1944" (re: OSS use of T Forces as cover for "unacknowledgeable activities") Box 52, Entry 115, Folder 3, RG 226, NA, Washington, D.C.

17. Pash, op. cit., p. 99; Lasby, op. cit., pp. 16–17. On Alsos, see also Leslie R. Groves, *Now It Can Be Told* (New York: Harper & Row, 1962), and Samuel Goudsmit, *Alsos* (New York: n.p., 1947).

Chapter Three

1. Dornberger's own account of his wartime career is in Walter Dornberger, *V-2* (New York: Viking, 1958). For another flattering view, see Dieter Huzel, *Peenemünde to Canaveral* (Englewood Cliffs, N.J.: Prentice-Hall, 1962). For a slave laborer's perspective, see Jean Michel with Louis Nucera, *Dora* (New York: Holt, Rinehart & Winston, 1980). For brief basic biographies of Dornberger, including awards and positions, see R. Turner, ed., *The Annual Obituary—1980* (New York: St. Martin's Press, 1980), and *Current Biography 1965*, p. 125ff. See Lasby, op. cit., pp. 32, 113, and 259, for basic biography and discussion of work at Wright Field.

2. Dornberger, op. cit., p. 99ff.

3. Original documentation concerning conditions at the Nordhausen works is found in the case record of the war crimes trial *U.S. Army* v. *Kurt Andrae et al.*, August 7 to December 30, 1947, microfilm M1079, NA. On this point see also U.S. Army INSCOM dossier on factory administrator Arthur Rudolph, loc. cit., available through FOIA request. Secondary sources: Pierre Durand, *Les Français à Buchenwald et à Dora* (Paris: Editions Sociales, c. 1977); Christine Somerhausen, *Les Belges déportes à Dora* (Brussels: Centre Guillaume Jacquemyns, 1979); and Michel, op. cit.

4. On authority at the Nordhausen works, see *U. S. Army* v. *Kurt Andrae et al.*, loc. cit. Dornberger largely confirms his pivotal role in production scheduling, though ignoring its significance; see Dornberger, op. cit., pp. 211 and 239.

5. Dornberger, op. cit., p. 259; on Dornberger's knowledge of atrocities, see "Niederschrift über die Besprechung um 6.5.1944 im Büro Generaldirektor Rickhey ["Transcript Dealing with the Conference of May 6, 1944, in the Office of Director General Rickhey"]," Imperial War Museum, London, reproduced in Eli Rosenbaum, [*Arthur*] *Rudolph: The Speer Analogy* (New York: s.p., 1985).

6. "German Civilians Compelled to Bury Victims of Nazis," *New York Times*, April 23, 1945, p. 5; and "Atrocity Films Released," *New York Times*, April 27, 1945, p. 3. Also noteworthy in the shaping of American opinion concerning Nazi atrocities was the liberation of the somewhat smaller concentration camps at Ohrdruf (April 4, 1945) and at Gardelegen (April 14, 1945). U.S. Generals Dwight D. Eisenhower and George Patton visited Ohrdruf amid heavy publicity; see Gilbert, *Holocaust*, p. 790ff.

7. Lasby, op. cit., pp. 37–49, and 85, with $400–$500 million figure on p. 42.

8. Ibid., pp. 83–87. On Soviet acquisition of scientists, see also Office of Strategic Services, "General Situation Report No. 2., 15 July to 1 September 1945" (top secret).

9. Hunt, op. cit.

10. Lasby, op. cit., pp. 77–79.

11. Ibid., pp. 80–81.

12. Ibid., pp. 58–59.
13. Hunt, op. cit., Lasby, op. cit. pp. 151–60 and 176–78. Former OMGUS official quote: confidential informant.
14. Lasby, op. cit., p. 159; Hunt, op. cit., with underlying documentation in "Report on Conference with State," to Director JIOA from Commander C. R. Welte, May 26, 1947; Wev to Chamberlin, July 2, 1947; and Intelligence Division GSUSA from JIOA Deputy Director Walter Rozamus, November 28, 1947.
15. Reporter Linda Hunt was the first to unearth records concerning the Pentagon's efforts to suppress military records of the Nazi pasts of certain of the German scientists it was then recruiting; see: Hunt, op. cit. On this point see also "Application of Denazification Procedures to German Scientists," from Lucius Clay to Noce, September 20, 1947, in which General Clay provides 1,000 blank *Meldebogens* (denazification interview forms) to Noce and argues: "It would be much better to permit them [German scientists] to remain in the U.S. as Nazis without bringing them to trial than to establish special procedures not now within the purview of German law," in Lucius Clay, *Papers of General Lucius D. Clay,* ed. Jean Edward Smith (Bloomington, Ind.: Indiana University Press, 1947), vol. III, pp. 432–33, hereinafter *Clay Papers.*
16. Hunt, op. cit. Quote is from cable from JIOA Deputy Director Rozamus to Intelligence Division GSUSA.
17. Hunt, op. cit., also Lasby, op. cit., pp. 113, 159, 209, and 245. On Arthur Rudolph: U.S. Department of Justice press statement, October 17, 1984; Ralph Blumenthal, "German-born NASA Expert Quits U.S. to Avoid a War Crimes Suit" and "NASA Refuses to Comment on Its Former Official," *New York Times,* October 18, 1984, pp. 1 and A-13; James M. Markham, "Ex-Nazi Denies Role in Deaths of Slave Laborers," *New York Times,* October 21, 1984, p. 8; Thomas O'Toole and Mary Thorton, "A Long Trail to Departure of Ex-Nazi Rocket Expert," *Washington Post,* November 4, 1984, p. 1. See also Rudolph's extensive U.S. Army INSCOM dossier, available through the Freedom of Information Act.

On Rickhey, see *U.S. Army* v. *Kurt Andrae et al.,* loc. cit.

On Schreiber, see Nuremberg Assistant Prosecutor Alexander Hardy's memo, "The Case of Walter Schreiber," February 17, 1952.

Chapter Four

1. Reinhard Gehlen, *The Service,* tr. D. Irving (New York: World Publishing, 1972), pp. 3–10, with quoted statement on p. 6. On Gehlen's surrender, see U.S. Army records, "Report of Interrogation: Gehlen, Reinhard, 28 August 1945," G-2 MIS-Y, Gehlen folder (secret), Box 472, RG 165, NA. This interrogation report also discusses Bokor's role. Bokor's name is reported there as "Capt. Boka." For physical description at time of arrest, see "Basic Personnel Record #3WG-1300: Gehlen, Reinhard," in the same folder. See also: Cookridge, op. cit. pp. 111–23; Höhne and Zolling, op. cit., pp. 61–72; Alain Guerin, *Le Général Gris* (Paris: Julliard, 1969); and Charles Whiting, *Gehlen: Germany's Master Spy* (New York: Ballantine, 1972).

For Himmler's "peace proposals" mentioned in text, see Höhne, op. cit., p. 583ff.

2. Gehlen, op. cit., p. 6ff. Also: Richard Harris Smith, *OSS* (Berkeley: University of California Press, 1972), pp. 239–41, hereinafter cited as Smith, *OSS.*

On Bokor: interview with retired Colonel John A. S. Bokor, Captain Bokor's son, June 9, 1984.

For original documentation on standing U.S. orders regarding relations with German POWs who had formerly been intelligence officers, see "Counter-Intelligence Screening of the German Armed Forces," Supreme Headquarters of the Allied Expeditionary Forces, March 1945 (secret), Folder GBI/CI/CS/091.711-2 (Germany), "C. I. Control and Disposal of German Forces," Box 110, Entry 15, RG 331, NA.

3. Smith, *OSS,* p. 240.

For biographic details on Generals Sibert and Bedell Smith, see Department of Defense Office of Public Information Press Branch reports on Sibert (April 3, 1952) and Smith (July 31, 1951), available through the Center for Military History, Washington, D.C. Sibert's obituary appeared in the *Washington Post* on December 23, 1977, and Smith's career is discussed in *Webster's American Military Biographies* (Springfield, Mass.: G & C Merriam, 1979), p. 400.

4. See Gehlen, "Report of Interrogation."

5. On starvation camps, see Werth, op. cit., p. 643ff., and Davidson, op. cit., p. 568. On Gehlen's wartime role in German POW interrogation programs, see David Kahn, *Hitler's Spies: German Military Intelligence in World War II* (New York: Macmillan, 1978), pp. 142–51, 428–35 passim.

6. For Gehlen "on principle" quote, see Höhne and Zolling, op. cit., p. 196, or Jürgen Thorwald, "Der Mann im Dunkeln," *Welt am Sontag,* December 18, 1956.

On Sommer, Krichbaum, and Schmidt, see Cookridge, op. cit., pp. 144–45; Höhne and Zolling, op. cit., p. 199.

7. Bokor interview, June 9, 1984.

8. Höhne and Zolling, op. cit., p. 172.

9. On Dr. Franz Alfred Six: For quote on "solving the Jewish Question," see *Trials of War Criminals,* vol. IV, p. 525, with a summary of Six's war crimes on p. 521ff. On wartime role, see Central Intelligence Agency, *Study of Intelligence and Counterintelligence Activities on the Eastern Front and Adjacent Areas During World War II* (confidential), Addendum G: "Members of the SS Who Participated in Mass Executions and Atrocities," p. 7, RG 263, NA, hereinafter cited as *CIA Eastern Front Study.* See also State Department Propaganda Investigation Team, "Investigation Report," April 30, 1946, interrogation of Franz Six and Horst Mahnke, RG 238, NA; and State Department Special Interrogation Mission, interrogation of Fritz E. A. von Twardowsky, October 3, 1945, Box 745, Entry 179 (G-2 ID MIS-Y records), RG 165, NA. Six's SS and NSDAP dossier is available through the Berlin Document Center, SS No. 107480, NSDAP No. 245,670.

On Six's "eager beaver" relationship with Himmler: *Das Eichmann-Protokoll* (Berlin: Severin und Siedler, 1982); or *Eichmann Interrogated* (New York: Farrar, Straus & Giroux, 1983), pp. 27 and 29. See also Twardowsky interrogation, loc. cit.

Six's writings circulated by the Nazis include *Europa: Tradition und Zu-*

kunft (1944) and *Freimaurerei und Judenemanzipation* (1938), both published by Hanseatische Verlagsanstalt, Hamburg; *Les Guerres Intestines en Europe et la Guerre d'Union du Présent*, n. d. (1941?); and *Dokumente der deutschen Politik* (Berlin: Deutsches Auslandswissenschaftliches Institut, 1942).

On Augsburg's role noted in the text, see Emil Augsburg records at the Berlin Document Center, SS No. 307925.

10. For an overview of Amt VI, see Kahn, op. cit., pp. 253–71; Höhne and Zolling, op. cit., pp. 368–69; and Walter Schellenberg, *The Labyrinth*, tr. Louis Hagen (New York: Harper Bros., 1956), pp. 273–76.

On Poppe: Author's interviews with Nikolai N. Poppe, October 26 and December 4, 1984, and Nicholas Poppe (Nikolai N. Poppe), *Reminiscences*, ed. Henry Schwartz (Bellingham, Wash.: Western Washington University Center for East Asian Studies, 1983), p. 163ff.

Archival material on the Wannsee Institute includes interrogations of Six, Mahnke, and Twardowsky cited in source note 9, above; and "Interrogation Summary No. 1989: Walter Schellenberg," Office of U.S. Chief Counsel for War Crimes Evidence Division, April 30, 1947, with text in German and summary in English. See also: *Records of the Reich Leader of the SS and Chief of the German Police*, microfilmed at Alexandria, Va., RG T-175, Roll 455, Frame 2971560ff., for documentation concerning Wannsee's role in the looting of libraries and bookdealers; Roll 456, Frame 2972093ff., for correspondence, security passes, lists of employees, etc., from the institute; and roll 457, Frame 2973523ff., for Amt VI-G correspondence concerning use of concentration camp inmates for custodial work. This collection is on microfilm in the NA and in a number of leading libraries. Office of U.S. Chief Counsel for War Crimes, *Staff Evidence Analysis, Doc. No.: NO-3022*, in the Nuremberg records at the NA, documents SS General Berger's response to one Wannsee study by Akhmeteli.

For a surviving example of a Wannsee study, see Wannsee Institute, *Kaukasus* (Berlin: Herausgegeben vom Chef der Sicherheitspolizei und des SD, 1942), now in the Library of Congress.

For Eichmann's recollection of Wannsee Conference: *Life* (November 28, 1960), pp. 24 and 101. An English translation of the Wannsee Protocol itself can be found in John Mendelsohn, ed., *The Holocaust: The Wannsee Protocol and a 1944 Report on Auschwitz* (London and New York: Garland, 1982), which includes a commentary by Robert Wolfe of the Modern Military Branch at the NA. The translation of the protocol (known as Nuremberg Document No. NG-2586) was done by the Office of U.S. Chief Counsel for War Crimes.

On Role of Six, Ohlendorf, and Schellenberg as "Nazified professors and lawyers," see Höhne, op. cit., p. 154.

11. Interview with Benjamin Ferencz, July 20, 1984.

On postwar work with Augsburg and Hirschfield incident, see "Special Interrogation Report No. 65," File CI-SIR/66, subject: Barbie, Klaus (top secret), p. 4, Tab 29 of Ryan, *Barbie Exhibits*. East German claims against Six can be found in Albert Norden, *Brown Book, War and Nazi Criminals in West Germany* (DDR Documentation Center of State Archives Administration, Verlag Zeit im Bild, German Democratic Republic), pp. 79–80.

12. On need for specific approval by Clemency Board, see Charles Thayer, "Inquiries Concerning War Criminals," p. 6 (n.d.) in Thayer Papers, at Truman Library. On Six's clemency by McCloy, see *New York Times,* October 4, 1952.

On Six's defense testimony on behalf of Eichmann mentioned in footnote, see *New York Times,* May 3, 1961, p. 14; May 15, 1961, p. 16.

On Six's work for Porsche: Hilberg, op. cit., p. 713. Eichmann's work for Daimler-Benz: *Eichmann Interrogated,* loc. cit., p. 283.

13. Dr. Emil Augsburg: For "Jew-baiting," see Augsburg's records at the Berlin Document Center, SS No. 307925, NSDAP No. 5,518,743. On "special tasks," see Augsburg, "Beforderungsvorichlag: Hauptsturmführer Dr. Emil Augsburg," July 10, 1941, Document No. 23009–23010. See also interrogation of Six and Mahnke, loc. cit.

14. On Augsburg's work for SS General Bernau and other employers, see "Subject: Merk, Kurt," November 16, 1948, HQ CIC Region IV to HQ 7970th CIC Group, EUCOM, p. 2 (secret), Tab 33, Ryan, *Barbie Exhibits.* On Barbie connection, "Dr. Althaus" alias, etc., see Tabs 9, 18, 29, and 33 of Ryan, *Barbie Exhibits.* A sanitized version of Augsburg's CIC dossier is available through the FOIA at U.S. Army INSCOM; see File No. XE004390 16B036, Augsburg, Emil (secret). On wartime activities, including role in killing squads, see source note 13, above. Allan Ryan has told the author that he believes Augsburg also worked for British intelligence during 1947.

On Wannsee director Dr. Mikhail Akhmeteli, discussed in footnote: Akhmeteli's NSDAP Card No. 5360858, as well as some captured correspondence with SS General Berger, is available through the Berlin Document Center. On Akhmeteli's wartime role, see interrogation of Six and Mahnke, loc. cit.; interrogation of Schellenberg, loc. cit. (Schellenberg's testimony offers the physical description of Akhmeteli.) Secondary sources include: Alwin Ramme, *Der Sicherheitsdienst der SS* (Berlin: Deutscher Militarverlag, 1969?), pp. 95–97; Peter Kleist, *Zwischen Hitler und Stalin* (Bonn: Athenaum Verlag, 1950), pp. 134–35; and (in English) Dallin, *German Rule,* loc. cit., pp. 170n, 323n., and 357. On race theory, see Armstrong, op. cit., p. 574. On early life, see Höhne and Zolling, op. cit., pp. 368–69. On relationship with Gehlen, see Cookridge, op. cit., pp. 242 and 311.

15. On Augsburg's work for Gehlen: Höhne and Zolling, op. cit., p. 199; Cookridge, op. cit., pp. 194 and 242.

Chapter Five

1. Arthur Macy Cox interview, June 7, 1984.
2. Cookridge, op. cit., pp. 158 and 161. Dulles quote: Höhne and Zolling, op. cit., p. xv.
3. Rositzke comments: For "virtually empty," see Harry A. Rositzke, *The CIA's Secret Operations* (New York: Reader's Digest Press, 1977), p. 20. For "primary role" comment: Harry Rositzke interview, January 16, 1985.
4. W. Park Armstrong interview, June 17, 1983. On "retyping reports," see Cookridge, op. cit., p. 201. Höhne comment: Höhne and Zolling, op. cit., p. 107, or see original *Spiegel* series in spring and summer 1971.
5. Marchetti interview, June 7, 1984.
6. Cox comments, December 15, 1983.

7. The author is indebted to Matthew A. Evangelista's study, "Stalin's Postwar Army Reappraised," *International Security* (Winter 1982–1983), p. 110ff., from which a number of pertinent points in this section have been drawn. On railroads, see Evangelista, op. cit., pp. 120–23; on Soviet dependence on horse-drawn transport discussed in footnote, see ibid., p. 121; E. O'Ballance, *The Red Army* (London: Faber & Faber, 1964), p. 192; and Dr. Allen F. Chew, "Fighting the Russians in Winter, Three Case Studies," U.S. Army Command and General Staff College, *Leavenworth Papers,* December 1981, pp. 35–41. On 1946 estimates, see JWPC 432/7, "Tentative Over-all Strategic Concept and Estimate of Initial Operations—Pincher," June 18, 1946 (top secret), cited in Evangelista's study.

8. On MIS/OSS rivalry see, for example, Anthony Cave Brown, *The Last Hero: Wild Bill Donovan* (New York: Vintage, 1982), pp. 305–07.

9. For "opportunist" quote, see "Memorandum For: Chief of Staff, United States Army, Subject: Grombach, John V.," from James L. Collins, Acting Deputy AC of S for Intelligence, July 5, 1967 (confidential), in Grombach Dossier, No. 81177870, U.S. Army INSCOM, Fort Meade, Md.

For an overview of Grombach's career, including his accomplishments in sports, see Grombach's obituary in the West Point alumni magazine *Assembly* (June 1983), p. 132. NB: Grombach, who was born of French parents, was christened Jean Valentin Grombach. In his adult life, however, he generally preferred to use the form "John Valentine Grombach," which is what is used in this text.

10. INSCOM Dossier No. 81177870 is the best single source of documentation on Grombach's professional career. See particularly "Summary of Information (SR 380-320-10)" reports for the following dates and subjects: "G-2 SPS Grombach, John Valentine," June 1, 1955 (top secret); "N. V. Philips Co.," June 1, 1955 (top secret); "Grombach, John V.," September 23, 1958 (confidential); and memo from Brigadier General Richard Collins, director of plans, programs, and security to ASCoSI, Subject: Grombach, John Valentine, September 30, 1958 (secret). On Philips's role, see Grombach letter to Colonel George F. Smith, April 12, 1950, and Collins report of September 5, 1958 (secret). For quote on "pro-Marxist personnel," the purges of OSS R&A, and the Grombach-OSS R&A conflict generally, see "G-2 SPS Grombach, John Valentine," June 1, 1955 (top secret), and the April 12, 1950, Grombach letter to Colonel George F. Smith. On Katyn Forest massacre dispute, see Brigadier General Richard Collins memo of September 30, 1958.

On Duran case, see David Oshinsky, *A Conspiracy So Immense: The World of Joe McCarthy* (New York: Free Press-Macmillan, 1983), p. 126, and David Caute, *The Great Fear: The Anti-Communist Purge Under Truman and Eisenhower* (New York: Simon & Schuster, 1978), pp. 331–38. Grombach later claimed it had been he who first discovered the "Communist connections" of Carl Marzani, Alger Hiss, John Stewart Service, and several other well-known targets of 1940s security investigations.

For Grombach's comments discussed in footnote, see John V. Grombach, *The Great Liquidator* (Garden City, N.Y.: Doubleday, 1980), p. xvii. The aim of this book, Grombach writes, was to "convince the U.S. public that subversion and clandestine espionage activities cannot be controlled by normal, legal, and proper methods. The current limitations placed on both the CIA and FBI," he continues, "would more properly fit a Boy Scout organization" (p. xviii).

11. On Project 1641, ibid., pp. xvii–xviii, 109, and 114; Lyman Kirkpatrick interview, April 11, 1984; and "G-2 SPS Grombach, John Valentine," June 1, 1955 (top secret), and the April 12, 1950, Grombach letter to Colonel George F. Smith.

12. On resignation of McCormack and its significance, see William R. Corson, *The Armies of Ignorance* (New York: Dial/James Wade, 1977), p. 272; and Smith, *OSS*, pp. 364–66.

13. Interview with retired officer of the Office of National Estimates (ONE), June 30, 1986.

14. Lukacs comments: John Lukacs, "The Soviet State at 65," *Foreign Affairs* (Fall 1986), pp. 27–29. Höhne on "alarm signal": Höhne and Zolling, op. cit., pp. 100, 106–07.

15. Cable ".340: The Berlin Situation" (top secret), *Clay Papers,* vol. II, pp. 568–69. On Czech spring crisis, see Daniel Yergin, *Shattered Peace: The Origins of the Cold War and the National Security State* (Boston: Houghton Mifflin, 1977), pp. 343–54.

16. *Clay Papers,* pp. 568–69. See also Lucius Clay, *Decision in Germany* (Garden City; N.Y.: Doubleday, 1950), pp. 345–55.

17. On effects of Clay's (and Gehlen's) "alarm": *Final Report of the Select Committee to Study Governmental Operations with Respect to Intelligence Activities,* U.S. Senate, 94th Congress, 2d Session, 1976, hereinafter cited as *Church Committee Report,* book IV, p. 29; Yergin, op. cit., pp. 351–54; and interview with retired officer of the Office of National Estimates, June 30, 1986. The key role of these warnings in the political events that followed is also noted in Steven L. Rearden, *The Formative Years,* vol. 1 of *History of the Office of the Secretary of Defense,* ed. Alfred Goldberg (Washington, D.C.: Historical Office, OSD, Department of Defense, 1984), p. 281ff.

On supposed Soviet military superiority in early postwar Europe, see, for example (on "mobile spearhead" and estimate of divisions), Evangelista, op. cit., pp. 114–16; and JIC Report, December 2, 1948, p. 2, noted in Evangelista. Also Marchetti interview, June 7, 1984. For document quoted in footnote, see "Memorandum for Chief of Staff US Army, Subject: Soviet Intentions and Capabilities 1949–1956/57," January 4, 1949 (top secret), in Hot Files, Box 9, Tab 70, RG 319, NA, Washington, D.C.

18. Evangelista, op. cit., pp. 112 and 115. For *U.S. News* quote, see "Russia's Edge in Men and Arms," *U.S. News & World Report* (April 2, 1948), pp. 23–25.

19. Paul Nitze, "NSC 68 and the Soviet Threat Reconsidered," *International Security* (Spring 1980), pp. 170–76, noted in Evangelista, op. cit., p. 112.

20. Marchetti interview, June 7, 1984.

For role of "human sources" discussed in text, see *EUCOM Annual Report 1954,* pp. 128–32, 145, 148, and 485–88 (secret), Adjutant General's Office Command Report Files 1949–1954, RG 407, NA, Suitland, Md. For popular summaries on intelligence gathering using these methods, including some statistics, see James P. O'Donnell, "They Tell Us Stalin's Secrets," *Saturday*

Evening Post (May 3, 1952), p. 32; same author and magazine, "These Russians Are on Our Side" (June 6, 1953); also Höhne and Zolling, op. cit., pp. 94 and 107–08; and Cookridge, op. cit., p. 201. For Richard Bissell comment on the ineffectiveness of human source intelligence in totalitarian societies, see Leonard Mosley, *Dulles* (New York: Dial Press, 1978), p. 374.

On missile gap discussed in footnote: Marchetti interview, June 7, 1984. Rositzke disagrees with Marchetti on this point, arguing that German intelligence on Soviet rocket programs was generally good; see Rositzke, op. cit., p. 20. H. A. R. ("Kim") Philby, a Soviet double agent who penetrated the British Secret Intelligence Service, expressed his opinion of Gehlen's effectiveness after Philby had defected to the USSR. "I knew about the Gehlen unit from the summer of 1943 onwards . . ." he commented in 1977. "It seemed to be no better than the other sections of the *Abwehr,* which means it was very bad indeed. No exaggeration, no joke. So I was undismayed when CIA took it over." See Philby's April 7, 1977, letter to author Leonard Mosley published in Mosley, op. cit., pp. 493–96.

Dornberger's role in the missile gap affair is noted in John Prados, *The Soviet Estimate* (New York: Dial, 1982), p. 61, which offers a consistently valuable presentation of the intelligence estimation process.

21. Marchetti interview, June 7, 1984.

Chapter Six

1. On CROWCASS, see United Nations War Crimes Commission, *History of the UNWCC and the Development of the Laws of War* (London: HMSO, 1948), pp. 360–80; and Ryan, *Barbie Exhibits,* Tab 19. Copies of the now-rare CROWCASS index books are available at Boxes 3690 and 3692, RG 59, NA, Washington, D.C., and Box 1720, RG 153, NA, Suitland, Md. The U.S. Army INSCOM has released a dossier of typical CIC CROWCASS correspondence in response to an FOIA request by the author; see INSCOM Dossier No. XE 004643 D 20B 102 (secret).

2. Corson, op. cit., pp. 84 and 86–88.

3. Ibid., p. 87. On Thayer/Herwarth, see Thayer, *Hands,* p. 186; on Gehlen, see Gehlen, op. cit., pp. 8 and 11.

4. Bramel is quoted in Brendan Murphy, *The Butcher of Lyon* (New York, Empire Books, 1983), p. 230.

5. Herb Brucher interview, May 23, 1984.

6. On Catch-22, see, for example, Ryan, *Barbie Report,* pp. 50–51; on collection of clippings and similar "paper mill" type of information, see ibid., pp. 25–26.

7. On Camp King (Durchgangslager für Luftwaffe), Bokor interview, June 9, 1984; also JCS, "Dulag Luft," nonclassified, privately printed, n.d. (1976?), on Scharff (p. 75), killing of escapees (pp. 37–38), high-level POWs (p. 80), returning POWs (p. 82)—copy in author's collection. The author is indebted to John Bokor for bringing this manuscript to my attention. On the postwar reputation of the camp, see Victor Marchetti and John Marks, *The CIA and the Cult of Intelligence* (New York: Dell, 1974), pp. 187–88; and James P. O'Donnell, "These Russians Are on Our Side," loc. cit. On Dulag Luft, see also Philip Flammer, ed., "Dulag Luft: The Third Reich's Prison Camp for Airmen," and

James L. Cole, "Dulag Lüft: Recalled and Revisited," both in *Aerospace Historian* (June 1972), p. 58ff. On writing histories, see, for example, Gehlen "Report of Interrogation," pp. 2–4.

8. JCS, "Dulag Luft," p. 82.

9. For code names and brief descriptions of these operations, see P&O File 311.5 TS (Sections I, II, III), 1948, in 1946–1948 top secret decimal file, Records of Army General Staff, RG 319, NA. See also same citation in 1949–1950 decimal files; with additional details available via FOIA requests to Suitland archives.

10. Mark Aarons interview, June 20, 1985. Émigré sources claim that there were some 250,000 to 500,000 executions of anti-Communist Croats and Slovenes during 1944 and 1945. Although those figures are clearly exaggerated, they suggest that large-scale massacres did take place. Krunoslav Dragonovic's essay "The Biological Extermination of Croats in Tito's Yugoslavia," in Antun F. Bonifacic and Climent Miknovich, *The Croatian Nation* (Chicago: Croatia Cultural Publishing Center, 1955), discusses these killings in considerable detail.

The repatriation programs mentioned in the text remain the object of intense controversy. For reliable accounts, see Nicholas Bethell, *The Last Secret* (New York: Basic Books, 1974), and Mark R. Elliot, *Pawns of Yalta* (Urbana, Ill.: University of Illinois Press, 1982), p. 104ff. More controversial studies include Julius Epstein, *Operation Keelhaul* (Old Greenwich, Conn.: Devin-Adair, 1973), and Nikolai Tolstoy, *The Secret Betrayal* (New York: Charles Scribner's Sons, 1978).

For contemporary coverage of the breakdown of U.S.-Soviet cooperation on the war crimes issue, see, for example, "Soviet, Italy Raise Extradition Issue," *New York Times*, February 25, 1948, and Delbert Clark, "Red Push Must End, Clay Aide Asserts," *New York Times*, March 5, 1948 (on suspension of extradition of war criminals to Czechoslovakia).

11. On the murders at Katyn and the Polish deportations, see, Louis FitzGibbon, *Katyn* (New York: Charles Scribner's Sons, 1971); J. Heydecker, and J. Leeb, *The Nuremberg Trial*, tr. R. A. Downie (Cleveland and New York: World Publishing, 1962), pp. 293–307; George F. Kennan, *Memoirs 1925–1950* (Boston: Little, Brown, 1967), pp. 199–200, hereinafter cited as *Kennan vol. I*. For executions at Dubno, see *CIA Eastern Front Study*, "Addendum A: NKVD Operatives and Persons Connected with Them," particularly p. 2 entry for "Bronstein." On deportations from the Baltic states, see, for example, William Tomingas, *The Soviet Colonization of Estonia* (Kultuur Publishing House, 1973), p. 265ff.

12. Nikita Khrushchev, *Khrushchev Remembers*, tr. Strobe Talbot (Boston: Little, Brown, 1970), pp. 596–97; or see Joseph L. Nogee and Robert H. Donaldson, *Soviet Foreign Policy Since World War II* (New York: Pergamon, 1981), pp. 56–59.

13. On Iron Guardists in Romanian Communist party, see Ceauşescu's speech at the 1961 plenum in *Scinteis* (December 13, 1961), as noted in Paul Lendvai, *Eagles in Cobwebs* (Garden City, N.Y.: Doubleday, 1969), pp. 287–89.

14. "Statement of Mr. Djilas," *Official Records of the General Assembly*, Sixth Session, Ad Hoc Political Committee, Eighth Meeting, United Nations, No-

vember 26, 1951, A/OR 6/Ad Hoc Committee. On East German use of Nazis: for Grossmann and Bartsch, see John Dornberg, *The Other Germany* (Garden City, N.Y.: Doubleday, 1968), p. 297; for Erdely, see U.S. Dept. of State cable, Heidelberg to secretary of state, 862.20211/8-2045, August 21, 1948 (confidential), RG 59, NA; on Carl Clodius, see "Nazi Economist Used by Cominform," *Prevent World War II* (May–June 1948), Columbia University Library. For Rattenhuber, Bamler, and Heidenreich, see Cookridge, op. cit., pp. 271–72. For Bamler, Sanitzer, and Hagemeister, see Höhne and Zolling, op. cit., pp. 238–39 and 243–44.

Chapter Seven

1. Yergin, op. cit., pp. 288–96. Also: John Iatrides, *Revolt in Athens* (Princeton, N.J.: Princeton University Press, 1972).

2. On IDEA, see Ian McDonald, "Senator [Metcalf] Says Greek Leaders Aided Nazis," *Times* of London, November 17, 1971, and Jack Anderson, "The Junta and the Nazis," *New York Post,* November 16, 1971. On persecution of Greek Jews by Greek rightists, see Ivan Mihailoff, "Greece and the Jews of Salonika," *Balkania* (July 1967), particularly p. 15. On events during the Greek civil war generally, see Yergin, op. cit., pp. 279–95, and Todd Gitlin, "Counter-Insurgency: Myth and Reality in Greece," in David Horowitz, ed., *Containment and Revolution* (Boston: Beacon, 1967), p. 140ff. On wartime casualties of Jews and Greeks, see Eugene Keefe et al., *Area Handbook for Greece,* 2d ed. (Washington, D.C.: Government Printing Office, 1977), p. 28. Also author's interviews with Elias Demetracopoulos, who kindly provided the author with news clippings concerning events in his native country.

Original source material concerning the role of Nazi collaborators in Greece includes: "Seventh Army Interrogation Center Preliminary Interrogation Report: POULOS, Georg, OBST (Col), Greek Police Volunteer Bn," June 27, 1945, ref: SAIC/PIR/61 (secret), Box 721-A, Entry 179, MIS-Y Enemy Interrogation Files 1943–1945, RG 165, NA. American interrogations of SS RSHA Amt. VI leader Otto Skorzeny in 1945 also provide considerable background on relations among the SS, Abwehr, and Greek collaborators. See "Annex No. III: Invasion Nets in Allied Occupied Countries," "Consolidated Interrogation Report (CIR) No. 4, Subject: The German Sabotage Service," July 23, 1945 (confidential), for interrogation of Skorzeny and his adjutant Radl, and the attached "Consolidated Interrogation Report (CIR) No. 13, Subject: Asts in the Balkans." pp. 5–8, 17–18; both of which are in Entry 179, Box 739, Enemy POW Interrogation File MIS-Y, 1943–1945, RG 165, NA.

3. On Papadopoulos, Natsinas, and Gogoussis, see McDonald, op. cit. On Secret Army Reserve, see "Joint Outline War Plans for Determination of Mobilization Requirements for War Beginning 1 July 1949," Joint Strategic Plans Committee, JSPC 891/6. See particularly annex to Appendix "E," pp. 34, 42–43, and Office of Chief of Naval Operations Enclosure "A," n.d. (top secret) in P&O 370.1 TS (Case 7, Part IA, Sub Nos. 13), RG 319, Records of the Army Staff, NA. For later reporting from a critical perspective on CIA activities in Greece, see Yiannis Roubatis and Karen Wynn, "CIA Operations in Greece," and Philip Agee, "The American Factor in Greece: Old and New," both in

Philip Agee and Louis Wolf, eds., *Dirty Work: The CIA in Western Europe* (Secaucus, N.J.: Lyle Stuart, 1978), particularly p.154ff.

4. *Kennan vol. I,* pp. 294–95 ("Communist conspiracy"). Kennan's account of the Long Telegram and its results appears on pp. 271–97. For background on controversy surrounding State Department-White House disputes over policy toward the USSR prior to World War II, see "Ah, Sweet Intrigue! Or, Who Axed State's Prewar Soviet Division?," *Foreign Intelligence Literary Scene* (October 1984), p. 1.

5. *Newsweek* quote: "The Story Behind Our Russian Policy," *Newsweek* (July 21, 1947), pp. 15–17. Kennan quote is from the well-known "Mr. X" article: "Mr. X" (George F. Kennan), "The Sources of Soviet Conduct," *Foreign Affairs* (July 1947). See also *Kennan vol. I,* pp. 354–67, on the "Mr. X" article generally. For contemporary profiles noting key role of George Kennan and Charles Bohlen in formulation of U.S. policy during the early cold war, see the *Newsweek* article, above, and "Messrs. Bohlen and Kennan, Authors of Firm Policy to Russia," *U.S. News & World Report* (August 8, 1947), p. 50ff. See also Yergin, op. cit., pp. 163–92, and Walter Isaacson and Evan Thomas, *The Wise Men* (New York: Simon & Schuster, 1986), pp. 347–85.

6. *Kennan vol. I,* p. 359.

7. On role in propaganda programs, see Mickelson, op. cit., pp. 14–15. On role in guerrilla warfare programs, see Joint Strategic Plans Committee, JSPC 862/3 and JSPC 891/6. For a similar operation involving Finnish soldiers who volunteered for anti-Communist guerrilla operations, see Kennan correspondence with Gruenther, April 27, 1948 (secret), P&O 091.714 TS (Section I, Case 1), all at RG 319, NA.

8. JSPC 862/3 and JSPC 891/6.

9. *Kennan vol. I,* p. 81.

10. Ibid., p. 81. For background on this point, see also Charles Bohlen, *Witness to History* (New York, W. W. Norton, 1973), p. 71ff., and Paul Blackstock, *The Secret Road to World War II* (Chicago: Quadrangle, 1969), pp. 256–57 and 310–11, hereinafter cited as Blackstock, *Secret Road.*

11. Herwarth, op. cit., pp. 75, 77, 80, and photo section; Bohlen, op. cit., p. 67ff.; Charles Thayer, *Bears in the Caviar* (Philadelphia: J.B. Lippincott, 1951), p. 28ff., Thayers, *Hands,* p. 183ff; Isaacson and Thomas, op. cit., pp. 175–77.

12. Thayer, *Hands,* p. 185. Herwarth also told Thayer during his 1945 interrogation that he had played a major, heroic role in von Stauffenberg's July 20, 1944, plot against Hitler. Thayer appears to have accepted Herwarth's account without question, and eventually published it in *Hands,* pp. 196–200. Other postwar accounts from conspirators who survived the July 20th affair or from historians who have studied the matter closely do not support Herwarth's (and Thayer's) claim that he played a substantial role in the plot. On this point, see, for example, Hans Bernd Gisevius, *To the Bitter End,* tr. Richard and Clara Winston (Boston: Houghton Mifflin, 1947), p. 490ff.; Peter Hoffmann, *The History of the German Resistance, 1933–1945,* tr. Richard Barry (Cambridge, Mass.: MIT Press, 1979) pp. 397–535; Allen Dulles, *Germany's Underground* (New York: Macmillan, 1947); Hans Royce, ed., *20 Juli 1944* (Bonn: Herausgegeben von der Bundeszentrale für Heimztdienst, 1953); or Hans-Adolf Jacobsen, ed., *July 20, 1944, German Opposition to Hitler* (Bonn: Press and

Information Office of the Federal Government [of Germany], 1969). The Gestapo's massive contemporary investigation of the July 20th conspiracy also failed to turn up enough evidence against Herwarth to cause the police agency to bring him in for questioning.

13. Herwarth, op. cit., pp. 352–53.

14. Ibid., p. 353ff. (on Herwarth); Strik-Strikfeldt, op. cit., p. 238 (on Köstring and Hilger); *Trials of War Criminals,* vol. XI, pp. 600–01 (on Hilger in United States).

15. *Kennan vol. I,* pp. 175 and 177.

16. Ibid., p. 179.

17. Isaacson and Thomas, op. cit., p. 448.

18. Griffiths memo to Francis Cardinal Spellman, March 4, 1948, cited in John Cooney, op. cit., p. 159.

19. Ibid., p. 159ff., with Cardinal Tisserant statement on pp. 159–60 and Spellman quote drawn from undated Spellman memo to the Vatican concerning his meeting with Secretary of State George Marshall noted on p. 161.

20. On role of Exchange Stabilization Fund as funding source for clandestine operations: William Corson interview, March 26, 1984; Bokor interview, June 9, 1984, and Corson, op. cit, p. 299. For background and history of fund, see "Memo to Secretary [of the Treasury John] Snyder from F. A. Southard, Subject: History and Present Status of Exchange Stabilization Fund, 12/14/47," and similar studies titled simply "Exchange Stabilization Fund" dated December 1948, December 14, 1949, March 1950, January 1951, Office of the Assistant Secretary for International Affairs, U.S. Department of the Treasury; copies in collection of the author. Annual unclassified accounts of fund activity which establish the fund's size but conceal its clandestine role are available in the *Annual Report of the Secretary of the Treasury,* for 1947, 1948, 1949. On the fund's relationship to the Safehaven program and captured Nazi loot, see *Elimination of German Resources for War,* Hearings before the Committee on Military Affairs, U.S. Senate, June 25, 1945, pt. 2, pp. 135–36; *Change of Status Record, Title: Records of the Office of Economic Security Policy* and *Records of the Division of Economic Security Controls,* both 1945–1947, NA; and contemporary draft of Safehaven historical summary hand-titled "Safehaven History" (Department of the Treasury, 1946?), copy in collection of author.

21. William Colby, *Honorable Men: My Life in the CIA* (New York: Simon & Schuster, 1978), p. 115. For account of CIA role in Italian elections generally, see Corson, op. cit, pp. 295–301, with information on money laundering on p. 299. During 1975 the U.S. House of Representatives' Select Committee on Intelligence, chaired by Representative Otis Pike, prepared a highly critical report on CIA clandestine activities, including the secret financing of selected Italian political candidates and labor leaders over a thirty-five-year period. The CIA and the White House succeeded in suppressing the official publication of this study, but the document was leaked to the media and published in special supplements to the *Village Voice* on February 16 and February 22, 1976. See p. 86 of the February 16 "Special Supplement: The CIA Report the President Doesn't Want You to Read" for further discussion of agency intervention in the Italian elections.

22. On Rauff, see Ralph Blumenthal, "New Charges Made on Nazi," *New York Times*, May 10, 1984, and particularly *SS Col. Walter Rauff: The Church Connection 1943–1947* (Los Angeles: Simon Wiesenthal Center Investigative Report, May 1984), which includes copies of documentation concerning Rauff's crimes against humanity, his role in Operation Sunrise, and Bicchierai's part in Rauff's escape. See also U.S. Army INSCOM Dossier No XE 216719 I9B001, "Rauff, Walter," for data on his arrest and escape from U.S. custody; and unnumbered INSCOM dossier on Operation Circle (obtained via FOIA) concerning church role in mass escape of German and Italian Fascist prisoners from Rimini POW camp, 1946. The extradition of Rauff from Chile was a major campaign of the Wiesenthal Center until Rauff's death in May 1984. See, for example, press statement "Nazi Criminals in Latin America," from Dokumentationszentrum des Bundes Judischer Verfolgter des Naziregimes, Vienna, April 7, 1983.

   For Allen Dulles's own account of Rauff's role in Operation Sunrise, see Allen Welsh Dulles, *The Secret Surrender* (New York: Harper & Row, 1966), pp. 66, 83, 102, 107, and 192–93. For text of telegram discussed in footnote, see Jack D. Neal to USPOLAD, Berlin, September 17, 1947, at 740.00116 EW/8-1147 Secret File (top secret, no distribution), RG 59, NA, Washington, D.C. For postwar data on Dollman, Schellenberg, and Wolff, see Hilberg, op. cit., pp. 705, 713, and 715; and on Wolff: "SS-General Wolff gestorben," *Frankfurter Allgemeine Zeitung*, July 17, 1984.

23. Cooney, op. cit., p. 160.

24. For Mickelson comment regarding Kennan, see Mickelson, op. cit., p. 14.

Chapter Eight

1. Robert Bishop and E. S. Crayfield, *Russia Astride the Balkans* (New York: McBride & Co., 1948), p. 264ff., with quote on p. 266.

2. Full text of NSC 20/1 is available in Thomas Etzold and John Lewis Gaddis, eds., *Containment: Documents on American Policy and Strategy 1945–1950* (New York: Columbia University Press, 1978), p. 173ff.

   For Kennan's pivotal role in the creation of American clandestine action capabilities during this period, discussed in the text, see *Church Committee Report*, Book IV, pp. 29–31; Mickelson, op. cit., pp. 14–19; and Corson, op. cit., pp. 294–95 and 302–07.

3. NSC 20/1, quoted in Etzold and Gaddis, op. cit., pp. 176, 180, 190, 192, and 201.

4. For basic documentation on Bloodstone, including its cover story, see "Utilization of Native Anti-Communist Elements in Non-Western Hemisphere Countries Outside the Iron Curtain in the Interest of the United States," State, Army, Navy, Air Force Coordinating Committee (SANACC) 395 Document 10, undated (May 1948?, top secret). On assignment of Bloodstone as a code word for the project, see Document 28, June 18, 1948 (top secret). These records are now available through Scholarly Resources' microfilm edition of State, War, Navy Coordinating Committee (SWNCC) and SANACC records. See Martin P. Claussen and Evelyn B. Claussen, *Numerical Catalog and Alphabetical Index for State-War-Navy Coordinating Committee and State-Army-Navy-Air Force Coordinating Committee Case Files 1944–1949* (Wil-

mington, Del.: Scholarly Resources, Inc., 1978), for a guide to these record collections. The document numbers noted here refer to the document numbers on the "List of Papers" which accompanies the original SANACC 395 dossier and which is reproduced in the microfilm collection. New SANACC 395 records, obtained by the author via the FOIA and not available in the microfilm collection, are noted separately.

5. On Wisner's role, see "Utilization of Refugees," Policy Planning Staff policy paper PPS 22/1, Department of State, March 4, 1948 (secret), and Wisner memo, March 17, 1948 (secret), both cited in SANACC document registers as SANACC 395 Document 1, March 4, 1948 (secret). On Lovett's role, see SANACC Document 13, May 26, 1948, and Saltzman memo to Lovett, May 27, 1948 (top secret).

6. SANACC 395, March 17, 1948, "Utilization of Refugees from the USSR in the U.S. National Interest" (secret), Document 2, pp. 1, 5, and 6. See also SANACC Document 12, May 25, 1948, Gardiner memo to Bohlen, Armstrong, etc. (top secret) and May 27, 1948, Saltzman memo (top secret), both in microfilm collection; and September 22, 1948, memo from Stone to Mosely re: SANACC 395/1 (top secret), obtained by author through the FOIA.

7. SANACC 395 Document 10, "Utilization of Native Anti-Communist Elements in Non-Western Hemisphere Countries Outside the Iron Curtain in the Interest of the United States," undated, (May 1948?, top secret); SANACC Secretary H. W. Moseley to Executive Secretary NSC, June 10, 1948, SANACC 395 Document 23.

8. JSPC 862/3 (Revised) August 2, 1948 (top secret), p. 5 (on relation to SANACC 395 and 396); Appendix "C," p. 35 (on SANACC 395 and 396 recruits for "special operations"); and Appendix "C," p. 27 ("special operations" defined) at P&O 352 TS (Section 1, Case 1), RG 319, NA.

Brief notes on Franklin Lindsay's career, mentioned in footnote, may be found in Smith, *OSS,* p. 161. Lindsay's role in the early proposals for training anti-Communist émigrés is noted in the JSPC 862 records noted above, enclosure "B."

9. JSPC 891/6, "Joint Outline War Plans for Determination of Mobilization Requirements for War Beginning 1 July 1949," September 17, 1948 (top secret), p. 36, "Psychological Warfare." For country-by-country review, see Tab "B," p. 39ff., with quoted portion at p. 40. Document is at P&O 370.1 TS (Case 7, Part IA, Sub Nos. 13), RG 319, NA.

10. NSC 10/2, loc. cit., or see *Church Committee Report,* Book IV, pp. 29–31.

11. Thomas Powers, *The Man Who Kept the Secrets: Richard Helms and the CIA* (New York: Simon & Schuster, 1979), pp. 37–39.

12. John Paton Davies interview, November 23, 1983.

13. *Church Committee Report,* Book IV, p. 30.

14. W. Park Armstrong memorandum to Kennan, Davies, Saltzman, Thompson, and Humelsine, subject: "Refugee Problem and SANACC 395," November 8, 1948 (top secret), obtained through the FOIA.

Armstrong comments: Armstrong interview, June 17, 1983. Armstrong died on June 2, 1985; see "W. Park Armstrong Jr.," *Washington Post,* June 6, 1985, p. C12, for obituary.

SANACC 395 and 396 were removed as "Agenda Items" from SANACC

Committee consideration shortly after the approval of SANACC 395 and NSC 10/2 in June 1948. As this memorandum clearly shows, however, these projects were by no means canceled; they were simply pushed under a deeper security cover, primarily inside Wisner's OPC.

15. For discussion of Bloodstone and Congress, see Charles Saltzman to Robert Lovett, May 17, 1948 (top secret), also cited as SWNCC 395 Document 14; and Charles Bohlen to Moseley, August 30, 1948 (top secret). For Charles Thayer's role in the approach to Congress and particularly in dealing with the problem of potential "sour apples" among the immigrants, see SANACC 395 memos dated September 22 and 20, 1948 (top secret), both obtained via FOIA from NA.

16. *Church Committee Report,* Book IV, p. 31.

17. "If an occasion arose" quote: Ibid., p. 31. "Dismay" quote: Yergin, op. cit., p. 284.

18. *Church Committee Report,* Book IV, p. 31.

Chapter Nine

1. Tom Clark: SANACC 395 memo, June 10, 1948 (top secret); W. Park Armstrong: Armstrong memorandum to Kennan, Davies, Saltzman, Thompson, and Humelsine, November 8, 1948 (top secret); both obtained through FOIA request. John Earman: SANA 6045, "Appointment of an Ad Hoc Committee," April 26, 1948 (secret), SANACC 395 Document 9; on Earman's later role at CIA, see "John S. Earman Jr., 60," obituary, *Washington Post,* April 11, 1974. On Boris Pash, see SANA 6045, "Appointment of an Ad Hoc Committee," April 26, 1948 (secret), SANACC 395 Document 9. On Pash's work for OPC, see *Church Committee Report,* Book IV, pp. 128–32.

Future ambassadors to the USSR involved in either planning or implementing SANACC 395 were George F. Kennan, Charles Bohlen, and Llewellyn Thompson; the VOA director was Charles Thayer; the future Radio Free Europe director was Howland H. Sargeant. The State Department's intelligence and policy apparatus was represented in Bloodstone planning or implementation by W. Park Armstrong (director of the Office of Intelligence and Research—INR), Evron Kirkpatrick (later deputy director of INR), George Fearing (director of intelligence collection and dissemination), and John D. Hickerson and Francis Stevens (both of the Office of Eastern European Affairs).

For a more complete picture of Bloodstone personalities and the role they played in the creation of this program, see the original documentation in Scholarly Resources microfilm SANACC file, cited above. For documentation on characterization of Bloodstone mentioned in text, see Chapter Eight.

2. "If practicable" quote: SANA 6083, dated May 25 and June 4, 1948 (top secret), SANACC Document 12. "Attorney General" quote: SANACC 395 memo, September 20, 1948 (top secret), obtained via FOIA from NA. For other Bloodstone documentation concerning Boyd, see SANA 6024, April 15, 1948 (secret), also cited as SANACC 395 Document 8; SANA 6107, Attorney General to Moseley, June 17, 1948 (secret); and SANA 6156, July 7, 1948 (top secret). For other data on Boyd's career: Immigration and Naturalization Service internal publication *INS Information Bulletin* (July–August 1973), and John Boyd interviews, May 27 and August 11, 1983.

3. "Summary of Provisions of the Displaced Persons Act of 1948," *IRO* [International Refugee Organization] *News Digest,* No. 13 (June 30, 1948), p. 6.
4. For Alexander's relationship to Bloodstone, see "State Department Implementation of SANACC 395/1," Gardiner to Hummelsine, June 10, 1948 (top secret), obtained through FOIA. For coverage of Alexander's testimony and the subsequent controversy discussed in footnote, see "Subversive Agents Believed in U.S. Under Wing of U.N.," July 21, 1948; "Marshall Knows No Agents in U.N.," July 22, 1948; "Those U.N. Communists" (editorial), July 24, 1948; "Vindication for the U.N." (editorial), August 28, 1948; "U.N. Spy Charges Called Baseless," September 2, 1948; "State Department Accuses Visa Aide," September 16, 1948; "U.S. Aide Threatens Suit," October 5, 1948; "Alexander Is Reprimanded for Charging Subversives Entered Country Through U.N.," October 22, 1948, all of which appeared in the *New York Times.* For Alexander's 1960 comments, see "Problem of Refugees" (letter), *New York Times,* December 11, 1960. Report of Alexander's death is based on Dennis Hayes (president, Foreign Service Association) interview, July 8, 1983.
5. Quoted comments from Kirkpatrick and Penniman from Evron Kirkpatrick interview, November 10, 1983, and Howard Penniman interview, November 10, 1983. Kirkpatrick's relationship to Bloodstone is established at "State Department Implementation of SANACC 395/1." For basic biographic information on Kirkpatrick, see *Contemporary Authors,* vol. 57–60, p. 321, and *Biographic Directory* of the American Political Science Association for 1968 and 1973. For critical statements mentioned in footnote, see Robert Walters, "Kirkpatrick Organization Linked to CIA Fund Outlets," *Washington Star,* February 19, 1967; Robert Sherrill, "The Professor and the CIA," *Nation* (February 27, 1967). "On Quoting 'The Nation,'" *Washington Star,* March 3, 1967 (Kirkpatrick's reply); Tom Lewis and John Freidman, "Is USIA Sponsoring a Hidden Curriculum?," *Harper's Weekly* (June 14, 1976); Allen Boyce (pseudonym), "The Market for Potted Expertise," *Nation* (November 11, 1978).
6. The criteria are drawn from the following: "Entry of Alien Specialists," Kirlin to Bohlen, August 2, 1948 (top secret), SANACC microfilm records; "State Department Implementation of SANACC 395/1"; Armstrong memo to Kennan, Davies, etc.; and SANACC 395/1, "Utilization of Refugees from the Soviet Union in the U.S. National Interest," May 25, 1948 (top secret).
7. "Operational Situation Report USSR No. 11," March 1 to March 31, 1942, Einsatzgruppen report, Prosecution Exhibit 13, *Trials of War Criminals,* loc. cit., vol. IV, pp. 188–91.

   Hilger's own brief presentation of his wartime role is in Gustav Hilger and Alfred G. Meyer, *The Incompatible Allies: A Memoir-History of German-Soviet Relations 1918–1941* (New York: Macmillan, 1953), p. 338, which is an English-language adaption of Gustav Hilger, *Wir und der Kreml, Deutsch-sowietische Beziehungen 1918–1941* (Frankfurt am Main: Metzner, 1955). Allen Dulles, then U.S. OSS chief in Bern, Switzerland, cabled to Washington in mid-1944 that "on Russian affairs . . . Ribbentrop listens mainly to Hilger." See "Bern to OSS," July 19, 1944, Washington Section R&C 78, Bern, June 1, 1944, to July 31, 1944, Entry 134, Box 276, RG 226, NA.
8. The Hungarian incident is discussed in captured Nazi correspondence dated

January 27, 1944, reproduced in Randolph Braham, *The Destruction of Hungarian Jewry: A Documentary Account* (New York: World Federation of Hungarian Jews, 1963), pp. 122–24. The reproduced file is Nuremberg evidence document NG 2594.

9. Data on Hilger's role in the Nazi Foreign Office and the murder of Italian Jews are found in Hilberg, op. cit., pp. 351 and 432–33; Nuremberg document NG-5026, "Hilger to Group Inland II"; and Charles Allen, "Nazi War Criminals Living Among Us," *Jewish Currents* (January 1963), pp. 5–9. For a contemporary OSS documentation of the role of the Foreign Ministry in the deportation of Italian Jews, see "Bern to OSS," December 30, 1943 (KAPPA series), Washington Sect. R&C 78, Entry 134, Folder 3, Box 274, RG 226, NA.

10. Dallin, *German Rule*, pp. 505 and 635; see also Fischer, op. cit., pp. 26, 137.

11. Hilger's CROWCASS entry is found on p. 168, Box 1719, RG 153, NA, Suitland, Md., a copy of which is in the author's collection.

12. Strik-Strikfeldt, op. cit., p. 238 (seen in Mannheim POW camp); and *Trials of War Criminals*, loc. cit., vol. XI, pp. 600–01, April 17, 1946 (in United States during Nuremberg trials).

The FBI, in response to several FOIA inquiries filed by the author, revealed that it holds at least twelve dossiers concerning Hilger's activities in the United States, including one acknowledging his role as an FBI informant (in 1950) and a second so secret that even its file number remains classified. Of the fragmentary information that the bureau did declassify, the most interesting is the record of its interrogations of Hilger dated November 22 and December 8, 1948, summarizing his work for the German government. There is no indication that the bureau inquired into Hilger's role in the Holocaust. The Department of State has also declassified a fragmentary collection of records concerning Hilger, most of which date from the late 1970s. Copies in the author's collection.

13. Telegram traffic concerning Hilger's 1948 transit into the United States includes: Berlin to Washington dispatch marked "Personal for Kennan," 862.00/9-2548, September 25, 1948 (top secret); Heidelberg to Washington dispatch marked "For Kennan," 862.00/9-2748, September 27, 1948 (top secret), which suggests use of false identities; Washington to Heidelberg, 862.00/9-2848, September 28, 1948 (top secret); Heidelberg to Washington, 862.00/9-3048, September 30, 1948 (top secret), all of which are found in RG 59, NA, Washington, D.C.

On this point, see also U.S. Army INSCOM dossier concerning Hilger, No. XE-00-17-80 I6A045, which the author obtained via an FOIA request from the Criminal Division of the U.S. Department of Justice. Document 46 in that dossier, "350.09: Transmittal of Classified Personal [illegible]," October 19, 1948 (confidential), notes that "Gen. Walsh or George Kennan State Department should be contacted in case of difficulty" during Hilger's travel to the United States. Document 37 of the same dossier ("subject: Background Investigation, HILGER, Gustav, 25 July 1951") indicates Hilger was issued nonimmigrant Visa No. 324 at the U.S. Consulate in Munich on October 6, 1948.

For subcommittee specializing in false identification for Bloodstone émigrés discussed in footnote, see "Utilization of Refugees," SANACC 395/1, May 25, 1948 (top secret), pp. 11–16, with quote from p. 16.

14. Poppe interview, October 26, 1984.

     On Eurasian Institute role in employing former Nazis mentioned in foot-note, see cable "For Offie from Davies," May 27, 1948 (secret) 800.43 Eurasian Institute/5-2748 secret file; "From Tehran to Secretary of State, attention John Davies," re: Ulus and Sunsh, July 27, 1948 (secret), 800.43 Eurasian Institute/7-2748 secret file; "Department of State to AMEMBASSY, Tehran," re: Sunsh, July 27, 1948 (secret), 800.43 Eurasian Institute/7-2748; "For Davies from Dooher," re: Ulus, August 12, 1948 (secret), 800.43 Eurasian Institute/8-1248; "Department of State to AMEMBASSY, Athens," initialed by Kennan, October 12, 1948 (secret), 800.43 Eurasion *(sic)* Institute/10-1248; etc. All in RG 59, NA.

15. On Hilger's relationship with Bohlen and the Office of National Estimates, see Bohlen, op. cit, p. 292; and Meyer interview. See also *Church Committee Report,* Book IV, pp. 18–19 re: early days of Office of National Estimates and its role.

16. Kennan correspondence, August 12, 1982; see also "Help for Nazis Held Not Unusual," *New York Times,* February 20, 1983.

17. For "stigma" comment: Meyer interview, December 30, 1983; see Hilger and Meyer, op. cit., pp. viii–ix for data on "generous grant." Kennan's role in obtaining Hilger's security clearance is found in Hilger's U.S. Army INSCOM file no. 84066.3224, also numbered as INSCOM dossier XE 001780 D 20A042 (secret), Document 15, 51–52. A number of records implicating Hilger in crimes against humanity had, in fact, been introduced as evidence in war crimes trials at Nuremberg, though there is no indication that they were reviewed prior to Hilger's being granted a security clearance; see, for example, Nuremberg evidence documents NG 2594 and NG 5026, noted above.

18. On Hilberg's protest and 1962 incident with Charles Allen, see Allen, op. cit. Hilger's death: Letter to author from Christoph Brummer, press counselor, Embassy of the Federal Republic of Germany, September 4, 1984.

19. Poppe, op. cit., pp. 163–64.

20. Ibid., pp. 165–66. On the Judeo-Tats, see also Rudolph Lowenthal, "The Judeo-Tats of the Caucasus," *Historia Judaica,* vol. XIV (1952), p. 61ff.

21. For a surviving example of a Wannsee study, see Wannsee Institute, op. cit. On activities and staffing of the Wannsee Institute, including Poppe's role, see *Records of the Reich Leader of the SS and Chief of the German Police,* loc. cit., Roll 456, Frame 2972093ff., for correspondence, security passes, lists of employees, etc., from the institute.

22. *Records of the Reich Leader of the SS and Chief of the German Police,* loc. cit., Roll 455, Frame 2971560ff., for documentation concerning Wannsee's role in the looting of libraries and bookdealers; and Roll 457, Frame 2973523ff, for Amt VI-G correspondence concerning use of concentration camp inmates for custodial work.

     Poppe's comments: Poppe interviews, October 26 and December 4, 1984, and Poppe, op. cit., pp. 170 and 174–75.

23. Poppe, op. cit., pp. 170 and 175–76.

24. Rodes memo to DDI Frankfurt, May 22, 1947 (top secret), copy in author's collection. On Poppe's work for British and American agencies: Poppe, op. cit., pp. 191, 193–96, and 197–98.

25. State Department records concerning Poppe's immigration may be found at: "For [Carmel] Offie from [John Paton] Davies," 800.4016 DP/3-848, March 8, 1948 (secret); "For Offie from Davies," 893.00 Mongolia/3-1848, March 18, 1948 (secret); "For [James] Riddleberger from [George] Kennan," 861.00/10-2248, October 22, 1948 (secret—sanitized); "Personal for Kennan from Riddleberger," 861.00/11-248, November 2, 1948 (secret—sanitized); and "Personal for Riddleberger from Kennan," 800.4016 DP/5-449, May 3, 1949 (secret), signed also by Robert Joyce, all at RG 59, NA. The sanitized correspondence was obtained through the FOIA.

On Poppe's immigration, also: author's interviews with Poppe, October 26 and December 4, 1984; Davies, November 28, 1983; and Evron Kirkpatrick, November 10, 1983.

Poppe's U.S. Army INSCOM file is available via the FOIA and is No. 84107.3224. For British Foreign Office correspondence on the Poppe affair, see *British Foreign Office: Russia Correspondence 1946–1948, F. O. 371* (microfilm collection of British records), Scholarly Resources, Wilmington, Del., 1982, particularly 1946 File 911, Document 12867, p. 80ff., and 1946 File 3365, Document 9647, p. 22ff. It is interesting to note that U.S. Political Adviser in Germany James Riddleberger, who played a role in the escape of Klaus Barbie, was directly involved in arranging Poppe's immigration to the United States. (Riddleberger is deceased.) Robert Joyce, who assisted in the American end of the transit arrangements, also played a key role in the immigration of Albanian émigrés with backgrounds as Nazi collaborators; see source note 34, below.

An account of Poppe's immigration to the United States, including a direct admission that "a U.S. intelligence agency" sponsored his resettlement in this country, appears in *Nazis and Axis Collaborators Were Used to Further U.S. Anti-Communist Objectives in Europe—Some Immigrated to the United States,* report by the Comptroller General of the United States, U.S. General Accounting Office, June 28, 1985, p. 35. This report, prepared by GAO investigator John Tipton following limited access to CIA records, neither names Poppe nor identifies the intelligence agency that sponsored him. The anonymous "Subject E" of Tipton's report, however, is without a doubt Poppe, and the agency is the CIA. This study is hereinafter cited as *1985 GAO Report.*

26. Poppe interview, October 26, 1984; see also Poppe, op. cit., pp. 199–200.

27. For a brief official biography on Poppe, see *Directory of American Scholars,* 1974 edition, p. 368, and *The Writers Directory, 1982–1984,* p. 754, which discusses Poppe's literary accomplishments. A Russian-language interview with Poppe concerning his career is available at the Hoover Institution at Stanford University. See also Arista Maria Cirtautas, "Nicholas Poppe, a Bibliography of Publications from 1924 to 1977," *Parerga* (Seattle, Wash.: University of Washington, Institute for Comparative and Foreign Area Studies, 1977), for an extensive bibliography of Poppe's work, which is unfortunately silent on Poppe's production for the SS, British, and American intelligence agencies. Poppe's own account is in Poppe, op. cit., p. 199ff.

28. For Poppe's testimony on Owen Lattimore, see "Institute of Pacific Relations," *Hearings before the Subcommittee to Investigate the Administration of*

the *Internal Security Act and Other Internal Security Laws,* U.S. Senate, 82nd Congress, February 12, 1952, pp. 2691–2707, 2724–31, with quoted passages on pp. 2725–26. For overviews of Lattimore case, see Oshinsky, op. cit., p. 136ff., and Caute, op. cit., p. 317ff. See also C. P. Trussell, "Senate Unit Calls Lattimore Agent of Red Conspiracy," *New York Times,* July 3, 1952, p. 1. For Poppe's statements concerning Lattimore's role in opposing Poppe's immigration, see Poppe, op. cit., pp. 191, 197, and 214–16.

29. Poppe interview, December 4, 1984.

30. Ibid. For points discussed in footnote, *1985 GAO Report,* p. 35, and U.S. Department of Justice Criminal Division correspondence re: FOIA request CRM-11132-F, January 9, 1986.

31. "Axis Supporters Enlisted by U.S. in Postwar Role," *New York Times,* June 20, 1982.

32. Joyce memo: "Robert Joyce to Walworth Barbour," 875.00/5-1249, May 12, 1949 (top secret), RG 59, NA. Background information on Robert Joyce may be found in his obituary, which appeared in the *Washington Post,* February 10, 1984.

On character of Albanian collaboration, see OSS R&A report L38836, "Albania: Political and Internal Conditions," July 10, 1944 (secret), which states in part that "Xhafer Deva, Rexhep Mitrovic and Midhat Frasheri are with the Germans. . . . Anti-Semitic measures are being adopted now," RG 226, NA. See also "Axis Supporters Enlisted by U.S. in Postwar Role," loc. cit., and Hilberg, op. cit., pp. 451 and 451n.

33. Dosti comment: "Axis Supporters Enlisted by U.S. in Postwar Role," loc. cit. On Assembly of Captive European Nations funding by CIA through Radio Free Europe: Price, op. cit., pp. CRS 9–10, and see Chapter 1, source note 9, for further documentation. On Philby's role: Bruce Page et al., *The Philby Conspiracy* (New York: Signet, 1969), pp. 177–89, and Kim Philby, *My Silent War* (New York, Ballantine, 1983), pp. 155–65.

Chapter Ten

1. On origins of RFE and RL, see Mickelson, op. cit., pp. 11–22, 59–75; David Wise and Thomas Ross, *The Invisible Government* (New York: Vintage/Random House, 1964), p. 326ff.; Marchetti and Marks, op. cit., pp. 174–78; and Cord Meyer, *Facing Reality* (New York: Harper & Row, 1980), pp. 110–38. On the CIA's controlling role in RFE and RL throughout the cold war, see also John Crewdson and Joseph Treaster, "Worldwide Propaganda Network Built by the CIA," *New York Times,* December 26, 1977, p. 1; "Defector Had Job Tied to CIA," *Washington Post,* September 15, 1966; "Help for Radio Free Europe," *Washington Post,* February 5, 1966; "CIA Cash Linked to Broadcasts," *Washington Post,* March 12, 1970; "Ban Sought on CIA Aid for Radio Free Europe," *New York Times,* January 24, 1971; Michael Getler, "CIA Runs Radio Free Europe, Ex-Employee Says in Prague," *Washington Post,* January 31, 1976.

2. Mickelson, op. cit., pp. 14–17. Mickelson identifies the source of the first $2 million of National Committee for a Free Europe funds (plus printing presses, propaganda balloons, etc.) as Frank Wisner's OPC, which in turn had inherited that "nest egg," as Mickelson puts it, from the Special Projects Group (SPG),

the institutional umbrella for the $10 million in U.S. clandestine funding allocated for manipulation of the Italian election. Mickelson does not discuss where the SPG got its funds, however. For details on that point, see Chapter Seven, source note 20.

3. For Carey comment, see *New York Herald Tribune,* January 29, 1950, and Richard Boyer and Herbert Morais, *Labor's Untold Story* (New York: United Electrical Radio & Machine Workers of America Publishing Division, 1973), p. 362. On Kennan's role in creating the NCFE board, see Mickelson, op. cit., pp. 14–15. On early NCFE board members, see Price, op cit., p. CRS-7, and National Committee for a Free Europe, *President's Report for the Year 1954* (New York: National Committee for a Free Europe, 1954). The most complete presentation of backgrounds and careers of early NCFE directors available at present is in Collins, op. cit., p. 362ff. Mickelson offers a useful table of key NCFE and American Committee for Liberation personalities on p. 257ff. For roles of Yarrow, Grace, and Heinz, see Comptroller General of the United States, *U.S. Government Monies Provided to Radio Free Europe and Radio Liberty,* General Accounting Office Report No. 72-0501, (Washington, D.C.: Government Printing Office, 1972) pp. 79–81 and 109.

4. Mickelson, op. cit., pp. 18, 20.

5. James Burnham, *Containment or Liberation?* (New York: John Day Co., 1953), p. 188. For Burnham's relationship with OPC, see Smith, *OSS,* p. 367. For official, but sanitized, funding estimates, see also Comptroller General of the United States, *U.S. Government Monies Provided to Radio Free Europe and Radio Liberty,* loc. cit.

6. The history of the various corporate covers employed by the OPC and the CIA to conceal their relationship with RFE, RL, and other psychological warfare programs is complex.

The corporate parent of the agency's Eastern European broadcasting arm, for example, has variously been called the Committee for a Free Europe (1948–1949); the National Committee for a Free Europe (1949–1954); the Free Europe Committee, Inc. (1954–1976); and, finally, RFE/RL, Inc. (1976–   ). Each of these companies had a broadcasting division named Radio Free Europe (circa 1950–   ).

The CIA's parallel effort aimed at the USSR has included the American Institute for the Study of the USSR (1950); Institute for the Study of the History and Culture of the Soviet Union (1950); American Committee for the Freedom of the Peoples of the USSR (1951); American Committee for the Liberation of the Peoples of Russia, Inc. (1951–1953); and American Committee for Liberation from Bolshevism, also often known as AMCOMLIB (1953–1956). The latter had officially changed its name to Radio Liberation, Inc. by 1963, although correspondence from 1956 to 1963 indicates that the parent company also did business as AMCOMLIB, Inc. during that time. Next came the Radio Liberty Committee (1963–1976). The radio broadcasting arm of this operation was variously known as the Radio Station of the Coordinating Center of Anti-Bolshevik Struggle (1953); Radio Liberation from Bolshevism (1953–1956); Radio Liberation (1956–1963); and Radio Liberty (1963–   ).

The Radio Free Europe and Radio Liberty organizations finally merged into RFE/RL, Inc. in 1976. The author has attempted to simplify references in the text to these changing corporate cover entities as much as possible for clarity's sake.

On clandestine CIA funding of educational and charitable foundations mentioned above in the text, see "Groups Channeling, Receiving Assistance from CIA," *Congressional Quarterly Almanac 1967*, pp. 360–61; *Church Committee Report*, Book VI, p. 263ff; Gloria Emerson, "Cultural Group Once Aided by CIA Picks Ford Fund Aide to Be Its Director," *New York Times*, October 2, 1967, p. 17; Hans J. Morgenthau, "Government Has Compromised the Integrity of the Educational Establishment," and Irving Louis Horowitz, "Social Scientists Must Beware the Corruption of CIA Involvement," both in Young Hum Kim, ed., *The Central Intelligence Agency: Problems of Secrecy in a Democracy* (Lexington, Mass.: D. C. Heath & Co., 1968).

Of particular interest in this regard is George Kennan's presidency of the Free Russia Fund and, later, of the East European Fund, major conduits for Ford Foundation money to approved scholars seeking to define U.S./Soviet relations during the cold war. Both funds placed particular stress on émigré affairs. For an early Free Russia Fund publication, see George Fischer, ed., *Russian Émigré Politics* (New York: Free Russia Fund, Inc., 1951). On Kennan's role, see also "The Men of the Ford Foundation," *Fortune* (December 1951), p. 117.

For an overview of clandestine CIA funding of media assets, see Daniel Schorr, "Are CIA Assets a Press Liability?," *More* (February 1978), p. 18ff.

7. On clandestine U.S. funding for foreign governments' exile programs, see "U.S. Policy on Defectors, Escapees and Refugees from Communist Areas," NSC 5706 (secret), February 13, 1957, p. 6, a sanitized version of which is available in RG 273, NA, Washington, D.C. For $100 million estimate, see *U.S. Government Monies Provided to Radio Free Europe and Radio Liberty*, loc. cit. On the CIA's use of RFE/RL covers to pass funds to exile committees, see Price, op. cit., p. CRS-1 (for CIA funding of RFE) and p.CRS-10 (for RFE funding of the ACEN). See also NCFE, *President's Report for the Year 1954*, pp. 18–21, for a surprisingly frank presentation of the committee's Division of Exile Relations' work with the ACEN, International Peasant Union, Christian Democratic Union of Central Europe, and others.

8. For source material on CIA funding of exile programs, see source note 7, above. On clandestine CIA funding of the extreme-right Paris Bloc of the Anti-Bolshevik Bloc of Nations (ABN) exile organization, see A. Tchilingarian, "The American Committee and the Struggle Against Bolshevism," *Armenian Review* (March 1955), p. 3ff., and Crewdson and Treaster, op. cit., p. 37, for agency funding of book by extreme right ABN leader Suzanne Labin. Although Labin worked closely with numerous outspoken Nazi collaborators and sympathizers in the leadership of ABN, there is no indication that she collaborated with or is sympathetic to Nazi Germany. For a more complete discussion of the dominant role of Nazi collaborators in the ABN, as well as their role in more moderate CIA-funded organizations, such as the ACEN and the exile committees, see Chapters Fifteen and Seventeen.

9. For an example of political controversy over the "left" tilt of some RFE/RL-financed émigré associations, see Kurt Glaser's attack on the Council for a Free Czechoslovakia titled "The 'Russia First' Boys in Radio Free Europe," *Na-*

tional Republic (February 1953). This article found its way into Immigration and Naturalization Service records as INS "Memorandum for File 56347/ 218," May 6, 1953, retyped word for word by an unidentified investigator for the Subversive Alien Branch. That memo, in turn, led to a series of watch reports and even arrest warrants for pro-Zenkl Czech leaders. See INS classified file on Council for a Free Czechoslovakia, obtained by author via FOIA. On "liberal" tilt, see also Smith, *OSS*, p. 389, n. 63; Colby, op. cit.; and Kurt Glaser, "Psychological Warfare's Policy Feedback," *Ukrainian Quarterly* (Spring 1953), p. 110ff. For Durcansky group's view of Tiso regime, see Ferdinand Durcansky, "The West Shut Its Eyes to Tiso's Warning," *ABN-Correspondence*, No. 5–6 (1953), p. 6.

10. On Nižňanský and Csonka, see Milan Blatny, *Les Proclamateurs de Fausse Liberté* (Bratislava: L'Institut d'Études de Journalisme, 1977), pp. 16 and 30. Kennan quote: George F. Kennan, *Memoirs 1950–1963* (Boston: Little, Brown, 1967), p. 96, hereinafter cited as *Kennan vol. II.*

11. On selection of name for American Committee for the Liberation of the Peoples of Russia, see Mickelson, op. cit., pp. 63–64 and 69. On origins of Radio Liberation generally, see Joseph Whelan, *Radio Liberty: A Study of Its Origins, Structure, Policy, Programming and Effectiveness* (Washington, D.C.: Congressional Research Service, 1972); with discussion of evolution of American Committee for Liberation of the Peoples of Russia name at p. CRS-8ff. See also William Henry Chamberlin, "Emigre Anti-Soviet Enterprises and Splits," *Russian Review* (April 1954), p. 91ff.

On founding of Vlassovite Komitet Osvobozhdeniia Narodov Rossii, or KONR (Committee for the Liberation of the Peoples of Russia), see Dallin, *German Rule*, pp. 628–36. George Fischer reports that the name KONR was originally chosen by Himmler himself.

12. Mickelson, op. cit., p. 69, n. 2. For a more detailed examination of internal émigré splits and conflicts through 1952, see Dvinov, *Politics of the Russian Emigration*, loc. cit., p. 285ff. For a Ukrainian nationalist point of view on this question, see, for example, "Court Justice or Political Vengeance," *Ukrainian Quarterly* (Spring 1952), p. 101ff., which concerns a beating of a pro-American Committee for Liberation Ukrainian leader at the hands of three young nationalists.

13. Hans-Erich Volkmann, "Main Political Trends Among Russian Émigrés in Germany After World War II," tr. RFE/RL, *Osteuropa* (April 1965), p. 20. The extremist Russian nationalist organization NTS reported a number of similar bombing incidents during the same period that it also blamed on the KGB or its predecessors, the MGB and MVD. On murders, kidnappings, and other violence against émigrés, see *MVD-MBG Campaign Against Russian Émigrés* (Frankfurt: Possev Publishing House, 1957), and Central Intelligence Agency, "Soviet Use of Assassination and Kidnapping," February 17, 1966, FOIA review 8/76, Document No. 570-254 (obtained via FOIA), which is so similar in content to the Possev publication as to suggest derivative authorship. Possev served as the official publishing house of the extreme Russian nationalist group NTS for more than twenty years, although today it asserts it is an independent organization. On confessed Soviet double agents among the émigrés, see, for

example, Konstantin Cherezov, *NTS, a Spy Ring Unmasked* (Moscow: Soviet Committee for Cultural Relations with Russians Abroad, n.d. [1963?]). Cherezov was a leading NTS activist in Western Europe until he defected to the Soviets.

14. Mickelson, op. cit., p. 35, with quote from Poole on pp. 40–41.
15. Paul Blackstock, *Agents of Deceit* (Chicago: Quadrangle Press, 1966), pp. 141–46, with original publication of "Document" at *News from Behind the Iron Curtain,* magazine of NCFE (January 1952).
16. Blackstock, *Agents of Deceit,* p. 146.
17. CBS television, *60 Minutes* transcript for May 17, 1982, on Hazners, Stankievich.

On Trifa, see Jack Anderson, "RFE's Bishop Interview Is Probed," *Washington Post,* February 20, 1980.

Chapter Eleven

1. Fletcher Prouty interview, April 12, 1984. See also Fletcher Prouty, *The Secret Team* (Englewood Cliffs, N.J.: Prentice-Hall, 1973). On pivotal role of Brigadier General Robert McClure, see Colonel Alfred H. Paddock, *U.S. Army Special Warfare* (Washington, D.C.: National Defense University, 1982), pp. 17–20 and 44–51.
2. Prouty interview, April 12, 1984. For archival documentation on this point, see JIC 634/1, "Joint Intelligence Committee: Vulnerability of Soviet Bloc Armed Forces to Guerrilla Warfare," September 8, 1953 (top secret), now available on microfilm through University Publications of America, *Records of the Joint Chiefs of Staff,* Part 2: *The Soviet Union,* Reel 7, Frame 0184ff., which discusses in detail U.S. insurgency operations inside the USSR in the event of war, including assassinations, contamination of water supplies, destruction of communications, and other techniques.
3. "Subject: Evaluation of Effect on Soviet War Effort Resulting from the Strategic Air Offensive," June 1, 1949 (top secret), Box 9, Tab 67-OSD, Hot Files, RG 319, NA, Washington, D.C., declassified following author's review request. On this point, see also "Dir of Log to Dir of P&O, Subject: JCS 1920/1," March 1, 1949, P&O 350 06 TS through 381 FLR TS, 1949 Hot File, RG 319, NA, Washington, D.C.
4. On Labor Service units, see *Labor Services and Industrial Police in the European Command 1945–1950* (Karlsruhe, Germany: Historical Division EUCOM, 1952), pp. 112–15 and the chronology on pp. 236–46. This study was formerly classified as secret security information but is now declassified and available at the NA and the Center for Military History, both in Washington, D.C. It is cited hereinafter as *Labor Service History.*

   For data in footnote concerning USSR use of Labor Service units, see Central Intelligence Agency, "Memorandum for Mr. John D Hickerson, Department of State," November 19, 1947 (secret), 861.20262/11-1947 RG 59, NA, Washington, D.C. For Nazi use of Labor Service groups, see B. Dmytryshyn, "The Nazis and the SS Volunteer Division 'Galicia,' " *American Slavic and East European Review* (February 1956), pp. 2–3, and C. L. Lundin, "Nazification of Baltic German Minorities," *Journal of Central European Affairs* (April

1947), p. 25. See also L. Poliakov, "The Vatican and the 'Jewish Question,' " *Commentary* (November 1950), p. 442, for information concerning genocidal activities by German Labor Service gangs during the Holocaust in Poland.

On Special Forces secrecy discussed in the text and footnote, see Paddock, op cit., p. 194, n.84, and p. 196ff., n. 13, 14, 17, and 26. See also *Newsweek* (January 21, 1952). Paddock also offers an excellent discussion of interservice rivalry over the Special Forces on pp. 131–42. He does not, however, clarify the Special Forces' role in nuclear war planning, perhaps because of lingering security restrictions. On interservice rivalry: Colonel Charles M. Simpson, *Inside the Green Berets: The First Thirty Years* (Novato, Calif.: Presidio, 1983), pp. 17, 21, 48, and 53; also Prouty interview, April 12, 1984. On continuum of prewar psychological warfare programs with postnuclear guerrilla operations, see "Comments on Proposal for Establishment of a Guerrilla Warfare Group, Appendix 'B,' " pp. 2–4 (top secret), Hot Files, RG 319, NA, sanitized version in collection of author, and NSC 20, loc. cit.

5. *U.S.* v. *Talivaldis Karklins,* U. S. District Court Central California, civil action CV 81 0460 LTL; and U.S. Department of Justice, Office of Special Investigations, op cit., p. 44. On émigré nationalists and the Labor Service Divisions, see also depositions of Edward O'Connor and Col. Philip Corso (ret.), *U.S.* v. *Liudas Kairys,* U.S. District Court Northern Illinois, civil action 80-C-4032, and the defendant's posttrial brief in the same case. Kairys had served during the war in the SS Commando Lublin and as an SS guard at the Treblinka forced-labor camp. He joined a U.S. Army-sponsored Lithuanian labor service unit in 1947, and it was through that channel that he entered the United States. "The Army took Kairys and 18 to 20 men from his [Labor Service] unit to Stuttgart," Kairys's defense brief reads. "They were taken to the head of a long line waiting to see the [U.S.] consul and after only two or three minutes of processing, he was given an oath" and shortly thereafter put on a transport to the United States. The Treblinka forced-labor camp where Kairys served is not to be confused with the better-known Treblinka extermination center, which was nearby. Thousands of Jewish prisoners were murdered by the SS at the forced-labor camp; hundreds of thousands were killed at the extermination center.

On Zegners, see "Aplilciba 1941 y 20 Augusta," "Aplilciba 18 Dec. 1941," and "RIGAER E-G der Sicherheitspolizei den 7 Okt. 1942 Nr.1098," copies in author's collection, which document Zegners's role in the Latvian security police in Riga.

6. The American colonel quoted in the text spoke with the author on the condition he not be identified.

7. For record of Busbee's correspondence, see "Item 1, 2 February 1951" and "Item 1, 27 April 1951," European Command Labor Services Division Classified Decimal File, 1950–51 (secret), now at RG 338, NA, Suitland, Md.; and *Labor Service History,* p. 151.

8. *Labor Service History,* p. 117 (on suppression of disturbances); pp. 181–82 (on weapons and training); p. 198 (on chemical warfare preparations). On strength of units, see *EUCOM Annual Narrative Report 1954* (secret), RG 338, NA, Suitland, Md., pp. 85–88, 95–98. On secrecy of mission, see "Subject: Letter to General Eddy from K. W. Von Schlieben, Major, 31 Oct 1950" (restricted), RG 338 Decimal Files, NA, Suitland, Md.

9. On Albanian unit, see *EUCOM Annual Narative Report, Labor Services Division, 1950,* European Command Labor Services Division Classified Decimal File, 1950–51 (secret), p. 22, RG 338, NA, Suitland, Md.

10. "Geheimorganisation des Bundes Deutscher Jugend in Hessen Ausgehoben," *Frankfurter Allgemeine Zeitung,* October 9, 1952; "Oberbundesanwalt Fordert BDJ-Akten," *Frankfurter Rundschau,* October 14, 1952, p. 1; "Alleged Secret Organization: Guerrilla Training in Germany," *Times* of London, October 9, 1952.

11. " 'Partisans' in Germany: An Arms Dump in the Odenwald," *Times* of London, October 11, 1952; "German Says U.S. Set Up Saboteurs," *New York Times,* October 9, 1952; "More Germans Hit U.S. Sabotage Plan," *New York Times,* October 12, 1952.

12. "German Saboteurs Betray U.S. Trust," *New York Times,* October 10, 1952.

13. "German Socialist Fears Subversion," *New York Times,* October 14, 1952.

14. Thomas Braden interview, September 12, 1984; Meyer, op. cit.

15. Select Committee [Church Committee] to Study Governmental Operations With Respect to Intelligence Activities, U.S. Senate, 94th Congress, *Alleged Assassination Plots Involving Foreign Leaders: An Interim Report* (Washington, D.C.: Government Printing Office, 1975).

16. Military Intelligence Division, "History of the Military Intelligence Division, 7 December 1941—1 September 1945," *ACMH Manuscripts, 1946,* pp. 307–08, ACMH Manuscripts (secret), RG 319, NA, Washington, D.C.

17. Colonel R. W. Porter to Major General R. C. Lindsay et al., "Psychological Warfare Study for Guidance in Strategic Planning," with annex, March 11, 1948 (top secret), P&O 091.42 TS (Section I, Cases 1–7), Hot Files, RG 319, NA, Washington, D.C. On this point, see also JIC 634/1, Reel 7, frame 0184ff., particularly Paragraph 5c, "Command of MVD Security Units." "The command of MVD security troops is extremely centralized," the JIC recommendation states. "[T]herefore, [MVD] headquarters would be profitable targets. The higher the MVD official that could be removed, the greater the loss of security control, and the greater the intimidation of other officials."

For an intriguing study of the "benefits" of systematic assassination of America's political opponents, see Captain John T. Stark, *Unconventional Warfare—Selective Assassination as an Instrument of National Policy* (Air University, Maxwell Air Force Base, Alabama: Command and Staff College Special Study, n.d. [1962?]), official use only.

18. Wisner correspondence with the INS, 1951, as reproduced in John Loftus, *The Belarus Secret* (New York: Knopf, 1982), pp. 102–03.

19. *Church Committee Report,* Book IV, p. 132n.

20. Prouty interview, April 12, 1984. For information on the "medical experiments" discussed in footnote, see John Marks, *The Search for the Manchurian Candidate* (New York: Times Books, 1979), pp. 22–29. For CIA role in assassination plots on foreign leaders, see *Church Committee Report,* interim report, November 20, 1975, and *Church Committee Report,* Book IV, p. 121ff.

21. John S. Guthrie memorandum for the secretary, Security Control Section, JIG, "Subject: Assignment of Code Word," December 8, 1947 (top secret), (for Hagberry) and November 21, 1947 (for Lithia), both in 1946–1948 Decimal File, P&O 311.5 TS (Section II), 1948, RG 319, NA, Washington, D.C.

22. Maris Cakars and Barton Osborn, "Operation Ohio," *WIN* (September 18, 1975). See also Miles Copeland, *Without Cloak or Dagger* (New York: Simon & Schuster, 1974), p. 241, in which former CIA operative Copeland praises the "no-nonsense handling of occasional traitors" by an unidentified émigré group on the OPC payroll as a desirable contrast with what was "allowed in the OPC itself." For Army comments on missing records mentioned in text: author's FOIA correspondence with the National Archives and U.S. Army concerning Hagberry, Lithia, and Rusty, 1984.

More recently the CIA has sidestepped objections to its role in the murder of political opponents by defining "assassination" so narrowly as to be meaningless in most circumstances. Although the CIA's use of assassination is barred by a presidential order, in 1985 there came to light a CIA *Psychological Warfare Manual*, prepared for anti-Communist Nicaraguan rebels, in which the agency directs its client soldiers to employ "selective use of violence" to "neutralize" Nicaraguan officials such as local and regional leaders, doctors, judges, and police. The CIA manual also suggests hiring professional criminals to carry out "selective jobs" against local Nicaraguan government officials and sympathizers and advocates murdering other anti-Communist sympathizers in order to create "martyrs." When U.S. congressional hearings were held on the matter, the former chief of CIA clandestine operations in Latin America, Dewey Claridge, testified that these murders were not "assassinations" and therefore not barred by the presidential order. According to Claridge, "these events don't constitute assassinations because as far as we are concerned assassinations are only those of heads of state." The (U.S.) National Council of Teachers of English awarded its 1985 "Doublespeak" Awards to both Claridge and the CIA itself as "an appropriate form of recognition" for the agency's "misuse of public language"; see National Council of Teachers of English, *Quarterly Review of Doublespeak* (January 1986), p. 2.

23. Franklin Lindsay interview, January 25, 1985.

24. *Church Committee Report*, Book IV, p. 128ff.

For data on Soviet use of assassination discussed in footnote, see, for example, CIA, "Soviet Use of Assassination and Kidnapping," loc. cit., "16 Anti-Communist Leaders Died the Death of Bandera," *ABN Correspondence*, n.d. (1962?); Nikolai Khokhlov and Milton Lehman "I Would Not Murder for the Soviets," *Saturday Evening Post* (November 20 and 27, December 4 and 11, 1954); and particularly *MVD-MGB Campaign Against Russian Émigrés*, loc. cit.

25. For biographic material on Pash: Boris Pash interview, February 1985; and Pash, op. cit., for World War II role and photos. For role in Oppenheimer case, see James Reston, "Dr. Oppenheimer Is Barred from Security Clearance, Though 'Loyal,' 'Discreet,'" *New York Times*, June 2, 1954, p. 1ff.

26. For documentation of Pash's role in Bloodstone, see SANACC 395, Document 8 (SANA 6024: Appointment of Committee), April 15, 1948 (secret). On assassination as a designated Bloodstone mission, see Joint Strategic Plans Committee, JSPC 862/3, loc. cit.

27. *Church Committee Report*, Book IV, p. 129. According to the CIA, Pash was assigned to that agency from March 3, 1949, to January 3, 1952, and worked with the CIA on several operations after that date; see ibid., p. 128.

28. Pash interview, February 1985.
29. SANACC 395 Document 8 (SANA 6024: Appointment of Committee), April 15, 1948 (secret), and *Church Committee Report,* Book IV, p. 128ff.
30. *Church Committee Report* Book IV, p. 129ff.
31. Ibid., p. 130.
32. Pentagon document: JSPC 862/2, loc. cit., Appendix "C," pp. 27, 35. Pash: SANACC 395 Document 8 (SANA 6024: Appointment of Committee), April 15, 1948, and *Church Committee Report,* Book IV, p. 130. Albanian role: see Chapter Nine, source notes 31 through 33. Murder of double agents: Cakars and Osborn, op. cit.; Copeland, op. cit., p. 241, with quoted comment from OPC supervisor in *Church Committee Report,* Book IV, p. 312.
33. Corson, op. cit., p. 361.

Chapter Twelve
1. Carroll, op. cit., pp. 80 and 85.
2. Ibid.
3. Dallin, *German Rule,* p. 680.
4. Rositzke interview, January 16, 1985.
5. Lindsay interview, January 25, 1985.
6. For Soviet reportage, see, for example, V. Styrkul, *The SS Werewolves* (Lvov: Kamenyar Publishers, 1982), Yuri Melnichuk, *Judas's Breed* (Kiev: Dnipro Publishers, 1978); Mykola Horlenko, *Fake Patriots* (Odessa: Mayak Publishers 1983); Olexander Vasylenko, "The Brand of Criminals," *Ukrainian News,* no. 20 (1986).
7. For the Western reportage, see, for example, United Committee of the Ukrainian-American Organizations of New York, *The Ukrainian Insurgent Army in Fight for Freedom* (New York: Dnipro Publishing, 1954), hereinafter cited as *Ukrainian Insurgent Army.*; Edward M. O'Connor, "A New Look at Nationalism," *Ukrainian Quarterly,* vol. XII, no. 4 (1957); Supreme Ukrainian Liberation Council, "The Policy of Liberation," November 4, 1953; Mykola Lebed, *UPA, Ukrainska Povstanska Armiia* (Uydannia Presovoho Biura UGVR, 1946); and, on a more careful and scholarly level, Armstrong, op. cit. "Dnipro Publishers" of Kiev (note 6 above) is not affiliated, obviously, with "Dnipro Publishing" of New York, which put out the *Ukrainian Insurgent Army* text mentioned in this note.
8. Dallin, *German Rule,* p. 107ff.; Wilhelm Canaris, "Kriegstagebuchaufzeichnung über die Konferenz im Führerzug in Ilnau am 12.9.1939," Nuremberg document No. 3047-PS, NA, Washington, D.C., and Kahn, op. cit., p. 453. For historical overviews of Ukrainian nationalism, see Philip Friedman, "Ukrainian-Jewish Relations During the Nazi Occupation," *YIVO Annual of Jewish Social Science,* vol. XII, p. 259ff.; Alexander Motyl, *The Turn to the Right: The Ideological Origins and Development of Ukrainian Nationalism* (Boulder, Colo.: East European Monographs, Columbia University Press, 1980); St. J. Paprocki, "Political Organizations of the Ukrainian Exiles After the Second World War," *Eastern Quarterly,* vol. V, nos. 1–2 (January 1952); John S. Kark, "The Ukraine and Its Supreme Liberation Council," master's thesis, University of Maryland, 1955; and Armstrong, op. cit. On anti-Semitism, see Friedman, op. cit.; Dallin, *German Rules,* p. 119, n. 2; Malcolm MacPherson, *The*

Blood of His Servants (New York: Times Books, 1984); and Hermann Rasch-hofer, *Political Assassination: The Legal Background of the Oberlander and Stashinsky Cases* (Tübingen: Fritz Schlichtenmayer, n.d. [1963?]). Raschhofer, a German rightist, defends former SS officer Teodor Oberlander on the ground that Ukrainian nationalist extremists, not Germans, were primarily responsible for anti-Semitic outrages during the opening months of the German occupation of Lvov. Raschhofer's study is perhaps the most sophisticated defense of Nazi genocide in the Ukraine available in the English language. The only source for this unusual volume in the United States, so far as the author is aware, is John Birch Society bookstores.

9. Dallin, *German Rule* p. 119ff. On the assassination of Pieracki and the subsequent careers of Lebed and Bandera, see Mykola Lebed, U.S. Army INSCOM Dossier No. C 804 3982, obtained by the author via FOIA. Note particularly "Memorandum for the Officer in Charge, Subject: Mikola Lebed," September 30, 1948 (secret), 7970th Counter Intelligence Corps Group, Region IV; "Personality Report, Subject: LEBED, Mykola," by CIC Special Agent Randolph Carroll, December 29, 1947; and "Personality Card, LEBED, Mykola," Ref. D 82270 memo, July 22, 1948 (Document 08).

10. Wolodymyr Stachiw to Adolf Hitler, June 23, 1941, Reich Chancery registry No. RK 9380A, U.S. government's evidentiary exhibit, *U.S.* v. *Bohdan Koziv,* U.S. District Court Southern Florida and 11th Circuit Court of Appeals docket no. 79-6640-CIV-JCP, copy in author's collection.

    On funding and arms for OUN, see Dallin, *German Rule,* pp. 115ff.; 621–27.

11. Dallin, *German Rule,* pp. 115ff., 621–27. For self-acknowledgment by nationalist sources of recruiting among Nazi-sponsored militia groups, see Lev Shankowsky, "Ten Years of UPA Struggle," in *Ukrainian Insurgent Army,* p. 26. Shankowsky's account asserts that the UPA "operate[d] on a large scale against Nazi Germany," a position that is at best a one-sided presentation of the facts. This volume is generally regarded as the "official" history of the UPA by Ukrainian nationalists in the United States, and it fails to discuss the role of the group in anti-Semitic pogroms and pro-Nazi activities.

12. Dallin, *German Rule,* pp. 625, 645–46, 654.

13. On Operation *Sonnenblume,* see Otto Skorzeny, "Consolidated Interrogation Report No. 4," loc. cit., pp. 38–39. See also "General Situation Report No. 2, 15 July to 1 September 1945," Office of Strategic Services Mission for Germany (top secret), p. 5, for further details drawn from an interrogation of prisoner Bruno A. C. Nikoll.

14. *Ukrainian Insurgent Army,* p. 40.

15. *Village Voice* reporter Joe Conason, working independently from the author, published an extensive exposé of the Lebed affair, including the Kosakivs'kyy account, as this book was in preparation. See Joe Conason, "To Catch a Nazi," *Village Voice* (February 11, 1986), p. 1. For a reply to these charges from the Ukrainian Supreme Liberation Council with which Lebed is affiliated, see "Statement from the Foreign Representation of the Ukrainian Supreme Liberation Council," *America* (March 3, 1986), p. 2ff. Also Mykola Lebed interviews, October 9 and December 10, 1985. For an authoritative account of the atrocities at the Zackopane Gestapo school near Krakow, see *Urteil vom 15*

August 1968 in der Strafsache gegen Wilhelm Karl Johannes Rosenbaum, Landgericht Hamburg, Schwurgericht (50) 21/67 (judgment in the Wilhelm Rosebaum war crimes case), p. 22ff.

16. Mykola Lebed, INSCOM Dossier No. C 804 3982. St. J. Paprocki, op. cit., cites Lebed as security chief of the OUN and "the man pulling the strings within the [OUN] party" (p. 44). Yaroslav Bilinsky also notes Lebed as "an outstanding organizer and the chief of the OUN security service"; see Yaroslav Bilinsky, *The Second Soviet Republic: The Ukraine After World War II* (New Brunswick, N.J.: Rutgers University Press, 1964), p. 122.

17. [German] Army Field Police Group Report No. 1, July 7, 1941, published in Raschhofer, op. cit., p. 41ff.

18. On events in Lvov, see Leon W. Wells, *The Death Brigade (The Janowska Road)* (New York: Holocaust Library and Schocken Books, 1978), and Philip Friedman, *Roads to Extinction: Essays on the Holocaust: The Destruction of the Jews of Lwow 1941–1944* (Jerusalem: Yad Vashem, 1979). See also MacPherson, op. cit., p. 101ff. According to captured SS records, a later purge of Jews in Lvov (one of several) yielded "20,952 kilograms of golden wedding rings . . . 35 wagons of furs . . . 11.73 kilograms of gold teeth and inlays," and a long list of other items, each of which was dutifully tallied up and turned over to the SS "Special Staff Reinhard." See International Military Tribunal, *Trials of the Major War Criminals Before the International Military Tribunal* (Nuremberg, Germany: 1947), vol. 3, p. 532. See also N. M. Gelber, *The Encyclopedia of the Jewish Diaspora* vol. 1, *Lwow,* (Jerusalem: n.p., 1956), in Hebrew.

   Lebed's account discussed in the footnote is based on Mykola Lebed interview, December 10, 1985, and Lebed's correspondence with the author, March 1, 1985. For U.S. Army account, see Mykola Lebed INSCOM dossier no. C 804 3982.

19. Mykola Lebed, INSCOM Dossier No. C 804 3982. Note particularly "Memorandum for the Officer in Charge, Subject: Mikola Lebed"; "Personality Report, Subject: LEBED, Mykola"; and "Personality Card, LEBED, Mykola." A second INSCOM dossier concerning Lebed, No. D-201967 24B2190, includes copies of Lebed's postwar appeals to U.S. Secretary of State George Marshall and a complete copy of Lebed's own account of the UPA during the war, which unfortunately is presently available only in the Ukrainian language. See Lebed, op. cit.

20. Mykola Lebed INSCOM Dossier No. C 804 3982, "Personality Card, LEBED, Mykola."

21. Lebed interview, December 10, 1985.

22. Mykola Lebed INSCOM Dossier No. C 804 3982, "Extract from par 2, MOIC Sub-Region MARBURG, file III-M-1928 Subject: Formation of a Ukrainian Government in Exile," July 7, 1948 (secret); Document 43 in the Lebed dossier.

23. Central Intelligence Agency Act of 1949, Section 7 [50 USC 403h]. On Lebed's life in Germany, see Lebed INSCOM dossier.

24. Agency correspondence with author: INS, June 5, 1984, and Office of the Attorney General, June 25 and December 31, 1984. For denial of congressional request, author's interview with former Congresswoman Elizabeth Holtz-

man, June 7, 1983. In June 1985 the CIA released a small group of heavily censored records concerning the 100 Persons Act in response to an FOIA request by the author. They acknowledge in passing that the CIA and the INS "have cooperated on mutual problems for many years" and that the authority to sponsor aliens for 100 Persons immigration had been delegated by the CIA director to Deputy Director Marshall Carter in 1962. Author's FOIA request No. F84-0414.

25. *1985 GAO Report.* Mykola Lebed is the anonymous "Subject D" discussed in this study.

26. U.S. Displaced Persons Commission, *List of Organizations Considered Inimical to the United States Under PL 774* (Frankfurt: U.S. Displaced Persons Headquarters, n.d.) (secret), pp. 29–30.

27. On procedures and the transmittal of information concerning Lebed, see *1985 GAO Report* p. 34. Also Lebed interviews, October 9 and December 10, 1985. On archives, see INSCOM Dossier No. ZF010016.

28. *Newsweek* (March 19, 1951), and Mykola Lebed, "Ukrainian Insurgent Army," speech at Yale Political Union, February 13, 1951, in *Vital Speeches of the Day,* April 1, 1951, p. 370ff.

29. *1985 GAO Report,* p. 34.

30. "SHANDRUK, General Paul," CIC Region III report, May 14, 1951, in IN-SCOM Dossier 148204 25 B/679 (secret), Documents 042–045. On Shandruk's wartime career see also *Final Interrogation Report: The Polish-Ukrainian Military Staff,* U.S. Seventh Army Interrogation Center, August 28, 1945 (confidential), Box 721A, Entry 179, MIS-Y Enemy POW Interrogation Files, RG 165, NA, Washington, D.C.

31. Shandruk was living in Trenton, New Jersey, as of 1959. See Pavlo Shandruk, *Arms of Valor,* tr. Roman Olesnicki (New York: Robert Speller & Sons, 1959), p. xxxiv. The U.S. Army was well aware that Shandruk had lied on his application for a U.S. visa; see "Memo for Major Abraham, Visa Section" from Captain Charles Hoagland, June 29, 1950[?] (confidential), which states: "Subject's case file seems to indicate that SZYNDRUK [a standard transliteration of Shandruk] supplied false information in connection with his visa applications . . . [and] it would appear that CIC may be subject to criticism if it became general knowledge that SZYNDRUK was allowed to emigrate to the United States in spite of his SS background. . . . For example, the Soviet line of propaganda could center upon a U.S. move, say, to harbor from justice a 'famous Nazi collaborator'" (Documents 049–050 in Shandruk INSCOM dossier). Shandruk nevertheless entered the United States and remained there without difficulty.

32. On registers of Ukrainians willing to fight in guerrilla operations, see JCS 1844/144, "Civil Affairs and Military Government Plan in Support of the Joint Outline Emergency War Plan for a War Beginning 1 July 1952" (top secret), available on microfilm through University Publications of America title *Records of the Joint Chiefs of Staff,* Part 2: *The Soviet Union,* Reel 7, Frame 1078ff.; see particularly original document, p. 1308. See also Powers, op. cit., p. 52.

33. Intelligence Research Report, "Nature and Extent of Disaffection and Anti-Soviet Activity in the Ukraine," March 17, 1948 (secret), pp. 12–13. This report

is available on microfilm through *A Guide to OSS/State Department Intelligence and Research Reports,* and its underlying microfilm collection published by University Publications of America, at Reel VIII, Item 7.

34. On the CIA's stockpiles of explosives mentioned in text, most of the CIA's own documentation concerning its sabotage and guerrilla operations in Eastern Europe remains classified. Recent amendments to the Freedom of Information Act suggest that these records may well remain buried forever—or, more likely, selectively leaked to sympathetic scholars—despite their obvious relevance to present-day American policy debates over U.S.-Soviet relations. The quotes here are drawn from army staff records: P&O 040 CIA 1949–1950, correspondence of December 27, 1949, and January 4, 12, and 19, 1950 (top secret), RG 319, NA, Washington, D.C.

35. Rositzke, op cit., p. 169. Lindsay interview, January 25, 1985; Rositzke interview, January 16, 1985.

36. For army estimates of numbers of Soviet guerrillas, see top secret decimal File 370.64 1951–1954, Army Chief of Special Warfare Brigadier General Robert McClure, "Memorandum to Asst. Chiefs of Staff G-3, subject: Staff Studies;" June 12, 1951, Box 15, RG 319, NA, Washington, D.C., and Paddock, op cit., p. 125.

37. Lindsay interview, January 25, 1985.

38. On airdrops of agents, see United Nations, *Official Records of the General Assembly,* Eleventh Session, Annexes, vol. II, November 12, 1956, to March 8, 1957, New York, Agenda Item 70 (hereinafter cited as "UN Debate Item 70") pp. 1–14; William J. Jorden, "Soviet Assails U.S., Produces 4 'Spies,' " *New York Times,* February 7, 1957, p. 1; Rositzke, op. cit., pp. 18–38, 168–74; Rositzke interview, January 16, 1985; Mosley, op. cit., p. 289 (comments by Howard Roman), pp. 325, 346, 374 (comments by Richard Bissell), p. 495 (comments by Kim Philby); Philby, op. cit., p. 164; Dvinov, *Politics of the Russian Emigration,* pp. 188–89; Ohletz interrogation, loc. cit; Cookridge, op. cit., pp. 237–64; Powers, op. cit., pp. 46ff. and 404; and Thomas Bell Smith, *The Essential CIA* (self-published [?], n.d. [1976?]) available through the Library of Congress at JK468.I6554.

39. "UN Debate Item 70," p. 3. See also Jorden, op. cit.

Chapter Thirteen

1. Benno W. Varon, "The Nazis' Friends in Rome," *Midstream* (April 1984), Charles Allen, "The Vatican and the Nazis," *Reform Judaism* (Spring–Summer 1983), and Gitta Sereny, *Into That Darkness* (New York: Vintage, 1983). See particularly: Vincent LaVista, "Illegal Emigration Movements in and Through Italy," May 15, 1947 (top secret), FW 800.0128/5-1547, RG 59, NA, Washington, D.C., hereinafter cited as *La Vista.* Charles Allen deserves credit for first unearthing the *La Vista* records. The identities of prelates who were reported to have been involved in illegal emigration, in some cases including Nazi smuggling, appear in *La Vista* Appendix "A." Appendix "B" was written by U.S. Army CIC Special Agent Leo J. Pagmotta in December 1946 in connection with Operation Circle, an investigation into a mass escape of prisoners from the Rimini POW camp north of Rome. The prisoners were reported to

have fled Europe with Vatican assistance. Further documentation on those events can be found in Case No. 4111, CIC Rome Detachment, Zone Five: "Operation Circle: Investigation of Illegal Emigration Movements,". December 26(?), 1946 (secret). Also Ivo Omercanin interview, January 9, 1986. See also Tomas Eloy Martinez, "Perón and the Nazi War Criminals," Colloquium Paper of the Woodrow Wilson International Center for Scholars, Washington, D.C., April 26, 1984, p. 2.

2. For official confirmation concerning the CIA's role in RFE, RL, and the ACEN, see *Price,* op. cit.

   For notes on prominent Intermarium personalities, see Ferenc Vajda, U.S. Army INSCOM Dossier No. XE232094I9C003, Document 55, "Prominent Members of Intermarium," and Documents 49–51, "Memorandum for the Officer in Charge, Subject: Intermarium," June 23, 1947 (secret). On role of prominent Intermarium personalities to Christian Democratic Union of Central Europe (CDU/CE), see *Freedom, Prerequisite to Lasting Peace* (New York: CDU/CE, 1957), p. 121ff., and Charles R. Dechert, "The Christian Democratic International," *Orbis* (Spring 1967), p. 106ff. For CDU/CE's relationship with the Free Europe Committee, see NCFE, *President's Report,* particularly for 1953 and 1954, chapters headed "Division of Exile Relations." See also Zygmunt Nagorski, "Liberation Movements in Exile," *Journal of Central European Affairs* (July 1950), pp. 139–40. Also, Charles Dechert interview, April 16, 1984.

3. On the role of clerical-Fascist parties in the Holocaust, see Levin, op. cit, pp. 507–17 (on Ustachis in Croatia) and 527–47 (on Slovakia). Yeshayahu Jelinek's "Storm Troopers in Slovakia: The Rodobrana and the Hlinka Guard," *Journal of Contemporary History,* vol. 6, no. 3 (1971), p. 97ff., is a good review of Slovakian clerical-Fascist history, including its complex internal political feuds; see particularly pp. 97–98, 103–04, and 111ff. on Catholic ideology and role of Hlinka Guards in Holocaust. For postwar U.S. government acknowledgment of Hlinka collaboration, see U.S. Displaced Persons Commission, op. cit., p. 6. On renewed killings of Jews in Slovakia, see Levin, op. cit., and Dawidowicz, op. cit, pp. 509–17 and 527–30.

   For text and commentary on 1941 Vichy document discussed in footnote, see L. Poliakov, "The Vatican and the Jewish Question," tr. Rosa Mencher, *Commentary* (November 1950), pp. 444–45. Poliakov was at the time of the article research director for the Centre de Documentation Juive Contemporaine in Paris.

   For useful summaries of examples of Vatican efforts on behalf of European Jewry, see Poliakov, op. cit., pp. 440–43, and A. Rhodes, *The Vatican in the Age of Dictators* (London: Hodder & Stoughton, 1973). See also Alexander Ramati, *The Assisi Underground* (New York: Stein & Day, 1978).

4. Benno W. Varon, "The Nazis' Friends in Rome," *Midstream* (April 1984), p. 13.

5. *La Vista,* Appendix A.

6. Ibid., pp. 2, 10.

7. For notes on Intermarium personalities, see VAJDA, Ferenc, INSCOM dossier no. XE232094I9C003, Documents 45, 49–51.

   On the rescue of the Ukrainian Waffen SS Division discussed in the footnote, see Shandruk, op. cit., pp. 290–96, with correspondence from Archbishop Buchko reproduced on pp. 295–96. Also based on author's interview with Buchko's former secretary Wacyl Lencyk, July 30, 1984. On the activities of the Ukrainian SS division, see Stein, op. cit., pp. 185–88. On the Ukrainian division's enlistment of concentration camp guards and *Einsatzkommandos,* see pp. 258–64. See also Basil Dmytryshyn, "The Nazis and the SS Volunteer Division 'Galicia,' " *American Slavic and East European Review,* vol. 15 (February 1956), pp. 1–10, and "The Polish-Ukrainian Military Staff," *Final Interrogation Report,* Ref. No. SAIC/FIR/34, August 28, 1945 (confidential), Enemy POW Interrogation File, Box 721, RG 165, NA, Washington, D.C.

On Archbishop Ivan Buchko (sometimes transliterated as Buczko), see U.S. Army INSCOM Dossier No. XE232094I9C003, Document 55, concerning Buchko's role in Intermarium and as "leader of UK [Ukrainian] resistance movement." LaVista's note concerning Buchko is in *La Vista,* Appendix A, and includes address of refugee relief agency in Rome. Walter Dushnyck's glowing "Archbishop Buchko—Arch-Shepherd of Ukrainian Refugees," *Ukrainian Quarterly* (Spring 1975), pp. 32–43, written shortly after Buchko's death, is the most comprehensive review of his life available in English at present; see p. 41 for Dushnyk's account of Buchko's role in halting Operation Keelhaul. See also Armstrong, op. cit., pp. 60–61.

8. Ferenc Vajda, INSCOM Dossier No. XE232094I9C003, Documents 49–51, "Memorandum for the Officer in Charge, Subject: Intermarium," June 23, 1947 (secret).

9. For Intermarium's program, see "The Ideological Basis of the Confederation of Central-Eastern Europe," and Gustav Celmin, "From the Idea of Intermarium to Its Realization," both in *Intermarium Bulletin* (Rome), no. 5 (January 1947); quote on crushing Soviet military is from the latter article. For map of desired territories, see *Miedzymorze* (Rome: 1946). For examples of repression of the group in Eastern Europe, see "Political Aspirations of Emigrants and Their Homeland Reactions," *Intermarium Bulletin,* no. 9 (1948), pp. 9–10.

Intermarium's own publications are scarce, but those that are available remain a rich source of information on the personalities and politics of the movement. FBI File No. 65-38136, Serials 117 and 132, obtained via the FOIA, contain copies of *Intermarium Bulletin,* no. 4 (December 1945) and no. 5 (January 1947), in French and English, as well as a copy of *The Free Intermarium Charter* (1945) and some fragmentary sanitized bureau correspondence concerning the group. The New York Public Library holds a collection of early French-language *Intermarium Bulletins.* The Library of Congress holds nos. 4 through 12 and 14–16.

Internal evidence in both the Vajda and Dragonovic INSCOM files indicates that a specific group of intelligence reports concerning Intermarium was prepared by U.S. Army CIC in Vienna and Rome. INSCOM, unfortunately, asserts that it is not able to locate that material. Department of State coverage of the evolution of this organization includes Report 800.43 International of Liberty/7-1548, July 15, 1948, from Frankfurt, RG 59, NA, Washington, D.C. OSS reporting appears to have been limited to Report 3145, "Central European Federal Club," RG 226, NA, Washington, D.C. No CIA reports are known to be publicly available.

10. Ferenc Vajda, INSCOM Dossier No. XE232094I9C003, Documents 49–51, "Memorandum for the Officer in Charge, Subject: Intermarium." The incident discussed at this point in the text concerns the escape of Olivar Virtschologi-Rupprecht, an associate of Vajda's.

11. On Vajda affair, including his role in looting and other crimes, ibid. Quoted reference letter by Gowen is at "From: HQ Dept of the Army from Dir Intelligence Div, to: EUCOM," February 11, 1948 (confidential), on Document 36; on Castel Gandolfo incident, see "Summary of Information: VAJTA, Ferenc," September 9, 1947 (secret), Documents 42–43. See also U.S. Department of State, "Subject: Vajda, Ferenc," 111.20A/3-2448 (secret) and "Subject: Comments re: Biographical Data," 111.20A/3-3048 (secret) and "Subject: Ferenc Vajda," 111.20A/4-1048 (with attachments in French written by Vajda), (secret), all dating from 1948 in RG 59, NA, Washington, D.C. See also Department of State's cable from Budapest to the secretary of state (no decimal file number; obtained via FOIA) January 10, 1948 (secret) re: Ferenc Vajda and Richard Wilford's long memorandum on Intermarium titled "Recent Developments Concerning the Establishment in Madrid of an Anti-Communist 'Eastern European Center,' " December 20, 1947 (secret). The latter document includes a detailed essay by Vajda titled "The History of the Exile Groups" as an appendix, which is particularly useful in its discussion of the political alignments of major Intermarium personalities. Wilford's study suggests that Vajda may have been plotting to lead a breakaway movement within Intermarium and was traveling to the United States in the hopes of securing substantial U.S. aid for his group. For contemporary coverage of the Vajda affair, see "Ferenc Vatja [*sic*] Arrested" *New York Times,* January 10, 1948, p. 6, and "Plan to Hear Consul in Vajta [*sic*] Case," *New York Times,* January 12, 1948, p. 4.

12. "Nagy Calls Vatja [*sic*] Nazi," *New York Times,* January 16, 1948, p. 4. For Gowen quote concerning Pearson, see Gowen's "Summary Report of Investigation: VAJTA, Ferenc," March 22, 1948 (top secret) in Vajda INSCOM dossier, Documents 9–13, with quoted portion in Document 13.

The FBI has recently released a heavily censored group of files concerning Vajda's stay in the United States. These include copies of a considerable amount of contemporary newspaper coverage and memos complaining that the Department of Justice was being blamed in the media for the entry of Nazis into the United States, when in fact, "the responsibility for [this] clearly lies with other Government departments or agencies" (Ladd memo to director, FBI, February 11, 1948, secret). Among the more interesting bureau records is a copy of a newspaper column by Spencer Irwin noting that Vajda "claimed that he was brought over here by the War Department and would be consulted by it to formulate a plan. This assertion," Irwin continues, "will bear the most thorough investigation." In reality, however, the entire matter was quickly dropped following a brief and largely secret congressional inquiry. See Spencer Irwin, "Behind the Foreign News," *Cleveland Plain Dealer,* January 4, 1948.

The Hungarian government attempted to extradite Vajda for war crimes on July 20, 1950, but was rebuffed on the grounds that he was no longer in U.S.

custody. See Department of State records 211.6415, Vajtha [*sic*], Ferenc/7-2050, with attachments, obtained by the author via FOIA.

13. On congressional inquiry, "Inquiry Finds Vajta [*sic*] Lacked Passport," *New York Times*, January 15, 1948, p. 11. On Vajda's refuge at College of the Andes, see declassified State Department records: "Memorandum for the files on Ferenc Vajta, 3/27/56" with attached correspondence from Vajda (confidential), 911 6221/4-1756, RG 59, NA, Washington, D.C. Also Allan Ryan interview, May 9, 1984.

On Adolf Berle's role as a conduit for agency funds, see Jim Schachter, "Adolf Berle, Late Professor of Law, a Founder of 50's CIA Drug Test Front," *Columbia* [University] *Daily Spectator* October 31, 1977, p. 1.

14. Gustav Celmins's role in Intermarium is established in Ferenc Vajda, INSCOM Dossier No. XE23209419C003, Document 55, and in Gustav Celmins's "From the Idea of Intermarium to Its Realization," *Intermarium Bulletin* (Rome), no. 5 (January 1947). For later teaching role and expulsion from the United States, see *CIA Eastern Front Study*, Addendum E: "The Baltic States," p. 3, for data concerning Celmins's Fascist record, entry into the United States, work in Syracuse, and eventual flight to Mexico. On the genocidal role of the Perkonkrusts, see *List of Organizations Considered Inimical to the United States Under PL 774*, loc. cit. p. 19.

15. For staffing of ACEN, see Assembly of Captive European Nations, op cit., p. 177ff.; note roles of Alfreds Berzins (p. 183) and Boleslavs Maikovskis (p. 186). For U.S. government statements concerning wartime role of these individuals, see CROWCASS, *Wanted List No. 14*, loc. cit. (on Berzins); Office of Special Investigations, op. cit., pp. 34–35 (on Maikovskis).

16. Assembly of Captive European Nations, op. cit., pp. 132, 139, 170–171, 180, and 187 (on Dosti); pp. 153, 183, 187, and 189 (on Berzins).

17. Ivo Omrcanin interview, January 9, 1986. On Krunoslav Dragonovic's role in Intermarium, see Ferenc Vajda, INSCOM Dossier No. XE23209419C003, Case No. 5080, "Subject: Intermarium," June 23, 1947 (secret), Document No. 50. On Dragonovic's wartime role, see *Martyrdom of the Serbs* (Serbian Eastern Orthodox Diocese, n.d. [1943?]), p. 274. On Dragonovic's role in escape routes for Croatian Fascist Ustachis, see Krunoslav Dragonovic, INSCOM Dossier XE 207018, CIC Special Agent Robert C. Mudd, "Summary of Information: Father Krunoslav DRAGANOVIC [*sic*]," February 12, 1947 (secret), Document Nos. 311–313. See also Mudd's report of September 5, 1947 (secret) for list of Ustachi fugitives under Dragonovic's care in 1947, Document nos. 307–310. Dragonovic's organization, the Istituto di St. Jeronimus in Rome, is also cited in *La Vista*, Appendix A, as a channel of illegal immigration. For further information on Ustachi participation in Intermarium, see also "Croatian Activities in the Emmigration [*sic*]," Report No. R-3-50, January 3, 1950, source: ODDI Hq USFA (Rear) (secret), which notes that "some high ranking personalities of the Ustacha in Austria, in conjunction with . . . the Catholic Church, are assertedly attempting to establish the 'Intermarium' or 'Inter-Danube States,' to be composed of all the Catholic nations of Southeastern Europe"—obtained from U.S. Army INSCOM via the Freedom of Information Act. On escape of Ustachi, see 860H.20235/7-2347, July 23, 1947 (secret), with

attachments, RG 59, NA, Washington, D.C. Also of interest is an exchange of diplomatic notes between J. Graham Parsons (U.S. Embassy, Rome) and Walter Dowling (EE Division, State Department HQ), dated May 22, 1947, and July 26, 1947, concerning the escape of Ante Pavelic disguised in priest's robes. On escape of Pavelic and Artukovic, see Ryan, *Barbie Report,* pp. 136n.–37n., and Howard Blum, *Wanted: The Search for Nazis in America* (Greenwich, Conn.: Fawcett, 1977), pp. 187–88.

18. Ryan, *Barbie Report,* p. 135ff.
19. For Lyon quotes and role of Lyon and Crawford, see CIC Agent Paul Lyon, "Rat Line from Austria to South America," July 12, 1948 (top secret), and Paul Lyon, "History of the Italian Rat Line," April 10, 1950 (top secret), obtained via FOIA from U.S. Army INSCOM, Fort Meade, Md. Department of Justice's version: Ryan, *Barbie Report,* p. 135ff.
20. CIC Special Agent Robert C. Mudd, op. cit. See also Mudd's report of September 5, 1947 (secret) for list of Ustachi fugitives under Dragonovic's care in 1947, Document Nos. 307–310. Both are in Dragonovic, INSCOM Dossier XE 207018.
21. Ryan, *Barbie Report,* p. 28ff. On Barbie, see also Magnus Linklater, Isabel Hilton, and Neal Ascherson, *The Nazi Legacy* (New York: Holt, Rinehart & Winston, 1984); Murphy, op. cit.; Tom Bower, *Klaus Barbie* (New York: Pantheon, 1984).
22. Klaus Barbie CI Special Interrogation Report 62 (CI-SIR/62), April 15, 1948 (secret), reproduced in Ryan, *Barbie Exhibits,* Tab 27.
23. Lieutenant Colonel Ellington Golden to commanding officer, Hq 970th CIC Detachment, "Subject: Klaus BARBIE," December 11, 1947 (top secret); and E. Dabringhaus, "Agents' [*sic*] Monthly Report," September 15, 1948 (top secret), reproduced in Ryan, *Barbie Exhibits,* Tabs 18 and 31.
24. Russ Belant, "Prof. Discusses US Ties to Postwar Nazis," (Wayne State University) *The South End* (February 14, 1983). Erhard Dabringhaus interview, January 1986.
25. Ryan, *Barbie Report,* p. 69n. On Reny Hardy Affair, see Linklater et al., op. cit. pp. 77–96 passim.
26. Ibid., p. 78.
27. Ibid., pp. 150–54. See also George Neagoy, "Memorandum for the Record, Subject: Disposal of Dropped Intelligence Informant," March 27, 1951 (top secret), reproduced in Ryan, *Barbie Exhibits,* Tab 104.
28. Konrad Adenauer, *Memoirs 1945–1953,* tr. Beate Ruhm von Oppen (Chicago: Henry Regnery Co., 1966), p. 445, cited in Tom Bower, *Blind Eye to Murder* (London: Paladin-Grenada, 1983), p. 421, hereinafter cited as Bower, *Blind Eye.* For accounts of McCloy's amnesties from varying perspectives, see Bower, *Blind Eye,* pp. 411ff., and Benjamin Ferencz, *Less Than Slaves* (Cambridge, Mass.: Harvard University Press, 1979), p. 72ff. On U.S. consideration of a nuclear attack in the Korean War, see Gregg Herken, *The Winning Weapon* (New York: Vintage, 1982), pp. 332–335.
29. Bower, *Blind Eye,* p. 415.
30. Office of the U.S. High Commissioner for Germany's Office of Public Affairs, "Landsberg: A Documentary Report," *Information Bulletin* (February 15, 1950) p. 1ff.

31. Ibid.

32. Bower, *Blind Eye*, p. 418. See also Joseph Borkin, *The Crime and Punishment of I. G. Farben* (New York: Free Press, 1978).

33. Ryan, *Quiet Neighbors*, pp. 280–84. See also following correspondence obtained via FOIA for documentary background: Representative Peter Rodino to comptroller general, February 17, 1983; Allan Ryan to Joseph Moore (FBI), February 18, 1983; and GAO Director William Anderson to FBI Director William Webster, March 2, 1983. A sanitized version of Barbie's FBI file available via FOIA includes similar internal DOJ correspondence on this investigation; see FBI File No. 105-221892 on Klaus Barbie.

34. Ryan, *Barbie Report*, p. 212.

35. Lyon, "History of the Italian Rat Line," loc. cit.

36. Lyon, "Rat Line from Austria to South America," loc. cit.

37. Lyon, "History of the Italian Rat Line," loc. cit.

38. Ryan, *Barbie Report*, p. 158, and Allan Ryan interview, May 9, 1984.

39. Lyon, "History of the Italian Rat Line," loc. cit. Bishop's name has been removed from the version of this document published by the Department of Justice; see Ryan, *Barbie Exhibits*, Tab 94.

40. Bishop and Crayfield, op. cit., p. 7. See Brown, op. cit., pp. 679–81, on Bishop's work in Bucharest. On Bishop's intelligence work, see also "American Military Unit in Bucharest" (secret), *Mediterranean Theater of Operations Security Histories*, Folder 195b, Box 39, Entry 99, RG 226, records of the OSS, NA, Washington, D.C.; based also on Seraphim Buta interview, April 18, 1985. Bishop's own recounting of the liberation of Romania is found in Colonel Robert Bishop, "I Saw the Reds Taste Freedom," *Collier's* (December 25, 1948). Bishop's ongoing work for U.S. intelligence is not mentioned in the *Collier's* text. The National Personnel Records Center reports that its records indicate that Bishop died on November 28, 1958.

41. Lyon, "History of the Italian Rat Line," loc. cit.

42. John M. Hobbins, "Memorandum for the Record, Subject: Informant Disposal, Emigration Methods of the 430th CIC Detachment," n.d. (top secret), reproduced in Ryan, *Barbie Exhibits*, Tab. 96, with quote on pp. 7–8. On Justice Department's denial of CIA involvement mentioned above in the text, see Ryan, *Barbie Report*, p. 145n.

43. Neagoy transfer to the CIA: Ryan, *Barbie Report*, p. 145n. Dragonovic and U.S. intelligence: Dragonovic, INSCOM dossier XE 207018, "Operational Work Sheet, 20 Oct '60, Subject: Krunoslav Stefano Dragonovic" (confidential), Document 127.

44. Linklater et al., op. cit., pp. 195–96. On currency smuggling trial, see documents 038–043 of Dragonovic's CIC dossier. On association with Bonifacic, see Bonifacic and Mihnovich, op. cit., p. 293ff.

45. Nathaniel Sheppard, "Arrest of Nine Terror Suspects Brings Uneasy Calm to Croatian-Americans," *New York Times*, July 23, 1981, p. 8; Arnold Lubasch, "10 Croatians on Trial on Racketeering Charge," *New York Times*, February 21, 1982, p. 6; "Six Croatians Convicted in NY of Plots Against Countrymen," *Washington Post*, May 16, 1982, p. 12; "6 Croatian Nationalists Given Long Prison Terms by Judge," *New York Times*, July 4, 1982, p. 13; Arnold Lubasch, "Use of Racketeering Law Is Barred in Case Against Croatian Terrorists," *New*

York Times, January 27, 1983, p. 5. Croatian terrorists have also been very active in Australia and are reported to have been involved in a complex scandal involving tacit sponsorship by the Australian Secret Intelligence Organization (ASIO); see "Australian Police Raid Secret Service," *Washington Star,* March 16, 1973, and Joan Coxsedge, "One, Two, Three—Ustasha Are We!" Melbourne (Australia) Unitarian Peace Memorial Church Pamphlet No. 1, 1972.

Chapter Fourteen

1. Virtually all National Security Council documentation concerning NSC 86, NSCID 13, and NSCID 14 remains classified. Brief declassified discussions of the status and general program of these decisions can be found, however, at *National Security Council, Status of Projects Report,* for January 18, and 30, 1950 (p. 2); March 13, 1950 (p. 1); October 2, 1950 (p. 4); October 16, 1950 (p. 14); October 23, 1950 (pp. 14–15); November 20, 1950 (pp. 15–16); February 26, 1951 (p. 14); March 26, 1951 (pp. 11–12); April 2, 1951 (pp. 9–10); April 23, 1951 (p. 1); July 28, 1952 (p. 3); August 11, 1952 (p. 1). A small collection of heavily sanitized correspondence and memos concerning NSC 86 was released following an FOIA request by the author. Of this group, see particularly "Memorandum for the Ad Hoc Committee on NSC 86, Subject: U.S. Policy on Defectors," February 8, 1951 (top secret), with attachments, and Francis Stevens, "In the Present World Struggle for Power . . . [title and date deleted, 1950?]," Document 10205 (secret), NSC 86 file, RG 273, NA, Washington, D.C., which, although largely censored, outline the main purposes and tactics of the defector program. Stevens argues that the return of General Vlasov and his senior officers to the USSR at the close of World War II was an error. Extending asylum to ROA veterans was later undertaken "at first clandestinely and recently more openly," he writes. See also National Security Council, *Policies of the Government of the United States of America Relating to the National Security,* vol. III, 1950 (top secret), p. 148, and vol. IV, 1951 (top secret), pp. 40–41, RG 273, NA, Washington, D.C. Additional documentation is at National Security Council, *Record of Actions,* January 19, 1950 (No. 274); March 3, 1950 (No. 281); October 12, 1950 (No. 364); April 18, 1951 (No. 462); and Actions No. 662–663 (all top secret), now at RG 273, NA, Washington, D.C. See also NSC 5706, loc. cit. On the escapee program, which was a major component of U.S. handling of defectors during this period, see Edward W. Lawrence, "The Escapee Program," *Information Bulletin,* Office of the U.S. High Commissioner for Germany (March 1952), p. 6ff. See also James P. O'Donnell, "They Tell Us Stalin's Secrets," *Saturday Evening Post* (May 3, 1952), p. 32ff.

2. NSC 5706, loc. cit. On International Rescue Committee, see John M. Crewdson, "Group Led by CIA Board Nominee Reportedly Got $15,000 from Agency," *New York Times,* February 20, 1976, and U.S. Displaced Persons Commission, *The DP Story: Final Report of the U.S. Displaced Persons Commission* (Washington, D.C.: Government Printing Office, 1952), pp. 270, 285–86, 289, and 292–93 on the IRC, National Catholic Welfare Conference, Tolstoy Foundation, Latvian Relief, Inc., United Lithuanian Relief Fund of America, and other beneficiaries of U.S. government refugee relief aid. See

also NCFE, *President's Report*, for 1953 (p. 18ff.) and 1954 (pp. 18–24), on aid to groups primarily underwritten by the NCFE.

3. For Saltonstall comment and McCone's reply, see Wise and Ross, op. cit., p. 130n. On use of CIA funds to lobby Congress mentioned above in text, see Price, op. cit., p. CRS-10, and documents released through Department of State FOIA Case no. 8404249, September 25, 1986, loc. cit.

For congressional testimony and lobbying activities by ACEN leaders, see Committee on the Judiciary, U.S. Senate, *A Study of Anatomy of Communist Takeovers Prepared by the Assembly of Captive European Nations* (Washington, D.C.: Government Printing Office, 1966); Committee on Un-American Activities, U.S. House of Representatives, *International Communism* (Washington, D.C.: Government Printing Office, 1956); Select Committee to Investigate the Incorporation of the Baltic States into the USSR, U.S. House of Representatives, *Hearings* (Washington, D.C.: Government Printing Office, 1953); see also National Committee for a Free Europe, *President's Report*, 1953, p. 18ff., and 1954, p. 18ff. For discussions of the role of Eastern European exile associations in lobbying Congress, see "[Representative] Kersten's Investigatory House Committee Meets in Munich," *ABN Correspondence* (May–September 1954), p. 1; "Lithuanian American Council," *Lituanus* (July 1955), p. 23, about lobbying against the genocide treaty and in favor of creation of congressional investigating committees; and V. S. Vardys, "Congressional Investigations of Communists Abroad," *Lituanus* (February 1956), concerning the Katyn investigation, the Kersten Amendment, creation of Escapee Program, role in congressional elections; and Mathias, op. cit., p. 975ff.

A particularly valuable source is a 600-page U.S. Department of State dossier on the ACEN released under the FOIA. It includes correspondence between State and the ACEN, plus a number of reports and other material concerning ACEN lobbying on Capitol Hill and in the executive branch that are unavailable elsewhere. For an example of ACEN lobbying, see ACEN correspondence with Senator John F. Kennedy, March 3, 1958 (thanking him for receiving ACEN delegation); ACEN solicitation of Kennedy endorsement and support, March 17, 1958; Kennedy telegram of support, April 24, 1958; ACEN letter to Kennedy, July 1, 1960; reply, July 13, 1960; in John F. Kennedy Pre-Presidential Collection, Legislative Files, Box 687, John F. Kennedy Library, Boston, Massachusetts.

4. On "thousands of Waffen SS veterans and other Nazi collaborators," see Ryan, *Quiet Neighbors*, pp. 26–27. On political role of these people within the broader Eastern European immigration, please see the detailed discussion that follows in the text and source notes.

5. *1985 GAO Report;* see also Ralph Blumenthal, "2 War Criminals Had Official Help in Getting to U.S., Study Finds," *New York Times*, June 29, 1985; Thomas O'Toole, "The Secret Under the Little Cemetery," *Washington Post*, May 23, 1982; Charles Allen, *Nazi War Criminals in America: Facts . . . Action* (Albany, N.Y.: Charles Allen Productions, Inc., 1981).

On CIA desire for thousands of informants and covert operations, see "Explanatory Background Information for the Guidance of Consular Officers in Implementing Section 2, Subsection (d) of the Displaced Persons Act," February 24, 1950 (confidential), AG 383.7 1948–1949–1950, RG 407, NA, Washington, D.C. These State Department records are contained in the files of the Army Adjutant General's Office.

6. Ibid.
7. Ibid.

The Council for a Free Czechoslovakia boasts of receiving such "in blank" visas in its publication *In Search of Haven* (Washington, D.C.: Council for a Free Czechoslovakia, 1950). On political use of these visas, see also Kurt Glaser, "Psychological Warfare's Policy Feedback," *Ukrainian Quarterly* (Spring 1953), p. 175. Glaser contends that the visas were extended too freely to the more liberal groupings among Eastern European émigrés such as the Council for a Free Czechoslovakia, resulting in a supposedly "soft" line on the USSR among U.S. intelligence analysts in 1953. For data on CIA funding of exile groups mentioned in text, see source note 2, above.

8. NSC 5706, loc. cit., p. 2 (paragraph 5), 6 (paragraph 16, 17), 9 (paragraph 26), 13ff., and 23 (CIA coordination of defector cases).
9. For funding data, see NSC 5706, loc. cit.; "Operations Coordinating Board Report on U.S. Policy on Defectors, Escapees and Refugees from Communist Areas," of July 9, 1958, January 21 and July 15, 1959, and September 14, 1960, National Security Council Policy Papers file, RG 273, NA, Washington, D.C.; U.S. Displaced Persons Commission, op. cit.; and Comptroller General of the United States, *U.S. Government Monies Provided to Radio Free Europe and Radio Liberty,* loc. cit.

In a nutshell, the NSC's committee responsible for authorization and coordination of CIA clandestine operations (named the Operations Coordinating Board during the Eisenhower administration) was given responsibility for oversight and coordination of both clandestine and "overt" refugee aid funds channeled through the CIA, International Cooperation Administration, Department of Agriculture's surplus food programs, and others. These funds were then extended to private refugee relief agencies favored by the government for their ability to "contribut[e] to the achievement of U.S. national security objectives both toward Communist-dominated areas and the Free World" (NSC 5706, p. 2). Many aspects of this large program remain secret to this day. Even so, the available records clearly establish that, first, intelligence-gathering and national security objectives were the government's central rationale for funding relief programs serving Soviet bloc refugees and, secondly, that refugee programs were an integral part of the U.S. government's broader covert action strategy during the 1950s.

10. NSC 5706, pp. 2, 13.
11. On Vanagis' postwar role in Displaced Persons camps, see *Daugavas Vanagi Biletens* (November 1955), available in the New York Public Library. On Latvian militia participation in pogroms and mass murders, see Hilberg, op. cit., pp. 204–205 and 254, and Gilbert, *Holocaust,* pp. 155–57 and 388. On their flight to Germany at war's end, Dallin, *German Rule,* p. 621n. For the Vanagis' own version of their role in the SS and in Nazi collaboration in Latvia, see *Daugavas Vanagi Biletens* (November 1951, January 1953, February 1953, March 1953, and April 1953).
12. *Daugavas Vanagi Biletens* (November 1955). See also L. R. Wynar, *Encyclope-*

dic Directory of Ethnic Organizations in the United States (Littleton, Colo.: Libraries, Inc., 1975).

13. On IRC, see U.S. Displaced Persons Commission, op. cit., pp. 285–86 and 293. See also NCFE, *President's Report,* 1953, p. 22, and 1954, p. 18ff. For documentation concerning use of RFE for funding of exile leaders, see the correspondence released through Department of State FDIA Case No. 8404249, loc. cit.

14. On Hazners, see U.S. Department of Justice, Office of Special Investigations, op. cit. p. 25, and CBS television, *60 Minutes* transcript for May 17, 1982, pp. 8–9, which includes reporting of Hazners's wartime role and on Hazners's successful defense against an effort by the U.S. Justice Department to deport him. Hazners reproduces his Iron Cross award, signed by Adolf Hitler, in his autobiography: Vilis Arveds Hazners, *Varmacibas Torni* (Lincoln, Neb.: Vaidava, 1977).

15. For Hazners's role in the Committee for a Free Latvia, see Wynar, op. cit., and *Daugavas Vanagi Biletens,* loc. cit. On ACEN/CIA link, see Chapter Fourteen, source note 3, above.

16. *Daugavas Vanagi Biletens,* loc. cit.

17. U.S. Department of Justice, Office of Special Investigations, op. cit. pp. 34–35, and U.S. Department of Justice press statement of August 16, 1984. On Maikovskis's ACEN role, see Assembly of Captive European Nations, op. cit., p. 186. See also "Soviets Demand U.S. Extradite L. I. Man," *New York Times,* June 12, 1965; "Latvia Opens Trial of 61 on Charges of War Killings," *New York Times,* October 12, 1965, p. 5; "Riga Court Dooms 5 for Nazi Crimes," *New York Times,* October 31, 1965, p. 22; and Ralph Blumenthal, "U.S. Opens New Drive on Former Nazis," *New York Times,* December 30, 1973, p. 1. Maikovskis's attorney, Ivars Berzins, declined comment on this issue in a telephone interview, November 25, 1985.

18. Berzins's CROWCASS entry is found at CROWCASS, *Wanted List No. 14,* loc. cit., p. 14. See also Alfreds Berzins, INSCOM Dossier No. XE 257645 D 25A 2664 (secret); and Berzins's "Declaration of Intention" in INS File A7-845-451 concerning his arrival in the United States and subsequent application for citizenship.

19. Alfreds Berzins, INSCOM dossier no. XE 257645 D 25A 2664. Berzins's publications in the United States include Alfreds Berzins, *I Saw Vishinsky Bolshevize Latvia* (Washington, D.C.: Latvian Legation, 1948); Alfreds Berzins, *The Two Faces of Co-Existence* (New York: Robert Speller & Sons, 1967); *Latvia* (Washington, D.C.: American Latvian Association in the U.S., Inc., 1968); *The Unpunished Crime* (New York: Robert Speller & Sons, n.d.), with an introduction by Senator Thomas Dodd that features a brief—and erroneous—account of Berzins's wartime activities. On positions in Latvian organizations, see *Daugavas Vanagi Biletens* and ACEN, op. cit., pp. 153, 183, 187, and 189. See also Assembly of Captive European Nations, FBI file No. 105-32982 (obtained in sanitized form via the FOIA).

It is worth noting that the "Latvian Legation" in Washington, D.C., that financed many of Berzins's early postwar activities was actually a U.S. sponsored "government-in-exile" for Latvia created when the State Department refused to recognize the USSR's forcible annexation of Latvia (and Lithuania and Estonia) during the Hitler-Stalin pact period immediately prior to World War II. All Latvian financial assets in the United States were frozen, then turned over to an émigré "government," led primarily by former Latvian Ambassador to the U.S. Alfred Bilmanis. A full accounting of this money has never been made public, but it is clear that the émigrés spent substantial sums on publishing and diplomatic receptions throughout the 1940s and 1950s. An émigré Latvian "legation" continues to operate in Washington.

20. *Daugavas Vanagi Biletens* (February 1951). Hazners was editor of the *Biletens* at this point; the president of the organization at the time was V. Janums, who is also accused of war crimes by the present Soviet Latvian government.

21. U.S. Displaced Persons Commission, op. cit., pp. 100–02. For more on lobbying by religious groups in favor of admission to the United States of Baltic SS legions, see "Church Unit Denies War Is Inevitable," *New York Times,* January 18, 1951.

22. U.S. Displaced Persons Commission, op. cit. See also "Freedom Forecast for Baltic States," *New York Times,* June 17, 1951, p. 38; "Dr. Edward M. O'Connor, 77, Former NSC Staffer, Dies," *Washington Post,* November 27, 1985; and particularly "R.M.," "Edward O'Connor Remembered in Cleveland Ceremonies," *America* (January 27, 1986), p. 3.

23. Joseph Boley, "United Lithuanian Relief Fund of America," *Lituanus* (October 1956), p. 20ff. See also "Lithuanian Aid Sought, Relief Fund Plans to Bring 5,000 More D.P.'s Here," *New York Times,* January 17, 1951. For documentation on funding of BALF by the government and the Catholic Church, see U.S. Displaced Persons Commission, op. cit., p. 293.

24. On Lithuanians facing deportation for participation in Nazi crimes, see U.S. Department of Justice, Office of Special Investigations, op. cit., and U.S. Department of Justice press statements of July 8, 1983, March 27, June 1, and November 9, 1984, and April 29, 1985, concerning cases against ten Lithuanian veterans of the SS and members of collaborationist militia forces.

25. "Priest in Brooklyn as Soviet Tries Him on Wartime Charge," *New York Times,* March 9, 1964; "Soviet Lithuania Orders 7 Jailed as Nazi Aides," *New York Times,* March 16, 1964; and Ralph Blumenthal, "U.S. Opens New Drive on Former Nazis," loc. cit. For the Soviet Lithuanian government's account of Jankus's wartime activities, see *Who Is Hiding on Grand Street?* (Vilnius: Mintis Publishing House, 1964).

26. Comptroller General of the United States, *Widespread Conspiracy to Obstruct Probes of Alleged Nazi War Criminals Not Supported by Available Evidence—Controversy May Continue* (Washington, D.C.: Government Printing Office, 1978), GAO Report No. GGD-78-73, pp. 34–39. On Belorussian (White Russian) émigrés discussed in footnote above, see William Doherty, "Author: Documents Prove U.S. Recruited Russian Nazis," *Boston Globe,* February 19, 1985, p. 5; and John Loftus, "Covert Violations of Congressional Restrictions," paper (with archival facsimiles) prepared for media release, February 18, 1985.

27. Paddock, op. cit., pp. 121–23 and 129ff. Also Prouty interview, April 12, 1984.

28. Paddock, op. cit., pp. 121–23 and 149, and Simpson, *Inside the Green Berets,* loc. cit., pp. 24–25. See also "AG 342.18 GPA Subject: Enlistment in the

Regular Army of 2500 Aliens," June 1, 1951 (secret), RG 407, NA, Washington, D.C.

29. "File No. ID 907, Analysis of Available DP Manpower," February 25, 1948 (top secret), P&O 091.714 TS (Section 1, Case 1), RG 319, NA, Washington, D.C.

30. Ibid.

31. For assignments to atomic, chemical, and biological warfare missions, see "(M) 342.18 (10 Apr 52) Priorities and Special Qualifications for Enlistment of Aliens Under Public Law 597" (secret—security information), AG 342.18, 1948–1949–1950, RG 407, NA, Washington, D.C. For arrival and disposition of Lodge Act recruits, see series of surveys of various dates from 1951 to 1954 headed "AGTP-P 342.18 Screening of Lodge Bill Personnel for Special Forces Activities" (confidential), AG 342.18, 1948–1949–1950, RG 407, NA, Washington, D.C. For a popular presentation of one group of recruits, see William Ulman, "1,000 Red Army Vets Train GI's," *Nation's Business* (June 1955), p. 46ff.

32. On Bank's role in special warfare, see Paddock, op. cit., pp. 119–59 passim. On Bank's role in Barbie affair, see Ryan, *Barbie Exhibits*, Tab. 36.

33. Simpson, *Inside the Green Berets*, loc. cit., p. 39.

34. On Witsell ruling, see "AGSE 342.18 Subject: Enlistment in the Regular Army of Aliens," November 7, 1952, Special Regulations (restricted—security information), Tab B, p. 7, AG342.18, 1948–1949–1950, RG 407, NA, Washington, D.C. For enlistment figures, see Paddock, op. cit., p. 149.

35. Richard Harwood, "Green Berets Dislike 'Image,' " *Washington Post*, August 17, 1969.

36. "AGPT-P 342.18, "Screening of Lodge Bill Personnel for Special Forces Activities: Special Orders Number 68," March 23, 1954, with enclosures (confidential), AG342.18 1948–1949–1950, RG 407, NA, Washington, D.C.

37. See Paddock, op. cit., pp. 150 (for stress on insurgency) and 73 (on American way of life). On slogan, see *The Green Beret*, vol. II, no. 9 (September 1967), p. 15.

38. Ryan, *Quiet Neighbors*, pp. 26–27.

Chapter Fifteen

1. Collins, op. cit., p. 256ff.; NCFE, *President's Report*, for 1953, p. 18ff., and 1954, p. 18ff. On CIA funding for Crusade for Freedom (CFF), see Mickelson, op. cit., pp. 41 and 58.

2. Isaacson and Thomas, op. cit., pp. 496–97. For a more complete picture of liberation thinking during the early 1950s, including acknowledgment of the pivotal role of Vlasov Army veterans and other World War II collaborators, see Burnham, op. cit. p. 196ff., and James Burnham, *The Coming Defeat of Communism* (New York: John Day Co., c. 1950), p. 211ff. Burnham was a consultant to Wisner's OPC during this period and offers perhaps the most detailed exposition of liberation theory available in nonclassified literature. On this latter point, see George H. Nash, *The Conservative Intellectual Movement in America Since 1945* (New York: Basic Books, 1976), pp. 96–97 and 372.

3. Telephone interview with Walter Pforzheimer, November 20, 1983.

4. Mickelson, op. cit., p. 52.

5. James T. Howard, "200 Exiles Hammer by Radio at the Iron Curtain," *Washington Post*, September 17, 1950.
6. Department of State, Office of Intelligence and Research, *NTS—The Russian Solidarist Movement*, External Research Paper, series 3, no. 76, December 10, 1951, and Dvinov, *Politics of the Russian Emigration*, pp. 113–194, both of which clearly establish the anti-Semitic roots of the NTS. The NTS's own *NTS: Introduction to a Russian Freedom Party* (Frankfurt am Main: Possev-Verlag, 1979) and *Let Your Conscience Decide*, JPRS No. 4425 (Washington, D.C.: Joint Publication Research Service, 1961) provide the organization's own bowdlerized version of its history.

  The NTS today calls itself Narodno-Trudovoy Soyuz Rossiyskikh Solidaristov (NTS), a name that avoids the unpopular National Socialist connotations of the former Natsional'no-Trudovoi Soyuz title. Despite the name change, the leadership of the organization remains in essentially the same hands that have guided the group for decades.
7. State Department, *NTS—The Russian Solidarist Movement*, loc. cit., pp. 2–3.
8. Dallin, *German Rule*, p. 526; Buchardt, op. cit.; Dvinov, *Politics of Russian Emigration*, p. 113ff.
9. CIC Special Agent William Russell, "Summary Report of Investigation: Constantin Boldyreff," December 27, 1948 (confidential); and CIC Special Agent Seymour Milbert, "Memorandum for the Officer in Charge," August 19, 1945 (confidential), both located in Boldyreff, Constantin, INSCOM Dossier No. D-3675 20B85. Additional material has been obtained from the Department of State via the FOIA.
10. Boldyreff, INSCOM Dossier No. D-3675 20B85.
11. On Common Cause and its roots in the same circles that gave birth to NCFE, see *New York Times:* "Mayor at Yule Fete," December 9, 1950, p. 16; "300 Attend Party for Common Cause," December 8, 1951, p. 7; "Anti-Reds to Hold 'Congress of Free' " December 27, 1951; "Freedom Plaque on Sale," September 26, 1952, p. 15; and "Medina Reverses Himself, Bars Role as Honor Guest at Anti-Red Dinner," February 25, 1950, p. 1. Boldyreff's connection with Common Cause is established in the author's interview with him, August 8, 1983, and in Constantine Boldyreff (as told to Edward Paine), "The Story of One Russian Underground Organization Attempting to Overthrow Stalin," *Look* (October 26, 1948), p. 25ff. See also "Chief of Intelligence to OMGUS (Hesse), Subject: Constantin BOLDYREFF," November 8, 1948 (secret), in the Boldyreff INSCOM dossier. Boldyreff's visa to the United States was arranged with the assistance of the Tolstoy Foundation, according to army CIC records.
12. For typical newspaper coverage of Boldyreff during his first tour of the United States, see "Russians Are Ready to Revolt Says Leader of Underground," *Boston Herald*, October 11, 1948; "Russians Seen Ready to Revolt Against Stalin," *Baltimore Sun*, October 11, 1948; Ralph de Toledano, "Man from Russia," *Newsweek*, October 25, 1948, p. 38.
13. See citations in source note 12 above. See also Dvinov, *Politics of the Russian Emigration*, pp. 174–91 passim.
14. "Russians Are Ready to Revolt Says Leader of Underground," *Boston Herald*, October 11, 1948.
15. Boldyreff (as told to Paine), op. cit., pp. 25ff.; C. W. Boldyreff (with O. K.

Armstrong), "We Can Win the Cold War—in Russia," *Reader's Digest* (November 1950), p. 9ff.; C. W. Boldyreff, "Whither the Red Army," *World Affairs* (Fall 1953); C. W. Boldyreff (with James Critchlow), "How the Russian Underground Is Fighting Stalin's Slavery," *American Federationist* (May 1951), p. 14ff., with quote drawn from p. 14. (Critchlow eventually became a career executive with RFE/RL and by 1976 had become sharply critical of the extreme Russian nationalism of many RL broadcasts; see Mickelson, op. cit., p. 201.)

16. Cookridge, op. cit., p. 250; Boldyreff interview, August 8, 1983. For Vlasov Army colonization plan discussed in footnote, see American Consulate General, Casablanca, Morocco, "DP Resettlement Project in French Morocco," October 7, 1947 (confidential), with enclosed report from Boldyreff, 800.4016 DP/10–747, RG 59, NA, Washington, D.C. On NTS leaders' backgrounds as Nazi collaborators discussed in footnote, see State Department, *NTS—The Russian Solidarist Movement,* loc. cit., p. 3; Dvinov, *Politics of the Russian Emigration,* p. 190. On Tenzerov's recruitment by Augsburg, see Augsburg, INSCOM Dossier no. XE 004390 16B036.

The Soviet government has published documents which it claims are a CIA/British SIS agreement on the employment of NTS as an intelligence asset; see Cherezov, op. cit., pp. 54–62. The CIA generally denounces such revelations as forgeries, although it is not known to have done so in this case.

17. Boldyreff, INSCOM dossier no. D-3675 20B85; Boldyreff interview, August 8, 1983.

18. For Boldyreff's commentaries, see Nicola Sinevirsky (pseudonym), *SMERSH,* eds. Kermit and Milt Hill (New York: Henry Holt & Co., 1950). For Boldyreff's congressional testimony, see Subcommittee to Investigate the Administration of the Internal Security Act, U.S. Senate, *Strategy and Tactics of World Communism,* Part 1, May 15 and 27, 1954 (Washington, D.C.: Government Printing Office, 1954), p. 2ff.; Un-American Activities Committee, U.S. House of Representatives, *Communist Psychological Warfare (Thought Control)* (Washington, D.C.: Government Printing Office, 1958), which is described as a "consultation" with Boldyreff.

19. Vladimir Petrov interview, July 29, 1985.

20. *Church Committee Report,* Book IV, pp. 35 and 36n.

21. *Kennan vol. II,* pp. 97–99.

22. On $180,000 seed money, see Mickelson, op. cit., p. 52. For CFF funding data during the early 1950s, see Collins, op. cit., p. 279ff.; Mickelson, op. cit., p. 52ff.; Comptroller General of the United States, *US Government Monies Provided to Radio Free Europe and Radio Liberty,* loc. cit.; and *Supplement to Report on U.S. Government Monies* (secret), May 25, 1972 (classified annex), a sanitized version of which is available via the Freedom of Information Act.

23. NCFE, *President's Report,* 1954, p. 35.

24. Herbert E. Alexander, *Financing Politics: Money, Elections and Political Reform* (Washington, D.C.: CQ Press, 1984), Table 1, p. 7.

25. "Freedom Crusade Opens East-West TV," *Washington Post,* September 24, 1951. For discussion of CFF propaganda events, see Collins, op. cit., p. 256ff.; or Mickelson, op. cit., p. 51ff. For typical contemporary news coverage, see, for example, *Washington Post:* "Freedom Crusade Launched at Meeting in

Maryland," September 14, 1950; "Freedom Bell Here Monday for Crusade," October 1, 1950; "Churches to Participate in Freedom Crusade," October 7, 1950; "Eisenhower Opens Crusade for Freedom Behind 'Curtain,' " September 4, 1951; "Freedom Crusade Rally Scheduled," September 14, 1951; " 'Place in Sun' Premiere to Aid D.C. Crusade for Freedom," October 2, 1951; "Freedom Bell Pierces Curtain," October 20, 1953; "Parade to Open 'Freedom' Drive," January 28, 1954. Collins reports that the *New York Times* featured ninety-seven news articles—all of them favorable—about the CFF during the campaign's first two years of operation.

26. James T. Howard, "200 Exiles Hammer by Radio at the Iron Curtain," *Washington Post,* September 7, 1950.
27. "Freedom Forecast for Baltic States," *New York Times,* June 17, 1951; "Baltic Groups Here Hold Freedom Rally," *New York Times,* June 16, 1952; also, "1,800 Here Mark Latvia's Founding," *New York Times,* November 18, 1951; "Exile Leaders Join in 'Bill of Rights' " and "Text of Declaration by 10 Exiled Leaders," *New York Times,* June 13, 1952.
28. Thorwald, *Illusion,* pp. xv–xxii. The Gehlen official Heinz Danlo Herre had also served as chief of staff to Köstring and Herwarth during the Caucasus campaign during the war; see Dallin, *German Rule,* p. 543n.
29. Petrov interview, July 29, 1985.
30. Dulles testimony before House Foreign Affairs Committee, 1952, quoted in "A Fresh Wind from the USA," *ABN Correspondence,* no. 3–4 (1953), pp. 1–2; Petrov interview, July 29, 1985.
31. Dallin, *German Rule,* p. 497ff.
32. SANACC 395/1 (Operation Bloodstone), loc. cit.
33. "Russians Are Ready to Revolt Says Leader of Underground," *Boston Herald,* October 11, 1948.
34. "Text of the Republican Party's 1952 Campaign Platform," *New York Times,* July 11, 1952, p. 8.
35. John Foster Dulles, "A Policy of Boldness," *Life* (May 19, 1952), p. 146ff.
36. For an excellent account of Lane's lobbying and internal Republican party politics on the "ethnic voters" issue, see Louis L. Gerson, *The Hyphenate in Recent American Politics and Diplomacy* (Lawrence, Kan.: University of Kansas Press, 1964), p. 178ff. See also Vladimir Petrov, *A Study in Diplomacy: The Story of Arthur Bliss Lane* (Chicago: Henry Regnery Co., 1971).
37. Gerson, op. cit., p. 193 ("Liberation Weeks," etc.); Collins, op. cit., p. 329ff.; "D.P. Charges Enslaving of 500,000 Lithuanians," *New York Times,* July 18, 1950; "Freedom Forecast for Baltic States," *New York Times,* June 17, 1951; "Freedom Crusade Rally Scheduled," *Washington Post,* September 14, 1951; "Exile Leaders Join in 'Bill of Rights,' " *New York Times,* June 13, 1952; "Baltic Groups Hold Freedom Rally Here," *New York Times,* June 16, 1952.
38. Petrov interview, July 29, 1985; Vladimir Petrov, *Escape from the Future* (Bloomington, Ind.: Indiana University Press, 1973), p. 337ff., with incidents discussed in footnotes at pp. 341–42, 349–51, 354, 360–61. On Petrov's relation to 1952 election: Gerson, op. cit., p. 229, and Petrov interview, July 29, 1985.
39. Gerson, op. cit., p. 194.
40. Republican National Committee, "The Margin of Victory in Marginal Districts," cited in Gerson, op. cit., pp. 198–99.

41. Grombach, INSCOM dossier. See particularly "Summary of Information (SR 380–320–10)" reports for the following dates and subjects: "G-2 SPS GROMBACH, John Valentine," June 1, 1955 (top secret); "N. V. Philips Co," June 1, 1955 (top secret); "Grombach, John V.," September 23, 1958 (confidential); and memo from Brigadier General Richard Collins, director of plans, programs and security to ASCoSI, Subject: GROMBACH, John Valentine, September 30, 1958 (secret). On Philips's role, see Grombach letter to Colonel George F. Smith, April 12, 1950, and Collins report, September 5, 1958 (secret).

42. "Memorandum for File: Subj: GROMBACH, John V.," December 21, 1952, Naval Intelligence Command files, Document No. 62-77306, with attachments, obtained through FOIA.

43. Ray Ylitalo interview, June 18, 1984.

44. Lyman Kirkpatrick, *The Real CIA* (New York: Macmillan, 1968), p. 149ff. Also Lyman Kirkpatrick interview, April 11,1984.

45. Ylitalo interview, June 18, 1984.

46. Lyman Kirkpatrick interview, April 11, 1984.

47. Lyman Kirkpatrick interview, April 11, 1984, and Ylitalo interview, June 18, 1984. On leaks from McCarthy's office, see Kirkpatrick, op. cit., pp. 151–53; and Oshinsky, op. cit., p. 288n.

48. Kirkpatrick, op. cit., pp. 152–53.

For background on Grombach's long-standing dispute with the CIA, see Committee on Expenditures in the Executive Departments, U.S. House of Representatives, 80th Congress, *National Security Act of 1947* (Washington, D.C.: Government Printing Office, 1947). These unusual hearings were held to discuss the founding of a proposed central intelligence agency and were originally published in 1947 with the names of the witnesses suppressed. General Hoyt Vandenberg was thus originally identified only as "Mr. A," Allen Dulles became "Mr. B," and so on. Grombach testified on pp. 49–53 as "Mr. D" and strongly opposed extending overall authority over clandestine intelligence collection to any one agency. These hearings were eventually republished with new appendices in 1982 by the Committee on Government Operations and the Permanent Select Committee on Intelligence.

49. For coverage of Thayer's resignation, see "19 Lose U.S. Posts on Morals Charge," *New York Times,* April 21, 1953, p. 32; "Aide Will Be Queried on Resignation Story," *New York Times,* April 28, 1953, p. 36; and Oshinsky, op. cit., p. 288n. See also Charles Wheeler Thayer, U.S. Army INSCOM Dossier no. X8889748 (secret).

50. On Davies's role in Hilger immigration, see Berlin to Washington dispatch marked "Personal for Kennan," 862.00/9-2548, September 25, 1948 (top secret); Heidelberg to Washington dispatch marked "For Kennan," 862.00/9-2748, September 27, 1948 (top secret), which suggests use of false identities; Washington to Heidelberg, 862.00/9-2848, September 28, 1948 (top secret); Heidelberg to Washington, 862.00/9-3048, September 30, 1948 (top secret), all of which are found in RG 59, NA, Washington, D.C.

On Davies's role in Poppe's immigration, see "For [Carmel] Offie from [John Paton] Davies," 800.4016 DP/3-848, March 8, 1948 (secret); "For Offie from Davies," 893.00 Mongolia/3-1848, March 18, 1948 (secret); "For [James] Riddleberger from [George] Kennan," 861.00/10-2248, October 22, 1948 (secret—sanitized); "Personal for Kennan from Riddleberger," 861.00/11-248, November 2, 1948 (secret—sanitized); and "Personal for Riddleberger from Kennan," 800.4016 DP/5-449, May 3, 1949 (secret), signed also by Robert Joyce, all at RG 59, NA, Washington, D.C.

On Davies's role on Ulus and Sunsh affair, see "For [Carmel] Offie from [John Paton] Davies," May 27, 1948 (secret), 800.43 Eurasian Institute/5-2748 secret file; "From Tehran to Secretary of State, attention John Davies," re: Ulus and Sunsh, July 27, 1948 (secret), 800.43 Eurasian Institute/7-2748 secret file; "Department of State to AMEMBASSY, Tehran," re: Sunsh, July 27, 1948 (secret), 800.43 Eurasian Institute/7-2748; "For Davies from Dooher," re: Ulus, August 12, 1948 (secret), 800.43 Eurasian Institute/8-1248; "Department of State to AMEMBASSY, Athens," initialed by Kennan, October 12, 1948 (secret), 800.43 Eurasion [*sic*] Institute/10-1248, all in RG 59, NA, Washington, D.C. Also Poppe interviews, October 26 and December 4, 1984, Davies interview, November 28, 1983, and Evron Kirkpatrick interview, November 10, 1983.

51. For *Times's* characterization of Davies's position, see *New York Times Index,* 1954, p. 1154; for Davies's characterization, Davies interview, November 28, 1983.

52. For an account of Tawney Pippet, see testimony of Lyle H. Munson in Subcommittee to Investigate the Administration of the Internal Security Act, U.S. Senate, *Hearings on the Institute of Pacific Relations* (Washington, D.C.: Government Printing Office, 1952), p. 2751ff., and Robert Steele (Lately Thomas), *When Even Angels Wept* (New York: Morrow, 1973), p. 376n.

53. Walter Waggoner, "Dulles Dismisses Davies as a Risk; Loyalty Not Issue," *New York Times,* November 6, 1954, p. 1; and "Text of Statements by Davies and Dulles on the Former's Ouster," *New York Times,* November 6, 1954, p. 8. For a concise overview of the Davies affair and its aftermath, see James Fetzer, "The Case of John Paton Davies," *Foreign Service Journal* (November 1977), p. 15ff., with quote from Dulles on p. 31. See also John Paton Davies, *Foreign and Other Affairs* (New York: W. W. Norton, 1966).

54. Bohlen, op. cit., p. 71ff.

55. Oshinsky, op. cit., pp. 286–93, with quote on p. 292.

56. Ibid.

57. Ylitalo interview, June 18, 1984. Also Petrov interview, July 29, 1985, and, for Bogolepov's own account of his life, see Subcommittee to Investigate the Administration of the Internal Security Act, op. cit., p. 4479ff.

58. William White, "Bohlen Confirmed as Envoy, 74 to 13, Eisenhower Victor," *New York Times,* March 28, 1953, p. 1.

59. Joseph and Stewart Alsop, "Matter of Fact," *Washington Post,* July 5, 1953, and Oshinsky, op. cit., p. 293n.

60. Oshinsky, op. cit., p. 293.

61. For Solarium documentation, see U.S. Department of State, *Foreign Relations of the United States,* 1952–1954, vol. II, National Security Affairs, Part 1 (Washington, D.C.: Government Printing Office, 1984), pp. 323–443; for Cutler comment, pp. 441 and 401. All the Solarium material was originally classified top secret.

62. Ibid., pp. 388–93 and 399–412. For Kennan's account of these events, see *Kennan vol. II*, pp. 180–81.
63. U.S. Department of State, op. cit., pp. 441 (summary of recommendations) and 439 (Albania project), and pp. 393 and 441 (actual acceptance of key Task Force C tactical recommendations). For material discussed in footnote, see Murrey Marder, "Eisenhower Rejected Plan to Disrupt Soviet," *Washington Post,* December 7, 1984, p. A22. For text of NSC 5412, see NSC 5412, March 15, 1954, NSC 5412/1, March 12, 1955, and NSC 5412/2, December 28, 1955 (top secret), at RG 273, Policy Papers File, NA, Washington, D.C.

Chapter Sixteen

1. Powers, op. cit., p. 159.
2. *1985 GAO Report,* pp. 32–34. Otto von Bolschwing is the anonymous "Subject C" discussed in this study.
3. Ibid., pp. 31–32. Stankievich is the anonymous "Subject B" of the GAO's study.
4. *1985 GAO Report,* pp. 31–32.
5. Ibid.
6. Ibid, pp. 26–27, on purge at RFE/RL. On purge of Eberhardt Taubert, see Tauber, op. cit., vol. 1, pp. 150, 323, and 644; vol. 2, pp. 1049–50, 1070–71, 1325, and 1328.
7. For Eichmann quote, see Simon Wiesenthal Center, *Membership Report,* Summer 1985. On Brunner's wartime career, see Berlin Document Center dossier on Alois Brunner, NSDAP no. 510,064; SS no. 342 767. See also Alois Brunner, U.S. Army INSCOM dossier no. XE064584 17B025.
8. Cookridge, op. cit., p. 354.
9. Ibid., p. 352.
10. Approximately 400 pages of original documentation on Skorzeny—some of it sanitized—is available through the FOIA at Otto Skorzeny, U.S. Army IN-SCOM dossier no. XE00 0417. Most of these records date from 1945 to 1950. This body of records, interestingly enough, was subjected to a "special purge" in 1973, according to army records. Additional postwar interrogations of Skorzeny may be found at "Skorzeny, Otto," Box 739, Entry 179, Enemy POW Interrogation File MIS-Y 1943–1945, RG 165, NA, Washington, D.C. The State Department, FBI, and INS have also released fragmentary records on Skorzeny following FOIA requests. The CIA has yet to release its records on Skorzeny, despite formal requests to do so. Considering Skorzeny's lifelong involvement in a variety of affairs that touched on CIA concerns—such as the Egyptian project mentioned in the text, the international arms trade, the African uranium industry, aid to Biafran rebels, and, allegedly, political assassinations, to name only a few—the presently available material on Skorzeny can only be considered the tip of a much larger iceberg.

Meanwhile, a reliable biography of Skorzeny's postwar career has yet to appear. Charles Whiting, *Skorzeny* (New York: Ballantine, 1972), is almost exclusively limited to Skorzeny's wartime exploits. Skorzeny's own *Meine Kommanounternehmen, Krieg ohne Fronten* (Wiesbaden: Limes Verlag, 1976), also available as Otto Skorzeny, *La Guerre Inconnue* (Paris: Albin Michel, 1975), focuses primarily on World War II events, with only a highly selective and flattering account of 1945 to 1950. For a popular account of Skorzeny's activities after 1945 that mixes occasional skilled reporting with considerable myth, see Glenn Infield, *Skorzeny: Hitler's Commando* (New York: St. Martin's Press, n.d.).

11. Skorzeny to Spruchkammer, Darmstadt Camp, July 26, 1948, at Document 026 in the Skorzeny INSCOM dossier.

12. Miles Copeland, *The Game of Nations* (New York: Simon & Schuster, 1970), p. 104.

13. Cookridge, op. cit., pp. 352–54.

14. Ibid. See also "Klarsfeld: Mitarbeiter Eichmanns Lebt in Damaskus," *Frankfurter Allgemeine Zeitung*, June 28, 1982; "Why Nazi Hunters Won't Give Up," *Newsweek* (February 21, 1983); James M. Markham, "In Syria, a Long-Hunted Nazi Talks," *New York Times*, October 29, 1985; and Beate Klarsfeld, *Wherever They May Be!* (New York: Vanguard Press, 1975), pp. 231–33.

15. Robert Fisk, "Syria Protects Eichmann Aide," *Times* of London, March 15, 1985. Also Markham, op. cit.

16. Copeland, *Game of Nations*, loc. cit., pp. 103 and 105.

17. Ibid.

18. Otto von Bolschwing, NSDAP and SS dossier at the Berlin Document Center, NSDAP No. 984212; SS No. 353603.

19. Sicherheitsdienst des RFSS SD-Hauptamt, *Palastinareise Bericht* (U.S. designation no. 173-b-16-14/61), now at Frames 2936012–2936068, microfilm roll 411, T-175, RG 242, NA, Washington, D.C.

20. *Eichmann Interrogated*, loc. cit., pp. 24–25 and 30.

21. Ryan, *Quiet Neighbors*, pp. 221–23.

22. The Nazis' program of racial definition of Jews, registration, taxation, expropriation of Jewish property, and eventually concentration and attempted extermination of the Jewish people was obviously a protracted process, involving many tens of thousands of perpetrators. The roots of this campaign stretch back to the beginning of the Nazi party and, in a broader sense, to the long tradition of European anti-Semitism. In this sense, Otto von Bolschwing was only one of a great many who played a role in the creation of Germany's campaign against the Jews.

Yet Adolf Eichmann clearly played a pivotal role in the development of Nazi persecution from the late 1930s on, and von Bolschwing's influence on Eichmann is testified to by Eichmann himself. Otto von Bolschwing had been trained as a banker and a lawyer, and his anti-Semitic writings during the 1930's helped Eichmann and the SS formulate the "practical" and "modern" measures that proved to be the centerpiece of Nazi persecution of the Jews during the years leading up to the extermination program itself. See Ryan, *Quiet Neighbors*, pp. 221–23 on von Bolschwing's recommendations. See Levin, op. cit., p. 95ff., particularly pp. 101–10, on Eichmann's role in Austria and its role as a model for Nazi persecution of Jews throughout the Reich. For the historical importance of the Austrian measures in the overall development of Nazi criminality, see World Jewish Congress et al., op. cit., pp. 96–97 and 488–98ff. The striking similarity between von Bolschwing's recommendations and Eichmann's Austrian measures can be established by comparing von Bolschwing's text in Ryan with the World Jewish Congress evidence.

23. Original documentation on the Bucharest events can be found in the report by von Killinger to Joachim von Ribbentrop, February 26, 1941, published in English in U.S. Department of State, *Documents on German Foreign Policy, 1918–1945,* vol. XII, pp. 171–76. See also Hilberg, op. cit., p. 489; Höhne, op. cit., pp. 327–29; and Ryan, *Quiet Neighbors,* pp. 227–31, with quoted comment on p. 238.

24. Von Killinger to von Ribbentrop, loc. cit. For original documentation from German Foreign Office archives tracing von Bolschwing's activities leading up to the abortive rebellion, see captured German correspondence: Für Vertr. Leg. Rat Luther. Bukarest, May 22, 1940; Luther [Berlin] to Schröder [n.d.]; Der Chef der Sicherheitspolizei und des SD (VI D 3) [SS Sturmbannführer Fischer?] to Picot, May 23, 1940; Luther to Bukarest, May 27, 1940; Der Chef der Sicherheitspolizei und des SD (VI A 42 Ke/Str.) to Luther, January 8, 1941, marked "Urgent!"; Luther to Vizenkonsul Beuttler, January 13, 1941; Der Chef der Sicherheitspolizei und des SD (VI A 42 Ke/Str.) to Luther, January 10, 1941; Picot to Luther, February 7, 1941. Copies in collection of author.

25. Hilberg, op. cit., p. 489.

26. U.S. Air Force, "Statement of Civilian Suspect, Otto Albrecht Alfred von Bolschwing," December 22, 1970 (secret), obtained via FOIA.

27. Ibid; with further details in U.S. Air Force, "Report of Investigation, Otto Albrecht Alfred von Bolschwing," p. 2. Primary documentation concerning von Bolschwing's activities during this period may be found in von Bolschwing's archives, portions of which have been obtained by the author. Of particular interest are a letter from Roy F. Goggin, June 7, 1945; a document dated June 1, 1948; and a recommendation concerning von Bolschwing to police HQ in Salzburg, May 20, 1948.

28. May 20, 1948, recommendation to police HQ, Salzburg, von Bolschwing archives.

29. Anthony Cave Brown, ed., *The Secret War Report of the OSS* (New York: Berkley, 1976), p. 286.

30. U.S. Department of Justice, "Record of Sworn Statement—Witness [Otto von Bolschwing]," file no. A8-610-051, June 26, 1979, and confidential informant.

31. U.S. Air Force, "Statement of Civilian Suspect Otto Albrecht Alfred von Bolschwing," loc. cit., pp. 14–15, and confidential informant.

32. *1985 GAO Report,* pp. 32–34. Otto von Bolschwing is the anonymous "Subject C" discussed in this study. On O'Neal's relationship to von Bolschwing, see U.S. Air Force, "Report of Investigation, Otto Albrecht Alfred von Bolschwing." On O'Neal's later career, see Agee and Wolf, op. cit., pp. 604–05.

33. *1985 GAO Report,* pp. 32–34.

34. Ibid.

35. "Application for Immigrant Visa and Alien Registration no. I-259338, von BOLSCHWING, Otto," December 22, 1953; Mrs. Roy Goggin interview, April 4, 1984.

36. Former OSI Deputy Director Martin Mendelson and former OSI trial attorney Eugene Thirolf deserve the credit for discovering von Bolschwing's presence

in the United States and initiating the prosecution against him. For journalistic accounts, see Carey, op. cit., and Christopher Simpson, op. cit. The author is particularly grateful to Peter Carey for his assistance with the Otto von Bolschwing research.

37. *1985 GAO Report,* pp. 32–34.
38. This can be determined by comparing Tipton's sanitized account with documentation concerning von Bolschwing obtained from public archives, court filings, and the Freedom of Information Act.
39. Höhne and Zolling, op. cit., p. xv.
40. Cookridge, op. cit., pp. 315–16; Höhne and Zolling, op. cit., pp. 229–30.
41. Ibid.
42. Cookridge, op. cit., pp. 320–34; Höhne and Zolling, op. cit., pp. 280–90.
43. Ibid.
44. Ibid.
45. For text of NSC 5412, see NSC 5412, NSC 5412/1, and NSC 5412/2, RG 273, Policy Papers File, NA, Washington, D.C.

Chapter Seventeen

1. For text of UPI and AP teletype transmissions, see *Time Capsule/1956* (New York: Time-Life Books, 1968), pp. 92–93.
2. Ibid., p. 90.
3. On Hungarian exiles' criticisms of Radio Free Europe's role, see "Anna Kethly Scores Radio Free Europe," *Washington Post,* November 30, 1956, and "Radio Free Europe Role in Hungary," *Washington Post,* November 13, 1956.
4. For documentation on RFE policy during the Hungarian events, see Elsa Bernaut, "The Use of Hungarian and Polish Material," American Committee for Liberation Research Library, October 29, 1956, now in RFE/RL Archives in New York.
5. "Set Up Is Revised at Anti-Red Radio," *New York Times,* April 29, 1957, p. 6.
6. Assembly of Captive European Nations, op. cit. p. 12. For documentation concerning CIA funding of the ACEN and of its exile leaders, see the ACEN correspondence released through Department of State FOIA case no. 8404249. See also National Committee for a Free Europe, *President's Report,* 1953, p. 22, and 1954, p. 18ff.
7. Assembly of Captive European Nations, op. cit. See comments from the *New York Herald Tribune, Christian Science Monitor,* and other publications reproduced on the flyleafs of this text.
8. Ibid., pp. 180–81 and 187 (Balli Kombetar officials, including Hasan Dosti), p. 184 (Lithuanian delegation), p. 186 (Balli Kombetar officials in Liberal Democratic Union), p. 187 (Berzins on Deportations Committee), and p. 188 (Maikovskis in International Peasant Union). For more on Maikovskis, see U.S. Department of Justice, Office of Special Investigations, op. cit., pp. 34–35; and U.S. Department of Justice press statement of August 16, 1984. Maikovskis's attorney, Ivars Berzins, declined comment on this issue in a telephone interview, November 25, 1985.

The FBI has recently declassified a heavily censored version of its dossier on the ACEN, withholding almost half the entire file on national security grounds.

The released portion does, however, concede in passing that the ACEN had become a key focus of the government's own inquiries into Nazi criminals in the United States as of 1982; see letter from GAO investigator John Tipton to Joseph Moore, FBI, August 26, 1982, FBI ACEN file.

9. Assembly of Captive European Nations, op. cit. p. 182ff.

10. See American Friends of the Captive Nations, *Hungary Under Soviet Rule* (New York: American Friends of the Captive Nations and the Assembly of Captive European Nations, 1959), for listing of American Friends officers and committee members. Also of note on the committee: Eugene McCarthy, Eugene Lyons, Sidney Hook, John Richardson, Jr.

11. *ABN Correspondence* (newsletter). For information on ABN personalities and activities, see, for example, Ferdinand Durcansky, "The West Shuts Its Eyes to Tiso's Warning," no. 5–6, 1953 (praise of Tiso regime); "Dr. Ante Pawelic [*sic*]," no. 7–8, 1957 (praise of Ustachi regime); "ABN Activities," no. 1–2, 1955; "Prof. R. Ostrowski Visits the USA," no. 5–6, 1958; "A.B.N. Congress in Toronto," no. 5–6, 1953; and "The Truth About ABN: Memorandum to the State Department," no. 10–11, 1955 (on Ostrowsky's and Berzins's role in the organization). See also Press Bureau of the ABN, *Our Alternative* (Munich: Anti-Bolshevik Bloc of Nations, 1972). For recent investigative reporting concerning the ABN, see Scott Anderson and Jon Lee Anderson, *Inside the League* (New York: Dodd Mead & Co., 1986), pp. 13–154 passim.

12. For examples of congressional influence by extremist émigré groups, see "Congressman Kersten Adopts Our Ideas," *ABN Correspondence*, no. 11–12 (1953); "Kersten's Investigatory House Committee Meets in Munich," *ABN Correspondence*, no. 5–9 (1954), on the House select Committee on Communist Aggression. For discussions of the role of Eastern European émigré associations in congressional affairs generally, see "Lithuanian American Council," *Lituanus* (July 1955), p. 23, on opposition to genocide treaty, creation of congressional investigating committees; and Vardys, op. cit., on Katyn investigation, Kersten Amendment, creation of Escapee Program, role in congressional elections. Vardys complains, however, that despite the congressional right wing's assiduous efforts to use anti-Communist investigations as an election ploy, the voting public was growing suspicious of its efforts by the mid-1950s. Three key House sponsors of a variety of the more extreme "liberation" measures lost in heavily ethnic Eastern European districts in Milwaukee, Chicago, and Wilkes-Barre during the 1954 congressional elections.

13. For more on O'Connor, see Edward Mark O'Connor, FBI File No. 62–88018 (and two cross-references), obtained via the FOIA; "Freedom Forecast for Baltic States," *New York Times*, June 17, 1951, p. 38; "Dr. Edward M. O'Connor, 77, Former NSC Staffer, Dies," loc. cit.; "Edward O'Connor Remembered in Cleveland Ceremonies," loc. cit.; and particularly Edward M. O'Connor, "Our Open Society Under Attack by the Despotic State," *Ukrainian Quarterly* (Spring 1984), p. 17ff. On role in Displaced Persons Commission, see U.S. Displaced Persons Commission, op. cit., p. 71; A. H. Raskin, "3 Agencies Resettling D.P.'s Told to End Contracts of Leftist Union," *New York Times*, May 2, 1951, and "Cut Leftist Union Ties," *New York Times*, May 3, 1951.

14. For activities and personalities of the 1960 parade, see commemorative pa-

rade program titled "Captive Nations Week, July 19–23, 1960," Captive Nations Committee, Washington, D.C., copy in collection of author.

15. See ibid. on App's role in the parade. On App's writings, see Anti-Defamation League of B'nai B'rith, *Extremism on the Right* (New York: Anti-Defamation League of B'nai B'rith, 1983), pp. 14, 130, and 159, and *Contemporary Authors*, vol. 101, pp. 23–24.

16. *Kennan vol. II*, p. 286.

17. Mathias, op. cit., p. 975ff.

18. Ibid., pp. 984–85.

19. *Kennan vol. II*, pp. 278–319 passim.

20. Correspondence with National Republican Heritage Groups (Nationalities) Council Executive Director Radi Slavoff, October 2, 1985.

21. Jack Anderson [and Les Whitten], "Nixon Appears a Little Soft on Nazis," *Washington Post*, October 11, 1971.

22. Ibid.

23. Wynar, op. cit. On Daumants Hazners and Ivan Docheff's role in Republican group, see Federal Election Commission filings, 1976. On Ivars Berzins, see also Anti-Defamation League of B'nai B'rith, *The Campaign Against the U.S. Justice Department's Prosecution of Suspected Nazi War Criminals* (New York: ADL Special Report, 1985), p. 5. On this issue, see also Jay Mathews, "Nazi-Hunt Methods Protested," *Washington Post*, March 23, 1985, and Mary Thornton, "East European Émigrés Are Accused of Impeding Hunt for Nazis in U.S.," *Washington Post*, April 6, 1985. Ivars Berzins has also served as defense attorney for accused Nazi criminals Arnolds Trucis and Boleslavs Maikovskis.

24. Nicholas Nazarenko interviews, July 21 and 22, 1984. On Nazarenko's role in Republican party group, see Nazarenko's resolution at the May 1984 National Republican Heritage Groups (Nationalities) Council annual convention, "Resolution: Whereas, Moscow Communism is the leading mortal enemy . . . ," May 18, 1984, copy in collection of author, and Federal Election Commission filings for 1975 and 1981.

25. Nicholas Nazarenko speech, July 21, 1984.

26. On mailing list, ibid. For a list of organizations belonging to the Coalition for Peace Through Strength, see American Security Council, "Model Peace Through Strength Resolution for Organizations," n.d. (1984–1986), promotional flyer, copy in collection of author. Member organizations that are on record as favoring Axis governments of World War II include the World Federation of Cossack National Liberation Movement of Cossackia, the Bulgarian National Front, the Croatian-American Committee for Human Rights, and the Slovak World Congress. At least five other coalition member groups have expressed points of view that many people would regard as sympathetic to the Nazi quisling regimes of World War II. See also coaltion chairman John M. Fisher correspondence with Nicholas Nazarenko, July 5, 1984, copy in collection of author.

27. Sidney Blumenthal, "The Reagan Doctrine's Strange History," *Washington Post*, June 29, 1986.

28. Ibid.

29. Burnham, *Containment or Liberation?*, loc. cit., p. 196ff., and Burnham, *Coming Defeat of Communism*, loc. cit., p. 211ff.

30. See, for example, "Captive Nations Week, 1984, a Proclamation by the President of the United States," July 16, 1984, and "Captive Nations Week, 1985, A Proclamation by the President of the United States," July 19, 1985, both published and distributed by the White House Office of Public Liaison. The original Captive Nations proclamation is 73 Statute 212, signed July 17, 1959.

31. Lasby, op. cit., p. 79ff.

32. On evolution of concept and term *national security state*, see Yergin, op. cit.; and Marcus Raskin, "Democracy Versus the National Security State," *Law and Contemporary Problems* (Summer 1976), p. 189ff. On Kennan, Thayer, and Magruder's role, see *Church Committee Report*, Book IV, pp. 28–31 (on Kennan); Paddock, op. cit., passim (on Magruder); JSPC 862/3 enclosure B. p. 4ff. (on Thayer). On containment's goal for dealing with the Soviets, see "The Analysis by Mr. X [Kennan]: It's America vs. Russia . . . Until Russia Is Forced to Cooperate or Collapse," *Newsweek* (July 21, 1947), p.16.

33. Bishop and Crayfield, op. cit., p. 264ff. (on Romania); Rositzke, op. cit., p. 169ff. (on Poland).

34. Ian McDonald, op. cit.; David Binder, "Odysseus of the Greek Left Feels Back 'in My Element,' " *New York Times*, October 18, 1986.

35. On role of NSC 10/2 and NSC 5412: *Church Committee Report*, Book IV, pp. 25–55. On murders by Nicaraguan contras, see Americas Watch, *Human Rights in Nicaragua 1986* (New York and Washington, D.C.: Americas Watch, 1986), p. 18ff.; see also Joe Pichirallo and Edward Cody, "U.S. Trains Antiterrorists," *Washington Post*, March 24, 1985.

36. *Church Committee Report*, Book VI, pp. 257–58.

37. Cookridge, op. cit., calls Gehlen the "Spy of the Century" and points out that Soviet and East German publications termed him the "biggest single factor in the prevention of a possible East-West détente" (p. 5). While it is unlikely that any one person truly deserves that description, it is nonetheless true that Gehlen played a substantial clandestine role in East-West affairs that has generally been ignored by historians.

38. On disposal programs, see Marchetti and Marks, op. cit., p. 257; *1985 GAO Report*. On murder of double agents, see *Church Committee Report*, Book IV, p. 130ff.

39. Ralph Blumenthal, "Nazi War Crimes Suspect Asserts CIA Used Him as Anti-Soviet Spy," *New York Times*, October 15, 1976. For quoted text, see Union of American Hebrew Congregations, *Keeping Posted* (October 1980), back cover, for reproduction of the CIA's letter to Laipenieks. Charles Allen supplied the facsimile of the CIA letter to *Keeping Posted*.

40. Dusko Doder, "New Charges, Admission on Waldheim's Record: '47 Soviet-Bloc Bid to Recruit Waldheim as Agent Described," *Washington Post*, October 30, 1986.

41. On CIA programs inside the United States, see John M. Crewdson and Joseph Treaster, "The CIA's 3-Decade Effort to Mold the World's Views," *New York Times*, December 25 to 27, 1977; Powers, op. cit.; Marchetti and Marks, op. cit. On clandestine CIA funding of educational and charitable foundations,

labor groups, and student organizations, see "Groups Channeling, Receiving Assistance from CIA," *Congressional Quarterly Almanac 1967*, pp. 360–61; *Church Committee Report*, Book VI, p. 263ff.; Morgenthau, "Government Has Compromised the Integrity of the Educational Establishment," and Horowitz, "Social Scientists Must Beware the Corruption of CIA Involvement," both in Kim, ed., op. cit. For an overview of clandestine CIA funding of media assets, see Schorr, op. cit.

42. Caute, op. cit., pp. 224–63.
43. On limitations of the laws against Nazi criminals in the United States, see Ryan, *Quiet Neighbors*.
44. Charles R. Allen, Jr., "OSI vs. Nazis: Success or Failure," *Reform Judaism*, (June 1981), and Charles R. Allen, Jr., "Odyssey of Nazi Collaborator," *Jewish Currents* (December 1977), both of which concern the Soobzokov case. See also Representative Elizabeth Holtzman, "Alleged Nazi War Criminals in America," *Congressional Record*, December 3, 1980, no. 169, pt. II (concerning Soobzokov, Hazners).
45. For official acknowledgment of 100 Persons cases with histories as Nazi criminals, see Neal Sher, "Statement Before the Subcommittee on Immigration . . . House of Representatives," October 17, 1985, p. 6.
46. Department of Justice press statement, July 9, 1980.
47. Christopher Simpson, op. cit.
48. U. S. Department of Justice, Office of Special Investigations, op. cit. p. 29.
49. *U.S.* v. *Liudas Kairys*, U.S. District Court Northern Illinois, civil action 80-C-4302, Government's post-trial brief, August 30, 1982, p. 41ff.
50 Anti-Defamation League of B'nai B'rith, *The Campaign Against the U.S. Justice Department's Prosecution of Suspected Nazi War Criminals.* loc. cit.
51. Ibid., pp. 24–25.
52. Ibid., p. 16n.
53. Simon Wiesenthal comment at press conference, May 9, 1984.
54. On present situation of Burnham, see Sidney Blumenthal, "The Reagan Doctrine's Strange History," loc. cit. For obituaries of persons mentioned in the text, see *Washington Post*, June 6, 1985 (W. Park Armstrong); November 27, 1985 (O'Connor); May 8, 1986 (Lovett); *New York Times*, February 15, 1984 (Joyce); *Assembly* (West Point, N.Y.), June 1983 (Grombach). Data on Evron Kirkpatrick and Lyman Kirkpatrick are from author's interviews, November 10, 1983, and April 11, 1984, respectively; the two Kirkpatricks are not known to be related.
55. Braden interview, September 12, 1984.
56. Powers, op. cit., pp. 91–97, with quote from Wisner on p. 95.
57. "Frank Gardiner Wisner Dead; Former Top Official of CIA," *New York Times*, October 30, 1965, p. 35. In response to an FOIA request the CIA has released approximately 400 pages of material on Wisner, including Wisner's own account of the events preceding his death. See particularly Richard Helms, "Frank Gardiner Wisner, In Memoriam," text of speech at commemorative ceremony, January 29, 1971, Langley, Virginia (Document 1 in Wisner CIA file); and two "recollections" by fellow CIA officers (names deleted), January 19, 1970, and n.d. [1970?] (documents 2 and 3 in Wisner CIA file).

58. For obituary, see "Charles Thayer, Soviet Expert, 59," *New York Times,* August 29, 1969.
59. Ronald Steel, "The Statesman of Survival," *Esquire* (January 1985), p. 68ff.
60. Ibid.

Selected Bibliography

Acheson, Dean. *Present at the Creation.* New York: W. W. Norton, 1969.

Adenauer, Konrad. *Memoirs 1945–1953,* tr. Beate Ruhm von Oppen. Chicago: Henry Regnery Co., 1966.

Agee, Philip, and Wolf, Louis, eds. *Dirty Work, The CIA in Western Europe.* Secaucus, N.J.: Lyle Stuart, 1978.

Alexander, Herbert E. *Financing Politics: Money, Elections and Political Reform.* Washington, D.C.: CQ Press, 1984.

Allen, Charles, Jr. *Nazi War Criminals in America: Facts . . . Action.* Albany, N.Y.: Charles Allen Productions, Inc., 1981.

American Political Science Association. *Biographic Directory.* Washington, D.C.: American Political Science Association, 1968 and 1973.

Anderson, Scott, and Anderson, Jon Lee. *Inside the League.* New York: Dodd, Mead & Co., 1986.

Anti-Bolshevik Bloc of Nations. *Our Alternative, ABN and EFC Conferences.* Munich: Press Bureau of the Anti-Bolshevik Bloc of Nations, 1972.

Armstrong, John A. *Ukrainian Nationalism 1939–45.* New York: Columbia University Press, 1955.

Armstrong, John A. ed. *Soviet Partisans in World War II.* Madison: University of Wisconsin Press, 1964.

Assembly of Captive European Nations. *First Session: Organization, Resolutions, Reports, Debate.* New York: ACEN publication No. 5, 1955.

Avotins, E.; Dzirkalis, J.; and Petersons, V. *Daugavas Vanagi.* Riga: Latvian Publishing House, 1963.

Bailey, Bernadine. *The Captive Nations: Our First Line of Defense.* Chicago: Charles Hallberg, 1969.

Bar-Zohar, Michel. *La Chasse aux Savants Allemands.* Paris: Librairie Arthème Fayard, 1965.

Beck, Melvin. *Secret Contenders.* New York: Sheridan Square, 1984.

Berzins, Alfreds. *I Saw Vishinsky Bolshevize Latvia.* Washington, D.C.: Latvian Legation, 1948.

———. *Latvia.* Washington, D.C.: American Latvian Association in the U.S., Inc., 1968.

———. *The Two Faces of Co-Existence.* New York: Robert Speller & Sons, 1967.

357

––––––. *The Unpunished Crime.* New York: Robert Speller & Sons, n.d.

Bethell, Nicholas. *The Last Secret.* New York: Basic Books, 1974.

Bilinsky, Yaroslav. *The Second Soviet Republic: The Ukraine After World War II.* New Brunswick, N.J.: Rutgers University Press. 1964.

Bishop, Robert, and Crayfield, E. S. *Russia Astride the Balkans.* New York: McBride and Co., 1948.

Blackstock, Paul. *Agents of Deceit.* Chicago: Quadrangle, 1966.

––––––. *The Secret Road to World War II.* Chicago: Quadrangle, 1969.

––––––, and Schaf, Frank L. *Intelligence, Espionage, Counterespionage and Covert Operations: A Guide to the Information Sources.* Detroit: Gale Research, 1978.

Blatny, Milan. *Les Proclamateurs de Fausse Liberté.* Bratislava: L'Institut d'Études de Journalisme, 1977.

Blum, Howard. *Wanted: The Search for Nazis in America.* Greenwich, Conn.: Fawcett, 1977.

Bohlen, Charles. *Witness to History.* New York: W. W. Norton, 1973.

Bonifacic, Antun F. (Ante Bonifacic), and Mihnovich, Clement. *The Croatian Nation.* Chicago: Croatia Cultural Publishing Center, 1955.

Borkin, Joseph. *The Crime and Punishment of I. G. Farben.* New York: Free Press, 1978.

Bower, Tom. *Blind Eye to Murder.* London: Paladin-Grenada, 1983.

––––––. *Klaus Barbie.* New York: Pantheon, 1984.

Boyer, Richard, and Morais, Herbert. *Labor's Untold Story.* New York: United Electrical Radio & Machine Workers of America Publishing Division, 1973.

Brown, Anthony Cave. *The Last Hero: Wild Bill Donovan.* New York: Vintage, 1982.

Buchardt, Friedrich. "Die Behandlung des russischen Problems wahrend der Zeit des national-sozialistischen Regimes in Deutschland," typescript, n.d. (1946?).

Burnham, James. *The Coming Defeat of Communism.* New York: John Day Co., 1950.

––––––. *Containment or Liberation?* New York: John Day Co., 1953.

Caute, David. *The Great Fear: The Anti-Communist Purge Under Truman and Eisenhower.* New York: Simon & Schuster, 1978.

Cherezov, Konstantin. *NTS, a Spy Ring Unmasked.* Moscow: Soviet Committee for Cultural Relations with Russians Abroad, n.d. (1963?).

Cherednichenko, V. *Collaborationists.* Kiev: Politvidav Ukraini, 1975.

Chew, Dr. Allen F. *"Fighting the Russians in Winter. Three Case Studies."* U.S. Army Command and General Staff College, "Leavenworth Papers," December 1981.

Christian Democratic Union of Central Europe. *Freedom. Prerequisite to Lasting Peace.* New York: Christian Democratic Union of Central Europe, 1957.

Cirtautas, Arista Maria. "Nicholas Poppe, a Bibliography of Publications from 1924 to 1977." *Parerga.* Seattle, Wash.: University of Washington Institute for Comparative and Foreign Area Studies, 1977.

Claussen, Martin P., and Claussen, Evelyn B. *Numerical Catalog and Alphabetical Index for State-War-Navy Coordinating Committee and State-Army-Navy-Air Force Coordinating Committee Case Files 1944–1949.* Wilmington, Del.: Scholarly Resources, Inc., 1978.

Clay, Lucius. *Decision in Germany.* Garden City, N.Y.: Doubleday, 1950.

———. *Papers of General Lucius D. Clay,* ed. Jean Edward Smith. Bloomington, Ind.: Indiana University Press, 1974. Cited here as *Clay Papers.* Vol. 1.

Cline, Marjorie W.; Christiansen, Carla E.; and Fontaine, Judith M., eds. *A Scholar's Guide to Intelligence Literature: Bibliography of the Russell J. Bowen Collection.* Frederick, Md.: University Publications, 1983.

Cohn, Norman. *Warrant for Genocide.* London: Penguin, 1970.

Colby, William. *Honorable Men: My Life in the CIA.* New York: Simon & Schuster, 1978.

Collins, Larry D. "The Free Europe Committee: American Weapon of the Cold War." Ph.D. dissertation, Carlton University, 1975 (Canadian Thesis on Microfilm Service call no. TC 20090).

Comptroller General of the United States (General Accounting Office). *Nazis and Axis Collaborators Were Used to Further U.S. Anti-Communist Objectives in Europe—Some Immigrated to the United States.* Washington, D.C.: Government Printing Office, 1985. GAO Report No. GAO/GGD-85-66. Cited here as *1985 GAO Report.*

———. *U.S. Government Monies Provided to Radio Free Europe and Radio Liberty.* Washington, D.C.: Government Printing Office, 1972. GAO Report No. 72–0501, with classified annex obtained through the FOIA.

———. *Widespread Conspiracy to Obstruct Probes of Alleged Nazi War Criminals Not Supported by Available Evidence—Controversy May Continue.* Washington, D.C.: Government Printing Office, 1978. GAO Report No. GGD-78-73.

Constantinides, George. *Intelligence and Espionage: An Analytical Bibliography.* Boulder, Colo.: Westview Press, 1983.

Cookridge, E. H. (Edward Spiro). *Gehlen.* New York: Random House, 1971.

Cooney, John. *The American Pope: The Life and Times of Francis Cardinal Spellman.* New York: Times Books, 1984.

Cooper, Matthew. *The Nazi War Against the Soviet Partisans 1941–1944.* New York: Stein and Day, 1979.

Copeland, Miles. *The Game of Nations.* New York: Simon & Schuster, 1970.

———. *Without Cloak or Dagger.* New York: Simon & Schuster, 1974.

Corson, William R. *The Armies of Ignorance.* New York: Dial/James Wade, 1977.

Council for a Free Czechoslovakia. *In Search of Haven.* Washington, D.C.: Council for a Free Czechoslovakia, 1950.

Coxsedge, Joan. *One, Two, Three—Ustasha Are We!* Melbourne, Australia: Unitarian Peace Memorial Church Pamphlet No. 1, 1972.

Daim, Wilfried. *Der Vatikan und der Osten.* Vienna: Europa-Verlag, n.d.

Dallin, Alexander. *German Rule in Russia,* 2d ed. Boulder, Colo.: Westview Press, 1981.

———. *The Kaminsky Brigade 1941–1944.* Cambridge, Mass.: Harvard University Russian Research Center, 1956.

Davidson, Eugene. *The Trial of the Germans.* New York: Macmillan, 1966.

Davies, John Paton. *Foreign and Other Affairs.* New York: W. W. Norton, 1966.

Dawidowiscz, Lucy. *The War Against the Jews.* New York: Bantam, 1976.

DeSantis, Hugh. *The Diplomacy of Silence.* Chicago: University of Chicago Press, 1979.

Detweiler, Donald, ed. Burdick, Charles B. and Rohwer, Jürgen, assoc. eds. *World War II German Military Studies.* New York: Garland, 1979.

Donovan, Robert J. *Tumultuous Years.* New York: W. W. Norton, 1982.

Dornberg, John. *The Other Germany.* Garden City, N.Y.: Doubleday, 1968.

Dornberger, Walter. *V-2.* New York: Viking, 1958.

Dulles, Allen Welsh. *The Craft of Intelligence.* New York: Harper & Row, 1963.

———. *The Secret Surrender.* New York: Harper & Row, 1966.

Dulles, John Foster, and others. Society of Friends of Romania. *Bulletin Dedicated to Her Majesty Queen Marie of Roumania.* New York: Fischer Publishing, 1926.

Dulles, John Foster. *War or Peace.* New York: Macmillan, 1950.

Durand, Pierre. *Les Français à Buchenwald et à Dora.* Paris: Éditions Sociales, 1977.

Dvinov, Boris (pseudonym). *Documents on the Russian Emigration: An Appendix to Rand Paper P-768.* Santa Monica, Calif.: Rand Corporation Study No. P-865, 1956.

———. *Politics of the Russian Emigration.* Santa Monica, Calif.: Rand Corporation Study No. P-768, 1955.

Elliot, Mark R. *Pawns of Yalta.* Urbana, Ill.: University of Illinois Press, 1982.

Epstein, Julius. *Operation Keelhaul.* Old Greenwich, Conn.: Devin-Adair, 1973.

Etzold, Thomas, and Gaddis, John Lewis, eds. *Containment: Documents on American Policy and Strategy 1945–1950.* New York: Columbia University Press, 1978.

Ferencz, Benjamin. *Less Than Slaves.* Cambridge, Mass.: Harvard University Press, 1979.

Fischer, George. *Soviet Opposition to Stalin.* Cambridge, Mass.: Harvard University Press, 1952.

———., ed. *Russian Émigré Politics.* New York: Free Russia Fund, Inc., 1951.

FitzGibbon, Louis. *Katyn.* New York: Charles Scribner's Sons, 1971.

Forrestal, James. *The Forrestal Diaries,* ed. Walter Mills. New York: Viking, 1951.

Friedman, Leon, ed. *The Law of War: A Documentary History.* New York: Random House, 1972.

Friedman, Philip. *Roads to Extinction: Essays on the Holocaust; The Destruction of the Jews of Lwow 1941–1944.* Jerusalem: Yad Vashem, 1979.

Gehlen, Reinhard. *The Service,* tr. D. Irving. New York: World Publishing, 1972.

Gelber, M. N. *The Encyclopedia of the Jewish Diaspora,* vol. 1, *Lwow.* Jerusalem: n.p. 1956.

Gerson, Louis L. *The Hyphenate in Recent American Politics and Diplomacy.* Lawrence, Kan.: University of Kansas Press, 1964.

Gilbert, Martin. *Atlas of the Holocaust.* New York: Macmillan, 1982.

———. *The Holocaust.* New York: Holt, Rinehart & Winston, 1985.

Goudsmit, Samuel. *Alsos.* New York: pub. unknown, 1947.

Greenspan, Morris. *The Soldier's Guide to the Laws of War.* Washington, D.C.: Public Affairs Press, 1969.

Grombach, John V. *The Great Liquidator.* Garden City, N.Y.: Doubleday, 1980.

Groves, Leslie R. *Now It Can Be Told.* New York: Harper & Row, 1962.

Guérin, Alain. *Le Général Gris.* Paris: Julliard, 1969.

Gutman, Yisrael, and Rothkirchen, Livia. *The Catastrophe of European Jewry.* Jerusalem: Yad Vashem, 1976.

Handlin, Oscar. *Race and Nationality in American Life.* Boston: Little, Brown, 1957.

Hazners, Vilis Arveds. *Varmacibas Torni.* Lincoln, Neb.: Vaidava, 1977.

Herken, Gregg. *The Winning Weapon.* New York: Vintage, 1982.

Herwarth von Bittenfeld, Hans Heinrich. *Zwischen Hitler und Stalin.* Frankfurt: Verlag Ullstein, 1982.

Heydecker, J., and Leeb, J. *The Nuremberg Trial,* tr. R. A. Downie. Cleveland and New York: World Publishing, 1962.

Hilberg, Raul. *The Destruction of the European Jews.* New York: Harper & Row, 1961.

Hilger, Gustav. *Wir und der Kreml, Deutsch-sowjetische Beziehungen 1918–1941.* Frankfurt am Main: Metzner, 1955.

———, and Meyer, Alfred G. *The Incompatible Allies: A Memoir-History of German-Soviet Relations 1918–1941.* New York: Macmillan, 1953.

Historical Division, European Command (EUCOM). *Labor Services and Industrial Police in the European Command 1945–1950.* Karlsruhe, Germany: Historical Division, EUCOM, 1952.

Hoffmann, Joachim. *Die Geschichte der Wlassow-Armee.* Freiburg im Breisgau: Verlag Rombach, 1984.

Höhne, Heinz. *The Order of the Death's Head.* New York: Ballantine, 1971.

———, and Zolling, Hermann. *The General Was a Spy.* New York: Bantam, 1972.

Homze, Edward L. *Foreign Labor in Nazi Germany.* Princeton, N.J.: Princeton University Press, 1967.

Horowitz, David. *The Free World Colossus.* London: Macgibbon & Kee, 1965.

———, ed. *Containment and Revolution.* Boston: Beacon, 1967.

———, ed. *Corporations and the Cold War.* New York: Monthly Review Press, 1969.

Huzel, Dieter. *From Peenemünde to Canaveral.* Englewood Cliffs, N.J.: Prentice-Hall, 1962.

Iatrides, John. *Revolt in Athens.* Princeton, N.J.: Princeton University Press, 1972.

International Military Tribunal. *Trial of the Major War Criminals Before the International Military Tribunal.* Nuremberg, Germany: International Military Tribunal, 1947.

Isaacson, Walter, and Thomas, Evan. *The Wise Men.* New York: Simon & Schuster, 1986.

JCS. "Dulag Luft," privately printed manuscript, n.d. (1976?).

Kahn, David. *Hitler's Spies: German Military Intelligence in World War II.* New York: Macmillan, 1978.

Kark, John S. "The Ukraine and Its Supreme Liberation Council," master's thesis, University of Maryland at College Park, 1955.

Keefe, Eugene K.; Coffin, David P.; Mussen, William A., Jr.; and Rinehart, Robert. *Area Handbook for Greece,* 2d ed. Washington, D.C.: Government Printing Office, 1977.

Kennan, George F. *Memoirs 1925–1950.* Boston: Little, Brown, 1967. Cited here as *Kennan vol. I.*

———. *Memoirs 1950–1963.* Boston: Little, Brown, 1967. Cited here as *Kennan vol. II.*

Kent, Sherman. *Strategic Intelligence for American World Policy.* Hamden, Conn.: Archon Books, 1965.

Khrushchev, Nikita. *Khrushchev Remembers,* tr. Strobe Talbott. Boston: Little, Brown, 1970.

Kim, Young Hum, ed. *The Central Intelligence Agency: Problems of Secrecy in a Democracy.* Lexington, Mass.: D. C. Heath & Co., 1968.

Kirkpatrick, Lyman. *The Real CIA.* New York: Macmillan, 1968.

———. *The U.S. Intelligence Community: Foreign Policy and Domestic Activities.* New York: Hill and Wang, 1973.

Kleist, Peter. *Zwischen Hitler und Stalin.* Bonn: Athenaum Verlag, 1950.

Kovrig, Bennett. *The Myth of Liberation.* Baltimore: Johns Hopkins University Press, 1973.

Lang, Jochen von, and Sibyll, Claus, eds. *Eichmann Interrogated.* New York: Farrar, Straus & Giroux, 1983. Originally *Das Eichmann-Protokoll.* Berlin: Severin und Siedler, 1982. Here cited as *Eichmann Interrogated.*

Lasby, Clarence. *Project Paperclip.* New York: Atheneum, 1975.

Lebed, Mykola. *UPA. Ukrainska Povstanska Armiia.* Uydannia Presovoho Biura UGVR, 1946.

Lendvai, Paul. *Eagles in Cobwebs.* Garden City, N.Y.: Doubleday, 1969.

Levin, Nora. *The Holocaust.* New York: Schocken, 1973.

Linklater, Magnus; Hilton, Isabel; and Ascherson, Neal. *The Nazi Legacy.* New York: Holt, Rinehart & Winston, 1984.

Loftus, John. *The Belarus Secret.* New York: Knopf, 1982.

MacPherson, Malcolm. *The Blood of His Servants.* New York: Times Books, 1984.

Marchetti, Victor, and Marks, John. *The CIA and the Cult of Intelligence.* New York: Knopf, 1974.

Marks, John. *The Search for the Manchurian Candidate.* New York: Times Books, 1979.

May, Ernest R., ed. *Knowing One's Enemies: Intelligence Assessment Before the Two World Wars.* Princeton, N.J.: Princeton University Press, 1986.

Mendelsohn, John, ed. *The Holocaust: The Wannsee Protocol and a 1944 Report on Auschwitz.* London and New York: Garland, 1982.

Meyer, Cord. *Facing Reality.* New York: Harper & Row, 1980.

Michel, Jean, with Nucera, Louis. *Dora.* New York: Holt, Rinehart & Winston, 1980.

Mickelson, Sig. *America's Other Voice: The Story of Radio Free Europe and Radio Liberty.* New York: Praeger, 1983.

Miedzymorze. Rome: n.p. (Intermarium) 1946.

Morse, Arthur D. *While Six Million Died.* Woodstock, N.Y.: Overlook Press, 1983.

Mosley, Leonard. *Dulles.* New York: Dial, 1978.

Motyl, Alexander. *The Turn to the Right: The Ideological Origins and Development of Ukrainian Nationalism.* Boulder, Colo.: East European Monographs, Columbia University Press, 1980.

Murphy, Brendan. *The Butcher of Lyon.* New York: Empire Books, 1983.

MVD-MBG Campaign Against Russian Émigrés. Frankfurt am Main: Possev Publishing House, 1957.

Nash, George H. *The Conservative Intellectual Movement in America Since 1945.* New York: Basic Books, 1976.

National Committee for a Free Europe. *President's Report for the Year 1953.* New York: National Committee for a Free Europe, 1954.

———. *President's Report for the Year 1954.* New York: National Committee for a Free Europe, 1955.

Natsional'no-Trudovoi Soyuz. *Let Your Conscience Decide.* Washington, D.C.: Joint Publication Research Service, 1961. JPRS No. 4425.

Natsional'no-Trudovoi Soyuz. *(Narodno-Trudovoy Soyuz Rossiyskikh Solidaristov) NTS: Introduction to a Russian Freedom Party.* Frankfurt am Main: Possev-Verlag, 1979.

Nogee, Joseph L., and Donaldson, Robert H. *Soviet Foreign Policy Since World War II.* New York: Pergamon Press, 1981.

Norden, Albert. *Brown Book: War and Nazi Criminals in West Germany.* DDR Documentation Center of State Archives Administration: Verlag Zeit im Bild.

O'Ballance, E. *The Red Army.* London: Faber & Faber, 1964.

Omrcanin, Ivo. *Dramatis Personae and Finis of the Independent State of Croatia in American and British Documents.* Bryn Mawr, Pa.: Dorrance, 1983.

———. *The Pro-Allied Putsch in Croatia in 1944 and the Massacre of Croatians by Tito Communists in 1945.* Bryn Mawr, Pa.: Dorrance, 1975.

Oshinsky, David. *A Conspiracy So Immense: The World of Joe McCarthy.* New York: Free Press-Macmillan, 1983.

Paddock, Colonel Alfred H. *U.S. Army Special Warfare.* Washington, D.C.: National Defense University, 1982.

Page, Bruce; Leitch, David; and Knightley, Phillip. *The Philby Conspiracy.* New York: Signet, 1969.

Pash, Boris. *The Alsos Mission.* New York: Award House, 1969.

Petrov, Vladimir. *Escape from the Future.* Bloomington, Ind.: Indiana University Press, 1973.

———. *A Study in Diplomacy: The Story of Arthur Bliss Lane.* Chicago: Henry Regnery Co., 1971.

Philby, Kim. *My Silent War.* New York: Ballantine, 1983.

Pike, Representative Otis. "Special Supplement: The CIA Report the President Doesn't Want You to Read." *Village Voice* (February 16 and 22, 1976). This is the leaked text of a U.S. House of Representatives Select Committee on Intelligence report on clandestine CIA activities; the text was withheld from official publication by presidential request.

Poppe, Nicholas (Nikolai N. Poppe). *Reminiscences,* ed. Henry Schwartz. Bellingham, Wash.: Western Washington University Center for East Asian Studies, 1983.

Powers, Thomas. *The Man Who Kept the Secrets: Richard Helms and the CIA.* New York: Pocket Books, 1979.

Prados, John. *The Soviet Estimate.* New York: Dial, 1982.

Price, James R. *Radio Free Europe: A Survey and Analysis.* Washington, D.C.: Congressional Research Service Document No. JX 1710 US B, March 1972.

Prouty, Fletcher. *The Secret Team.* Englewood Cliffs, N.J.: Prentice-Hall, 1973.

Ramati, Alexander. *The Assisi Underground.* New York: Stein & Day, 1978.

Ramme, Alwin. *Der Sicherheitsdienst der SS.* Berlin: Deutscher Militarverlag, n.d. (1969?).

Raschhofer, Hermann. *Political Assassination: The Legal Background of the Oberlander and Stashinsky Cases.* Tübingen: Fritz Schlichtenmayer, n.d. (1963?).

Rearden, Steven L. *The Formative Years,* vol. 1, *History of the Office of the
Secretary of Defense,* ed. Alfred Goldberg. Washington, D.C.: Historical Office
of the Secretary of Defense, 1984.

Reitlinger, Gerald. *The House Built on Sand.* London: Weidenfeld & Nicolson,
1960.

———. *The SS: Alibi of a Nation.* Englewood Cliffs, N.J.: Prentice-Hall,
1981.

Rhodes, A. *The Vatican in the Age of Dictators.* London: Hodder & Stoughton,
1973.

Ringelblum, Emmanuel. *Polish-Jewish Relations During the Second World War,*
eds. Joseph Kermish and Shmuel Krakowski; tr. Dafna Allon et al. New York:
Howard Fertig, 1976.

Rogger, Hans, and Weber, Eugen, eds. *The European Right. A Historical Profile.*
Berkeley: University of California Press, 1965.

Rositzke, Harry A. *The CIA's Secret Operations.* New York: Reader's Digest Press,
1977.

———. *The KGB: The Eyes of Russia.* Garden City, N.Y.: Doubleday, 1981.

Ryan, Allan. *Klaus Barbie and the United States Government.* Washington, D.C.:
Government Printing Office, 1983. Cited here as Ryan, *Barbie Report.*

———. *Klaus Barbie and the United States Government. Exhibits to the Report.*
Washington, D.C.: Government Printing Office, 1983. Cited here as Ryan, *Barbie Exhibits.*

———. *Quiet Neighbors.* New York: Harcourt Brace Jovanovich, 1984. Cited here
as Ryan, *Quiet Neighbors.*

Schatoff, Michael. *Bibliography on [the] Vlasov Movement in World War II.* New
York: All Slavic Publishing House, 1961.

Schellenberg, Walter. *The Labyrinth,* tr. Louis Hagen. New York: Harper & Bros.,
1956.

Schmidt, George. *The American Federation of Teachers and the CIA.* Chicago:
Substitutes United for Better Schools, 1978.

Serbian Eastern Orthodox Diocese. *Martyrdom of the Serbs.* Serbian Eastern
Orthodox Diocese, n.d. (1943?).

Sereny, Gitta. *Into That Darkness.* New York: Vintage, 1983.

Shandruk, Pavlo. *Arms of Valor,* tr. Roman Olesnicki. New York: Robert Speller
& Sons, 1959.

Simon Wiesenthal Center. *SS Col. Walter Rauff: The Church Connection 1943–
1947.* Los Angeles: Simon Wiesenthal Center Investigative Report, May 1984.

Simpson, Colonel Charles M. *Inside the Green Berets: The First Thirty Years.*
Novato, Calif.: Presidio, 1983.

Sinevirsky, Nicola (pseudonym). *SMERSH,* eds. Kermit and Milt Hill. New York:
Henry Holt & Co., 1950.

Six, Franz Alfred. *Dokumente der Deutschen Politik.* Berlin: Deutsches Auslandswissenschaftliches Institut, 1942.

———. *Europa: Tradition und Zukunft.* Hamburg: Hanseatische Verlagsanstalt,
1944.

———. *Freimaurerei und Judenemanzipation.* Hamburg: Hanseatische Verlagsan-stalt, 1938.

———. *Les Guerres Intestines en Europe et la Guerre d'Union du Présent.* n.p., n.d. (1941?).

Smith, Richard Harris. *OSS.* Berkeley: University of California Press, 1972.

Smith, Thomas Bell. *The Essential CIA.* Self-published, n.d. (1976?). Available through the Library of Congress at JK468.I6554.

Somerhausen, Christine. *Les Belges déportes à Dora.* Brussels: Centre Guillaume Jacquemyns, 1979.

Stark, Captain John T. *Unconventional Warfare—Selective Assassination as an Instrument of National Policy.* Air University, Maxwell Air Force Base, Ala-bama: Command and Staff College Special Study, n.d. (1962?).

Steele, Robert (Lately Thomas). *When Even Angels Wept.* New York: Morrow, 1973.

Stehle, Hansjakob. *Eastern Politics of the Vatican 1917–1979,* tr. Sandra Smith. Athens, Ohio: Ohio University Press, 1981.

Stein, George H. *The Waffen SS.* Ithaca, N.Y.: Cornell University Press, 1966.

Stephan, John J. *The Russian Fascists.* New York: Harper & Row, 1978.

Strik-Strikfeldt, Wilfried. *Gegen Stalin und Hitler: General Wlassow und die rus-siche Freiheitsbewegung.* Mainz: Hase & Koehler Verlag, 1970. In English: *Against Stalin and Hitler,* tr. David Footman. New York: John Day Co., 1973.

Styrkul, V. *The SS Werewolves.* Lvov: Kamenyar Publishers, 1982.

Tauber, Kurt P. *Beyond Eagle and Swastika.* Middletown, Conn.: Wesleyan Uni-versity Press, 1967.

Thayer, Charles. *Bears in the Caviar.* Philadelphia: J. B. Lippincott, 1951.

———. *Guerrilla.* New York: Harper & Row, 1963.

———. *Hands Across the Caviar.* Philadelphia: J. B. Lippincott, 1952.

Thorwald, Jürgen (Heinz Bongartz). *Flight in the Winter.* New York: Pantheon, 1951.

———. *The Illusion: Soviet Soldiers in Hitler's Armies.* New York: Harcourt Brace Jovanovich, 1974.

Tolstoy, Nikolai. *The Secret Betrayal.* New York: Charles Scribner's Sons, 1978.

Tomingas, William. *The Soviet Colonization of Estonia.* Kultuur Publishing House, 1973.

Trials of War Criminals Before the Nuremberg Military Tribunals Under Control Council Law No. 10. Washington, D.C.: Government Printing Office, 1949–1953.

Turner, R., ed. *The Annual Obituary—1980.* New York: St. Martin's Press, 1980.

United Committee of the Ukrainian-American Organizations of New York. *The Ukrainian Insurgent Army in Fight for Freedom.* New York: Dnipro Publishing, 1954. Here cited as *Ukrainian Insurgent Army.*

United Nations War Crimes Commission. *History of the UNWCC and the Develop-ment of the Laws of War.* London: HMSO, 1948.

U.S. Chief Council for Prosecution of Axis Criminality. *Nazi Conspiracy and Ag-gression.* Washington, D.C.: Government Printing Office, 1946.

U.S. Congress. House of Representatives. Committee on Expenditures in the Executive Departments. *National Security Act of 1947*. Washington, D.C.: Government Printing Office, 1947.

————. Select Committee to Investigate the Incorporation of the Baltic States into the USSR. *Hearings*. Washington, D.C.: Government Printing Office, 1953.

————. Committee on Un-American Activities. *International Communism*. Washington, D.C.: Government Printing Office, 1956.

————. Committee on Un-American Activities. *Communist Psychological Warfare (Thought Control)*. Washington, D.C.: Government Printing Office, 1958.

————. *Bicentennial Captive Nations Week*. Washington, D.C.: Government Printing Office, 1977.

————. Subcommittee on Immigration. *Alleged Nazi War Criminals*. Washington, D.C.: Government Printing Office, 1978.

U.S. Congress. Senate. Subcommittee to Investigate the Administration of the Internal Security Act. *Hearings on the Institute of Pacific Relations*. Washington, D.C.: Government Printing Office, 1952.

————. Subcommittee to Investigate the Administration of the Internal Security Act. *Strategy and Tactics of World Communism*. Part 1, May 15 and 27. Washington, D.C.: Government Printing Office, 1954.

————. Committee on the Judiciary. *A Study of the Anatomy of Communist Takeovers Prepared by the Assembly of Captive European Nations*. Washington, D.C.: Government Printing Office, 1966.

————. Select Committee (Church Committee) to Study Governmental Operations with Respect to Intelligence Activities. Ninety-fourth Congress. *Alleged Assassination Plots Involving Foreign Leaders: An Interim Report*. Washington, D.C.: Government Printing Office, 1975.

————. Select Committee to Study Governmental Operations with Respect to Intelligence Activities. Ninety-fourth Congress, Second Session. *Final Report*. Washington, D.C.: Government Printing Office, 1976. Cited here as *Church Committee Report*.

U.S. Department of State. *Foreign Relations of the United States*. 1952–1954, vol. II, National Security Affairs, Part 1. Washington, D.C.: Government Printing Office, 1984.

U.S. Displaced Persons Commission. *The DP Story: Final Report of the U.S. Displaced Persons Commission*. Washington, D.C.: Government Printing Office, 1952.

Wannsee Institute. *Kaukasus*. Berlin: Herausgegeben vom Chef der Sicherheitspolizei und des SD, 1942.

Webster's American Military Biographies. Springfield, Mass.: G. and C. Merriam, 1979.

Wells, Leon W. *The Death Brigade (The Janowska Road)*. New York: Holocaust Library and Schocken Books, 1978.

Werth, Alexander. *Russia at War 1941–1945*. New York: Avon, 1965.

Whelan, Joseph. *Radio Liberty: A Study of Its Origins, Structure, Policy, Programming and Effectiveness*. Washington, D.C.: Congressional Research Service, 1972.

Whiting, Charles. *Gehlen: Germany's Master Spy*. New York: Ballantine, 1972.

Wiesenthal, Simon. *The Murderers Among Us,* ed. Joseph Wechsberg. New York: McGraw-Hill, 1967.

Wise, David, and Ross, Thomas. *The Espionage Establishment.* New York: Bantam, 1968.

————. *The Invisible Government.* New York: Vintage/Random House, 1964.

Woolf, S. J., ed. *Fascism in Europe.* London: Methuen, 1981.

Woolston, Maxine. *The Structure of the Nazi Economy.* New York: Russell & Russell, 1968; reprint of 1941 edition.

World Jewish Congress et al. *The Black Book: The Nazi Crime Against the Jewish People.* New York: Nexus Press, 1981; reprint of the 1946 edition.

Wynar, L. R. *Encyclopedic Directory of Ethnic Organizations in the United States.* Littleton, Colo.: Libraries, Inc., 1975.

Wytwycky, Bohdan. *The Other Holocaust.* Washington, D.C.: Novak Report on the New Ethnicity, 1980.

Yergin, Daniel. *Shattered Peace: The Origins of the Cold War and the National Security State.* Boston: Houghton Mifflin, 1977.

Zimmels, H.J. *The Echo of the Nazi Holocaust in Rabbinic Literature.* Ktav Publishing House, 1977.

Selected Archival Sources

Selected declassified U.S. government records of interest now in the National Archives (NA) or available through the Freedom of Information Act (FOIA).

DEPARTMENT OF COMMERCE

U.S. Department of Commerce. Office of Technical Services. *Report of the Combined Intelligence Objectives Subcommittee.* Washington, D.C., 1944.

DEPARTMENT OF JUSTICE

Case Records

U.S. v. Vilis Hazners. Board of Immigration Appeals, file no. A10 305 336.

U.S. v. Liudas Kairys. U.S. District Court Northern Illinois, civil action 80-C-4302 and U.S. Immigration Court, Chicago, Ill., file no. A7 161 811.

U.S. v. Talivaldis Karklins. U.S. District Court Central California, civil action CV 81 0460 LTL.

U.S. v. Bohdan Koziy. U.S. District Court Southern Florida and U.S. 11th Circuit Court of Appeals docket no. 79-6640-CIV-JCP.

U.S. v. Edgars Laipenieks. U.S. Immigration Court, San Diego, California, file no. A11 937 435 and U.S. 9th Circuit Court of Appeals docket no. 83-7711.

U.S. v. Boleslavs Maikovskis. U.S. Immigration Court, Manhattan, New York, and Board of Immigration Appeals, file no. A8 194 566.

U.S. v. Otto Von Bolschwing. U.S. District Court Eastern California, civil action no. 81-308 MLS.

Federal Bureau of Investigation

Assembly of Captive European Nations. FBI File No. 105-32982.

Barbie, Klaus. FBI File No. 105-221892.

Intermarium. FBI File No. 65-38136 serials 117 and 132.

Grombach, John Valentine. FBI File No. 62-221892.

Hilger, Gustav. FBI files nos. 62-118313 serial x2; 64-31609 serial 227; 100-358267 serial 6; 100-364882 serial 48; 100-412348 serial 24; (deleted file no.); 105-70374 serial 4551; 105-115409 serial 3; 109-12-232 serial 408; and 105-10868.

O'Connor, Edward Mark. FBI File No. 62-88018.

Vajda, Ferenc. FBI file nos. 40-83378-A; 62-118313 serial x2; (deleted file no.); 65-62842 serials 89, 99; 77-63190 serial 8; 100-89-35 serials 48, 76, 79; 100-392404 serial 2; 105-0 serial 2346; 105-11044 serials 11, 12, 20, 23; 105-11669 serial 70; 105-22605 serial 1; (deleted file no.).

Immigration and Naturalization Service
Council for a Free Czechoslovakia classified file, "Memorandum for File 56347/218," May 6, 1953, INS Subversive Alien Branch, obtained via FOIA.

Office of Special Investigations
U.S. Department of Justice. Office of Special Investigations. *Digest of Cases in Litigation July 1, 1984.* Washington, D.C.: 1984.

DEPARTMENT OF STATE

Assembly of Captive European Nations
For documentation concerning payments to émigré leaders, the following records were released through FOIA:
Uldis Grava, American Latvian Association, to President Richard Nixon, January 14, 1972.
Lucius D. Clay, Radio Free Europe, to Secretary of State Henry Kissinger, October 10, 1971.
Secretary of State Henry Kissinger, to Lucius D. Clay, Radio Free Europe, November 1, 1971, with attached correspondence.
Six-hundred-page dossier of State Department records from 1954 to 1970 concerning the assembly.
ACEN Lobbying Activity: ACEN to Senator John F. Kennedy, March 3, 1958; ACEN to John F. Kennedy, March 17, 1958; Kennedy reply, April 24, 1958; ACEN to John F. Kennedy, July 1, 1960; Kennedy letter to ACEN chair Peter Zenkl, July 13, 1960; All at John F. Kennedy Pre-Presidential files, Legislative file: "Captive Peoples," Box 687, John F. Kennedy Library, Boston, Massachusetts.

Albanian Case
Robert Joyce to Walworth Barbour, May 12, 1949 (top secret), 875.00/5-1249, RG 59, NA, Washington, D.C.

Boldyreff Case
American Consulate General, Casablanca, Morocco, "DP Resettlement Project in French Morocco," October 7, 1947 (confidential), with enclosed report, 800.4016 DP/10-747, RG 59, NA, Washington, D.C.

Erdely Case
Heidelberg to secretary of state, August 21, 1948 (confidential), 862.20211/8-2045, RG 59, NA, Washington, D.C.

Eurasian Institute

For documentation concerning the Eurasian Institute, the following records are available at RG 59, NA, Washington, D.C.

"For Offie from Davies," May 27, 1948 (secret), 800.43 Eurasian Institute/5-2748 secret file.

"From Tehran to Secretary of State, attention John Davies," re: Ulus and Sunsh, July 27, 1948 (secret), 800.43 Eurasian Institute/7-2748 secret file.

"Department of State to AMEMBASSY, Tehran," re: Sunsh, July 27, 1948, also dated August 10, 1948 (secret), 800.43 Eurasian Institute/7-2748.

"For Davies from Dooher," re: Ulus, August 12, 1948 (secret), 800.43 Eurasian Institute/8-1248.

"Department of State to AMEMBASSY, Athens," intitialed by Kennan, October 12, 1948 (secret), 800.43 Eurasion *(sic)* Institute/10-1248.

Hilger Case

For telegram traffic, the following records are available at RG 59, NA, Washington, D.C.

Berlin to Washington dispatch marked "Personal for Kennan," September 25, 1948 (top secret), 862.00/9-2548.

Heidelberg to Washington dispatch marked "For Kennan," September 27, 1948 (top secret), 862.00/9-2748.

Washington to Heidelberg, September 28, 1948 (top secret), 862.00/9-2848.

Heidelberg to Washington, September 30, 1948 (top secret), 862.00/9-3048.

LaVista Report

Vincent LaVista, "Illegal Emigration Movements in and Through Italy," with appendixes, May 15, 1947 (top secret), FW 800.0128/5-1547, RG 59, NA, Washington, D.C. Cited herein as *LaVista*.

Lodge Act

"Explanatory Background Information for the Guidance of Consular Officers in Implementing Section 2, Subsection (d) of the Displaced Persons Act," February 24, 1950 (confidential), AG 383.7 1948–1949–1950, RG 407, NA, Washington, D.C.

Office of Intelligence and Research

External Research Paper, Series 3, No. 76, *NTS—The Russian Solidarist Movement.* Office of Intelligence and Research, Department of State, December 10, 1951.

Poppe Case

For documentation concerning the Poppe case, the following records are available at RG 59, NA, Washington, D.C. (correspondence designated "secret—sanitized" was obtained through FOIA):

"For [Carmel] Offie from [John Paton] Davies," March 8, 1948 (secret), 800.4016 DP/3-848.

"For Offie from Davies," March 18, 1948 (secret), 893.00 Mongolia/3-1848.

"For [James] Riddleberger from [George] Kennan," October 22, 1948 (secret—sanitized), 861.00/10-2248.

"Personal for Kennan from Riddleberger," November 2, 1948 (secret—sanitized), 861.00/11-248.

"Personal for Riddleberger from Kennan," signed also by Robert Joyce, May 3, 1949 (secret), 800.4016 DP/5-449.

Rauff Case

Jack D. Neal to USPOLAD, Berlin, September 17, 1947 (top secret, no foreign distribution), 740.00116 EW/8-1147 Secret File, RG 59, NA, Washington, D.C.

Vajda Case

211.6415 Vajtha (*sic*), Ferenc/7-2050, with attachments, obtained by the author via FOIA.

Department of State cable Budapest to secretary of state, January 10, 1948 (secret), no decimal file number, obtained via FOIA, with attached memorandum by Richard Wilford titled "Recent Developments Concerning the Establishment in Madrid of an Anti-Communist 'Eastern European Center,' " December 20, 1947 (secret).

800.43 International of Liberty/7-1548, July 15, 1948, RG 59, NA, Washington, D.C.

State Department Interrogation Mission

"Russian Émigré Organizations," United States Political Advisor for Germany, May 10, 1949 (secret), 861.20262/5-1049 Secret File, RG 59, NA, Washington, D.C.

Six, Franz, and Mahnke, Horst. "Investigation Report," April 30, 1946, State Department Propaganda Investigation Team, RG 238, NA, Washington, D.C.

Twardowsky, Fritz E. A. von, interview by State Department Special Interrogation Mission, October 3, 1945, Box 745, Entry 179, G-2 ID MIS-Y records, RG 165, NA, Washington, D.C.

DEPARTMENT OF DEFENSE

Department of Defense. Office of Public Information. Press Branch report on Edwin L. Sibert, April 3, 1952. Washington, D.C.: Center for Military History.

————. Press Branch report on Walter Bedell Smith, July 31, 1951. Washington, D.C.: Center for Military History.

Joint Intelligence Committee. JIC 575/1D, "The Defector Program." CCS 385-(6-4-46) (Section 21), RG 218, NA, Washington, D.C.

Joint Intelligence Committee. JIC 634/1, "Vulnerability of Soviet Bloc Armed Forces to Guerrilla Warfare," September 8, 1953 (top secret), available on microfilm through *Records of the Joint Chiefs of Staff.* University Publications of America, Frederick, Md.

Joint Chiefs of Staff. JCS 1735/104, "Escapee Provision of the Mutual Security Act of 1951" (top secret), CCS 385 (6-4-46) (Section 31), RG 218, NA, Washington, D.C.

————. JCS 1844/144, "Civil Affairs and Military Government Plan in Support of the Joint Outline Emergency War Plan for a War Beginning 1 July 1952" (top secret), available on microfilm through *Records of the Joint Chiefs of Staff.* University Publications of America, Frederick, Md.

————. JCS 1969, "Estimate of Indigenous Force Levels for Unconventional Warfare Programming" (top secret security information), CCS 385 (6-4-46) (Section 76), RG 218, NA, Washington, D.C.

Joint Strategic Plans Committee. JSPC 808/59/D, "Psychology Strategy Board Request for List of Problems to Be Considered," (top secret) CCS 385 (6-4-46) (Section 25), RG 218, NA, Washington, D.C.

————. JSPC 808/67/D, "Service Responsibilities for Covert Operations and Guerrilla Warfare" (top secret) CCS 385 (6-4-6) (Section 26), RG 218, NA, Washington, D.C.

Joint War Plans Committee. JWPC 432/7 "Tentative Over-all Strategic Concept and estimate of Initial Operations—PINCHER," June 18, 1946 (top secret), RG 219, NA, Washington, D.C.

U.S. AIR FORCE

Otto Albrecht Alfred von Bolschwing. "Report of Investigation," September 25, 1970 (secret); form OSI6, file HQD74(32)-2424/2.

Otto Albrecht Alfred von Bolschwing. "Statement of Civilian Suspect," December 22, 1970 (secret); form 1168a.

U.S. ARMY INTELLIGENCE AND SECURITY COMMAND (INSCOM) (INCLUDES U.S. ARMY COUNTERINTELLIGENCE CORPS [CIC] RECORDS) FORT MEADE, MARYLAND

Augsburg, Emil. INSCOM Dossier No. XE004390 I6B036 (secret).

Barbie, Klaus. *Special Interrogation Report No. 65.* File CI-SIR/66, subject: Barbie, Klaus (top secret).

Berzins, Alfreds. INSCOM Dossier No. XE 257645 D 25A 2664 (secret).

Boldyreff, Constantin. INSCOM Dossier No. D-3675 20B85 (secret), also code-numbered 84221 3248.

Brunner, Alois. INSCOM Dossier No. XE 064584 I7B025.

Buchardt, Friedrich. INSCOM Dossier No. XE 077406 D 216906.

CIC CROWCASS correspondence. INSCOM Dossier No. XE 004643 D 20B 102 (secret).

Dragonovic, Krunoslav. INSCOM Dossier No. XE 207018 (top secret).

Grombach, John Valentine (Jean Valentin Grombach). INSCOM Dossier No. 81177870 (secret).

Hilger, Gustav. INSCOM Dossiers No. XE-00-17-80 I6A045 and No. 84066.3224 (secret), also designated INSCOM Dossier No. XE 001780 D 20A042.

Lebed, Mykola. INSCOM Dossiers No. C 804 3982 and No. D 201967 24B2190 (secret).

Operation Brandy. INSCOM Dossier No. XE080352 Z 17D105 (secret).

Operation Circle. Investigation of Illegal Emigration Movements. Case No. 4111, CIC Rome Detachment, Zone Five, December 26 (?), 1946, (secret).

Organization of Ukrainian Nationalists. INSCOM Dossier No. ZF010016 (secret).

Poppe, Nikolai N. INSCOM Dossier No. 84107.3224 (secret).

Ratlines. CIC agent Paul Lyon, "Rat Line from Austria to South America," July 12, 1948 (top secret), and Paul Lyon, "History of the Italian Rat Line," April 10, 1950 (top secret), obtained via FOIA.

Rauff, Walter. INSCOM Dossier No. XE 216719 I9B001 (secret).

Rudolph, Arthur. INSCOM Dossier No. AE 529655 (secret).

Shandruk, Pavlo. INSCOM Dossier No. D 148204 25 B/679 (top secret).

Skorzeny, Otto. INSCOM Dossier No. XE00 0417.

Thayer, Charles Wheeler. INSCOM Dossier No. X8889748 (secret).

Vajda, Ferenc. INSCOM Dossier No. XE23209I9C003 (secret).

Verbelen, Robert Jan. INSCOM Dossiers No. AE 502201 and No. H 8198901, with accompanying cables (secret).

U.S. ARMY RECORDS AT THE NATIONAL ARCHIVES, WASHINGTON, D.C.

Central Registry of War Criminals and Security Suspects (CROWCASS)

U.S. Office of Military Government, Berlin Command. CROWCASS, *Wanted List No. 14,* November 1946.

Copies of the now rare CROWCASS index books are available at Boxes 3690 and 3692, RG 59, NA, Washington, D.C., and at Box 1720, RG 153, NA, Suitland, Md.

Code Word Assignments

Designations for Operations Panhandle, Credulity, Dwindle, Apple Pie, etc.: P&O file 311.5 TS (Section I, II, III), 1948, in 1946–1948 Decimal File (top secret), Records of Army General Staff, RG 319, NA, Washington, D.C. See also 1949–1950 decimal files.

John S. Guthrie memorandum for the secretary, Security Control Section, JIG, "Subject: Assignment of Code Word," November 21 and December 8, 1947 (top secret), P&O 311.5 TS (Section II), 1948, 1946–1948 Decimal File, RG 319, NA, Washington, D.C.

Enemy POW Interrogation Records

Supreme Headquarters of the Allied Expeditionary Forces, "Counter-Intelligence Screening of the German Armed Forces," March 1945 (secret), folder GBI/CI/CS/091.711-2 (Germany), "C.I. Control and Disposal of German Forces," Box 110, Entry 15, RG 331, NA, Washington, D.C.

Gehlen, Reinhard. "Report of Interrogation: Gehlen, Reinhard. 28 August 1945" (secret), Box 472, Entry 179 (G-2 MIS-Y records), 1943–1945, AC of S, G-2 Intelligence Division, RG 165, NA, Washington, D.C. Includes "Basic Personnel Record no. 3WG-1300: Gehlen, Reinhard," in the same folder.

Goettsch, Werner. "Final Interrogation Report No. 8: O/Stubaf Goettsch, Werner, July 24, 1945 (top secret), U.S. Forces European Theater Interrogation Center. Obtained from the CIA through FOIA.

Jung, Igor. "Preliminary Interrogation Report, Source: Jung, Igor," U.S. Seventh Army Interrogation Center, July 12, 1945 (confidential), Box 721 A, Entry 179 (G-2 MIS-Y records), 1943–1945, AC of S, G-2 Intelligence Division, RG 165, NA, Washington, D.C.

Köstring, Ernst. "Final Interrogation Report: Köstring, Gen D Kav, CG of Volunteer Units," U.S. Seventh Army Interrogation Center (ref: SAIC/FIR/42), September 11, 1945 (confidential), Box 721 A, Entry 179 (G-2 MIS-Y records), 1943–1945, AC of S, G-2 Intelligence Division, RG 165, NA, Washington, D.C.

Köstring, Ernst. MS C-043: "Eastern Nationals as Volunteers in the German Army." Foreign Military Studies records of RG 338, NA, Washington, DC.

Poulos, Georg. "Preliminary Interrogation Report: Poulos, Georg, OBST (Col), Greek Police Volunteer Bn," U.S. Seventh Army Interrogation Center (ref: SAIC/PIR/61), June 27, 1945 (secret), Box 721 A, Entry 179 (G-2 MIS-Y records), 1943–1945, AC of S, G-2 Intelligence Division, RG 165, NA, Washington, D.C.

Schellenberg, Walter. "Interrogation Summary No. 1989: Walter Schellenberg," Office of U.S. Chief Counsel for War Crimes Evidence Division, April 30, 1947, with text in German and summary in English.

Skorzeny, Otto, "Consolidated Interrogation Report (CIR) No. 4, Subject: The German Sabotage Service" (interrogation of Skorzeny and his adjutant Radl), July 23, 1945 (confidential); "Annex No. III: Invasion Nets in Allied Occupied Countries"; and the attached "Consolidated Interrogation Report (CIR) No. 13, Subject: Asts in the Balkans," pp. 5–8, 17–18; all of which are in Box 739, Entry 179 (G-2 MIS-Y records), 1943–1945, AC of S, G-2 Intelligence Division, RG 165, NA, Washington, D.C.

Twardowsky, Fritz E. A. von. Interview by State Department Special Interrogation Mission, October 3, 1945, Box 745, Entry 179 (G-2 MIS-Y records), 1943–1945, AC of S, G-2 Intelligence Division, RG 165, NA, Washington, D.C.

Polish-Ukrainian Military Staff. "Final Interrogation Report," U.S. Seventh Army Interrogation Center, August 28, 1945 (confidential), Box 721A, Entry 179 (G-2 MIS-Y records), 1943–1945, AC of S, G-2 Intelligence Division, RG 165, NA, Washington, D.C.

Guerrilla Warfare

Joint Strategic Plans Committee. JSPC 862/3 "Proposal for the Establishment of a Guerrilla Warfare School and a Guerrilla Warfare Corps," August 2, 1948 (top secret), P&O 352 TS (Section 1, Case 1), RG 319, NA, Washington, D.C.

———. JSPC 891/6 "Joint Outline War Plans for Determination of Mobilization Requirements for War Beginning 1 July 1949," September 17, 1948 (top secret), P&O 370 1 TS (Case 7, Part IA, Sub No. 13), RG 319, NA, Washington, D.C.

George F. Kennan correspondence with General Alfred Gruenther, April 27, 1948 (secret), P&O 091.714 TS (Section 1, Case 1) (top secret), RG 319, NA, Washington, D.C.

"Comments on Proposal for Establishment of a Guerrilla Warfare Group, Appendix 'B' " (top secret), P & O 350.06 TS through 381 FLR TS 1949 Hot Files, RG 319, NA, Washington, D.C.

Lodge Act

"AG 342.18 GPA Subject: Enlistment in the Regular Army of 2500 Aliens," June 1, 1951 (secret), RG 407, NA, Washington, D.C.

"File No. ID 907, Analysis of Available DP Manpower," February 25, 1948 (top secret), P&O 091.714 TS (Section 1, Case 1), RG 319, NA, Washington, D.C.

"AGPT-P 342.18 Screening of Lodge Bill Personnel for Special Forces Activities:

Special Orders Number 68," March 23, 1954, with enclosures (confidential), AG342.18 1948–1949–1950, RG 407, NA, Washington, D.C.

"AGSE 342.18 Subject: Enlistment in the Regular Army of Aliens," November 7, 1952, Special Regulations (restricted—security information), AG342.18 1948–1949–1950, RG 407, NA, Washington, D.C.

"(M) 342.18 (10 Apr 52) Priorities and Special Qualifications for Enlistment of Aliens Under Public Law 597" (secret—security information), AG 342.18 1948–1949–1950, RG 407, NA, Washington, D.C.

Psychological Warfare Operations

For documentation concerning psychological warfare, the following records are available at RG 319, NA, Washington, D.C. (declassified in sanitized form following author's FOIA request):

JCS 1735 series. "Guidance on Psychological Warfare Matters" (secret), Box 10, Entry 154, U.S. Army P&O Hot Files 091.412TS through 334WSEGTS.

Major General Charles Bolté to Brigadier General Robert A. McClure, July 7, 1949 (secret), Box 10, Entry 154, U.S. Army P&O Hot Files 091.412TS through 334WSEGTS.

Brigadier General Robert A. McClure to Major General Charles Bolté, July 20, 1949, with enclosure and subsequent correspondence (secret); Box 10, Entry 154, U.S. Army P&O Hot Files 091.412TS through 334WSEGTS.

Colonel R. W. Porter to Major General R. C. Lindsay et al., "Psychological Warfare Study for Guidance in Strategic Planning," with annex, March 11, 1948 (top secret), P&O 091.42 TS (Section I, Cases 1–7), Hot Files.

Army Chief of Special Warfare Brigadier General Robert McClure, "Memorandum to Asst. Chiefs of Staff G-3, subject: Staff Studies," June 12, 1951 (top secret) decimal file 370.64 1951–1954, Box 15.

OTHER ARMY RECORDS
(WASHINGTON, D.C.)

"Memorandum for Chief of Staff US Army, Subject: Soviet Intentions and Capabilities 1949–1956/57," January 4, 1949 (top secret), Box 9, Tab 70, Hot Files, RG 319, NA, Washington, D.C.

U.S. Army v. *Kurt Andrae et al.*, August 7 to December 30, 1947, NA microfilm M1079.

"Subject: Evaluation of Effect on Soviet War Effort Resulting from the Strategic Air Offensive," June 1, 1949 (top secret), Box 9, Tab 67-OSD, Hot Files, RG 319, NA, Washington, D.C.

"Dir of Log to Dir of P&O, Subject: JCS 1920/1," March 1, 1949, P&O 350.06 TS through 381 FLR TS, 1949 Hot File, RG 319, NA, Washington, D.C.

Military Intelligence Division. *History of the Military Intelligence Division, 7 December 1941–1 September 1945,* 1946 (secret), ACMH Manuscripts, RG 319, NA, Washington, D.C.

OTHER ARMY RECORDS
(OTHER REPOSITORIES)

Canham, Doris. *History of AMC Intelligence. T-2*, Wright Field, Ohio, 1948.

EUCOM Annual Narrative Report. Labor Services Division. 1950 (secret),

EUCOM Labor Service Division Classified Decimal File, 1950–51, RG 338, NA, Suitland, Md.

EUCOM Annual Narrative Report 1954 (secret), RG 338, NA, Suitland, Md.

EUCOM Annual Report 1954 (secret), Adjutant General's Office Command, Report files 1949–1954, RG 407, NA, Suitland, Md.

Historical Division, European Command (EUCOM). *Labor Services and Industrial Police in the European Command 1945–1950* (Karlsruhe, Germany: Historical Division EUCOM, 1952). Center for Military History, Washington, D.C. Cited herein as *Labor Service History.*

"Subject: Letter to General Eddy from K. W. von Schlieben, Major, 31 Oct 1950" (restricted), RG 338, Decimal Files, NA, Suitland, Md.

"Item 1, 2 February 1951" and "Item 1, 27 April 1951," European Command Labor Services Division Classified Decimal File, 1950–51 (secret), RG 338, NA, Suitland, Md.

DEPARTMENT OF THE TREASURY

"Memo to Secretary [of the Treasury John] Snyder from F. A. Southard, Subject: History and Present Status of Exchange Stabilization Fund, 12/14/47," copy in the collection of the author.

Office of the Assistant Secretary for International Affairs, U.S. Department of the Treasury. "Exchange Stabilization Fund." Dated December 1948, December 14, 1949, March 1950, January 1951, copies in collection of the author.

Annual Report of the Secretary of the Treasury for 1947, 1948, 1949.

DISPLACED PERSONS COMMISSION

List of Organizations Considered Inimical to the United States Under PL 774. Frankfurt: U.S. Displaced Persons Headquarters, n.d. (secret).

INTERAGENCY COMMITTEES, SWNCC, SANACC

Scholarly Resources microfilm collection of State, War, Navy Coordinating Committee and State, Army, Navy, Air Force Coordinating Committee case files, case nos. 395 and 396. The guide to these records is: Claussen, Martin P., and Claussen, Evelyn B., *Numerical Catalog and Alphabetical Index for State-War-Navy Coordinating Committee and State-Army-Navy-Air Force Coordinating Committee Case Files 1944–1949.* Wilmington, Del., Scholarly Resources, Inc., 1978.

W. Park Armstrong memorandum to Kennan, Davies, Saltzman, Thompson, and Humelsine re: "Refugee Problem and SANACC 395," November 8, 1948 (top secret), obtained through FOIA from NA, Washington, D.C.

SANACC 395 memos of September 22 and 20, 1948 (top secret), both obtained through FOIA from NA, Washington, D.C.

NATIONAL SECURITY COUNCIL

NSC 4. "Coordination of Foreign Information Measures," December 9, 1947 (confidential), Records of the NSC, RG 273, NA, Washington, D.C.

NSC 4a. "Psychological Operations," December 9, 1947 (top secret), Records of the NSC, RG 273, NA, Washington, D.C.

NSC 10/2. "Office of Special Projects," June 18, 1948 (top secret), NSC Policy Papers File (No. 10), RG 273, NA, Washington, D.C.

NSC 17. "The Internal Security of the United States," June 28, 1948 (confidential), NSC Policy Papers File, RG 273, NA, Washington, D.C.

NSC 20/1 and NSC 20/4. "U.S. Objectives with Respect to Russia," in *Containment. Documents on American Policy and Strategy 1945–1950,* edited by Thomas Etzold and John Lewis Gaddis (New York: Columbia University Press, 1978), or in the NSC Policy Papers File, RG 273, NA, Washington, D.C.

NSC 43. "Planning for Wartime Conduct of Overt Psychological Warfare," March 9, 1949 (secret), NSC Policy Papers File, RG 273, NA, Washington, D.C.

NSC 58. "United States Policy Toward the Soviet Satellite States in Eastern Europe," September 14, 1949 (top secret), NSC Policy Papers File, RG 273, NA, Washington, D.C.

NSC 59/1. "Foreign Information Program and Psychological Warfare Planning," *Progress Reports,* March 9, 1950, July 31, 1952, and February 20, 1953 (top secret), NSC Policy Papers File, RG 273, NA, Washington, D.C.

National Security Council. "National Psychological Warfare Plan for General War," May 8, 1951 (top secret), President's Secretary's files, Subject file 193: "Memo Approvals 283," Truman Library, Independence, Missouri.

National Security Council. "Progress Report by the Under Secretary of State on the Implementation of The Foreign Information Program and Psychological Warfare Planning (NSC 59/1)," May 7, 1952 (top secret), President's Secretary's files, Subject file 198, Truman Library, Independence, Missouri.

National Security Council. "Progress Report by the Acting Secretary of State on the Implementation of The Foreign Information Program and Psychological Warfare Planning (NSC 59/1)," July 31, 1952 (top secret), President's Secretary's files, Subject file 198, Truman Library, Independence, Missouri.

NSC 68. "United States Objectives and Programs for National Security," April 14, 1950 (top secret), Records of the NSC, RG 273, NA, Washington, D.C.

NSC 74. "A Plan for National Psychological Warfare," July 10, 1950 (top secret), President's Secretary's files, NSC Meetings Files, Truman Library, Independence, Missouri.

NSC 86. "U.S. Policy on Defectors" (top secret—sanitized), RG 273, NA, Washington, D.C. See particularly "Memorandum for the Ad Hoc Committee on NSC 86, Subject: U.S. Policy on Defectors," February 8, 1951, with attachments (top secret); and Francis Stevens, "In the Present World Struggle for Power . . . [title and date deleted, 1950?]," document 10205 (secret), NSC 86 file, RG 273, NA, Washington, D.C.

NSC 135/3. "Reappraisal of United States Objectives and Strategy for National Security," September 25, 1952 (top secret), Records of the NSC, RG 273, NA, Washington, D.C.

NSC 5412. "Covert Operations," March 15, 1954 (top secret), Records of the NSC, RG 273, NA, Washington, D.C.

NSC 5706. "U.S. Policy on Defectors, Escapees and Refugees from Communist Areas," February 13, 1957 (secret—sanitized), Records of the NSC, RG 273, NA, Washington, D.C.

National Security Council. *Status of Projects Reports* (top secret), RG 273, NA, Washington, D.C.

National Security Council. *Record of Actions* (top secret), RG 273, NA, Washington, D.C.

National Security Council. *Policies of the Government of the United States of America Relating to the National Security,* vol. III, 1950, and vol. IV, 1951 (top secret), RG 273, NA, Washington, D.C.

Office of the Assistant Secretary for Public Affairs. "Emergency Plan for Psychological Offensive (USSR)," April 11, 1951 (secret), President's Secretary's files, Subject file 188, Truman Library, Independence, Missouri.

OFFICE OF STRATEGIC SERVICES AND CENTRAL INTELLIGENCE AGENCY

Office of Strategic Services. "Bern to OSS," December 30, 1943 (KAPPA series), Washington Section, R&C 78, Folder 3, Box 274, Entry 134, RG 226, NA, Washington, D.C.

————. Research and Analysis Report L38836: "Albania: Political and Internal Conditions," July 10, 1944 (secret), RG 226, NA, Washington, D.C.

————. "Bern to OSS," July 19, 1944, Washington Section, R&C 78, Bern, June 1 to July 31, 1944, Box 276, Entry 134, RG 226, NA, Washington, D.C.

————. "Minutes of Meeting Held 20 December 1944," Folder 3, Box 52, Entry 115, RG 226, NA, Washington, D.C.

————. "General Situation Report No. 2. 15 July to 1 September 1945" (top secret), RG 226, NA, Washington, D.C.

————. OSS Report No. 3145: "Central European Federal Club," RG 226, NA, Washington, D.C.

————. *Mediterranean Theater of Operations Security Histories.* "American Military Unit in Bucharest" (secret), Folder 195b, Box 39, Entry 99, RG 226, NA, Washington, D.C.

"Memorandum for Mr. John D Hickerson, Department of State," from the Central Intelligence Agency (secret), 861.20262/11-1947, RG 59, NA, Washington, D.C.

Intelligence Research Report. "Nature and Extent of Disaffection and Anti-Soviet Activity in the Ukraine," March 17, 1948 (secret); available on microfilm through *OSS/State Department Intelligence and Research Reports.* University Publications of America, Frederick, Md.

Central Intelligence Agency. "Radio Free Europe," November 11, 1956 (secret). Obtained via FOIA.

————. Personnel dossier of Frank Wisner. Obtained via FOIA.

————. *Study of Intelligence and Counterintelligence Activities on the Eastern Front and Adjacent Areas During World War II* (confidential), Addendum A: "NKVD Operatives and Persons Connected with Them"; Addendum G: "Members of the SS Who Participated in Mass Executions and Atrocities," n.d., RG 263, NA, Washington, D.C. Cited herein as *CIA Eastern Front Study.*

"Soviet Use of Assassination and Kidnapping," February 17, 1966, FOIA review 8/76, Document No. 570-254. Obtained via FOIA.

Central Intelligence Agency. CIA deputy director for plans to assistant chief of staff, intelligence, Department of Defense, re: Otto von Bolschwing, n.d., August 21, 1970 (?) (top secret), released in sanitized form through FOIA.

BRITISH FOREIGN OFFICE RECORDS

British Foreign Office: Russia Correspondence 1946–1948. F.O. 371. Scholarly Resources, Wilmington, Del., 1982 (microfilm collection of British records), particularly 1946 File 911, Document 12867, p. 80ff. and 1946 File 3365, document 9647, p. 22ff.

CAPTURED GERMAN RECORDS

Microfilmed Archives in the United States
Records of the Reich Leader of the SS and Chief of the German Police, microfilmed at Alexandria, Va., RG T-175, NA, Alexandria, Va.

War Crimes Trials Exhibits
"Operational Situation Report USSR No. 11," March 1 to March 31, 1942 *(Einsatzgruppen* report), Prosecution Exhibit 13, *Trials of War Criminals Before the Nuernberg Military Tribunals Under Control Council Law No. 10.* Washington, D.C.: Government Printing Office.

Berlin Document Center
Akhmeteli, Mikhail. NSDAP Dossier No. 5360858; includes NSDAP party records and miscellaneous correspondence.
Augsburg, Emil. SS Dossier No. 307925, NSDAP Dossier No. 5518743. On "special tasks," see "Beforderungsvorichlag: Hauptsturmführer Dr. Emil Augsburg," July 10, 1941, Document No. 23009-23010.
Bolschwing, Otto von. SS Dossier No. 353603, NSDAP Dossier No. 984212.
Brunner, Alois. SS Dossier No. 342, 767, NSDAP Dossier No. 510064.
Krallert, Wilfried. SS Dossier No. 310323, NSDAP Dossier No. 1529315.
Mahnke, Horst. SS Dossier No. 290305, NSDAP Dossier No. 5286024.
Six, Franz Alfred. SS Dossier No. 107480, NSDAP Dossier No. 245670.

UNITED NATIONS RECORDS

"Statement of Mr. Djilas." *Official Records of the General Assembly,* Sixth Session, Ad Hoc Political Committee, Eighth Meeting, United Nations, November 26, 1951, A/OR 6/Ad Hoc Committee.
Official Records of the General Assembly, Eleventh Session, Annexes, vol. II, November 12, 1956, through March 8, 1957, Agenda Item 70. Cited herein as "UN Debate Item 70."

Illustrations have been supplied and are reproduced by permission of the following: GEORGE KENNAN (1966): UPI/Bettmann Newsphotos; GEORGE KENNAN (1938): UPI/Bettmann Newsphotos; FRANK WISNER: National Archives; CHARLES THAYER: AP/Wide World Photos; JOHN PATON DAVIES: AP/Wide World Photos; CARMEL OFFIE: AP/Wide World Photos; HANS HEINRICH HERWARTH: AP/Wide World Photos; HILGER, MOLOTOV, VON RIBBENTROP: AP/Wide World Photos; KÖSTRING: Ullstein Bilderdienst; VLASOV: Ullstein Bilderdienst; VLASOV'S ARMY CAVALRY: AP/Wide World Photos; LATVIAN SS VOLUNTEERS: Bilderdienst Suddeutscher Verlag; JEWISH WOMEN: Archiv Gerstenberg; HANGED ANTI-NAZI PARTISANS: Archiv Gerstenberg; GEHLEN AS COMMANDER OF FREMDE HEERE OST: Bilderdienst Suddeutscher Verlag; GEHLEN WITH STRIK-STRIKFELDT: Archiv/INTERFOTO; GEHLEN AT STAFF CHRISTMAS PARTY: Ullstein Bilderdienst; SIBERT: AP/Wide World Photos; SIX: AP/Wide World Photos; BRUNNER: AP/Wide World Photos; SKORZENY (1943): Bilderdienst Suddeutscher Verlag; SKORZENY (1959): UPI/Bettmann Newsphotos; DORNBERGER AND VON BRAUN: Bilderdienst Suddeutscher Verlag; NORDHAUSEN CONCENTRATION CAMP: AP/Wide World Photos; DORNBERGER (1954): AP/Wide World Photos; BOLDYREFF: AP/Wide World Photos; POPPE: AP/Wide World Photos; BARBIE PASSPORT: AP/Wide World Photos; BOHLEN: AP/Wide World Photos; DULLES: UPI/Bettmann Newsphotos; VON BOLSCHWING IN SS: Berlin Document Center; VON BOLSCHWING (1946): collection of the author; VON BOLSCHWING (1981): AP/Wide World Photos; LEBED: James Hamilton; MAIKOVSKIS IN UNIFORM: UPI/Bettmann Newsphotos; MAIKOVSKIS (1977): AP/Wide World Photos; LAIPENIEKS: AP/Wide World Photos; HAZNERS: UPI/Bettmann Newsphotos; FIRST CAPTIVE NATIONS DAY (WITH CARDINAL SPELLMAN): AP/Wide World Photos; CAPTIVE NATIONS DAY DINNER: collection of the author; SCRANTON, PA., GATHERING: *Scranton Tribune*.

Maps by Jaime Samilio.

Photo research by Toby Lee Greenberg.

Index

About the Author

CHRISTOPHER SIMPSON, 36, is the winner of the Judith McKown Excellence in Journalism Prize and the Newsletter Association award for investigative reporting. He served as Research Director for Marcel Ophuls' documentary *Hotel Terminus: The Life and Times of Klaus Barbie,* winner of the International Critics Prize at the Cannes Film Festival. His essays have appeared in four books and in dozens of major magazines and newspapers, including *The Washington Post. Blowback* is the winner of the 1988 Investigative Reporters and Editors Award as well as the *Present Tense*/Joel H. Cavior Award in the Category of History. He lives in Mt. Rainier, Maryland.